THE
SECRET
OF THE
HARDY BOYS

MARILYN S. GREENWALD

THE
SECRET
OF THE
HARDY BOYS

· · · · · · ·

Leslie McFarlane
and the
Stratemeyer Syndicate

OHIO UNIVERSITY PRESS
ATHENS

Ohio University Press, Athens, Ohio 45701
© 2004 by Marilyn S. Greenwald

Printed in the United States of America
All rights reserved

Ohio University Press books are printed on acid-free paper ⊗ ™

12 11 10 09 08 07 06 05 04   5 4 3 2 1

Library of Congress Catologing-in-Publication Data

Greenwald, Marilyn S.
  The secret of the Hardy boys : Leslie McFarlane and the Stratemeyer Syndicate
  / Marilyn S. Greenwald.
    p. cm.
  Includes bibliographical references and index.
  ISBN 0-8214-1547-6 (alk. paper)
    1. McFarlane, Leslie, 1902– 2. Authors, Canadian—20th century—Biography.
  3. Detective and mystery sotries, American—History and criticism. 4. McFarlane,
  Leslie, 1902– —Characters—Hardy Boys. 5. Young adult fiction, American—His-
  tory and criticism. 6. Young adult fiction—Publishing—United States. 7. Hardy
  Boys (Fictitious characters) 8. Teenage boy in literature. 9. Brothers in literature.
  10. Stratemeyer Syndicate. I. Title.
  PR9199.3.M3148Z67 2004
  813'.52—dc22
                                                              2004008033

To Tim

CONTENTS

Photographs follow page 106

ACKNOWLEDGMENTS

Leslie McFarlane was a prolific writer who used the written word to express himself personally and professionally. In addition to the hundreds of short stories, essays, books, documentaries, scripts, and poems he created, he also left behind thousands of pages of personal letters and diary entries. It would have been impossible to tell the story of his life without having access to his personal correspondence and diaries.

I am especially grateful to his two surviving children, Norah Perez and Brian McFarlane, for giving me access to his personal correspondence, as well as photos, tapes, books, and articles. They imposed no restrictions on these materials, went out of their way to make them available to me, and were always candid and open during the many discussions I had with them about their father's life and career. They opened their homes to me, and I very much appreciate their insights, their generosity, and their warmth. I could not have started or completed this project without them; I consider them friends and hope our relationship will continue.

I am also indebted to Leslie McFarlane's other relatives who talked to me about his life and who provided lively anecdotes: they include his stepdaughters, Kathy Palmer and Anne Yarrow (and Claire Campbell, to whom I did not speak directly); his sisters-in-law, Bertha McFarlane and Else Maddock; and his niece, Eleanor Huff.

Leslie McFarlane's writings were greatly influenced by his hometown of Haileybury, Ontario, and I gained an understanding of his love for that community after a visit there in 2001. My thanks go to the many friendly residents of Haileybury who are proud of their beautiful town, including Chris Oslund, curator of the Haileybury Heritage Museum.

The largest collection of McFarlane's professional letters is housed at the New York Public Library in the Stratemeyer Syndicate Records collection. Many people there helped me gather and sort information from this large repository. My thanks, also, to Carl Spadoni at the Mills Memorial Library at McMaster University for his aid in sorting out the newspaper and magazine articles stored there. I am also grateful for the assistance of the staff at the Thomas Fisher Rare Book Library at the University of Toronto, where McFarlane's letters to book critic William Deacon are stored.

ACKNOWLEDGMENTS

It would have been impossible to write this book without an understanding of the background of the Hardy Boys series and the Stratemeyer Syndicate. Much has been written in books, articles, and websites about the history, politics, and plots of series books. I sincerely appreciate the help of James Keeline, one the nation's foremost researchers on the subject, who invested a great amount of time corresponding with me and providing me with useful material. I thank him for his tremendous patience and great suggestions.

I also relied heavily on several detailed written sources. These include a website run by Ilana Nash (www.stratemeyer.net); two online newsletters, *The Bayport Times* and *The Bayport Gazette;* and the writings of Deidre Johnson. For detailed plot outlines and history of the Hardy Boys series, I am particularly grateful to Robert L. Crawford.

I realize I could not have completed this project without the support of my friends at the Ohio University Press. I am particularly grateful to Nancy Basmajian for her talent and patience. My thanks also go out to Gillian Berchowitz, Richard Gilbert, David Sanders, Judy Wilson, and the others at the press whom I greatly respect for their dedication and love of books.

Finally, I am very appreciative for the encouragement of many longtime and loyal friends whose excitement about this project helped me launch it in the first place. Thanks so much to Fred and Sarah Heintz, Doug Daniel, Nancy Lewis, and many others.

And, as always, to my husband Tim, who once again put in long hours as editor, researcher, and travel companion. I thank him for his support and love.

INTRODUCTION

When *Toronto Star Weekend Magazine* reporter Bob Stall visited Charles Leslie McFarlane's home to interview him one day in 1973, the seventy-one-year-old McFarlane assumed he would be asked the same questions he had answered over and over again.

An award-winning writer of fiction during the heyday of slick magazines in the 1920s, Les was also a pioneering director and writer for the National Film Board of Canada, a scriptwriter and drama editor for radio and the early "golden" days of television in Canada, and the author of several juvenile books and adult mysteries and novellas.

The kindly and patient Les knew, however, why reporter Bob Stall had come to his home near Toronto that day: to talk to Les about what he considered the most dubious of his many achievements—his authorship of the first sixteen books in the Hardy Boys series, one of the best-selling children's book series in history. It was a job he had undertaken to make ends meet forty-five years previously. Working for a flat fee of a hundred dollars or so per book, he had signed away all royalty rights and had written the books under the pen name Franklin W. Dixon.

Les had heard all the questions over the last few decades: Why had he agreed to write the books for such a low fee? Why had he signed away all the royalties? Had he considered taking legal action to reclaim those royalties? Did he mind that his books were modified in 1959 to update them and eliminate outdated references to "roadsters," "chums," and "gay speed-wagons"? He probably planned to give Stall his standard answers: He had accepted low fees for writing the books because that was the going rate at the time and wasn't bad pay in the 1920s for a few weeks' work; he had signed away the royalties to get the work, which he needed at the time as a young husband and father of three; no, he never planned to renege on a contract that he had signed with his eyes open; and, no, he didn't particularly mind the minor updating of the books to make them conform to contemporary language and customs.

In addition to asking the usual questions, however, Bob Stall offered Les some new information about the books—information that shocked and saddened the man who thought that he knew everything there was to know about the Hardy Boys.

***

Leslie McFarlane's life as a writer, film director, and father and stepfather made him a practical man. After fifty years, on and off, as a freelance writer and editor, Les had learned a long time before to make a decision and never look back. Decisions, right or wrong, must be made, and regretting them or rethinking them after the fact accomplishes nothing, he believed.

His sometimes difficult life also made him appreciate and savor some of the more mundane aspects of living that many others take for granted: holidays with family and all the ceremony that goes with them; searching for the perfect presents for those he loved; the beauty and grandeur of nature, and the joy of eating good food.

Les derived great happiness from being a father, and was happy to give practical advice to his children about their relationships, their lives, and their careers. Chief among this advice was that hard work is a reward in itself and that one's accomplishments will, ultimately, speak for themselves. By the time he reached his seventies, though, he may have discovered some flaws in this philosophy. Perhaps he was rethinking late in his life the value of a little self-promotion and whether the true achievements in his life, did, in fact, end up speaking for themselves.

The Hardy Boys mystery books were among the top-selling young-adult books of the twentieth century, selling more than 50 million copies. The Hardy Boys, like Nancy Drew, are household names. Both sets of books, although seemingly innocuous—featuring earnest, squeaky-clean young protagonists and natural settings—generate their share of controversy. Librarians and educators throughout much of the twentieth century debated the value of the books, which many think are mindless and repetitive. Many librarians banned them from shelves, and some continue to do so.

The Hardy Boys books in particular, though, held a special mystique for their young readers. Boys who grew up to succeed in a variety of careers, including as writers and English professors, are happy to admit that those were the books that first got them hooked on reading. Many of those men passed the books on to their own children. Perhaps this loyalty stems from the fact that boys who had been reluctant readers were excited to find books they genuinely enjoyed. More surprising, though, is the fact that the books live on, despite dramatic upheavals in culture, technology, and society.

As many scholars, reporters, and Hardy Boys fans have acknowledged, a good part of the reason for the exceptional popularity of the series was

Leslie McFarlane. As a twenty-four-year-old newspaperman who wanted to supplement his low salary, Les agreed to write the books for a small literary organization known as the Stratemeyer Syndicate. Edward Stratemeyer, its founder, hired freelance ghostwriters to write formulaic series fiction aimed at a young-adult audience. The writers worked from brief, rather stilted plot outlines supplied by the syndicate. Stratemeyer's aim was to create a boys' adventure series driven by plot turns and action; any distinctive personalities or character idiosyncrasies would be secondary.

Instead, Les created characters who were often quirky, sly, and certainly far from wooden—characters young readers could identify with because of their sense of humor, resourcefulness, and, at times, irreverence. They played practical jokes on each other, loved a good (or not so good) pun, and took no umbrage at good-natured kidding.

Further, McFarlane believed that Hardy Boy readers were up to literary challenges: he routinely used words like "ostensible," "ambling," and "propounded" ("jawbreakers," as he once called them). He had confidence that his readers were smart enough to understand them—or curious enough to look up their meaning, patting themselves on the back for doing so. He also inserted occasional allusions to the work of Shakespeare and Dickens.

At his own initiative, Les subtly and stealthily transformed some standard stereotypical characters, including three respectable policemen and a kindly maiden aunt, into subversives. The policemen were not pillars of society but instead bumbling Keystone Kops who could barely show up for work on time, let alone solve a case. And the stereotypical "kindly" maiden aunt was transformed into a comic dictatorial Cassandra, who always predicted a violent and tragic ending to her nephews' adventures.

In short, Les respected his adolescent audience and refused to write down to them. Although he endured his time as "Franklin W. Dixon" only to earn a few extra dollars, his years as a newspaper reporter cultivated in him a respect for the craft of writing, an eye for detail, and an appreciation for iconoclastic and unconventional personalities. All of this came through in the series fiction he wrote.

The financial reward for all this was a few thousand dollars over a period of about twenty years. The syndicate work did help him support his family in rural northern Ontario. But it also helped subvert his life's dream, which was to write the great Canadian novel—the story of the development of northern Ontario and all the romance and adventure that went with it. He returned to this project periodically throughout his life, but simply never had the time to make it gel.

Les's Canadian heritage was a source of pride for him, and despite several flirtations with living permanently in the United States, he was always drawn back home. Les himself may have seen the irony in the fact that he managed to master nearly all aspects of the American Dream but one: he worked hard, created something unique that filled a need, and persevered through adversity. He achieved everything but fame and riches.

Still, Leslie McFarlane was rewarded with a measure of recognition as a television writer and author, and ultimately he gained the self-confidence to be content with his talent and versatility as a writer. But he never made the "major strike," as one of his fellow writers called it, and he never wrote a critically acclaimed, best-selling work of fiction. Ultimately, by the end of his life, it was always his "Hardy Brats" that came first in one way or another.

Les was too gentle a man and respected children too much to turn them down when they traveled to his home seeking his signature as "Franklin W. Dixon" on their Hardy Boys books. Les did eventually take some pride in the fact that his writing had led many children to love and value books. But in his heart, he was disappointed that it was Joe and Frank Hardy and not the many other multidimensional characters he created that drew attention to him. He was not bitter—that was not his nature—but he was, as his stepdaughter recalled, "confused" about the phenomenon and never truly understood how his real accomplishments were overshadowed by grunt work he did once for a few dollars. A literate and erudite man, he never could figure out how fictional characters he had nurtured could achieve an immortality that eluded him.

But Leslie McFarlane believed a deal was a deal, and never looked back, even when he saw the image of his creation on lunchboxes, on television screens, and in comic strips. Instead, he took joy in his work, valued his family over any possession, and assumed that professional rewards would take care of themselves. Only months before his death at age seventy-four, he was still working on projects, including a novel, hoping for that major strike.

1

· · · · · · ·

TWO LIVES INTERSECT

By the time Edward Stratemeyer published the first Tom Swift book in 1910, at the age of forty-eight, the elusive Stratemeyer had already deeply influenced what children read—and he would have an even greater influence on what they would read for the remainder of the twentieth century. Tom Swift, "born" in Stratemeyer's Newark, New Jersey, offices, would become a household name for much of the twentieth century, as would his literary cousins Nancy Drew, Frank and Joe Hardy, the Bobbsey Twins, and other Stratemeyer creations. These fictional characters became far more famous than the men and women who created and wrote about them—authors whose names are familiar only to those with a particular interest in the subject of series books. Although Stratemeyer never achieved worldwide fame under his own name, his innovative mind, combined with cleverness, a willingness to work hard, and, perhaps most important, an ability to predict the changing whims of the reading public, made him a rich and quietly influential man.

When the first Tom Swift book came out, Charles Leslie McFarlane was about to turn eight years old. The son of John Henry McFarlane, a public school teacher and principal, and Rebecca Barnett McFarlane, a former seamstress, Les—as he was called throughout his life—was born in Carleton Place in northeast Ontario, near Ottawa, and had just moved with his parents and three brothers from nearby Arnprior to the tiny northern Ontario town of Haileybury, about one hundred miles north of North Bay in the Temiskaming Lake district. Haileybury, once a small lumber depot called Humphry's Landing, was founded in 1885 by Charles Cobbold (C.C.) Farr, a former trader for the Hudson's Bay Company. Farr purchased land for a homestead and within a few years had also opened a store and a post office. Naming the place Haileybury after a school in his native England, Farr worked hard to promote the area as a good location for settlement.

The picturesque lake district, once nearly inaccessible, had in 1904 become part of the T&NO (Temiskaming and Northern Ontario) rail line from North Bay. Seven years before the McFarlanes moved there, silver was discovered in Cobalt, five miles south of Haileybury. As the story goes, a blacksmith by the name of Joe LaRose threw his hammer at a fox one day when he was working in the bush. When he picked up his hammer, he found silver on the head. The rest is northern Ontario history. Although the discovery came in Cobalt, Haileybury was dramatically affected for one main reason: a law at the time prohibited the sale of liquor within five miles of mining camps, and Haileybury was located exactly five miles north of Cobalt.

Mining and the extension of the railroad system forever changed the complexion of the region, triggering a chain of events that brought thousands of prospectors there in a short time and ended in tragedy. The population boom and lack of proper sewage facilities led to a typhoid epidemic in the early years of the discovery; cheap housing fueled a devastating fire two decades later that nearly destroyed the town.

In the meantime, however, the discovery of silver, combined with the rustic terrain of Haileybury, turned the town into an author's dream—wild country full of quirky miners, prospectors, lawyers, engineers, and scam artists who were all out to get rich quick and who partied nonstop in the town's newly built hotels as they waited for the rivers to thaw. The antics of these men did not escape the sharp eye of young Leslie McFarlane, who apparently remembered them by name nearly seventy years later when he wrote about them in a brief childhood memoir. And they no doubt appeared in fictionalized form in the children's and adult books, short stories, plays, and radio, film, and television scripts that Les would write during his six-decade career. The theme of men and women shaped by their environment, for better or worse, was one that consistently ran through his fiction. The physical settings of his writings often became major characters in them.

It was a quirk of fate that first united Leslie McFarlane and Edward Stratemeyer, a happenstance that would have repercussions for both men and, ultimately, for millions of youngsters. On the surface, the two seemed very different. Stratemeyer, who was born in 1862 in Elizabeth, New Jersey, was the son of German immigrant Henry Julius Stratemeyer, who joined the California gold rush in 1849. Edward grew up in a middle-class environment in Elizabeth, where his family owned tobacco stores. In 1890, Edward opened a stationery store, but his true love was literature. Stratemeyer had always loved reading: he was partial to adventure tales and stories of boys who overcame adversity despite great odds. In 1883, at age twenty-one, he had created his own story paper—a type of newspaper/magazine of the era that featured poems, puzzles, fictional stories, and the like. Stratemeyer wrote all the content for that primitive effort, and it soon led to sales of stories to existing story papers. Between 1884 and 1889 he sold several works of fiction to various publications for low sums. Stratemeyer's most impressive sale came in 1889 when he received seventy-five dollars from *Golden Days for Boys and Girls* magazine for a story called "Victor Horton's Idea." These early efforts launched a literary career that eventually encompassed as many as 1,600 series books published in more than a dozen languages.

Throughout his career, Stratemeyer benefited from his own resourcefulness, fortuitous timing, and willingness to adapt to a rapidly changing market. After his success with *Golden Days,* Stratemeyer began working for Street & Smith, a prolific publisher of popular fiction and dime novels. The literary format known as the dime novel had come of age by the 1890s. Dime novels, usually sixteen- to thirty-two-page adventure stories for adolescents, issued weekly or semiweekly, often focused on the exploits of a series character. The ever-observant Stratemeyer formed his own ideas from watching how things were done at Street & Smith. He learned from dime novels the conventions of formulaic fiction and the usefulness of stock characters. And, because many of the characters in adventure dime novels were pranksters and jokesters, Stratemeyer came to realize how much adolescent readers appreciated these small doses of humor.

Stratemeyer also found inspiration in the Horatio Alger Jr. tales that were first published in the mid-1800s. Alger's 1867 story *Ragged Dick,* which traces a boy's career from newsboy to businessman, was the classic rags-to-riches tale that focused on the ingenuity and hard work of a courageous, self-reliant boy. Alger had always been a favorite author of the young Edward Stratemeyer, and the two later corresponded. Ultimately, Stratemeyer edited a manuscript for the ailing Alger. (On the original manuscript were Alger's handwritten notes and the continued typed copy by Stratemeyer). A year after Alger's death in 1899, Stratemeyer wrote eleven volumes of unfinished Alger manuscripts using the pen name Arthur M. Winfield. His efforts were anonymous as far as readers were concerned, but he earned money for the venture. Still, Stratemeyer's reasons for doing the work were not merely mercenary; he admired Alger, and appreciated how much the author had taught him.

Despite his attention to detail, Stratemeyer was always able to see the big picture. While working with Alger and for Street & Smith, he learned a valuable lesson: that the real money in the dime-novel and story-paper industry at that time went not to the authors but to the owner of the copyright. It was a lesson that would help make him a very wealthy man and create for him an enduring legacy in children's literature.

Stratemeyer's experiences as an author and editor of series fiction, and especially the spectacular success of his Rover Boys and Motor Boys series at the turn of the century, gave him the idea in 1906 to create his literary syndicate, headquartered in East Orange, New Jersey. In what some people later called a "fiction factory," Stratemeyer, in essence, paid a group of freelance writers book by book to write series books based on plot outlines he provided. He then had them published under pseudonyms, paying the authors a flat fee of $75 to $150 (depending on the era and book length) and having them sign away all rights to the books' authorship. By 1918, Stratemeyer's literary syndicate had taken off. He had moved his quarters from New Jersey to Manhattan and had marketed such characters as the Bobbsey Twins, the Rover boys, and Dorothy Dale, the first girls' series.

***

Leslie McFarlane and his three brothers were growing up in rural Haileybury and reading such children's periodicals as the well-known *Chums* volumes. As he portrays himself in two autobiographical sketches, Les, despite his deep love of reading, was not much of a student, even though his father was a popular principal in the Haileybury school district. (What he fails to note, though, is that he did graduate second in his class.) Les and his brothers spent most of their time in the Ontario countryside, with its long and freezing winters and short summers. They sledded down its steep hills, played hockey in subzero temperatures, fished, picnicked, and picked fruit. To the McFarlane boys, life centered around church, family meals at the dinner table, and, most of all, the outdoors. Consequently, during most of his years in high school, Les had no concrete plans about what he was going to do after graduation—that is, until he entered the International Order of the Daughters of the Empire essay contest, a move that would, indirectly, influence the rest of his life.

Each year, students in the Haileybury school district could compete in an essay contest sponsored by the IODE, as it was known, choosing one of two historical topics: the "development of the North" or the "British Navy." In 1916, Les, then thirteen, and three other students were honored for their essays. Les's thousand-word essay focused on the

quick and recent development of the Temiskaming Lake district and offered a strong hint of the writing style and point of view that he would
cultivate for most of his adult career. The essay was part descriptive travelogue, part timely news story, and most of all, a loving tribute to his
hometown. Les indicated he was wise beyond his years in his contention
that one's physical environment shapes one's destiny. He described how
the vast and beautiful region had nurtured a thriving, active boomtown.
But Les was not critical about such developments, and in fact sings the
praises of both the wilderness and of progress. The region, he wrote,

> was once nature's playground. In summer it was a great
> expanse of green woods and silvery lakes, in spring a
> rather desolate, rainy wilderness, in autumn a riot of
> color and in winter an ever-reaching sheet of purest
> white on which the evergreens stood out like gems. The
> only footsteps which sounded on the forest floors were
> those of the animals and the only sounds which dis-
> turbed the great silences were those caused when a fish
> jumped in the lake, when a Canada bird would lift its
> voice in praise of our country.

With the advent of the railroad and the discovery of silver, he wrote,
the area became "civilized" but remained beautiful:

> The "inpenetrable" North . . . sprang up over
> night. . . . Visions of fortunes awaiting them lured men
> to Cobalt and the surrounding district as a magnet
> draws a piece of iron. . . . Where once the deer stood to
> drink there is now a saw mill. The street car line ex-
> tends between Kerr Lake and New Liskeard where was
> once perhaps a forest trail. And all in few years.

The honor of winning the award and his pride in it provoked in Les
the need to write, and to never stop. He had now found a vocation, and
despite what would be years of hardship and heartbreak, he never wavered from it. Years later, after he became a father, he would tell his children of the tremendous flush of excitement a writer feels from seeing
his words in print or being recognized publicly for them. And he must
have been persuasive; two of his three children also became writers.

***

Leslie McFarlane and Edward Stratemeyer were both drawn to careers in writing, and writing gave them both tremendous satisfaction—each for different reasons. Even as a young man, McFarlane suspected he would never get rich from a career as a writer, but the independence, the prestige, and the occasional accolades sustained him over sixty years. Stratemeyer, on the other hand, saw his talent for writing and publishing as the means to becoming a respected, successful—and ultimately very rich—businessman. As a 1934 *Fortune* article declared, as "oil had its Rockefeller, literature had its Stratemeyer." The "meeting" in 1926 of McFarlane and Stratemeyer through a help-wanted ad would eventually spawn one of the most widely read series of juvenile books in the twentieth century.

The way the two men became acquainted was certainly unorthodox. Working as a reporter on the *Republican* in Springfield, Massachusetts, in 1926 and attempting to moonlight as a writer of adult fiction, Les spotted in a trade publication a want ad for a freelance writer. He remembered the ad in detail nearly half a century later: "'Experienced fiction writer wanted to write from outlines,'" it read. "It was the first time I'd ever seen such an ad for an experienced fiction writer." Having replied to the ad and getting a positive response in return, he still did not realize the significance of the man who had placed the ad. "I didn't know this was Edward Stratemeyer—the great Edward Stratemeyer, author of the Rover Boys, a fabulous man," he said. The thought of "becoming" author "Roy Rockwood" both thrilled and befuddled Les, who had thought of the author as a living, breathing human being. Stratemeyer sent Les a few copies of the adventures of Rockwood creation Dave Fearless. Les was impressed and looked at the bigger picture: "Among boys, Roy Rockwood was a name to conjure with," he said. "Roy Rockwood, creator of *Bomba the Jungle Boy,* the descendant of *Tarzan of the Jungle.* It would be an honor to be Roy Rockwood."

No one was more surprised than Les to learn that Roy Rockwood, a staple of his childhood, was not, in fact, a real person. As he wrote in his autobiography, he had established years before this revelation a sturdy mental picture of the man: "I pictured him seated at his desk, pen in hand, white shirt open at the throat, a bulldog pipe in his teeth. The creator of Bomba the Jungle Boy had a steady gaze, a firm mouth, a determined jaw. . . . True, I had never actually seen a picture of the great author but I didn't have to. I just knew that's how he would look." (It should be noted, though, that Les's memory may have lapsed a bit in recalling the Bomba series. Les was born in 1902, and the series was launched in 1926, so it would have been impossible for him to have read the books as a child. But he may have been familiar as a boy with several other series written by "Roy Rockwood," including the Speedwell Boys and Dave Dashaway series.) Les and his brothers bought into the marketing strategy that Stratemeyer had painstakingly established: to subtly camouflage the fact that these famous "writers" did not really exist, and that it was a series of often ephemeral ghostwriters who played their roles. So it was with a mixture of disappointment, surprise, and amusement that Les learned the truth. He decided he wanted to try his hand at becoming Roy Rockwood.

Les and his brothers read Alger's books as children, but their main source of reading material came at Christmas when, he remembered, "every normal Canadian lad felt neglected if he failed to receive a five-pound volume of either *The Boys' Own Annual* or *Chums.*" These were both collections of stories from weekly magazines for boys, which, like the Rockwood and Alger books, came from the United States. Les indicated sixty years later in his autobiography that while he read these books, he was skeptical of their quality even as a child: "There was a copious supply of reading matter—admittedly uncertified, unpasteurized and probably unhealthy . . . printed on 1,000 pages of eyestraining type."

What truly delighted young Les, however, were not these juvenile books, but some of the volumes he found in his father's bookcase—and decades later he recalled the richness and feel of those books: "I can recall my father's bookcase with its leather-bound one-volume editions of Longfellow, Milton, Tennyson, Wordsworth and Shakespeare." John Henry McFarlane loved poetry, but his oldest son did not share that preference; what delighted Les were the volumes of Charles Dickens: "I fell upon the *Complete Works of Charles Dickens* with absolute joy the day the set arrived in the house," he recalled in his autobiography. "Those red-bound volumes introduced me to a world of imagination and magic that can be evoked by a master." Indeed, the influence of Dickens can be seen both subtly and overtly in many of his short stories and, to a limited degree, in some of his Hardy Boys books. In his adult works, this homage to Dickens is evident at times in the names of characters (for instance, Flannelfoot Foster and Gideon McCrabb), in their often humble beginnings, and in their ability to overcome adversity, often because of twisted but fortuitous circumstances. Of course, the "characters" who inhabited Les's world when he was a child were Dickensian in their own right, as he would note in later writings. Even their names—Sarah Flegg, Otto Knapp, Ambrose O'Brien—fit the bill.

But John Henry McFarlane's influence on his son Les was not just literary. The intelligent, wry, and sometimes rigid John Henry—and his apparent dominant role in the family—influenced to some degree Les's portrayal of the imposing yet gentle Fenton Hardy. The controlled chaos of McFarlane home life also may have served as a model for Les when he wrote about the Hardy family.

Although he was barely eight years old when he moved to Haileybury with his parents and three brothers, Les had vivid memories of their arrival in the town; and based on the descriptions in his memoirs, one has to wonder whether it is more likely that the quirky characters of his childhood indeed affected his writing or that sixty years of writing fiction colored his remembrances. Either way, Les's portrait of his early years in his memoir *A Kid in Haileybury* is hilarious and poignant, as he describes the brave new world the family entered when his school-teacher father decided to uproot his family and take a high-paying job as public-school principal in the newly rich small town.

As a young man, John Henry McFarlane was a country teacher who taught in a one-room schoolhouse outside Lanark, Ontario, in the Ottawa Valley, where he was born in 1870. His star began to rise at the turn of the century, however, shortly before his marriage to Rebecca Barnett, when he was offered $600 a year to be principal of the public school in Carleton Place, about thirty miles southwest of Ottawa. The salary enabled him to marry Rebecca and, after a few years and three children, he became head of a larger school in Arnprior. After several years in that post, a want ad caught his eye: the Haileybury school board sought a principal of its public school and was willing to pay $1,500 a year. Even as a child, Les appreciated the impressive salary. In August of 1910, John Henry and Rebecca McFarlane boarded the train to North Bay and ultimately Haileybury, with their four sons, Les, the oldest; Frank, six; Wilmot (known as Dick), four; and baby Graham, ten months.

As the train chugged west toward North Bay, they saw the green valleys, vast meadows, and regal maples of Arnprior give way to bush country: "Small lonely lakes under the sullen clouds of a sunless sky, forlorn shacks in scrubby clearings," and, most of all, infinite formations of rock, "sheer walls of it, tumbled fields of it, jagged mountains of it," as

Les would later write. To little Les, the landscape brightened considerably when the train arrived in rainy Haileybury—at least the chaos and bustle indicated the family had arrived in civilization. "You sensed the energy of it the moment you stepped onto the railway platform into the crowd of men surging to climb on board, when you saw the packsacks and trunks and boxes and tents, and canoes being loaded into the baggage car, when you saw the confusion of horses and wagons that plunged and lurched in the mud and rains. You heard it in the bedlam of shouting and scrape of wheels, in the sounds of sawing and hammering that came from the skeletons of new buildings," he wrote.

What remained foremost in Les's mind decades after the family's arrival in Haileybury was the mud on the street that measured up to a foot deep after rains; mud that stopped horses in their tracks as they pulled carriages; and mud that was a permanent fixture on the floors of Rebecca McFarlane's kitchen. Haileybury was located in the middle of what the locals called the Clay Belt, and during the rainy season, the mud was unrelenting. "Our impression was that we had never seen so much mud in our lives, nor so many mud-spattered citizens, horses, and conveyances. Haileybury seemed to have struggled into being in a valiant effort to escape the clutches of a bog," he wrote. Before they found a house, the six McFarlanes first moved into the Matabanick Hotel in the center of downtown, at the intersection of a bus and trolley stop. The Matabanick and nearby government offices, grocery store, bars, and other commercial establishments made Haileybury seem downright bustling to them. As they trooped through the lobby for the first time, men were drinking, making deals, and lounging next to the enormous stone fireplace and under a moose head that, as Les remembered, "gazed benevolently into space." The Matabanick was the center of the social and business life in Haileybury. As Les and his brothers sat in their room, absorbing the atmosphere and watching the boats in the harbor, they eagerly greeted the promise of novelty and excitement.

Although John Henry McFarlane earned considerably more in Haileybury than he had in Arnprior, the cost of living in the new city was also higher. As soon as possible, the family moved into a small home on Latchford Street, near downtown, and paid, in Rebecca's view, the appalling sum of twenty dollars a month, twice their rent in Arnprior. Much to her chagrin, some of the walls in the house were so thin that she could see daylight through them, and the windows were ill fitting. Oddly, the entire house was backward: the back door in the kitchen faced the street, and the front door was inaccessible because it opened onto a verandah facing a creek. The vista from the "front" door consisted of two identical and very expensive brick homes that were owned by the Timmins brothers, two of Haileybury's richest citizens, who achieved their wealth in the nearby Cobalt silver camps. A scenic view from their home may have been lacking, but the McFarlane boys were duly impressed by their proximity to wealth.

Mining and lumber, indeed, had drawn many people to Haileybury and made them rich. In 1912, according to city records, thirty-five millionaires lived in Haileybury—the most per capita for any town in the province of Ontario. Many of the most beautiful houses were built along the main Lakeshore Road, which ran parallel to the Temiskaming. The city was divided into informal economic groups; the north side was considered the upper class. Latchford Street, also, was considered the north side, but it admitted people of "modest" income like the McFarlanes, Les recalled.

Because of all the problems with the Latchford Street house, and its high rent, John Henry McFarlane bought his own home as soon as he saved enough money to do so. The family soon moved into a three-bedroom, two-story house at 105 Marcella Street. The house, whose front verandah faced the right way, had a living room, dining room, and basement. And John Henry McFarlane must have loved the home. After it burned down in the catastrophic fire that devastated the town in 1922, he had it rebuilt exactly as it had been. The house still stands.

As Les recalled his childhood life, the biggest influences on him and his brothers appear to have been the people of Haileybury and the outdoors. At the time, children in Haileybury seemed oblivious to the long winters whose pounding blizzards and subzero temperatures frequently closed businesses and schools and paralyzed the town. The children took advantage of the season with sleigh rides, cut their own Christmas trees, fashioned their own bobsleds, and of course played hockey. As he reflected on his early life when he was in his seventies, Les remembered in detail the fun he had without the benefit of organized sports or adult supervision.

> I realize . . . that by today's standards any kid brought up in a remote northern town during the second decade of this century was underprivileged. It was a good thing that we didn't know it. . . . In summer we

could play ball in a lumpy vacant lot (without a certified coach to show us how and a gallery of howling parents to inspire us), go swimming in a lake frigid enough to turn us blue in five minutes. In winter we could play a scrambly kind of hockey . . . on a backyard rink.

Some of the adventures of Les, his brothers, and other boys in the neighborhood served as models for those of Frank and Joe Hardy and their friends. One particular risky, and illegal, activity was comically outlined at length in Les's childhood memoirs: the rapid descent by bobsled down a huge hill in Haileybury, through intersections in the center of town. As Les described it, the thrill was in the danger as the boys mounted their homemade bobsleds at the top of the Browning Street hill:

> On a good day the course would be coated with ice. If you got away to a flying start and crossed Rorke Avenue and Georgina without mishap you could count on bouncing past Davey John's assay plant at the approximate speed of Haley's comet. . . . You simply flashed across the intersection like a scalded cat. Any streetcar motorman, any driver of a horse drawn sleigh, or any coon-coated pedestrian . . . could take such measure as he deemed fit. If he had time.

The town council, alarmed at this activity, passed a law against it, but boys posted "lookouts" in strategic locations to warn of the constable's approach. Predictably, few were apprehended for this illegal activity even though many practiced it through the years.

The idea of children improvising activities in the outdoors, usually without close adult supervision, is of course one that recurs in the Hardy Boys books. The adults enter the picture when the boys return indoors, as was the case with Les and his brothers.

But Les's fond memories of his boyhood extend beyond simply the memories of athletic activities. He also recalled in detail the sensual pleasures of the land, the sounds, the sights, and even the tastes and the smells. In his childhood memoir, he recounts the tremendous pleasure he took from eating the berries that grew wild in Haileybury, and how the children went berry picking in warm weather and returned with pails full. And the intensity of the remembrance is deep. His mother would put some up in jars to be opened the following winter. The remainder would be staples of nearly every meal: berries and cream for breakfast, raspberry pie a few times a day, and bottles of nonalcoholic raspberry vinegar on hot days. The taste of the natural berries, he wrote, far surpassed any concoction of the world's greatest chefs: "No breakfast served in a Cordon Bleu café can equal a bowl of Temiskaming wild strawberries doused with cream and sugar, fortified by a toasted slice of my mother's homemade bread. . . . No dessert ever created by a chef in a tall white hat can ever eclipse a fat slab of her wild strawberry pie and no wine from the vineyards of Champagne could possibly ravish the tastebuds as exquisitely as a tall red glass of her raspberry vinegar, tinkling with ice, on a warm summer's afternoon."

If the environment in which he was raised stood out in Les' mind decades later, memories of the people he knew as a child were even more vivid. *A Kid in Haileybury* is inhabited by a variety of rogues, gamblers, eccentric tough guys, gentle teachers, and others etched in his mind—and later in his writings. Not coincidentally, colorful gamblers and sportsmen frequently populated the freelance articles he wrote for *Maclean's* and other magazines in the 1930s and 1940s.

The men and women who traveled to the Temiskaming Valley during Les's childhood may have provided material for the stories he wrote later in his life, but it was some of the teachers and his father who served as his early role models. The one who stands out in his mind was the intimidating Sarah Flegg, who, it appears, simply scared her students into high achievement. Miss Flegg, he notes, was "a yeller who ruled by fear." Usually hoarse from yelling by the end of the day, she frightened even the most irreverent student into silence, and all learned quickly not to incur her wrath. Miss Flegg's teaching methods were the opposite of the gentle school principal John Henry McFarlane's, but she did earn Mr. McFarlane's respect. Few if any of her students failed the yearly June exams, because they dared not repeat her class, as Les remembered: "Flegg Fugitives always reached his [Mr. McFarlane's] class poetically bulging with knowledge and thoroughly subdued to discipline, grateful to have reached the Entrance Class alive. It always took them a couple of years to recover and achieve a normal state of rebellion."

One of the most famous characters in the Hardy Boys series was Aunt Gertrude, who started out as a peripheral character but ended up, through Les's portrayal of her, as one of the most enduring and memorable characters in the Hardy circle. Like Miss Flegg, Aunt Gertrude was irascible and respected. And, just as Miss Flegg stood out among Les's other teachers, Aunt Gertrude was a much stronger and more visible character than the boys' mother, Laura Hardy.

Rebecca Barnett McFarlane, like other women of her era, spent most of her time raising her family and tending to her home. She is described by some people who knew her as a shy woman, although in her son's childhood memoirs, she is portrayed as a hard worker with a subtle and somewhat wry sense of humor. A seamstress before she married, Rebecca grew up in the small village of Clayton, a town so small that people bought their shoes from cobblers and housewives made their families clothes from fabric that came from the woolen mill. It was Rebecca Mc-Farlane who always insisted that her four boys be neat and well dressed in public. She is portrayed by Les as being frequently in the kitchen cooking delicious meals, and as maintaining a spotless home despite the ever-present mud in Haileybury and the presence of four lively boys. Like Laura Hardy, she is described by Les as quiet but loving and dependable.

Born in 1873, Rebecca was one of eight children of Rebecca Mc-Munn and Aaron Barnett, a barrelmaker. Rebecca Barnett's paternal grandmother, Jane Tully Barnett, born in 1812 in County Sligo, Ireland, left her home in County Cork with her father, Dr. William Tully, when she was six, bound for Quebec City. The rough trip, likely by steamboat, took about six weeks. When she was sixteen, she married Moses Barnett, and the couple lived in Ramseyville (now Almonte), Ontario. Moses and Jane had thirteen children, including son Aaron Barnett, who was born in 1831. Rebecca McMunn, Aaron's wife and Rebecca Barnett's mother, also made the rough journey from Ireland to Canada, and survived a shipwreck getting there.

John Henry McFarlane's ancestors also came to Canada from Ireland in the nineteenth century. George McFarlane, his grandfather, left Londonderry in County Cork in 1819. The fate of his first wife—Caroline Moore, whom he married in Ireland—is unknown. George McFarlane and Letitia Cunningham were married in Canada and had a son, William McFarlane, who married Mary Jane Graham. John Henry, the sixth of nine children of William and Mary Jane McFarlane, was born in 1870 near the town of Perth and grew up in Lanark County in the Ottawa Valley.

John Henry had been a teacher since the age of sixteen, teaching large numbers of students in one-room rural schools in several villages in the Ottawa valley. During one of his stints as a country teacher, in the village of Clayton, John Henry McFarlane boarded at the home of Aaron Barnett, the town cooper (barrelmaker). There he met the pretty brown-eyed Rebecca. It did not take long for him to propose, and after they were married, they moved to the larger town of Carleton Place, where John Henry was offered a job.

Despite the era, and the fact that he taught in rural communities, John Henry was probably ahead of his time in his philosophy about learning and earning a living. When he was sixty-four years old, in 1934, he was invited to return to one of the rural schools where he had taught from 1893 to 1897. During a reunion held there in his honor, he noted that "a child should be taught how to live rather than make a living."

John Henry McFarlane became a well-known and much-beloved educator in Haileybury. In his childhood memoirs, Les notes that his father's seemingly stern exterior hid a wry personality and gentle nature, though few people were fooled for long: "He was a good teacher himself, largely because pupils soon found that his stern appearance masked a baffling sense of humor. . . . Early training and family influence had made my father a master of deadpan delivery, highly esteemed by stand-up television comics even today." Les apparently inherited this dry sense of humor, as his writings—both personal and professional—would reveal, but he did not inherit even a superficially stern demeanor. Les was cheerful and friendly most of the time and avoided confrontation. Nor did he share the elder McFarlane's devotion to religion.

John Henry McFarlane was a devout Presbyterian who insisted that Sundays be devoted to attending church and all the activities associated with it. Rebecca Barnett was Anglican, and Les was later confirmed in the Anglican church when he was seventeen. Nearly six decades later, however, Les remembered vividly the boredom associated with the day of rest: "Kids didn't find it all that restful. If resting means forbidden to go fishing or swimming or playing cowboys and Indians or baseball or skating or bob-sledding then indeed Sunday offered—or let us say demanded—leisure of an excruciatingly boring kind." The day was strictly regimented: the boys cleaned their shoes, dressed in their Sunday clothes (which had to pass parental inspection), and walked to church. There they "pretended" to sing hymns, heard the pastor pray for them (where they wondered if, with all the "thees" and "thous," God's knowledge of the language was defective), sang another hymn, and then heard various announcements about religious activities during the week. Still not over, the minister would read his text, then "harangue us for an hour," after which they would sing still another hymn, he recalled.

As Les noted in a tongue-in-cheek passage in his autobiography, neither his father's deep religious faith nor his skill as an educator could help him instill in Les a very important quality: proficiency in math. Les indicates that while he was not a poor student, his interest in school hardly dominated his life. And his skills in math were indeed sadly lacking: "During the period of prayer he must have asked the Almighty to give him a hand," Les wrote. "And when Divine help failed to materialize he must have asked God just where he had gone wrong . . . what exactly he had done to deserve me."

John Henry was a prolific writer and poet who frequently put his personal thoughts on paper—a trait inherited by Les, who kept personal diaries for decades, and who was a voracious letter writer. John Henry frequently wrote about his own memories of his young adulthood, specifically about life in the Ottawa Valley, and some of his remembrances were published in newspapers there at the time. His articles continued to appear in Ottawa Valley newspapers even after he moved to Haileybury; he contributed articles about his new hometown. John Henry's favorite literary form, however, was poetry, and he wrote many poems throughout his life—poems that, again, spoke of his personal experiences.

John Henry McFarlane's most outstanding work, however, was probably the 10,000-word memoir he wrote after his retirement. The memoir is bittersweet, offering humorous and detailed anecdotes about his early teaching career, his students, and his move to Haileybury. It is an affectionate and poignant portrait of his life and career, and his narrative is frequently interspersed with original poetry. John Henry's memoir is remarkably similar in style to the memoir, autobiography, and letters his son Les would write. John Henry remembers facts and feelings in detail (such as the number of students in his first classroom, as well as the breakfast he ate before he arrived to teach for the first time), and he becomes nostalgic about the places he lived and the students he taught. His cheerful and optimistic attitude prevails in the memoir.

Throughout the memoir, he reflects on his mission and duties as an educator: "The teaching profession is a noble profession. We are dealing with life, not only physical life but Life Eternal, things that live, things that make for happiness. I sometimes think we are teaching our boys and girls only those things that enable them to make money. Is money lasting? Is character lasting? For which goal should we teach?"

John Henry McFarlane felt compelled to write so his memories of his life would last: "Cultivate the memory," he advises; "it is more easily carried than books. Fill it with golden gems that will stand the storms of time and the chilling waves of adversity." To John Henry McFarlane, the urge to write could not be denied. It was another personal quality his oldest son, Les, inherited.

2

. . . .

A WRITER IS BORN

Les's victory in the high school essay contest in Haileybury was a turning point in his life. Although he was only thirteen, the honor and prestige of winning hit him hard. Before he graduated second in his high school class, more honors came. When he was seventeen, he placed second in an Ontario-wide literary competition, and he won first place in a high school oratory competition. That year he also became editor of the newly formed high school newspaper, *The Hail-O*, which he helped found.

In school photos, the diminutive, dark-haired Les is usually the shortest in his class. He grew to only five-foot-three, and as a young man weighed about 105 pounds. His height later ruled him out for army service, but it did not stop him from participating in a variety of outdoor activities throughout most of his life. Les's slight stature never seemed to bother him—in fact, as he once noted, in could be an advantage to him as a reporter because it allowed him to slip into places he was not supposed to be. He accepted his short stature in the same manner he accepted most aspects of his life: on the surface, he was cheerful about it. But in his autobiography, he notes that if given his choice, he would have added a few inches to his height: "When you stop growing at five feet three you have problems," he wrote. "It is all very well to console oneself with the thought that Napolean was a very short man, but Napolean had a horse."

These events during his later high school years clearly paved the way for his writing career. For many young men in the Temiskaming Lake region, the promise of wealth made mining a natural draw; two of Les's brothers, Frank and Dick, went into prospecting as adults, although they were cautious enough not to quit their "day jobs" as pharmacist and watchmaker, respectively. Of his three brothers, in temperament and appearance Les most closely resembled Dick, the third of the McFarlane boys. Dick's wife, Bertha, recalled that Dick and Les were both natural storytellers who enjoyed the response they received to their stories, and both loved practical jokes. The infrequent reunions of all four grown brothers were usually raucous events, Bertha McFarlane recalled.

Les never was drawn to mining, apart from using the characters from his childhood in his fiction. Nor did he want to teach, despite the great respect and admiration he felt for his father. Various summer jobs did not help him make up his mind, either. Les was a tallyman in a lumber mill, a job that entailed sitting for ten hours each day, recording the dimensions of the spruce and pine boards that came from the saws. He was also a cook's helper in a road camp in the bush, serving four meals a day to, as he described them, "a fifty-man crew of dour and silent roadbuilders"; he was assistant projectionist at a movie theater, a junior bank clerk, and a sales representative for the Curtis Publishing Co. of Philadelphia, selling the *Saturday Evening Post* door to door. Despite this variety of odd jobs, he never forgot the thrill of seeing his words in print. He decided to become a writer.

A love of writing, however, did not translate into a lucrative career, as Les and many others knew. Having the nebulous title of "writer" was a luxury that few people of the era could afford. So Les, like others who felt as he did, decided to go into newspaper work. The job allowed him to exercise his creativity, meet eccentric and odd people, and still make a living, albeit a modest one.

Les had no illusions about spending his life as a newspaper reporter. Even as he took his first job in the field, he knew he would not do it for long. The ephemeral quality of the stories he wrote did not appeal to him, nor did the long hours and necessity of pleasing an often temperamental boss. To Les, writing was a solitary occupation that allowed one to leave a mark on the world; it was a noble profession that might not make one rich but could lead to respect and perhaps a limited amount of celebrity. As a young man of eighteen, he knew newspaper work, in the short run, was none of these things, but in the long run, could lead to them. For the moment, it was something he enjoyed doing, something for which he had talent, and something that he believed would help hone his skills.

***

Unlike many of the ghostwriters who formed the backbone of his book syndicate, Edward Stratemeyer did not have an extensive background in newspaper reporting. Stratemeyer's success stemmed from the fact that he took the formula of the dime novel and altered it to fit the changing cultural milieu. In the late nineteenth century, adolescent readers, often bound to jobs that kept them long hours, had little time for a childhood and enjoyed the escapism of these books. As the twentieth century dawned, however, adolescent readers were getting more time, more education, and more resources; boys were more interested in school, sports, and more middle-class pursuits. Stratemeyer apparently noted these cultural shifts and designed new ideas for his boys' books. In 1899, under the pen name Arthur M. Winfield, Stratemeyer created the Rover Boys series, which established a formula he would use for years to come. The three Rover boys, Dick, Tom, and Sam, attended Putnam Hall, a military school. Stratemeyer released the first three volumes at once, a tactic he designed to create interest in the series.

The Rover Boys caught on, and the series sold about 6 million copies before it was discontinued in 1926. But, even more important, its success had established for Stratemeyer a method of doing business in series books. In the early twentieth century, he established the pseudonyms of many other authors, including Clarence Young, author of the Motor Boys, and Victor Appleton, author of the Movie Boys series about teenagers who owned and operated a chain of theaters. During this busy time for Stratemeyer, the automobile, the airplane, motion pictures, and other technical innovations became the vogue. He made sure to incorporate them into his tales—indeed, they formed the backbone of many series, as Arthur Prager notes: "He took his basic Rover figures, changed the names, associated them with some kind of speedy vehicle or popular scientific device, and slipped them into his formula." The Rover Boys series was also innovative in the way it was distributed. By the time of its creation, Stratemeyer began bypassing magazine publishers and had the books published directly by Grosset & Dunlap.

Stratemeyer did not disregard his female readers. Although many of the earlier series books were geared to boys, girl characters began emerging gradually until they had series of their own: girls appeared in major roles in the Rover books, but Stratemeyer established the pen names Alice B. Emerson, for the Betty Gordon and Ruth Fielding series, and Laura Lee Hope, for the Moving Picture Girls, the Outdoor Girls, the Bunny Brown series, the Bobbsey Twins, and others. The Bobbsey Twins, established in 1904, was one of his most successful series, living on through the century until many years after his death. The Bobbseys, aimed at a younger and both male and female market, were about the antics of two sets of twins: Flossie and Freddie, age four, and Nan and Bert, eight. His most famous pseudonym, Carolyn Keene, was not launched until 1930.

It would be hard to overstate the impact culture and society had on Stratemeyer's ideas and his methods of business, and it is clear that he observed closely the activities at Street & Smith when he was there. Not one to let technological advances get ahead of his characters, Stratemeyer in 1910 created boy inventor Tom Swift, whose imagination knew few limits when it came to science and technology. The Tom Swift series sold 6.5 million copies, even more than the Rover Boys.

By about 1910, Stratemeyer was finding that he could not keep up with his own success. The series he created and wrote under a variety of pseudonyms were so popular that his publishers were demanding more, and he could not meet that demand. He started farming out work to freelance writers who wrote the tales from outlines he supplied. From the start, Stratemeyer had a rigidly organized operation and insisted on excellence and conformity in his writers. One of his earliest and most trusted ghostwriters was Howard Garis, a reporter for the *Newark Evening News*. Garis may have set the tone for the rest of Stratemeyer's writers: he wrote the first Tom Swift book for seventy-five dollars; took a set sum for each book he wrote, with no royalties; and wrote for the syndicate under a pen name, agreeing not to reveal his true identity. Over the years, Garis wrote other Stratemeyer Syndicate books, including some in the Bobbsey Twins, Tom Swift, and Motor Boys series. Unlike the other authors, he went beyond the role of ghostwriter and also wrote some plot outlines. Interestingly, Garis, who kept his job on the newspaper throughout his career with the Stratemeyer Syndicate, initially had no interest in writing under a pseudonym. When he met Stratemeyer, he had already written a novel, and his son recalls that part of the pleasure he took in writing came from the fact that people would be aware that he was an author. After meeting Stratemeyer, however, and learning about the workings of the syndicate, he agreed to Stratemeyer's terms which, of course, included writing under pen names. Garis's life soon revolved around writing series fiction, although his most famous children's books, the *Uncle Wiggily* series, were not written for the syndicate. His family, too, became involved. His wife, Lilian, and son, Roger, also wrote for the syndicate. Garis, like the other ghostwriters, walked a fine line. Although they were not given detailed written instructions, all the writers had to produce absorbing stories based on detailed outlines while at the same time achieving a uniformity of style that other ghostwriters could follow. Anyone who wrote the Tom Swift books, for instance, had to write so other Tom Swift authors could step into that author's shoes. It was an odd mixture of creative and formulaic writing. Garis noted the difficulty of the job, calling it "laying the pipes." As media historian Bruce Weber observes, "This meant knowing when and how to insert elements in a story that later could be picked up in what would seem the inevitable movement to the story's big climax. It was well-laid pipes that made a story hang together, and these along with the 'hooks' that propelled readers from chapter to chapter and book to book." Further, each book was uniform in length and format—twenty-five chapters and about two hundred pages.

Finding authors who could do this job quickly and effectively was imperative to Stratemeyer, and he did not take the selection process lightly. Leslie McFarlane describes a tryout in which he had to submit sample chapters; other sources report that Stratemeyer often looked at applicants' other writing. And although Stratemeyer did not actually make his writers sign secrecy clauses, he considered the syndicate pseudonyms to be brand names and did not want his ghostwriters to advertise their involvement in the writing of the series. When Les was in his seventies, nearly thirty years after he stopped writing for Stratemeyer, he still worried about the legality of revealing his ghostwriting experiences in his autobiography and correspondence. Stratemeyer was well aware that the young readers of series fiction had fixed mental pictures of Victor Appleton, Franklin W. Dixon, Carolyn Keene, and the other authors. Knowledge of their true identities—or, more accurately, awareness of their lack of identities—would destroy the mystique. A story circulated that Stratemeyer carefully staggered appointments when his writers came to visit him at his New York offices so they would never meet each other. It is unlikely, however, that the story is true, in part because his authors rarely visited him.

Stratemeyer's timing was fortunate, however, because in the early part of the twentieth century, many who had the itch to write professionally knew they had few opportunities outside of newspapers, and many had a desire to write the great American novel. In fact, many now-famous writers began as newspaper or magazine writers of the era. Like Les and Garis, other Stratemeyer Syndicate writers cut their teeth at newspapers. Mildred Wirt, who wrote the first Nancy Drew mystery and many others in the series as Carolyn Keene, moved to New York from an Iowa newspaper, seeking a writing job. She was the first woman to get a master's degree in journalism from the University of Iowa.

It is not surprising that these newspaper reporters found fiction writing so inviting. The story lines were usually fast paced, with an emphasis on adventure, danger, fast cars, or sports—more elaborate and glamorous versions of what they covered every day. While dime novels for juveniles provided outlets for many of these authors, those who longed to write for adults also found opportunities in what was called pulp fiction. Frank Munsey, known as the father of pulp, published the juvenile magazine *Golden Agosy* in the 1880s. Based on its success, he determined that adults, too, would be interested in plot-driven adventure stories. *Golden Argosy*, renamed *Argosy* in 1888, eventually became an all-fiction adventure magazine printed on rough wood-pulp paper. Its success prompted other publishers to follow suit, and eventually many of them abandoned the dime novel format to focus on magazines that sold for ten to twenty-five cents under names like *Adventure, Detective Fiction,* and *Action Stories.*

As Bruce Weber notes, the expansion of these magazines near the end of the nineteenth century provided a great many markets for writers. Experienced writers earned as much as two cents a word, meaning they could get $100 for a 5,000-word story. Weber writes, "What was required was an ability to deliver the 'goods,' to give editors the kind of never-a-dull-moment adventure yarns they wanted, and to supply them with speed and relentless regularity. This meant writers had to plunge in, plotting as they went along and rarely bothering with the niceties of editing and rewriting." Many writers earned their living through the pulps; some, like well-known muckraker Upton Sinclair and *Lad a Dog* author Albert Payson Terhune, used them to gain writing experience before they became full-time authors.

Stratemeyer in the early years offered working journalists a deal they found hard to refuse: like many publishers of the era, Stratemeyer did not make royalty deals with individual writers for popular fiction, but the flat fee he offered was frequently more than what other publishers would pay. So some reporters could moonlight for him and make twice as much money per month as they made on their newspapers. His relationship with his publisher, Grosset & Dunlap, was unique. Grosset, like many other publishers of the era, served essentially as a reprint house that bought its material from other publishers.

***

Les wrote the autobiographical *Ghost of the Hardy Boys* ostensibly to outline the events that led to his writing the Hardy Boys series, and to describe the process of the writing and how it affected his life. But much of the book is in fact devoted to his three years as a reporter on newspapers in northern Ontario and in Massachusetts. In *A Kid in Haileybury* he had described in detail the rogues and characters he met during his childhood days; in *Ghost of the Hardy Boys* he recalled the colorful characters he met in the newsroom and outside it as a young newspaper reporter. In *Ghost of the Hardy Boys* Les described how, at age seventeen, he began frequenting the offices of the local newspaper, the *Haileyburian,* to absorb the atmosphere. A kindly editor eventually asked him to write a few small stories on a freelance basis. Eventually, he wrote his first big story when he was asked to cover a fire in a nearby village. Les was pleased that the story was printed with little editing—until he learned that he had got the address wrong. "I had gone and burned down the wrong house," he recalled.

With a few freelance articles for the *Haileyburian* under his belt, Les took the trolley to Cobalt, where he interviewed for a job in that mining community five miles from his home. The editor of the *Cobalt Nugget*—a Mr. Browning, whom Les described as a gentle and kind man—hired him immediately at nine dollars a week, not bad pay considering he was still living at home. Immediately, the news editor, Dan Cushing, also offered him two pieces of advice: get names and addresses right, and do not use the word "very." Beyond that, Les was on his own.

Much to his regret, however, the Cobalt Les remembered from his childhood had changed. In ten or fifteen years, the novelty of silver mining had faded, and now it was gold exploration further north that drew the action. "Like one of her own aging madams with a little money in the bank and a lusty past to contemplate, the Cobalt mining camp had settled down and become respectable," he wrote.

Still, if it was writing experience he wanted, it was writing experience he got at the *Nugget.* Whether it was the right kind of experience for an aspiring magazine fiction writer, however, was a matter of debate. The experience on a daily newspaper certainly introduced him to the ways of the world, and Cushing always gave Les the straight story, whether it was about covering a news story or about his own career. When Les told him, for instance, that he periodically wrote short stories and poems and sent them to slick magazines like H. L Mencken's *Smart Set,* one of the more serious literary magazines of the era, Cushing pulled no punches. Any reporter who wanted to be a "writer" was wasting his time at both newspaper work *and* fiction writing, he said. A newspaper was no place for "fine" writing, he explained: "In the lead you put the who, the what, the where, the when and if necessary the how. . . . No fancy work. Try sneaking in any fine writing, any embroidery and I'll cut it out because it isn't good newswriting," he warned. Further, the jobs of reporter and fiction writer were completely at odds, he said. One dealt with facts and the other fiction. But, finally, the few hours a week the newspaperman has free should not be spent writing fiction, he warned: "An honest-to-God newspaperman is a newspaperman twenty-four hours a day," he said. "If he has any spare time he should be out screwing or drinking or hunting or fishing or what have you, maybe even spending a few hours with his family. One sure thing, he shouldn't be farting around with words." Cushing was not the only newspaperman to talk to Les about the fiction writing life. Several years later, when he worked on the *Sudbury Star,* an older journeyman called only Beckett, whom Les respected and thought of as a mentor, encouraged him. Beckett told Les that, indeed, fiction writers are good newspapermen who make things up. But he also told him that he needed luck and a lot of experience in life to be a successful writer, and that it could be a lonely life for the writer and his family.

The extensive writing experience he gained as a reporter taught Les to write tightly and quickly, and it taught him how to edit. Even the hundreds of personal letters he wrote later in his life were concise, clear, and grammatically correct and contained few if any typographical errors or misspellings. But there was some truth to what his early editor, Dan Cushing, said about the dramatic differences between newspaper writing and fiction writing. Newspapers were the training ground for many famous writers, including Mark Twain, Stephen Crane, Theodore Dreiser, John O'Hara, Sinclair Lewis, and Ernest Hemingway. Most learned that the long hours they put in left little time for the types of writing they wanted to do. Twain, for instance, found that reporting gave no "rest" or "respite." Willa Cather went even further, noting, like Dan Cushing, that the nature of newspaper writing was detrimental to fiction writing, calling journalism the "vandalism of literature" that "made an art a trade." Gertrude Stein told the young Hemingway that if he kept doing newspaper work, "you will never see things, you will only see words."

Still, to the nineteen-year-old Les McFarlane, newspaper work was a living, and, aside from the excruciatingly long hours, it was one he enjoyed. After cutting his teeth for a few months on the *Nugget,* he saw a want ad seeking experienced reporters at the *Sudbury Star.* The pay was a whopping twenty-five dollars a week, nearly three times what he earned at the *Nugget.*

But taking the job would mean Les would have to leave home. His brother Frank, who would now have a bed to himself, accompanied Les to the railway station, and, as the two waited, a dozen former classmates of Les's formed an impromptu band and played a song bidding him farewell. It was the first time he had left Haileybury and his family.

***

Les's real education about life began when he left home in 1920 to move to Sudbury. He was in the big leagues now—the *Star* was a newspaper full of grizzled veterans working in a loud, chaotic, and dingy newsroom. It was the type of newsroom, for example, where a blond society writer could burn her posterior as a result of brushing by a flaming wastebasket into which a careless reporter had flicked a lit match.

A tough and rowdy town, Sudbury, with a population of about fifty thousand, was a busy railway and mining center in the world's leading nickel-producing region. As Les noted in his autobiography, the town, with its beautiful lake, lawns, and flower gardens, may not have appeared too grim at first glance. But that vision of tranquility was deceptive: "The surrounding countryside was a forbidding jungle of barren rock that resembled a Wellsian vision of the mountains of the moon," he wrote. As he described it, the mining and "roasting" of nickel and copper ore just outside the town emitted huge clouds of sulphur and created a devastating fog in the outlying areas early each morning. Air pollution, he noted wryly, had not been "invented" yet, "but if it had they would have bragged that the nickel district was its original Canadian home."

Les soon discovered that if he had come to Sudbury to hone his fiction writing skills, he had come to the wrong place. His editor, Bill Mason, informed him immediately that he considered work for the *Star* a twenty-four-hour-a-day obligation. Les covered several beats, including police, school board, town council, and, to a limited degree, sports and theater. "I went flying around town like a small comet in orbit, from office to police court to town hall, to railway station to hotels, to provincial police office to fire hall to town police station and back to the office again, then out to fires, car crashes, ball games, school board meetings, town council sessions and the annual picnic of the Presbyterian Church Sunday School," he wrote. This was even more of a feat for a man who did not drive. Les never drove a car and, throughout his life, traveled on foot or by sleighs, streetcars, buses, and trains, or depended on others to transport him. Even his family is not sure why he never drove—whether he learned to and for some reason refused to do it, or never learned. It never seemed to cramp his style; "public" transportation in the form of streetcar, train, and sleigh was more widespread then.

Despite the frantic pace of his job, his five years in Sudbury did provide Les with some of the life experience he would need as a writer. There was no shortage of news in Sudbury, thanks mostly to the combination of two factors: Prohibition and the influx of miners and lumberjacks from all over the world who convened in the region. Illicit love affairs, bootlegging, fistfights, and even murder were not uncommon in Sudbury in the early twenties, and Les covered many of them for the paper. By his estimate he wrote about a half million words a year.

The job must have been eye-opening for the kid from Haileybury, whose knowledge of the world at the time had been gleaned mainly from his reading. But he was smart enough to realize that he did not have the life experience or sophistication required of most successful writers of fiction—a realization driven home to him by the numerous magazine editors who sent him rejection slips during his time in Cobalt. His former editor Dan Cushing had been brutally candid with Les after he found out his young reporter was writing a short story about a young man, long separated from his family, who by chance meets his sister at a house of ill repute. "You ever been in a whorehouse?" Cushing asked Les, who replied in the negative. "They won't buy your story," the editor predicted. "You've never been in a whorehouse. It won't be convincing."

Certainly life in Sudbury provided Les with some of the cold realities that would round out his writing. It is a testament to his drive and ambition that despite the long hours at the *Sudbury Star*, he did do some freelance writing. Most of it, he noted, was done at one to two in the morning in the newsroom, since he did not have a typewriter at home and it was easier for him simply to stay at work to write.

It was in Sudbury that Les met the young Ernest Hemingway, who as a reporter for the *Toronto Star* traveled north on a tip that a prospector had discovered a coal deposit next to a nickel mine. Nothing came of the tip, but Hemingway did do a story about Sudbury, mentioning, oddly and inaccurately, that the city seemed to have an inordinate number of streetwalkers.

Despite the long working hours and frequent disputes with a penny-pinching editor, the *Sudbury Star* did provide Les with several valuable opportunities—including the chance to write on a freelance basis for the *Toronto Star Weekly* magazine, and the chance to cover sports. He described many times later in his life the elation he felt after seeing his first *Star Weekly* article in print and getting paid ten dollars for it, his first sale as a freelance writer, at age seventeen. "I have no doubt a Nobel prize winner feels pretty good when he learns that he has made it but he can't feel any more elated than a novice writer who sees his story in print," he said. "For several days after an early sale, I made my rounds in a happy state of bemused idiocy. I was euphoric, imagining that everyone in town was saying: 'Look! Look! There's the chap who had a story in the *Toronto Star Weekly*.'" The kindly and sympathetic editor of the publication asked Les to submit more articles to his magazine and printed nearly all of them. "He had a soft spot in his heart for Canadian writers," Les recalled. "He knew they had to begin by getting their work into print." His minor success as a freelance writer for the *Star Weekly* simply whetted his appetite to do more writing; and the small victory of seeing his work in the magazine made him desire even more a career as a fiction writer.

Although editors at the *Sudbury Star* did not prohibit Les from writing for the *Star Weekly*, they certainly did not encourage it. In fact, in an attempt to keep him even busier, editor Bill Mason assigned Les the hockey beat—no small task for any Canadian reporter. Les had of course played hockey as a boy and had seen professional hockey in Haileybury. Even a native Canadian like Les, though, could not have overestimated the thirst northern Ontario fans had for hockey news during hockey season from November to March. Not only did readers want discussion of the game beforehand and results afterward, they wanted the paper to relive, play by play, games of the previous night. Even that was not enough to satisfy the demand of northern Ontario residents for hockey news.

Play-by-play accounts were soon carried by telegraph so residents throughout the region could hear about the progress of the games as they convened in public places to get the latest scores. Because he covered the games anyway, Les was hired on a freelance basis by the telegraph company to dictate play-by-play coverage to the telegraph operator so it could be translated into print and rushed to the movie theaters, lounges, hockey clubs, and other establishments where die-hard fans would gather. As Les noted in jest in his autobiography, he in effect became one of the first play-by-play "commentators," with the power to hold theaters full of people spellbound—even without benefit of radio or television. He also noted the irony of the situation—his son, Brian, would later become a household name as a hockey commentator on Canadian television's popular *Hockey Night in Canada*. And the irony was not lost on Brian seventy years later; in his own autobiography he retells with relish the story of his father and his adventures in hockey commentary. The chapter was titled "Dad Was a Stone-Age Broadcaster."

For his trouble, though, Les earned a grand total of five dollars a game—an amount his editor, Bill Mason, told him was much too low. Mason advised him to stand up for his rights and ask for at least twenty dollars, which Les promptly did. After some dickering, the telegraph people told him they no longer required his services. The lesson, he wrote, was that no one was indispensable (and that the employer frequently has the upper hand). It was a lesson he would remember ruefully when negotiating pay as a full-time freelance writer.

Les was certainly a jack-of-all-trades at the *Sudbury Star,* and his duties also included theater criticism. Like the other beats he covered, this one offered its share of drama and hilarious stories, and he recounts some in his autobiography. But the experience of covering theater would be invaluable to him. A lover of literature, he was naturally drawn to theater. Most of his life he attended plays and offered critiques of them to his children in letters when they were teenagers and adults. Les's exposure to the theater also led him to try his hand at playwriting—an art form that he soon learned was not as easy as it looked. After the publication of his short story "Impostor" in *Adventure* magazine, a popular American stage actor named Alan Dinehart expressed an interest in adapting it for the theater, offering him five hundred dollars for the rights. The request emboldened Les, prompting him to reject it in hopes of getting much more. Les contacted the actor, offering to write the play himself, and the two made a deal. But Les quickly learned, at age twenty-three, that he could not adapt to the limitations of playwriting. As he noted, characters in his short stories "are free to roam all over the place," while their actions on a small stage are much more limited. Because of these physical limitations, his characters were forced into artificial dialogue, announcing their attentions, thoughts, and motivations in an obvious way. And worst of all, Les could not coordinate the various exits and entrances of all the characters, despite the help of a playwriting manual. After a month of writing, he abandoned the project, admitting it was a humbling experience. It would be several decades before he would become versatile enough to master nearly every form of writing, including stage drama.

Meanwhile, Les's few years at newspapers taught him to write quickly, accurately, and, ultimately, in a descriptive and colorful way. But no story illustrated his talent as a reporter and writer more than one that would hit close to home for him: a devastating fire that nearly annihilated his childhood hometown of Haileybury.

Because of its unrestrained growth in such a short time, few building regulations were established in Haileybury and the surrounding areas. This, combined with the warm, dry summers, led to frequent brush fires in the area. They were so common that residents became used to seeing the mist of smoke from scattered fires. But some of the fires were more than mere nuisances. Les remembered one in the town of Matheson, a few miles from Haileybury, which swept through half a million acres of farmland and killed two hundred in several towns when he was fourteen. His memories of the fire, along with a news item at the time describing the deaths of twenty-two people who tried to escape the fire by hiding in a small shack, led to his writing years later of an award-winning short story called "The Root-House." The psychological study is set in a small shack, or root-house, as a family of three desperately tries to wait out a fire that sweeps their property. In this tale, however, the family emerges alive.

One fire that would remain vivid to him for the rest of his life was the devastating blaze on October 4, 1922, that destroyed much of Haileybury and killed eleven of its residents (although the number of casualties totaled forty-four in the region). The fire started after a long dry spell, when a high wind caused several small fires to merge and sweep through the area "like a red hot cyclone," Les wrote in his autobiography. At the time, he was working for the *Sudbury Star*, but because of his ties to Haileybury, Les was quickly dispatched by taxi to North Bay, eighty miles away, because rail centers at the time were centers for the distribution of news. Upon arriving there, he wrote five decades later, the news was sketchy, confusing, "and all bad." Worried for his parents and his brothers, Les remembers "patching together" a story for the front page of the *North Bay Nugget* (formerly the *Cobalt Nugget*), a newspaper owned by the owner of the *Star*. This patched together story across page one was a true illustration of Les's talents as a writer—concise, descriptive, and poignant, it conveyed perfectly the devastation and fear in the community. It ran a few days later in the *Star:* "A leering tornado of flame from the southwest roared down through a half-mile of underbrush upon the town of Haileybury, basking sleepily in the . . . sunlight on the shore of Lake Temiskaming early Wednesday afternoon, ate its way across the railway tracks and then, fanned by a 6o-mile-an-hour gale, ripped its way through the town to the water's edge, scattering the 4,000 inhabitants before its terrific blast veered to the south, leveled the town to the ground, swept into North Cobalt and reduced the place to cinders, and pursued its havoc-wreaking course to the borders of Cobalt, and subsided only when a heavy rainstorm quenched the terror." The story went on to describe some individual cases of families attempting to escape from the fire, and to describe the ruins: "At Mileage 104 the picture of desolation is complete. A pair of stray cattle nosed about for a bite of fodder yesterday as *The Star* correspondent motored over the road that winds through smoking heaps of former human habitation."

When he arrived in North Bay and gathered information for his first story, Les heard nothing but terrible rumors about the fate of Haileybury's residents, and tried desperately to learn the whereabouts of his family. He heard about a relief train that was carrying people from his hometown to North Bay; as he waited for the train, he caught a glimpse of his mother and youngest brother Graham. After his first flush of relief, he learned that the rest of his family would soon be on their way to North Bay by train. Mrs. McFarlane, however, became a wonderful firsthand source of information for Les's story as she described the confusion and terror in the town as it went up in flames. Les later learned that hundreds of people ran into the freezing lake and watched as the flames were ultimately swept away by a snowstorm. The fire raked 648 square miles of land and destroyed 90 percent of the city of Haileybury.

To Les, the Haileybury fire was more than just a chance to demonstrate his reporting and writing talents. It saddened him greatly that many of the remnants of his childhood were destroyed, and that some of the neighbors and friends he had grown up with had perished. The fire is considered one of the worst natural disasters in Canadian history. Still, the hardy Haileybury residents endured—new schools, churches, and government buildings were rebuilt within two years, and John Henry McFarlane, who had loved his family home, had it rebuilt on the same lot exactly as it was before the fire. To Les, however, Haileybury would never be the same.

3
. . . .
THE GHOST OF THE HARDY BOYS

Les did manage to do some freelance writing in Sudbury despite his hectic life there. According to detailed records he kept of his article and story sales, he sold two stories to *Adventure* magazine in late 1924 that earned him a total of $775, the equivalent of nearly eight months' salary as a reporter. These sales no doubt bolstered his confidence as a writer of fiction. Although the stories sold to a pulp publication rather than to the slick magazines like *Maclean's* or *Smart Set,* this early success indicated to him that he could possibly realize his dream of becoming a full-time writer of fiction. Clearly, Les could be on his way if he could keep up what were in essence two full-time jobs—as a reporter and as a fiction writer.

Les had the energy and the drive to do both, but he was of course reluctant to quit a job that provided a regular, albeit small, paycheck. And such a decision was not to be made lightly. It was a combination of fate, encouragement from a friend, and a momentary burst of frustration that led to his resignation from the *Star* one day.

As Les recounts in his autobiography, his friend and mentor at the paper, the man known as Beckett, calmly announced one day that he was leaving to become managing editor of the *Montreal Herald.* That news was not good for Les, who had come to admire and respect Beckett and use him as a sounding board. Beckett had told Les that most good writers need to write, and would do it for little or no money. On one of his last days at the paper, Beckett had found a want ad for a furnished summer cottage renting for one hundred dollars for the whole season. It was located on scenic and isolated Lake Ramsey, about three hundred miles north of Toronto and a few miles across the lake from Sudbury. Beckett thought it would make a perfect venue for his young friend to start a full-time fiction writing career.

Les wavered, telling Beckett that he was reluctant to give up a steady job for what would certainly be an unsteady existence. Beckett offered these words, which ultimately influenced Les's decision: "Don't wait too long," he said. "I've met scores of old newspapermen who wanted to be writers and never got around to it." With that, Beckett left. Les investigated the cottage, which was, indeed, rustic. It had no electricity, no roads nearby, and no indoor water. "It was a fine place," he recalled. Still, he hesitated to quit a paying job for the ascetic life of a writer. But the quandary resolved itself a few days later: one morning his editor and sometime-nemesis Bill Mason was again in a foul mood, criticizing his staff, its coverage of news, and particularly Les, who had come in late two days in a row. The tirade was all too familiar to the mild and non-confrontational Les, as he recalled in his autobiography:

> Perhaps an invisible Beckett tapped me on the shoulder and whispered, "Now is the time." So I put down my copy pencil, got to my feet, reached to the rack for my straw hat and put it on my head.
>
> Then to my infinite astonishment, I heard myself tell Mason to go fuck himself.
>
> I doubt if life holds any greater satisfaction.

He rented the cabin for the summer only, bought a secondhand type-writer, found a roommate, and moved in with a stock of provisions and beer. In addition to allowing him to write, the time away from a structured job also allowed him to read and get a closer view of the types of publications and writers popular in mid-1925. Always a voracious reader, he soon learned that the art of getting published was not simply restricted to the craft of writing itself. There was an art to pleasing editors, and in writing stories to match the available markets. He aspired to publishing his work not in pulp markets but in top-drawer American literary magazines such as *Harper's* and *Atlantic Monthly*. In these magazines, he noted, "it wasn't the story that counted but how you told it. Plots were for popular magazine writers, not for talented authors in embryo."

His time at the cabin introduced him to writers he would emulate and enjoy for the rest of his life: writers such as F. Scott Fitzgerald (with whom he corresponded later), Willa Cather, Somerset Maugham, and Theodore Dreiser. Les had always been a fan of H. L. Mencken's, and had read his magazine *Smart Set* when he was in high school. But as an adult on Lake Ramsey, he learned from Mencken the art of the essay and the value of literary criticism—even extremely negative criticism. Les was stunned and amused by how much Mencken could get away with in his criticism, and by the fact that he could berate and insult prominent men such as Billy Sunday, William Jennings Bryan, and even the president of the United States with no apparent repercussions: "Even the President . . . became a ward-heeler, a tool of crooks, a buffoon given to blather which made no sense to anyone at any time. This seemed pretty blasphemous to me and I kept a sharp eye on the news for a month after that, sure that Mencken would be arrested and shot as a traitor. . . . But no retribution fell upon Mr. Mencken. He stayed out of jail and went on smashing public idols." His reading on Lake Ramsey would influence Les for the rest of his life. He "discovered" Sherwood Anderson and his stories about small-town life—a subject with which Les was familiar—and took comfort in the fact that a figure no less famous than former dentist Zane Grey experienced humiliating rejection before his books were published.

Les's first few months as a full-time fiction writer were not without frustration. After shipping stories, one by one, to magazines like *Adventure,* he was dejected to have them returned, rejected, their margins littered with editors' criticisms. The detailed comments from *Adventure* editor Arthur Sullivant Hoffman, in particular, left him so depressed that he was tempted to take a walk after reading it—"straight into the lake," he joked in his autobiography. After the initial shock, however, Les was smart enough to reread the criticisms and profit from them: "I realized that this was advice with a value beyond rubies. Mr. Hoffman was . . . an editor who wasn't above taking time out to give a hand to a beginner who needed help. What he had done, simply, was to save this beginner about two years of trial and error." Even as a young man, Les was determined and practical. He listened to criticism and took it in the spirit in which it was given—a quality that would reap benefits throughout his life.

Having failed to sell any stories to the slicker publications, Les focused on *Adventure* magazine, where he had achieved a small measure of success the previous year. In his autobiography, he notes that the magazine, although printed on pulp paper, was not a "pulp" magazine in the strictest sense. Instead, it was a "respectable" journal that published the work of some skilled writers, including T. S. Stribling, who later won a Pulitzer Prize for fiction. And soon things did pick up for Les. In 1925, he sold five more stories to that magazine, as well as an article to a pulp magazine called *West.* His sales for that year totaled $1,540. What was more encouraging was that most of these were full-length stories, earning him as much as $480, as was the case with a 24,000-word mystery tale called "Agent of the Hawk" that he wrote for *Adventure*. (Also that year, Les wrote two smaller stories for which he earned $65 and $120.) And his sales were distributed throughout the year—his first story was published in February, and his last in December.

But whether for lack of self-confidence or a steady paycheck or for other reasons, Les was back at a newspaper in early 1926—this time in the United States at the *Springfield (Massachusetts) Republican*. Although he was only twenty-four, his employment and publishing record was impressive. He had covered a variety of types of stories at several newspapers and had several articles printed in magazines. All that meant little, however, to his new editor, Bill Walsh, who was not familiar with Haileybury, Cobalt, Sudbury, or the magazines for which Les wrote. But he hired Les at a salary of forty dollars a week, and included an advance of twenty dollars the first week. Les was not used to such generosity.

The *Republican* was a morning newspaper, and its rival, the *Union*, was published in the afternoon. Little real competition existed between the newspapers, each of which over the years developed its own audience. As at the other newspapers for which Les had worked, the newsroom was full of colorful characters; but these were not the rowdy, hard-drinking types he had met in Sudbury. Instead, each lived a type of alternative life. The Churches and Obits man, Les noted, wrote songs on the side and even had some published; the city hall reporter was an amateur actor waiting to be "discovered"; the police reporter was writing a novel; and of course Les was still honing his fiction-writing technique.

But he enjoyed working at the paper and liked his kindly editor, who gave the diminutive 118-pound Les the "hotel" beat, he suspected, so he could cover speakers at the many banquets in Springfield's one big hotel. "He thought I could do with a little fattening up," he recalled in his autobiography. Because of the long working days and continual colds he suffered because of the severe weather, he actually lost five pounds during his first few months in Springfield. As he wrote his future wife, Amy Arnold, weeks on the night shift made it difficult for him to make new friends. Still, he enjoyed the camaraderie in the newsroom and liked his fellow workers: "There is a pleasant informality about the life and the boys at the office are good-natured fellows, so I could be a lot unhappier." Les had always enjoyed the atmosphere of the newsroom, and he typed the letter to Amy as he sat in the newsroom at midnight, listening to the clattering linotype machines and few jangling phones.

It was also about this time that Les acquired an agent in New York, Bob Hardy, who would help him sell some of his freelance stories. The agent's last name would, ultimately, prove ironic.

***

By the time Les arrived at the *Springfield Republican,* Edward Stratemeyer's fiction syndicate was humming along—the economy was good, and many of his key series such as Tom Swift and the Bobbsey Twins were selling well. Stratemeyer's many series during the first quarter of the century fell into categories such as the "school series," including the Rover Boys (which ended in 1926); sports series, such as Baseball Joe; and girls' series, which by 1926 included the popular Ruth Fielding stories, the Outdoor Girls, and others.

By the mid-1920s, some of the books were beginning to gain a bit of sophistication. As one critic noted, the stilted and sometimes pretentious language of the highly popular Rover Boys series, written by Stratemeyer as Arthur M. Winfield, gave way to the concisely written and resourceful Tom Swift series. The style of the early Rover Boys was wordy and trite. No Rover boy, for instance, ever merely read a letter when he could "peruse its contents." Nor did any villain ever do anything but "tremble in his boots" when captured. On the other hand, the Tom Swift books—many of which were written by Howard Garis under the name of Victor Appleton—featured humor, concise description, and a higher level of writing overall, as several critics have noted. The true genius of that series, however, was its ability to capitalize so fully on the rapidly growing technology of the era. Tom invents whatever he needs, and the plots usually hinge on whether the invention will work and whether it will be stolen. Critic Russel Nye noted decades later that for the Tom Swift series, Garis and Stratemeyer "took the adventure story of the Rovers, combined it with Jules Verne, Thomas Edison, Marconi and all the others who contributed to the excitement of the machine age, and mixed into it the greatest assortment of gadgets known to man."

By this time, Stratemeyer had taken to placing ads in newspapers to attract new ghostwriters. He must have devoted considerable time to the task of separating the true writers who could complete the job he wanted from those who just fancied themselves writers. His million-dollar "syndicate" had a skeleton staff and was little more than an office to which authors sent their manuscipts. When he moved the office from New Jersey to New York City in 1914, he hired Harriet Otis Smith as his assistant;

Smith, among other duties, checked manuscripts to see that they conformed to the details of the plot outlines. Stratemeyer's older daughter, Harriet, did some editing for her father's syndicate shortly after she graduated from Wellesley College in 1914, but her father insisted she work from home because he was not keen on the idea of women holding jobs away from home. (The straight-arrow Stratemeyer believed in the sanctity of the family, attended church every Sunday, and did not drink.) Harriet Stratemeyer's limited involvement with the syndicate ended with her marriage to Russell Vroom Adams, an investment banker. Stratemeyer's younger daughter, Edna, was still in school during the height of her father's success. But the lack of help did not faze Stratemeyer, who was single-minded about the way he wanted things done. Unlike most of those who wrote for him—and his role model, Horatio Alger—Stratemeyer no longer had the desire to write the great American novel or to achieve celebrity. He simply wanted to run a successful and lucrative syndicate, a goal he certainly achieved by 1926.

Nothing illustrates Stratemeyer's unflappable nature better than the brouhaha raised early in the century by the Boy Scouts of America, whose self-described "chief librarian" undertook a serious campaign to undermine the series fiction of the era. Although his name is never mentioned in this effort, Edward Stratemeyer may have been one of the targets. Nearly a century later, the Boy Scouts' scare tactics and hyperbole seem comic, particularly since the books contained nothing prurient or off-color, and even the sanitized "violence" involved no blood. It is true that the boys and the villains repeatedly got tied up, hit on the head, or nearly drowned, and that they tumbled down cliffs or fell through trapdoors, but they never died brutal deaths. In his autobiography, Les noted that by the standards of the late twentieth century, the series books were remarkably tame and included no tobacco and not the slightest hint of sex, even on the part of the villains. If the villains did sneak a cigarette, he quipped, they did it "between chapters." (Even the socially conservative Les joked in his book that some illicit sex might not have hurt some of Stratemeyer's creations. After the success of the Hardy Boys, Les, as Carolyn Keene, wrote the initial books in a new series called the Dana Girls. Decades later, he reflected on the experience in an uncharacteristically off-color way: "I spent a couple of months banging away at the Dana sisters," he wrote. "Perhaps the expression is indelicate. Nobody every banged the Dana girls.")

But far tamer stuff bothered officials of the Boy Scouts in 1914. They did not take series fiction lightly and warned parents, teachers, and librarians of its dangers. In an attempt to stem what he deemed the reckless production of mindless adventure books that were harmful to adolescents, Boy Scouts librarian Franklin K. Mathiews went to publishers with various Scout-approved reading lists, which included classics like *Call of the Wild* and *20,000 Leagues under the Sea*. He also arranged for publication of the Boys Scouts' own series fiction. Known as the Tom Slade series by Percy Keese Fitzhugh, it supposedly told true-to-life Scout stories.

It is a measure of Stratemeyer's steely determination and his business acumen that he was unfazed by Mathiews's campaign. And it is a measure of Mathiews's evangelical zeal that he did not stop there. In 1914, he wrote a now-famous thousand-word essay in *Outlook* magazine that would be read by librarians for decades to come, titled "Blowing Out the Boy's Brains." By today's standards, the language and imagery of the essay are comical. Although he never mentions Stratemeyer by name, he angrily points out that the series books of the era were like explosives, guaranteed to "blow out the brains" of the boys who read them, and ought to carry a warning label on each one. The books are not written, he says, but "manufactured," not by one man, he implies, but by several people who turned out the books at breakneck speed, often one every two weeks. (Actually, Mathiews was not far from wrong on this point; some of Stratemeyer's ghostwriters could turn one out in three weeks or less, and it sometimes took only five weeks from conception of an idea for a book to typeset product.) Mathiews was probably one of the first to tiptoe around Stratemeyer's big secret: that each book in a series was not written by one author using his or her real name. Mathiews was more interested in the content of the books than in the method of production. He goes on to say,

> In almost all of this "mile-a-minute" fiction some inflammable tale of improbable adventure is told. Boys move about in aeroplanes as easily as though on bicycles; criminals are captured by them with a facility that matches the ability of Sherlock Holmes; when it comes to getting on in the world, the cleverness of these hustling boys is comparable only to those captains of industry and Napoleons of finance who have made millions in a minute.

With their formulaic writing style and plots, Mathiews writes, the "vile" series books may provide short-term cheap thrills, but will destroy the brain and the body, much as alcohol does. But Mathiews saves the best for last. In a breathless anecdote near the end of his essay, he tells the tale of a young man who disappeared suddenly from his quiet, middle-class home in Lansing, Michigan. Mathiews said the scoutmaster of the boy's hometown sent Boy Scout headquarters an ominous note, implying only one explanation for the disappearance: "cheap reading" in the form of series books.

The volatile language of Mathiews's tirade may owe something to writings by Anthony Comstock, a leading censor of the late nineteenth century. Mathiews's article recalls some passages from Comstock's book *Traps for the Young*, which attacks some literature of the 1880s and 1890s. Comstock notes, for instance, that light literature is "a devil-trap to captivate the child by perverting taste and fancy" and that by reading it, "your child is in danger of having its pure mind cursed for life." Comstock offers an anecdote of a young man who sent obscenity in the mail because he had read five-cent story papers.

Ironically, the conservative Mathiews was ahead of his time in at least one way. Criticism of the Stratemeyer series books by educators and librarians continued in one form or another throughout the twentieth century. Many of the arguments have repeated those first brought up by Mathiews—that the books have no literary value and are formulaic. But the Stratemeyer Syndicate and its series continued to grow during the century, and they certainly had their defenders and great word of mouth—millions of youngsters grew up and gave the books to *their* children. After 1959, the debate took a twist. That was the year the Stratemeyer Syndicate—long after the death of Edward Stratemeyer—changed some of the series fiction to update it and remove some passages and terms the publishers deemed racist or sexist. The rewrites had little effect on the libraries that had already removed the books from their shelves, or on those that had never carried them.

The true target of Mathiews's wrath may never be known. Some Syndicate researchers believe that it was not Stratemeyer, but producers of other juvenile fiction of the era. These researchers say many primary documents including letters indicate that the two men had a cordial—and certainly not hostile—relationship. But Mathiews's criticisms were widely known, and may even have given series books a blast of publicity. When Les was first introduced to the Stratemeyer Syndicate through a want ad seeking authors, he had never heard of Edward Stratemeyer, although the name was vaguely familiar to an older colleague, the literary critic for the *Republican*. After Les left the paper, the critic mailed him detailed accounts of the history of the syndicate and articles about the Boy Scouts controversy. It was only then, Les recalled in his autobiography, that he realized what he was getting himself into.

***

By the time Les became involved with the syndicate in 1926, it was clear that the efforts of Mathiews and others who criticized the books were nearly fruitless. The syndicate books had achieved commercial success, and no criticism by the Boy Scouts or librarians would stop children from reading them. In 1926 and 1927, the American Library Association published the Winnetka Grade Book List based on a survey of books read by schoolchildren in thirty-four American cities. It showed that series books were read by 98 percent of those surveyed. And it noted that "the books of one series [presumably the Bobbsey Twins] were unanimously rated trashy by our expert librarians and almost unanimously liked by the 900 children who read them." But Mathiews did make an enduring contribution to children's literature: teachers and librarians across the country embraced his creation of a Children's Book Week to encourage reading, and it exists today.

Certainly the millions of readers of Stratemeyer books exemplified the power children had when selecting reading material. The role of librarians and teachers in the selection and recommendation of children's books by schools and libraries was of course pivotal for most of the twentieth century, but for much of the first half of the century, publishing houses did not have separate children's divisions, and children's sections of public libraries were rare. The formation of these specialized departments would naturally have a profound effect on what children would read. In the 1920s, librarians found little that met their critical standards. Lewis Carroll's *Alice's Adventures in Wonderland,* published in 1865, was a watershed book, primarily because it was one of the first books written for children's pure enjoyment, rather than one designed to teach a lesson or instill a moral. Other books of the late nineteenth century were romantic and fey in nature, and were frequently aimed at a female audience— books like Lucretia Hale's the *Peterkin Papers* and of course the famous *Little Women* by Louisa May Alcott, which portrayed the warm family life of the Marches. Books for boys combined adventure with realism and humor. But the true watershed book of the genre was Robert Louis Stevenson's *Treasure Island,* published in 1883. The difference between

Treasure Island and other adventure novels of the era is, again, that Stevenson's book is pure adventure undiluted by what one group of children's literature critics called "ulterior" motives such as piety or morality. Critic Elizabeth Nesbitt notes that the beauty and craft of the writing "raises it to a level of art. . . . [Stevenson is] not just a lover of tales, but equally a lover of words and phrases, a meticulous searcher for the right word, a builder of phrases precise and exact."

Still, children's librarians of the early 1920s lamented the dearth of such richly textured books. "We are tired of substitutes for realities in writing for children," said Anne Carroll Moore, head of the New York Public Library's Children's Department in 1920. "The trail . . . [is] strewn with patronage and propaganda, moralizing self-sufficiency and sham efficiency, mock heroics and cheap optimism—above all, with the commonplace in theme, treatment and language." The end of World War I, however, brought many revolutionary changes in children's literature. Children's divisions were formed in publishing houses, magazines about children's literature (most notably *The Horn Book Magazine*) were published, and the John Newbery Medal was created by the American Library Association in 1922 to encourage high-quality juvenile books.

Most important, for the first time, the concept of "children's literature" as a genre was starting to be taken seriously. Moore, of the New York Public Library, began editing in 1924 a weekly page of criticism of children's books in the *New York Herald Tribune,* a section which included submissions from writers, illustrators, and librarians. A similar section was formed in the *New York Times Book Review* in 1930.

***

In 1926, when Les read the want ad in *The Editor* (which later became *Editor & Publisher*) seeking fiction writers, the Stratemeyer Syndicate was at its height: it had weathered the campaign by the Boy Scouts, it was quick to capitalize on the many technological and cultural changes of the era, and, thanks to Edward Stratemeyer and Howard Garis, syndicate activities and procedures were moving along smoothly. In his 1976 autobiography, Les describes at length his dealings with the syndicate, and his words have been quoted frequently in articles and books about the syndicate. Roger Garis, the son of Howard Garis, talks about life with Uncle Wiggily's alter ego and creator in his autobiography, *My Father Was Uncle Wiggily,* but nowhere besides Les's autobiography does a Stratemeyer author describe in such detail his experience with the syndicate. Stratemeyer himself, of course, took pains not to give away too much information about it, and his daughters, who took over after his death, gave few extensive interviews.

The reticence on the part of ghostwriters to discuss their experience probably stems from the copyright agreement they had accepted before they wrote the books, although they signed no secrecy clause; the agreements stated only that the ghostwriters could not use the pen names for their own work. Stratemeyer expected that the writers would not reveal their true identities, but he did encourage them to tell publishers about their work on the series in order to get other work. Indeed, the only penalty for going public may have been dismissal as a ghostwriter. Les acknowledges in his autobiography that this oath of silence was no problem for him—in fact, he noted wryly that he had no reservations in 1926 about making such a pledge, as long as the syndicate reciprocated and revealed to no one that he worked for it. Although he signed a legal document, Les never bothered to ask the penalty if he did, indeed, reveal the secret. "I assumed it had something to do with being boiled in oil," he wrote decades later. (If the Stratemeyers were ever to have boiled him in oil, it would most likely have happened in 1974, when Les appeared on the popular television game show *To Tell the Truth*. This time, he was the "real" Leslie McFarlane, aka Franklin W. Dixon, while the two men with him on the panel were impostors.)

When he was accepted by Stratemeyer and, shortly after, began writing the first Hardy Boys books, Les took the job very seriously. But Les's attitude about the syndicate and his role in it was ambivalent. After writing his first Hardy Boys book in late 1926, he had no intention of maintaining a long or serious relationship with the Stratemeyer Syndicate. Throughout his twenty-year association with it, he was continually on the brink of leaving it for good. But for one reason or another, he stayed.

In *Ghost of the Hardy Boys,* Les recounts in detail his tryout with the syndicate in 1926. Stratemeyer mailed him two of the syndicate's books: one from the Nat Ridley Rapid Fire Detective Stories (of which fifteen volumes had been published), by Nat Ridley Jr., and the other from the Dave Fearless series, an outdoor adventure series featuring underwater explorer and deep-sea diver Dave Fearless. Les's recollection in his autobiography indicates that he was mildly amused and somewhat astonished by several aspects of the situation, including the fact that Roy Rockwood was the author of the Dave Fearless series—the same author who wrote the Bomba the Jungle Boy books and several other series books that he had respected. He remembered distinctly the shock he felt when he began reading Dave Fearless: It was, as he described it, "bilge." Then it began to dawn on Les that "Roy Rockwood" had never existed in the first place. In the 1934 article in *Fortune* magazine, the writer notes ironically that the syndicate took great pains, sometimes to comical effect, to hide the fact that Stratemeyer himself wrote many of the books under various pseudonyms. *Fortune* told of a reader who wrote to the syndicate requesting a biographical sketch of May Hollis Barton, the name Stratemeyer used to write some of the Barton Books for Girls series. As Miss Barton was imaginary, so was the elaborate description of her that a syndicate assistant provided. "Little did the readers of this work know," the *Fortune* reporter noted sarcastically, "that she was a nervous, kindly, nearsighted stocky man who looked like a deacon and for whom books came forth like an interminable string of sausages."

Les decided to read the Dave Fearless book more closely. To his horror and relief, he saw that the book Stratemeyer had sent him was so badly written that it probably would take little effort to improve on it. The catch, however, was the difficulty in providing dialogue for someone like Fearless, who was perennially under water. It was clear to him that Stratemeyer had created Dave Fearless as a man of much action and few words.

Les learned from the book some of the strict formulaic aspects of syndicate books: all were between 204 and 218 pages in final book form, and all had the equivalent of commercials imbedded in them. The second chapter of each book began with a quick break from the action as the author summarized the activities of the protagonist in previous volumes. At the end of each book was another plug for the exploits of the hero or heroes in future volumes. Both tactics were designed to get youngsters to buy more books in the same series.

Despite what he considered the oddity and absurdity of the situation, Les decided to try his hand—for no pay—at a few practice chapters of a Dave Fearless book. If those were accepted, he would finish the book for pay. While Les had no illusions about the art of Stratemeyer Syndicate books, he admired their honesty: "Neither of the sample books had a smidgeon of merit," he wrote. "They had less content than a football bladder and no more style than a drunken camel. Garbage. But then, they didn't pretend to be works of literature. They were straightforward, cheap paperbacks for a public that would neither read nor relish anything better. And besides, I would be under no obligation to *read* the stuff. I would merely have to write it." With that, he began what would be one of the most enduring and frustrating relationships of his life.

***

As he described it in his autobiography, the initial outline for *Dave Fearless under the Ocean* consisted of three single-spaced typewritten pages of action-filled description, covering twenty-five chapters:

> CHAP. 1—Dave and Bob cruising off Long Island in launch Amos run into fog—mention first and second volumes of series—engine fails—ring reminds Bob of adventures on Volcano Island—mention other volumes—boys discuss Lem and Bart Hankers, believed dead—sound of foghorn is heard—ocean liner looms out of fog—collision seems inevitable.

Les was struck by the mile-a-minute frantic action and thrills in the book, which, he noted, seemed unrealistic: "[The outline] called for more perils and narrow escapes than a normal diver would encounter in several lifetimes." But after everyone left the paper for the day, Les rolled up his sleeves and began typing the story from the outline. Here's how part of that chapter 1 outline was translated onto his typewriter:

> Dave Fearless looked out over the rolling waves and frowned as he saw a greasy cloud rolling in from the horizon.
> "There's a fog coming up, Bob."
> "Looks like it. Do you think we had better turn back?"
> "Perhaps we should," agreed Dave. "We want to be back at Quanatack in time for supper."
> The two chums, Dave Fearless, young deep-sea diver, and Bob Vilett, marine engineer, were cruising off the coast of Long Island in Dave's motor boat, the *Amos*. Now, as Dave remarked, a fog was rising and they were a long way from home.

Of course, the fog gets worse, and by the end of chapter 1, a huge dark shape looms out of the fog; the ship is about to hit the *Amos* as the chapter ends.

Les found he had little trouble conforming to the standards set by Stratemeyer in the first two chapters of the book. Things happen "in the nick of time," the boys "breathe a sigh of relief" at their last-minute rescues, and the thrills continue throughout. Still, Les found that even formulaic writing for children was not without its intellectual challenges. In the first chapter of the book, for example, the boat's engine fails, but is of course miraculously fixed by Dave. Because Les knew little about the engineering of marine engines, he found it best to avoid the details of just how the engine was repaired—it just was.

He managed to complete the two chapters, pleased with himself, and packed them off to Stratemeyer. Before long, he received a letter from the syndicate head, informing him, in Stratemeyer's low-key manner, that the sample chapters were "satisfactory," and that he could finish the remaining chapters for $100. The confident Les had been so sure Stratemeyer would like his sample that he had already written five more chapters by the time the letter arrived. Shortly after he received the letter, he finished the book by working until 3 a.m. night after night in the *Republican* newsroom and packaged it for the mail. He never gave it a second reading or editing, nor did he keep a carbon copy of it: "The postal service would have been flattered by this manifestation of utter faith," he wrote years later. "Any professional writer would have been horrified."

With characteristic restraint, Stratemeyer's letter to Les called the book "a lively narrative." What was more important to Les, however, were the $100 check for *Dave Fearless under the Ocean* and another Dave Fearless story outline that accompanied the letter.

The remarkable ease of the situation struck Les. After doing some quick math, he calculated that if he quit his job on the paper, he could spend an hour a day to write four books a month for Stratemeyer, earning more than double his salary at the *Republican*. More important, he would have time to write some real works of literature without having to stay up most of the night. That spring, Les gave his notice at the paper, but managed to squeeze in one more Dave Fearless book—*Dave Fearless in the Black Jungle*—before he left the paper to head out of the United States and back to Lake Ramsey in Canada. This time he signed a year's lease on the cabin for a mere $100—the amount he earned for each Dave Fearless book.

***

Les enjoyed his new life at Lake Ramsey. He loved the cabin, the clean air and water, the woods and nearby beach with its birds and ducks. He loved the slower pace of his life that allowed him to enjoy a cup of coffee and some bacon and eggs before he began his work. In short, after working nearly six years on newspapers, he loved his freedom: "Never again would I work for a master, by hour, by day, by week or by year. Perhaps I had neither the talent nor the ability to make a living by writing, but such freedom was worth any sacrifice until I found out."

The freedom Les enjoyed did have its drawbacks. His newfound career as the author of the Dave Fearless books was taking off, but his true calling as a writer of adult fiction was coming along more slowly. Of the eight sales he made in 1926, seven were Dave Fearless books (each for $100). There was no shortage of rejections, however. According to his own meticulously kept records, he wrote seven stories and articles that were submitted to various publications and rejected. One 5,000-word story called "The Pillar of Fire" was rejected by the *Saturday Evening Post, Maclean's,* and a magazine called *Blue Book.* His earnings for fiction writing for the year were $1,225, slightly less than the $1,540 he had earned the previous year and nearly $800 less than what he would have earned at the paper.

By June, his optimism and enthusiasm were tempered by the flurry of rejection notices—and by the requests from his grocer and beer supplier for money he owed them. As would be the case throughout much of his life, a life raft arrived, this time in the form of a letter from an editor at *Everybody's,* who accepted "The Hill of Gold," a 25,000-word tale about a prospector, and sent him a check for $525. The story had been rejected by *Adventure,* a blow to Les, since he considered it perfect for that magazine.

The Dave Fearless books provided paychecks for Les, but little else. He did not think of them as indicators of his talent as a writer, so he was not hurt by any harsh words or requests for changes that came from Stratemeyer. Although Les and Stratemeyer would establish a warm relationship by mail over the next few years (the two never met), the publisher was hardly effusive with praise when it came to Les's writing, particularly during the early months of their relationship. In letters to Les, Stratemeyer always maintained a professional tone but was candid in his criticism of some of the early Dave Fearless books that Les wrote, criticizing everything from the length of the books to the way Les mailed them off.

For instance, Stratemeyer claimed to be surprised that he even received Les's second Dave Fearless book, *Dave Fearless near the South Pole:* "It was a miracle the MS. came through safely," he wrote back. "The envelope was wide open (evidently the glue didn't stick) and at first I was afraid some pages had dropped out—which would have caused both us and yourself a lot of trouble. Better seal well or tie up after this." But the packaging of the manuscript was the least of the complaints. Stratemeyer warned Les that he needed to follow the plot outlines more closely—and to pay attention to the diversity of the boats: "The main fault was in the fact that you did not read my letter carefully. In that I stated that the *Swallow* was a two-masted *steamer* and that Bob had been in the engine room when Dave met him. This was ignored (as was the fact in the other vols. that the *Falcon* was a *motor* yacht). What's the matter? Have they nothing but sails up your way?"

Stratemeyer brought up other points that Les would follow in his later books: in Stratemeyer's view, Les overused pronouns, prompting confusion in the reader; and he needed to add humor to his writing. "I think one element that has given such tremendous popularity to my own 'Rover Boys' books and 'Dave Porter' books is the fact that I never forgot boys love horse play and jokes, provided they are not spread on too thick."

Despite the criticisms, Stratemeyer accepted the books—even though he acknowledged that he had to make minor narrative revisions himself—and wanted more of them from Les. In subsequent letters, he told his new young writer in a rather urgent tone that due to the success of the series, he wanted one every three weeks for the next few months.

As Les pounded out the books, though, Stratemeyer found that his new author did not always follow Stratemeyer's—and publisher Garden City's—strict guidelines for length. Les's negligence would continue, much to Stratemeyer's annoyance. For instance, Stratemeyer complained about Les's third book, *Dave Fearless Caught by Malay Pirates:* "I am sorry to say that in looking the manuscript over and comparing it with the other books which have now been put in type, this manuscript is just about twenty pages short." Stratemeyer wrote that he was returning pages 123 to 138 so Les could add the needed pages and then receive his payment. But the length problem would continue: Les's fifth book, *Dave Fearless on the Ship of Mystery,* was, again, about nine typewritten pages short. ("Can't you drill in some extra pages which I can insert—either an adventure on the island or when Dave, Bob and Terry Fell take the board and escape the shark and row for Shark Cove?"

Stratemeyer asks in a letter.) Les's sixth Dave Fearless book, *Dave Fearless on the Lost Brig,* ran long, prompting another response from Stratemeyer, explaining that the published books must be 215 or 216 pages in length. At the end of 1926, Stratemeyer sent Les an urgent telegram urging him to add "twenty-seven" book pages immediately to *Dave Fearless at Whirlpool Point,* his seventh Dave Fearless book.

Les kept writing the Dave Fearless books at a furious pace. By late in the year, however, the public craving for the books was waning. Either the publishers overestimated the demand, or something changed the minds of the boys who devoured them. Les sensed as he was writing his seventh one, *Dave Fearless at Whirlpool Point,* that the series would be discontinued.

And he was right—the last Dave Fearless book he wrote was never published, although by that time he was so delighted at the sale of his short story "Hill of Gold" that he was not bothered. In fact, he briefly entertained the notion of writing Stratemeyer a letter telling him that he would be leaving the syndicate; after all, Les reasoned, if *Everybody's* accepted one of his stories, they probably would want more. And he was getting sick of pounding out the mindless adventures of the hyperactive deep-sea diver—a chore that never gave him much personal satisfaction.

Edward Stratemeyer, though, had always been a master of timing. There is no question that his success as a businessman was due largely to his ability to take advantage of changing societal, cultural, and literary values and incorporate them into his books for juveniles. Whether he knew it or not, his sense of timing was again impeccable when it came to the twenty-four-year-old Canadian writer he had recently employed as a ghostwriter. As Les was contemplating sending a letter of resignation to Stratemeyer, the syndicate chief sent a letter to him, informing him of a new series of books he had in mind featuring two teenaged detectives.

4

BIRTH OF A SERIES

Les was so excited to have his short story "Hill of Gold" published by *Everybody's* that he sent a copy of the magazine to Stratemeyer, who commented on it in two letters. He first noted that he had seen it, but apparently Les requested more of a critique of the story, and Stratemeyer obliged in his usual blunt manner: "Yes, I liked 'Hill of Gold,'" he wrote, adding that with the exception of one other story in the magazine, "it was the only thing I cared for in the magazine." Stratemeyer was more surprised by the short biographical sketch that accompanied the story: "Was somewhat astonished to learn that you are but twenty-three years of age [Les had just turned twenty-four when the story was published]," Stratemeyer wrote. "You are surely coming along finely and I wish you every success. One of my other writers is but twenty-two, just graduated as a lawyer, and he had written eight books for us in the past year. Strange to say, his father also writes for us!" (Stratemeyer apparently was referring to Roger Garis, whose father, Howard, was one of the syndicate's most prolific writers.) Stratemeyer noted that the syndicate also employed a woman who was twenty, and one "just a little older."

In many respects, Stratemeyer served as a father figure for some of his young writers, including Les. His relationship with most of them was conducted by mail and maintained a certain cordial formality, but he took pains to write his authors on his own. While Stratemeyer could be brusque, his letters indicate he was far from apathetic about the welfare and careers of his authors and he fully realized that most of them worked for him solely for the money. For instance, he once wrote Les that some Stratemeyer authors were respected for the work they did using their own names, and some were published by prestigious houses: "Writing our books on our outlines anonymously does not seem to hurt as our writers have books on the Harper list, the Lippincott list, the Little Brown list. . . . I like to see them get along, although many complain bitterly of the uncertainty of free lance production." Stratemeyer evidently was fond of Les, despite the young author's disregard of manuscript length requirements. Stratemeyer apparently believed Les was a competent author. In mid-December, at the end of a routine letter to him about the business of the syndicate, Stratemeyer told Les he was getting a Christmas bonus of fifty dollars: "At this time of year the Stratemeyer Syndicate remembers its old writers with some bonuses. . . . You aren't exactly one of the old writers but I wish you to feel yourself in the fold because of what you have done." In the latter part of their relationship, after Les was married with a family, he frequently asked Stratemeyer for advances on his pay, and Stratemeyer usually obliged.

His faith in Les was deep enough that he asked him to write the first three volumes of a new series to be started in early 1927. Establishing new series was of course nothing new to Stratemeyer by 1927, but this series was special in some ways. As Stratemeyer explained in a letter to Les, the books in this series would be bound in cloth rather than paper as the Dave Fearless books were, and would sell for fifty cents, a price slightly higher than that of the paperback books. (The Dave Fearless series was initially produced in hardcover editions in 1918.) Consequently, Les would receive $125 per book rather than the $100 he received for the Dave Fearless books. More important, the books would focus more on dialogue, plot, description, and narrative than on simple action. The protagonists would be two teenaged detectives who were the sons of a famous private investigator. The first book featuring the pair to be known as the Hardy Boys would be called *The Tower Treasure*. Stratemeyer described the premise in a letter to Les:

> You perhaps understand our cloth books go in a different field from the paper volumes and the stories are not quite so melodramatic—not quite such strong language and not much pistol play. . . . The boys are everyday schoolboys (not too young) and it will pay to liven it up here and there with a bit of fun or horseplay on their part.

Stratemeyer wanted to get the first three volumes of the new Hardy Boys series out as quickly as possible: having created the idea for the series and the initial outlines in late November, he hoped the first three volumes could be published by the following spring. Stratemeyer stressed to Les that the books should be uniform in length: 216 printed pages (each page being three lines longer than the pages of the Dave

Fearless books) and 25 chapters. This would require Les to submit exactly 165 typewritten pages. Usually, the first three volumes of a series, called "breeders," were published simultaneously or in rapid succession to establish interest in the series and to give readers an immediate opportunity to purchase more books in the same series.

Although Stratemeyer had favorites among his series, he was a businessman, and economics rather than sentimentality ruled his decisions. Whether he had affection for a particular series was irrelevant. If sales declined too sharply, a series was discontinued. The quantity of books sold at fifty cents apiece, for instance, had to generate the amount invested in the story. In the case of *The Tower Treasure*, for which Les was paid $125, sales needed to reach 6,250 copies, based on 2 cents per copy royalty, before the syndicate earned back its investment. The syndicate and the publishers of series books kept their profits and financial breakdowns secret, but as of 1934, seven years after the launch of the Hardy Boys series, *Fortune* magazine estimated the following profit breakdown on a fifty-cent series book: fifteen to twenty cents to the retailer; three- to five-cent royalty to the writer or syndicate; seven to twelve cents for overhead; three to five cents profit for the publisher, and thirteen to fifteen cents as the cost of manufacture.

When designing the idea for the Hardy Boys, Stratemeyer was, once again, keenly attuned to prevailing societal and cultural trends. Adult detective novels had been gaining immense popularity by the late 1920s. S. S. Van Dine, "father" of Philo Vance, published *The Benson Murder Case* in 1926, and writers such as Dashiell Hammett, Raymond Chandler and Charles M. Green (known as Erle Stanley Gardner) burst on the scene. Interestingly, despite the success of adult detective magazines and stories earlier in the century and in the late 1800s, Stratemeyer had not yet seriously ventured into that territory. Now, he decided, it was time.

Despite his cleverness and the bare-bones design of his business, Stratemeyer alone could not decide what was and was not publishable. He was at the mercy of his publishers, who by the 1920s consisted primarily of Cupples & Leon and Grosset & Dunlap. As he wrote to Grosset & Dunlap in 1927, "Detective novels are as interesting to boys as grown folks. I prefer two boys, brothers, as heroes." Whether or not Stratemeyer was aware of it, Les, too, was enthusiastic from the start about the new series featuring teenage detectives and about his new Stratemeyer identity as "Franklin W. Dixon." First, it allowed him to forgo the writing of the sensational action-packed Dave Fearless series, which by the end he had found boring and repetitive. With this new series, he wrote in his autobiography, there were "no man-eating sharks. No octopi. No cannibals, polar bears or man-eating trees. Just the everyday doings of everyday lads in everyday surroundings. . . . I was so relieved to be free of Dave Fearless and his dreary helpers that I greeted Frank and Joe Hardy with positive rapture." The idea of the series impressed him in other ways. When Stratemeyer described it to him, he referred to the mystery writer S. S. Van Dine, with whose works Les was familiar. Van Dine was the pseudonym of Willard Huntington Wright, whom Les knew as a sophisticated writer for H. L. Mencken's magazine *Smart Set*. Most important, however, was the realization for Les that even though detailed outlines were supplied to him and he still would be a ghostwriter, he could instill in this new series of books his own personality and his own style of writing. After all, Stratemeyer had certainly implied that Les would have more latitude than he had with Dave Fearless when writing this series. Rather than simply banging them out on his typewriter and stuffing them into an envelope with hopes of getting paid as soon as possible, Les had higher aspirations for these books. "It seemed to me that the Hardy boys deserved something better than the slapdash treatment Dave Fearless had been getting. It was still hack work, no doubt, but did the new series have to be all hack?" he asked. "There was, after all, the chance to contribute a little style, occasional words of more than two syllables, maybe a little sensory stimuli." As it turned out, Les *was* able to insert his own style into this series, as well as his views on such diverse issues as authority, family, and life's small pleasures. Les may have been a stepfather to the Hardy Boys, but, as generations of readers would see, he took the series and made it his own.

***

At any given time, Stratemeyer employed as many as twenty ghostwriters, all of whom wrote using Stratemeyer's plot and character outlines. Because they went by pseudonyms and signed away all rights, they could never claim full ownership, either publicly or to themselves. Thus, their relationship with their own work was an odd one. Les of course realized this, and even when he decided to take a little more time and effort with the Hardy Boy books than with the other syndicate books, he knew that the nonexistent Franklin W. Dixon would get the credit for it. And if the series became successful? "The writer who brought the skeleton outline to life wouldn't get a penny even if the books sold a million—which, of course, seemed impossible at the time," he noted years later.

By the end of 1926, Stratemeyer was busy planning for the new series and building a case for it with his publisher. As he told Grosset & Dunlap,

> In this line we have two boys, Joe and Frank Hardy, the sons of a celebrated detective. From their father they hear of various cases and gradually start to solve the mysteries. They get on to the "side issues" of the crimes, often bringing some boys or young men to the front and show them up as the criminals' aids. Thus while the father is the real detective, the brothers do their full share in exposing the wrongdoers and in regaining stolen goods. The boys' work as amateur detectives would furnish plenty of incident, exciting but clean.

The first three "breeder" books for the new Hardy Boy series were *The Tower Treasure,* in which the boys search the tower of a mansion where a crime has been committed; *The House on the Cliff,* in which the boys search for their father, who has mysteriously disappeared; and *The Secret of the Old Mill,* which sends the boys on a counterfeiting case. According to Stratemeyer Syndicate records, however, Stratemeyer sent publisher Grosset & Dunlap the summaries of seven Hardy Boy books that could be used as "breeders," including the three that were selected. The four that were not picked never became Hardy Boys books, even after the series achieved success: *The Ship of Mystery,* about an investigation by the boys of a ship said to be owned by smugglers; *The Missing Gold Nuggets,* about a theft at a mining camp; *The Stolen Horkar Diamonds,* about a diamond theft at a large jewelry store; and *The Missing Liberty Bonds,* about the theft of an elderly woman's savings. Stratemeyer's descriptions of the three that were selected, along with that of *The Ship of Mystery,* were sixty to seventy-five words in length, longer and more detailed than the others. The publisher suggested that the name of specific crimes not be used in the titles; further, a decision was made not to use the Hardy Boys name in the title, which was a departure for Stratemeyer series books.

The outlines for *The Tower Treasure* and *The House on the Cliff* that were sent to Les were about two pages in length, single spaced, but not divided into individual chapters, as later outlines would be. They were written primarily in brief or incomplete sentences, describing the action and the atmosphere of the narrative. They provide some specific details—they spell out the day of the week or month, sometimes describe a specific road, and occasionally offer a direct quote—but consist mainly of general plot points that serve to move the action. For instance, the opening paragraphs of the outline of *The Tower Treasure* establish the characters and scene specifically: "Joe and Frank Hardy are on their motorcycles on an errand for their father, Fenton Hardy, the famous detective. It is Saturday, a holiday from the Bayport High School which they attend, springtime." After the brief introductions, the action begins: "The shore road, the rocks below—the racing auto—will it hit them? Narrow escape—anger of middle aged man who ran car and anger of boys. 'A road hog,' they say."

The outline did leave much latitude for the writer. As it continued, "Boys at school—various doings—Frank and Callie—days pass. Mr. Hardy returns—tells important secret. The auto thief, a criminal named John ("Red") Jackley—called Red because of his fondness for red wigs—is under arrest."

Along with the story outline, Stratemeyer also sent Les a list of the characters and the setting of the new Hardy Boys series, in which he briefly describes the central personalities:

> *Frank Hardy*, age 16, tall, dark high school lad, brother to
> *Joe Hardy*, age 15, fair, curly hair, high school lad. Both sons of
> *Fenton Hardy*, a well-known private detective, age 40, tall, dark.
> *Mrs. Laura Hardy*, small, slim, light like son Joe. Sweet singer.

Perhaps because he considered himself a gentleman, Stratemeyer provided no age for Laura Hardy, nor did he elaborate on her vocal talents. Mrs. Hardy is portrayed in some of the books as the perpetually worried mother and it is spelled out repeatedly that she is none too pleased that her sons want to be detectives like their father—she would prefer they pursue careers in law or medicine.

The diverse cast of friends and relatives continued:

Aunt Gertrude, peppery and dictatorial, on visit to Hardys.
Chet Morton, school chum. Mr. Morton real estate dealer. Live mile outside Bayport. *Chet,* full of fun and jokes.
Perry Robinson, "Slim," school chum, likes to box.
Jerry Gilroy, Phil Cohen (Jew), *Tony Prito* (Italian) at school.

Tony's and Phil's religious and ethnic backgrounds would be alluded to periodically in the text of the Hardy Boy books—particularly in the first books of the series—and the appropriateness of these references would, over the years, become the subject of much debate among librarians, teachers, parents, and others who select reading material for children. Although Stratemeyer notes Phil's religion in the character list, it is referred to directly in the books only in the first reference to him as "dark haired and Jewish" and indirectly by his use of the exclamation "Oy" in *The Missing Chums,* the fourth book in the series. Tony's way of speaking, particularly early on, and references to his father's ethnicity indicate his Italian American heritage. Stratemeyer may have created these characters to establish diversity in the books, but some critics have maintained that the books used the defining of ethnic background in a negative way, too.

Stratemeyer gave no indication of what prompted his choice of names—including the name Franklin W. Dixon. In his autobiography, Les ponders how Stratemeyer came up with it and what the middle initial "W" represents: "certainly not 'wealthy,'" he concludes. The names of many characters—for instance, the villainous John "Red" Jackley in *The Tower Treasure* and the evil Ganny "Red" Snackley in *The House on the Cliff*—owe a debt to Charles Dickens, as do many names in other Stratemeyer series. They are frequently one or two syllables and often contain a hard "k" or "g" sound. The names of Bayport's two main law enforcement officers, Collig and Smuff—characters Les portrays as bumbling and comical—also sound as if they could have been the creations of Dickens.

Stratemeyer had used the name Frank Hardy for a character in one of the stories he finished in 1905 for Horatio Alger, called *A Young Book Agent; or, Frank Hardy's Road to Success,* but that was not the same character as the one in the Hardy Boys mystery series.

The character of Aunt Gertrude was a Leslie McFarlane creation in almost every way. Referred to by Stratemeyer only obliquely in the cast listing and not at all in the story outlines of the first few books, Aunt Gertrude was a favorite of Les, who would cultivate her persona during the twenty years he worked for the syndicate and ultimately mold her into one of the most famous and beloved characters in the Hardy fold.

Although there was no sex in the Hardy Boys books, and no references to it, Stratemeyer did include two teenage girls as regular characters: Callie Shaw, "brown eyes and hair, quick. Frank thinks her great," and Iola Morton, "plump and dark, sister to Chet, Joe thought her O.K. 'as a girl.'"

Also spelled out by Stratemeyer was the geography of the fictional Bayport, the city that was home to the Hardy Boys and the venue of much of the crime they investigated:

> Bayport, a city of fifty thousand, located on Barmet Bay, which opens three miles down on the Atlantic Ocean. Bayport has steamboat office and a railroad station, with trains to New York and South. Ships coal lumber and bricks, and has foundries. North, toward south opening of bay is Willow River, running back westward through farms and hills. (All fictitious.)

Whether Bayport was based on a specific American city has been the topic of debate for decades among fans and scholars of the Hardy Boys series. Some believe, because Stratemeyer lived in suburban New Jersey, outside of Manhattan, that it could be based on any number of small towns in Westchester County, New York, or New Jersey. Other readers have taken apparent clues in the text of some of the books (e.g., its distance from New York City) to try to determine its actual location. The elusive Stratemeyer does state in the outline, though, that the town and related geography are "all fictitious," and he never gave any indication that the details of his books were based on any real cities, situations, or people.

Finally, Stratemeyer described the Hardy home, located on the corner of High Street and Elm—an old stone house with lawn trees, a garage, and a barn with a gym. Most important, at least from the reader's point of view, was the Hardys' library, where Fenton Hardy worked and stored his impressive collection of files, disguises, and paraphernalia associated with cases. The library would be the setting for many conversations and revelations in the years to come.

Although Stratemeyer provided descriptions of the Hardy characters and locale, a clever writer still had creative leeway, and Les decided to take advantage of that. Les seemed to enjoy writing *The Tower Treasure*, in part because he was permitted to endow some of his characters with a sense of humor and fun, and in part because he could shape the narrative and characters as he liked despite the constraints imposed by the outline and the character summaries. Because the Hardy Boys series was new, he was not forced to conform to the style of existing books in the series. He embellished at will, possibly using some elements of his own childhood and certainly his own active imagination.

Les never acknowledged that any parts of the Hardy Boys books were based on Haileybury or on his experiences growing up there, and writes in his autobiography that situations and locations in the Hardy Boys books were not based on that town or any other real location. But some current Haileybury residents maintain that some situations and events in the series indicate that aspects of Haileybury were very much imbedded in Bayport, and that some of the experiences of Joe and Frank Hardy and their friends were reminiscent of those Les, his three brothers, and their friends in the northern Ontario town. Many years after he wrote those first Hardy Boys books, Les told his daughter, when giving her advice about writing, that all novelists use parts of their own life in their stories.

For instance, early in *The Tower Treasure*, Stratemeyer's outline described briefly how the boys, riding their motorcycles on a shore road adjacent to Barmet Bay, narrowly escape a head-on collision with a speeding car. But this was a closer call than even Stratemeyer had imagined. "Normally the situation would merely call for evasive action (taking to the shoulder), but a normal situation wouldn't do, as any old hand from the pulp diggings knows," Les recalls. "It is necessary to arrange the topography so that an abnormal situation will prevail." Les "rearranged the topography" to include a steep cliff to the immediate left of the boys—one that could lead to a two-hundred-foot drop into Barmet Bay for either the boys or the reckless driver. One of the breathtaking sites in Haileybury is Devil's Rock, a fault cliff rising three hundred feet above Lake Temiskaming. Devil's Rock is not immediately adjacent to the main north-south road in Haileybury, Lakeshore Road, but it is only about a quarter of a mile from it. The vaguely worded "shore road" Stratemeyer referred to in his outline for *The Tower Treasure* had been transformed into an actual street, "Shore Road," by the sixth Hardy Boys mystery, *The Shore Road Mystery*. By that book it had become a key locale. Lakeshore Road in Haileybury was the location of the large and palatial homes of those who made millions in the mining industry early in the twentieth century. Interestingly, Shore Road was also home to several of Bayport's wealthiest citizens, including Hurd Applegate of *The Tower Treasure* and Elroy Jefferson in *The Mystery of Cabin Island,* and it was the location of Purdy Place in *While the Clock Ticked.*

The sawmill on Mill Creek was a pivotal part of Haileybury's history, established by Haileybury founder C. C. Farr to provide lumber for the initial construction of the community. It was of course Stratemeyer and not Les who came up with the titles and story summaries of the books, so it was merely coincidence that the third book in the series was called *The Secret of the Old Mill.*

All writers of fiction may draw on their own experiences in one way or another. Whether Les used the leeway he was given to model some of his settings after Haileybury may never be known, but certainly his childhood years in that city influenced his writing. As he explained in *A Kid in Haileybury,* the natural resources of Ontario combined with the cooking talents of Mrs. McFarlane made for some fine meals in the household, and mealtimes were important to the family. Les described in detail the sensual pleasures of eating fresh berries and cream, berry pies, and warm homemade bread with fresh jam. Years after he lived alone on Lake Ramsey, he had distinct memories of the smell and taste of the eggs and bacon he prepared before beginning a day of writing. As a young man, Les wrote admiringly in his diaries of the delicious meals his wife Amy made for the family on holidays and special occasions. A continuing theme of the Hardy Boys books was the ubiquity of the food—for those involved in death-defying activities must still take time to nourish themselves. Even when the boys and their friends went on hikes or outings, they frequently had with them lunches carefully prepared for them. Equally rewarding, though, was the feeling of community that characterized family meals in Haileybury. Similarly, the Hardy Boys circle enjoyed the camaraderie that came with the tasty lunches and dinners—here were the true rewards of solving impossible cases and escaping near-death predicaments. At the end of *The Tower Treasure,* the boys, their friends, and the vindicated victims of the crime take comfort in a feast of roast chicken, mashed potatoes with gravy, and pie à la mode. Stratemeyer's outline merely calls for a celebratory dinner; the lavish banquet, Les noted decades later, was his own creation as Dixon: "He [Dixon] saw to it that young readers savored the sight, smell and taste of roast chicken, 'crisp and brown,' with huge helpings of mashed potatoes and gravy. He served them pickles, vegetables and sal-ads. He encouraged seconds. . . . Young readers learned then and there that when it came to food, Franklin W. was not a man to count the cost." Les's daughter Norah makes no bones about the fact that some aspects of the Hardy Boys books clearly reflected her father's personality. "He loved to eat, and most of the books ended with a big feast of some sort," she said in an interview.

She also linked her father's good sense of humor with the jokes he in-cluded in his books. Indeed, Chet Morton not only loved eating—as his physique reveals—but was a practical joker, as was Les. Of all the regular characters in the Hardy Boys series, it is not the principal characters of Frank and Joe who may have been modeled after the author himself, but the sidekick, Chet Morton. And the jovial Chet was one of the most pop-ular characters apart from Joe and Frank in the Hardy Boys series; in in-formal "surveys" taken on Hardy Boys websites, Chet is routinely named as one of the favorite characters.

Haileybury, with its rivers, lakes, forests, cliffs, hills, and fields, pro-vided a wonderful model for the rustic Bayport, but the real city was not quite as benign. The climactic extremes of northern Ontario, with its blizzards and bone-chilling cold, could be truly deadly. The cold seemed to cause perennial colds, flus, and respiratory ailments. The hot, dry air of summer caused deadly brush fires, and snow and ice frequently made winter travel nearly impossible. In the Hardy Boys books, the outdoors took on a type of gentle danger. Bodies of water, in particular, often served to move the action along as the protagonists and criminals alike were frequently diving into it, nearly drowning in it, and speeding their boats through it. But in the books that Les wrote, nobody ever died a bloody or brutal death outdoors. As series-book researcher Carol Billman writes, there was one main difference between adult detective novels and the juvenile ones. "There is a great difference between the 'mean streets' of the adult genre, where murder comes cheap and the entire world is stained by corruption, and the crime-ridden though ultimately comfort-able and serene world of Bayport. . . . Inordinate criminal activity notwithstanding, Bayport smells sweet. It is indeed a rarefied, almost fan-tastic place." Even though Bayport is a twentieth-century eastern U.S. city, Billman compares it to the fictional West, where lawbreakers who rode into town were invariably punished for their crimes, and where a type of genteel justice prevailed. Kennedy Gordon, who lived in Sudbury, where Les worked as a young reporter, believes that the crime-riddled waterfront in many of the Hardy Boys books was modeled after a region of Sudbury called the Borgia Market, a neighborhood of "cheap beer halls, dollar-a-night hotels and greasy diners," though not in fact a waterfront.

Les's upbringing and his father's emphasis on reading and independent thinking had a clear influence on the way he shaped the series. Although the Hardy Boys series and other books published by the syndicate would for years be the target of disapproving children's librarians and teachers who complained of the cumbersome writing and overreliance on action, much of the vocabulary and the literary allusions were quite sophisticated for the audience, boys aged eleven or twelve to sixteen. For example, in *The Tower Treasure*, as Mr. Hardy is stressing to his sons the importance of observation, he surmises that one of the boys' teachers was a fan of Charles Dickens. How did he know that? On three separate occasions, Mr. Hardy noted, the man had been carrying a copy of different Dickens books: one time *Oliver Twist*, another time *A Tale of Two Cities*, and a third time *David Copperfield*. Les inserted into the book a more subtle literary reference when he referred to the *Merchant of Venice* character Launcelott Gobbo: As the boys interview an actor in an attempt to track down a criminal, the actor notes that the wig he wore to play that Shakespearean character had been stolen. The vocabulary, also, may have forced some boys to consult dictionaries: "the newcomer, who was given the *prosaic* name of Henry J. Brown"; "Frank's *preoccupied* air had not gone unobserved. Callie Shaw had noticed his *abstraction*"; "Their disappointment had turned to *jubilation*, for now they felt that they were definitely on the trail of the mysterious man in the red wig, and while *ostensibly* there was no connection . . ."

Among Les's proudest creations in the Hardy Boys series were the three policemen, Chief of Police Ezra Collig, Detective Oscar Smuff, and Policeman Con Riley. None of the police officers appears in the character list or the outline for *The Tower Treasure*, although Collig is mentioned briefly in the outline for the second book, *The House on the Cliff*. In the three officers, Les created a trio of Keystone Kops who are comically gullible, lazy, inarticulate, and eager to take credit for work they have not done. These three Bayport law enforcement officers consistently show up late, miss obvious clues, and trip over themselves. Les saw their existence as a golden opportunity for comic relief. The police, when asked a question, tend to stray from the subject at hand and are prone to filibuster on completely unrelated topics. They are easily fooled, delayed, or otherwise humiliated by friend and foe.

Les's innocent comic portrayal drew the wrath of some adults, who were concerned that law enforcement officials were not treated with respect. Les believed that the bumbling Bayport cops, apart from providing humor, may have encouraged youngsters to question authority rather than accepting it blindly. To Stratemeyer, however, that was not the purpose of series fiction. Although Mssrs. Collig, Riley, and Smuff provided much comedy for the first few Hardy Boys books, they were much more serious and worthy of respect in the later books—at the request of Stratemeyer, who warned Les not to ridicule policemen, pillars of the community. Long after Les had stopped writing the books in the mid-1940s, the Bayport policemen became positively respectable.

In the first few Hardy Boys books, the comical Bayport police, like many of the criminals and lower-class characters in the books, spoke poorly; they frequently dropped the last few letters of their words, and did not use proper grammar: "Can't do no good and can't do no harm," Chief Collig says at one point. Or, "We've been hearin' about this Tower Mansion case. You've been workin' on it, eh?" Or, as Smuff said, "That's what we dedooce, anyway." Inarticulateness characterizes many of the criminals in the book and also is a trait of the many foreign characters. Rocco, an Italian immigrant who runs a fruit stand near the Bayport Police Station, speaks in *The House on the Cliff* in a manner reminiscent of Chico Marx: "'W'at you t'ink?" snickered the Italian, 'some boys come here a while ago and say da Blacka Hand [forerunner to the Mafia] t'ink I charga too much for da fruit.'"

Les at times was guilty not only of the stereotypical portrayals but also of the cumbersome writing that plagued many of the earlier Stratemeyer Syndicate books. Warned as a young newspaper reporter to use only the word "said" for utterances, he ignored that guideline in the Hardy Boys books: few if any characters "say" anything. Instead, they opine, observe, laugh, mutter, or otherwise colorfully utter; or they rely on overactive adverbs, admitting *heavily*, exclaiming *eagerly*, suggesting *fearfully*. And, defying what he had learned as a reporter about concise writing, Les would occasionally use a dozen words when three or four would suffice: "The Hardy boys were tense with a realization of their peril," he wrote in *The House on the Cliff*. Sometimes he just went on for no apparent reason, as he did in that same book: "Although Fenton Hardy was weakened by his imprisonment and privation and although the smuggler was strong and wiry, the detective had the advantage of a surprise attack, and Malloy had not time to collect his faculties."

Much of this may have stemmed from directives from Stratemeyer, who made it clear to his writers that all syndicate books must conform to certain rules of archaic prose. Stratemeyer also had a strict policy that early on, each book must refer to the previous book in the series, and near the end, each must offer a paragraph or two advertising the upcoming one. Although the authors attempted to slip this unobtrusively into the narrative, these "commercials" naturally become increasingly cumbersome as the series grew. In chapter 2 of *The Secret of the Old Mill,* the third of the "breeder" books, there is a brief but awkward break in the action as the previous two books are not-so-subtly reviewed:

> Already [the Hardy boys] had aided in solving two mysteries that kept Bayport by the ears. As related in "The Hardy Boys: The Tower Treasure," they had solved the mystery of the theft of jewelry and bonds from the Tower Mansion, even after Fenton Hardy had been unable to discover where the thief had hidden the loot. In the second volume of the series, "The Hardy Boys: The House on the Cliff," it has been told how the Hardy boys discovered the haunt of a gang of smugglers who were operating in Barmet Bay.

Interestingly, while the boys' father serves as a role model for their sleuthing, readers are reminded that Joe and Frank have solved cases that have stymied their famous dad, a nationally known sleuth. But Fenton Hardy remains in most of the books an active although offstage participant in Joe and Frank's activities

As evidenced by a letter he sent to Stratemeyer, in early January, Les was slightly late in turning in *The Tower Treasure* manuscript ("my illness and the usual festivities of the Christmas season somewhat interfered," he wrote). He told Stratemeyer, however, that he was beginning the second volume, *The House on the Cliff,* and would mail it to Stratemeyer in three weeks. Meanwhile, "if there are any points of criticism [with the Tower Treasure], I shall welcome them before I am too deeply into the new story." Stratemeyer answered Les's letter within three days, and the usually reserved syndicate head appeared unusually enthusiastic about *The Tower Treasure:* "All told I think this is a very good yarn—quite as good as anything you have turned in—and I think it will make an excellent initial volume for the series." Stratemeyer noted, however, that he

THE SECRET OF THE HARDY BOYS 4

changed the character of Hardy Boys chum Tony Prito so he would speak in "good English" but with an Italian accent. He also told Les that he was sending him the outline for the third volume, *The Secret of the Old Mill*, which he hoped could be completed within seven weeks.

By the time the first three Hardy Boys books were completed, Les and Stratemeyer had begun an extensive written correspondence that would last for the next three years, until Stratemeyer's sudden death. The two men never addressed each other by their first names, but Stratemeyer occasionally inquired about Les's health and commented periodically about pivotal events in Les's life, such as his marriage and his magazine writing career. In one letter written in May 1927, about eight months after Les began working for him, Stratemeyer wrote Les that he was "rather curious to know where Haileybury is located. When I first telegraphed to you, they seemed to make quite a job of routing the message." In return, Stratemeyer received a letter with a small, hand-drawn map of Haileybury and northern Ontario in the bottom left corner— along with a detailed description of the town's geography and an invitation to the cabin on Lake Ramsey, where Les stayed in the summer: "There are excellent motor roads to Sudbury, which is on the trunk highway to Sault Ste. Marie, and you can reach the town via Montreal, travelling up the Ottawa Valley," Les wrote. "It has occurred to me that perhaps you are taking a tour of this kind some summer, and if so I'm extending an invitation to the cottage. You are entirely welcome at any time and I think you would enjoy it." Les added that he lived alone in his cottage, with "three big rooms and two double beds. . . . Also, I am famous for my baked beans and Irish Stew." Les sent Stratemeyer a photo of the cabin. Stratemeyer thanked him in a letter and told him that he certainly would visit the "inviting" camp if he was in the vicinity. He, in turn, sent to Les a newspaper clipping about himself, which, the reserved and publicity-shy Stratemeyer wrote, "is the only thing available just now." Stratemeyer never took Les up on the offer, although the invitation itself illustrates the warm relationship between the two men, as well as the pleasure Les took in entertaining and socializing with his friends and relatives.

The relationship between Stratemeyer and Les was mutually beneficial, but far from perfect. Les's attitude about his writing for the syndicate would remain ambivalent for much of his life—and during particularly tough times, this attitude degenerated into antagonism toward the syndicate and disgust with his dependence on it. But Les continued to write for the syndicate for years to come, even after Stratemeyer's death.

5

. . . . . .

A WELL-OILED MACHINE

By the time he wrote *The Tower Treasure* in late 1926, Les had begun to establish himself permanently as a full-time freelance writer. During the warm weather, he stayed at his cabin on Lake Ramsey, and he moved back in with his parents in Haileybury during the winter. He was serious about his work: he rented a small second-floor office at the corner of Main Street and Ferguson Avenue in downtown Haileybury, and bought an old desk and chair for ten dollars from a politician who had just lost an election. He already had the Underwood typewriter.

The year 1926 was a good one for him. He earned $1,350, all of it, except the $525 he earned for his short story in *Everybody's* magazine, from Stratemeyer. But 1927 was to be an even better year for him, and one that gave him great encouragement about his future as a writer of a adult fiction.

Meanwhile, he was getting feedback on his Hardy Boys books in the form of the books themselves. Stratemeyer—who had many rules for his writers, including one requiring them to return all outlines with their finished manuscripts—dutifully mailed his authors the finished versions of the books they wrote. In early 1927, Les received through customs a neatly wrapped package from the Stratemeyer Syndicate containing the three volumes of the new Hardy Boys series. The author was less than impressed by the cover and frontispiece art by Walter S. Rogers, one of several artists Stratemeyer employed for his series books. The early Hardy Boys books had a red binding and a colorful dust jacket, which usually depicted Frank and Joe in an action scene. On the cover of *The Tower Treasure,* the boys, dressed rather formally in British driving caps, sweaters, and shirts with ties, stand behind some shrubs in the dark as they point to an ominous-looking Tower Mansion in the distance. The frontispiece of the book, depicting the boys in a discussion with Tower Mansion residents Hurd and Adelia Applegate, bothered Les, who had not pictured the characters quite the way Rogers had. It is probably fortunate that the staid Edward Stratemeyer was not around to read Les's interpretation of the scene fifty years later:

> Mr. Applegate was a weedy gent with a string tie and a vacant look. Miss Applegate, standing in a curtained archway with a flight of stairs in the background, was wearing elaborately flowing robes that seemed to have come right out of Godey's *Ladies Book* and the Hardy Boys were clutching their caps in a nervous sort of way. On the whole the scene appeared to represent an elderly pimp making a pitch on behalf of a couple of youthful clients to the madam of a fashionable whorehouse.

On the next page the three Hardy Boys titles were listed.

Les was pleased by the books despite the questionable artwork; after all, they were the first hardcover books he had written, in "good readable type" and copyrighted by the Library of Congress, he noted. He was impressed. And although the unorthodox arrangement he had with Stratemeyer—writing from outlines about characters he did not create—had its disadvantages, at least Les did not have to worry about book sales, which had no effect on what he was paid per book, although a series would of course be discontinued if it did not meet the syndicate's expectations. "Now they were launched on the sea of juvenile opinion," he wrote. "Would they be greeted with apathy, politely tolerated or rejected with scorn? Would they be received with enthusiasm, read with joy, applauded by boyish huzzahs? . . . It was of absolutely no concern to me. I was merely a ghost."

Indeed, the Hardy Boys series, along with the Nancy Drew series, would become the syndicate's top sellers. Eventually, the Hardy Boys would grow to become one of the best-selling children's book series of the twentieth century. But it got off to a rather slow start, and in fact the Ted Scott Flying series outpaced the Hardy Boys in both sales per year and sales per volume. (The Ted Scott series, about a mechanic turned pilot turned national hero, was launched in 1927, the same year as Charles Lindbergh's trans-Atlantic flight.) In 1927, for instance, when both series were launched, the Hardy Boys' average sales per volume were slightly below 9,000, compared to about 17,000 for the Ted Scott series. The Hardy Boys hovered at about 10,000 per volume until 1930 (when sales declined); the Ted Scott series grew to more than 20,000 per volume in 1928 and 1929. By 1931, both series sold about 8,000 copies per volume, and by 1932, the Hardy Boys outsold Ted Scott by several thousand copies per volume.

In the second and third books in the series, Les started to take a few more liberties with characters and situations. It was clear by then that the Hardy Boys' lives were not taken up entirely with solving crimes: repeated references were made to their schoolwork, sports, and life outside criminal investigations, and they and their friends enjoyed kidding each other and were not afraid to engage in puns or clever wordplay. Adults other than thieves, counterfeiters, and smugglers played a small role in the early books, and even the glamorous and famous Fenton Hardy usually let the boys figure things out on their own. Similarly, nothing was mentioned about church or Sunday school, perhaps because Les himself had such negative memories about his Sundays in church in Haileybury, although Edward Stratemeyer was a devout churchgoer.

And the characters in the book gradually began adopting distinctive characteristics. Dark-haired Frank, the older brother, was a bit more cerebral than the blond Joe, who was more athletic. Chubby Chet Morton was a practical joker, and references were made continually to his large appetite. Phil Cohen was quiet but smart, and Tony Prito was lively and enthusiastic. Each brother had a girlfriend of sorts: Iola Morton, in the case of Joe, and Callie Shaw, whom Frank likes.

As the series progressed through the first three books, Bayport's three chief law enforcement officers became increasingly buffoon-like. As smart as they were, Frank and Joe were reluctant to leave crime investigation to the three lazy policemen described in the books, although the Hardy Boys were much too polite to display their scorn for them in public. But Les was not. In the third book, *The Secret of the Old Mill,* Les goes to great lengths to describe the sloth and arrogance of Officer Con Riley, who walks down the street smoking a fat cigar, content with the fact that his wife and children are out of town and that he is clever enough to have a job where he works very little and gets the respect of many who greet him as he strolls along. He bristles as he spots Frank and Joe Hardy and their friends on the street—he feels they are know-it-alls who meddle too much in his police work—but beams as the boys heap false praise on him about his policework: "Perhaps he had been mistaken in his estimation of these lads after all," he thinks. "They were not mischievous young rascals, but bright, intelligent, high-minded boys who recognized human worth

THE SECRET OF THE HARDY BOYS 5

when they saw it and who respected achievement." His opinion of the boys rises even higher when Chet accidentally-on-purpose refers to him as "Lieutenant" Riley and is shocked that a man of his skill is not of that rank. All the while, the boys keep a straight face.

Stratemeyer's letters to Les during 1927 indicate that while he was pleased overall with the Hardy Boys manuscripts, he did have some minor criticisms. In one letter, he noted that he thought *The House on the Cliff* was "a very good story" but "a bit too melodramatic in the cave scenes—too much gun play and too much talk of murder. All those scenes I shall tone down." Stratemeyer tells Les that he should "give the boys their full share to do [evidently he meant activities outside of crime fighting], and glide over the action when it gets too raw or brutal. And lighten up on the heavy scenes now and then and add snatches of humor—and you'll have just what is needed." It was precisely the humor and lighthearted horseplay in the books that helped make them so popular among readers—and Stratemeyer knew this.

Also in that letter, Stratemeyer makes what would be a frequent criticism of Les's manuscripts: they were too short. He casually mentions this in his critique of *The House on the Cliff* ("Make full 156 pages long"), but the message is repeated in letters throughout the next few years; in some cases, Stratemeyer would send the manuscript back for Les to fill out the remaining pages. Other times, when he was on a tighter deadline, Stratemeyer himself or a syndicate worker would fill in the remaining pages. While Stratemeyer never appeared angry when bringing up the subject, he sometimes became impatient: "Please be sure to see to it that the story is the proper length to fill 216 text pages," he wrote in a critique of the fourth book, *The Missing Chums*. "Your other manuscripts were all a bit short—154 to 157 pages. They should be four to five pages longer, as I had to make additions in every instance to bring them up." Regarding the sixth book, the *Shore Road Mystery*, when the publishers reviewed the galley proofs, "we found that the story is about twelve printed pages short," he wrote. "You gave us 156 manuscript pages and I think your new story had better have about 165 manuscript pages." Stratemeyer added in a postscript that he was lengthening it, "as we are in a hurry."

Despite the annoyance caused by the short manuscripts, Les became one of Stratemeyer's most valued authors. Perhaps that is the reason Stratemeyer always complied when Les made his frequent requests for small advances of twenty-five or fifty dollars to meet expenses, although Stratemeyer usually paid authors after completion of their manuscripts.

These requests began in mid 1927, nearly a year after Les started working for the syndicate, but they grew in number over the next few years after he married and started a family, even though he noted after his request for the first one in July of 1927, "I hope you didn't mind the request and I don't think it'll happen again."

The spring of 1927 was pivotal for Les. In addition to earning a regular salary from his Hardy Boys books, he got a huge boost in his confidence from winning a Canadian national fiction contest sponsored by the prestigious *Maclean's* magazine. Les noted in his autobiography that as the rejection letters piled up, he received some good advice from his New York–based agent, Bob Hardy. Les said by that time his writing had overtones of bad Joseph Conrad—not a positive development, considering that even good work by the real Conrad was not selling well in 1927. His agent told Les that he should find a better model, or, better yet, simply write as himself. It was solid advice—and words by which Les would live the rest of his professional life. Meanwhile, the suggestion had positive short-term ramifications. Les had revised a long story he wrote called "The Root-House" about a couple and their small child who get trapped in a small shack while a brush fire rages outside. *Maclean's* entered it in its annual fiction contest, and it won third place and netted Les a $125 prize. While Les certainly needed the money, it was the prestige of the award—and the tremendous publicity it received in *Maclean's*—that thrilled him. Interestingly, he shared third place with the well-known Canadian writer Mazo de la Roche, author of the popular Jalna series, who by that time had already published three books. The editors noted they received 926 entries.

Les was proud of the award, and sent Stratemeyer a copy of the double-page award announcement that ran in *Maclean's*. ("I congratulate you on winning one of the MacLean's Magazine prizes, and trust this will give you more of an opening than ever," Stratemeyer responded.) Les joked in his memoir that the 7,000-word tale was a perfect Canadian story because it was downbeat and would thus appeal to Canadian judges: "It had a Canadian setting, was depressing in tone, studded in strong language and ended bleakly and without hope." "The Root-House" delves into the complaints and bleak life of a family as a fire outside sweeps through all their possessions and land. The couple, Mary and Joe, make a last-ditch effort to survive and argue bitterly and blame each other as they wait in the sweltering shelter while the world outside them is destroyed in an inferno:

They thought of the long, dull years that had passed
and of the long, dull years that loomed ahead, years of
struggling painfully again for nothing more that what
they had already struggled painfully to earn. It was bitter.
"All the workin' and scrapin' and savin.' All over
again."
In spite of herself, the reproach was wrung from
her. "Oh, if you hadn't started that fire in the slash!"
He turned on her, as by old habit. "There. Blame
me! I knew it!"

Some of the most beautiful writing in "The Root-House" focuses on
the devastation of the countryside and the power of nature—themes he
had sounded in his newspaper coverage of the Haileybury fire and, in
more elementary and innocent ways, in the Hardy Boys.

They huddled in their gloomy little hole in the ground
and wrangled, while outside the fire raged across their
farm and across the farms of the neighbors. Fields were
being blackened, trees were tumbling to the earth in
flurries of flame and smoke and dust, all the country
was wrapped in an impenetrable haze.

Still, Les may have been incorrect when he wrote decades later that
the story was without hope. The couple and their child survive, although all their possessions are destroyed. They do, however, resolve to
rebuild both their farm and their relationship.
"The Root-House" was a tremendous boost for Les's confidence and
drove up his stock as a freelance writer. After he won the prize, he sold
several detective stories to the magazines *Mystery Stories* and *Real Detective
Tales*. He also sold a brief piece to *Goblin*, a humor magazine. His sales
for 1927 were $1,815. More important, however, was the fact that only
$715 of that came from Stratemeyer. He earned the remainder from
other magazine sources, a comforting fact that may have encouraged
him to persevere as a freelance writer.

***

Listed on Les's sales record in 1927 is a $225 payment for a work called
Mystery Ranch, done for Stratemeyer. *Mystery Ranch* was an idea Strate-

meyer had for an adult mystery novel set on a ranch. Letters between Stratemeyer and Les indicated that both had high hopes for this 60,000-word story for which Stratemeyer hoped he could find a market.

Although it is unknown what efforts he made to find a publisher, several elements about the book are uncharacteristic of Stratemeyer: the syndicate had published a limited amount of adult fiction, but its forte by the late 1920s was children's series books—and the syndicate under Stratemeyer was certainly successful at arranging for these books to be written and sold. Also, by that time, most of Stratemeyer's ideas paid off. That ultimately was not the case with *Mystery Ranch.*

When he initially contacted Les about writing the book, he noted that the payment would be $225—about $100 more than Les was paid to write the Hardy Boys books, in part because *Mystery Ranch* would be 310 printed pages, about 100 pages longer than the Hardy Boys books. Stratemeyer wrote that he was looking for books for adults "with plenty of action and a good holding point at the end of each chapter. . . . I would also like to have some real cowboy humor."

Stratemeyer sent Les a single-spaced six-page outline telling the story of the mysterious murder of a ranch owner somewhere in the West. The protagonist, the victim's nephew, was raised by the rancher, and stands to inherit $5,000 if he can find who murdered him. (Fortunately, the old rancher had time to change his will right before he died.) Because *Mystery Ranch* would be a novel for adults, it comes complete with a love interest for the protagonist, cold-blooded murders with guns, and even a crooked pastor; certainly Stratemeyer would not have taken the liberty of creating these characters and situations in his books for juveniles.

The plot outline for *Mystery Ranch* sounds suspiciously like an outline for the Hardy Boys: it begins with the protagonist narrowly escaping uninjured after a train crash. (It opens, breathlessly: "A crash, a jar, and Brad Hawley, hurrying to attend one funeral, came close to another of his own. Wild confusion in the Pullman at night. Rain. Lightning. Brad crawls from the wreckage.") Brad Hawley, a college graduate who had plans to go into business, is suddenly transformed into a rancher and amateur detective, according to the outline: "The young collegian had now to change his entire program of life, giving up thought of business and getting back to life on the ranch, taking charge, as his uncle had before him. In this there was one compensation: Pearl." The outline comes complete with Dickensian character names—for instance, the lively cowboy, Snooky, and the ethically challenged minister, Paul Hosenberry (who is later revealed to be the criminal Philip Cross). As is the case in the Hardy Boys books, the heroes prevail at the end, despite many close calls. In this case, Brad and the shy Pearl walk in the moonlight at the end, and "all the difficulties of the past are washed away." (Because of the publication that year of Sinclair Lewis's *Elmer Gantry*, about a wayward minister, Stratemeyer treaded lightly when it came to the phony clergyman, warning Les that in order to avoid criticism like the kind aimed at Lewis's negative portrayal of the clergy, he should stress that the phony minister was an impostor "pure and simple" and never had any connection with any church.)

Judging from the intricate and rather silly outline, it is not surprising that Stratemeyer never could sell *Mystery Ranch*. After nearly two years, he gave up, writing to Les that he could attempt to sell it under his own name if he wished. If he did sell it, Stratemeyer, ever the businessman, told Les he thought it would be fair that he return the $225 payment to him, along with 20 percent of any sales revenues he received for it exceeding $450. The point was moot, however, because neither man sold the completed *Mystery Ranch* to a publisher.

***

It may have been by accident that one of the most popular characters in the Hardy Boys series was even created and nurtured. The feisty Aunt Gertrude may have been a creation of Stratemeyer's, but it was Les who gave her the colorful personality, brusque manner, and contrarian attitude that made her famous among Hardy Boys readers. Until the fourth book of the series, *The Missing Chums*, the benign Laura Hardy was the boys' only female role model—or at least the only adult female among the continuing characters. Laura Hardy was a likable and sympathetic character, warm and caring, but she appeared mainly to wring her hands over the boys' exploits, hoping that one day they would enter law or medicine.

Les had relied on Bayport's three policemen for comic relief, although by the time he sent in the manuscript for *The Missing Chums* he had learned that Stratemeyer had not been amused by the antics of Bayport's version of the Keystone Kops. When he sent the outline for the fifth book, *The Shore Road Mystery*, Stratemeyer mentioned to Les that he should avoid ridiculing Mssrs. Smuff and Collig. "In using the local police of Bayport, kindly remember that this is a good-sized town with a fair-sized force and be careful not to make a caricature of the chief and his head detective," he wrote. Although this admonition was hardly severe, Les took it to heart. In his autobiography, he wrote that he was shocked—and crushed. "I groaned," he remembered. "There went my best source of comedy material. I had been counting on the Bayport Bluecoats for at least four chapters of surefire laughs per book, and if I had any strong conviction about the Hardy Boys series at all, it was that where kid readers were concerned you couldn't go wrong by larding the action with a little funny stuff." What also bothered Les, though, was what Stratemeyer's criticism represented. He interpreted it to mean that young adults should not question authority and should accept what they are told. "Was it written in the Bible, the Talmud, the Koran, the British North America Act and the Constitution . . . that everyone in authority was inflexibly honest, pious and automatically admirable?" he asked. "Wouldn't every kid be the better for a little shot of healthy skepticism at an early age?"

Les may have taken Stratemeyer's words too seriously. After all, if Stratemeyer had severe objections to the way the officers were portrayed, he could have edited the copy and warned Les earlier. But the criticism stung Les, a firm believer that children, both boys and girls, be encouraged to think independently. Part of the appeal of Les's Hardy Boys books lies in the fact that, using puns, literary allusions, and sophisticated phrasing and sentences, he did not underestimate his readers or talk down to them.

While Les toned down slightly his portrayal of the policemen, the officers did not escape unscathed—they were still bumbling in most of the books he wrote. (In one of Les's last Hardy Boys books, *The Short-Wave Mystery*, written in 1945, Chet Morton is quoted as saying about Collig and Smuff, "If you bother to put their brains together you'd have enough for a half-wit!")

Disappointed as he was, though, Les found that Stratemeyer's criticism of his police portrayals closed one door but opened another. When he began to temper his satirical portrayals of the Bayport police, he found another target of humor—Fenton Hardy's spinster sister, the formidable Aunt Gertrude.

Aunt Gertrude first joins the Hardy Boys' world in a contentious scene in *The Missing Chums*. Unlike the other demure female characters in the series, she enters with both guns blazing, arguing about the fare with the taxi driver who delivers her and her yellow cat, Lavinia, to the Hardy home from the train station. She orders Frank and Joe to carry her luggage and chastises them when they drag their feet. Readers know early on that Aunt Gertrude is not one to be trifled with:

> She was a raw-boned female of 65, tall and commanding, with a determined jaw, and an acid tongue and an eye that could quell a traffic cop. She was as authoritative as a prison guard, bossed everyone within reach, and had a lofty contempt for men in general and boys in particular.

Aunt Gertrude, unlike her sister-in-law Laura Hardy, is not content to wring her hands and worry quietly about her two nephews. She is vocal about her opposition to their dangerous activities and pessimistic about the outcomes. In short, Aunt Gertrude tells it like it is, shows her emotions, and emerges as one of the most exuberant characters in the series. Les's portrayal of Aunt Gertrude no doubt was drawn from his imagination. But it is possible that when defining her as a character, he recalled his old grammar school teacher in Haileybury, Miss Sarah Flegg. As he wrote in his childhood memoir, *A Kid in Haileybury,* Miss Flegg was a teacher who ruled by fear—a "yeller" who made it clear that insubordination would not be tolerated. Yet Miss Flegg was widely admired and remembered when graduates met for reunions decades later.

In response to his portrayal of Aunt Gertrude in *The Missing Chums,* Les received instructions to make the visiting maiden aunt a permanent character. And he was only too happy to do it: "If there was a turning point in the series that was it," he remembered. "Maybe a turning point wasn't needed. Maybe the series would have plodded along without her but it wouldn't have been the same." Perhaps it was a self-fulfilling prophecy: as long as Aunt Gertrude made Les happy and provided him with a pleasant diversion, the books would then absorb that interest and enthusiasm.

Aunt Gertrude would become a versatile character whose appearances were not restricted to the pages of the Hardy Boys books. In an unsuccessful attempt in the 1930s to make a radio show about the Hardy Boys, she got top billing in the series that would have been called "Aunt Gertrude and the Boys." She made it onto television, with Frank and Joe, as a cartoon character and into at least one musical comedy based on the series. Years after he had stopped writing the series, Les was frequently told by Hardy Boys fans that Aunt Gertrude was one of their favorite characters.

By the time Les completed his fourth book in the series, his freelance career was well established. By the first part of 1928, he had sold nearly $2,000 worth of stories to more than six outlets, not including Stratemeyer's syndicate. To Les, however, the evidence that he was becoming "successful" lay not in the number of stories he sold, but in the markets to which he sold them. In addition to winning the short story competition in *Maclean's* and having "The Root-House" published there, he had sold two other short stories to that magazine by mid-1928 and had a 2,000-word piece published in *Vanity Fair* and another short piece in the *Toronto Star Weekly*. The slicker, more literate publications paid no more than the pulp publications *Real Detective Stories, Mystery Stories,* and others, but they were worth much more in prestige. Only "serious" writers had work published in those magazines. Les's sales for 1928 more than doubled to $3,928.

Perhaps it was the morale boost he received from his work by mid-1928, or the financial boost, or both that led to his wedding on May 3, 1928, to Amy Ashmore Arnold, a shy, reserved housekeeper who at the time of her marriage was working in the home of a family in Thetford Mines, Quebec. Amy, whose family lived in New Liskeard, near Haileybury, was the third of seven children of English immigrants Stephen and Amy Burton Arnold. Amy Arnold's mother was born in London and came to Montreal in 1893; the family moved to the Temiskaming Valley in northern Ontario in 1903, when Amy was seven years old, and took up farming.

The courtship of Les and Amy was apparently a long one, as indicated by one of Les's letters to her, but its details remain vague to surviving family members. Amy's sister, Else, and Les's younger daughter, Norah Perez, believe the two met at a dance or other social event in Haileybury or New Liskeard. The two dated for nearly nine years before they married. The letters Les wrote to Amy gave her updates about his work and activities, and usually told her how much he missed her. "It has been a lonely evening without you and I have missed you a great deal," he said in one handwritten letter. "I realize how much I love you when I can't be with you. I am glad you gave me that kerchief of yours last night for its fragrance and its softness seem to bring part of you to me through the storm and the night." Les, the compulsive writer who had always been able to express himself better in writing than orally, found words inadequate when it came to Amy: "I wanted to speak to you for letters are rather cold and formal looking affairs at best," he wrote in one. In another, he said he may pay her a surprise visit one day and "give you in person the many, many kisses I'm now obliged to send by letter and tell you what I now have to write—that you are everything to me and that I shall adore you always as I always adored you." He ended the letters with a series of *"xxxxxxxx"* to indicate kisses.

Another letter, typewritten on *Springfield Republican* stationery, refers to an argument the two had: "I'm glad everything is all right between us and we mustn't risk our happiness again by these misunderstandings," he wrote. "I think we both have confidence and faith in one another and in the love that has remained unshaken for seven years and keep the mutual trust and respect for one another's personalities that we had last autumn when we were together." In late 1927, Les indicated that he was still insecure about the relationship, even though the two had plans to marry. He writes that he had not received a letter from her in some time and "when you don't write, I often get the idea that is because you are losing interest. When a couple of weeks go by without hearing from you it seems you are in China or some distant place like that. I know we love each other deeply but the miles can so easily separate people in mind and thought" In the same letter, he tells her news about Thanksgiving and notes, "next year it will be my Thanksgiving dinner you will be cooking. I should say 'ours,' shouldn't I?"

In these letters, Les also wrote about the challenges of his life as a freelance writer. Many of these struggles—and triumphs—would repeat themselves over the years, and Amy's marriage would make her all too familiar with the dramatic ups and downs in the life of a writer.

In some ways the marriage of Amy and Les was an unlikely one, as the two had very different personalities and interests. Yet it endured for 27 years, until Amy's death, and Les considered it a happy one. His life revolved around literature and writing, so it is not surprising that even during their courtship he wrote her far more than she wrote him, and that he would wait impatiently for letters from her. Even in this way, according to their daughter, Norah, the two were dissimilar: Amy did not enjoy writing letters and found it difficult to express herself in writing. Her husband, on the other hand, was a compulsive writer, who in his lifetime would complete thousands of newspaper stories, short stories, novellas, magazine articles, novels, memoirs, plays, and letters. Indeed, as he grew older, his obsession with writing deepened.

But their differences stretched beyond that. While Les was outgoing, Amy was reserved; Les loved going out with friends and to social events and bars and restaurants, while Amy preferred staying home or gathering with family or close friends. And while Les was sentimental and occasionally extravagant, Amy was grounded and straightforward. And, perhaps most important, while Les could weather the uncertainty and vicissitudes that came with being a full-time writer, that lifestyle was sometimes intolerable for Amy.

Some of their differences may have resulted from their upbringing. Les was the oldest of four brothers, but he never played the role of caretaker to them nor was he responsible for their welfare. Further, his work as a newspaper reporter in several cities in the Canada and United States did instill in him a worldly outlook. Amy was the oldest daughter in a family of seven children and served as a role model and surrogate parent at times. Her youngest sister, Else, recalls that when Amy was working and the other Arnold girls were still at home, Amy would send money home to help the girls with their schooling, including money for room and board for her sister, Gladys, who was attending school in Cobalt, Ontario. Else remembers her oldest sister as "self-sacrificing"; similarly, Amy and Les's son, Brian, called her "almost martyr-like."

Leslie McFarlane, then twenty-five, and Amy Arnold, about to turn thirty-two, were married in Montreal on May 3, 1928, in a late-afternoon ceremony at the Church of St. James the Apostle. According to the wedding announcement in the newspaper, the bride "was very pretty in an ensemble costume of navy blue with hat to match. She wore a fox fur and carried a wedding bouquet of roses and lily-of-the-valley." Following the ceremony, the couple hosted a brief reception and left for their new temporary home, a cottage, in Coteau Landing, Quebec, near Montreal. Among those wishing them well was Edward Stratemeyer, who, upon learning of their nuptuals, sent the couple a $25 check as a wedding gift.

6
· · · · · · ·
THE GOLDEN HANDCUFFS

The timing of Les's and Amy's marriage was no coincidence: it occurred a year or so after his freelance writing career began to take off dramatically, and the prospect of financial security no doubt prompted them to marry after years of courtship. Amy's marriage to a writer raised some eyebrows among her friends and family. After the marriage, "their good wishes sounded more like condolences," Les wrote in his autobiography. "Especially a Canadian writer! One good woman said, 'God help you, my dear!' with compassion. We thought it was amusing at the time. Later we realized what she meant." His fiction sales totaled $3,928 for 1928, his best year for sales until that point. Unfortunately, his sales dropped below that in 1929 and 1931, and were only $157 higher in 1930.

Although the Hardy Boys series furnished a guaranteed paycheck, the idea of abandoning the Hardy Boys always brightened his outlook. As he notes in his autobiography, Les got into a writing groove after the fourth Hardy Boys book, *The Missing Chums:* "Without realizing it I had acquired systematic work habits and a professional attitude," he wrote. "The morning chapter rolled out of the typewriter every day until the book was done, the order filled, the merchandise delivered." He spent most mornings at his typewriter and, before his marriage, often spent the entire day writing. After Amy and he were married, Les noted, this momentum manifested itself as more sales of adult fiction to respectable magazines. "As time passed, more and more stories found their way into magazines in Canada, in the United States, even England, and some of them were good magazines indeed."

Throughout his early career, he thought continually of abandoning the Hardy Boys and allowing someone else to record their exploits. But no matter how he did the math, he could not figure out how to get along without the financial boost from Stratemeyer. Shortly before his marriage, he wrote to Stratemeyer asking him, slyly and indirectly, how many Hardy Boys books he could expect to write in a year and whether he could expect a raise, perhaps hoping that the answers would be "not many" and "no."

The even slyer Stratemeyer answered that the syndicate hoped to publish two Hardy Boys books a year. The other indirect question, however, went unanswered. Because he always hoped to make enough money with his adult fiction to sever ties with the Stratemeyer Syndicate, Les never imagined as a young man how long he would be tied to his Hardy Boys "anchor," as he called it. Thanks to a growing family, terrible economic conditions, and the resulting unstable freelance markets, "the sheet anchor was to hold far longer than I ever planned," he wrote fifty years later. "It held through several nasty squalls. . . . Nearly fifteen years went by before the rope was cut. It was considerably frayed by that time anyway." Stratemeyer no doubt knew that Les constantly contemplated abandoning his work for the syndicate—after all, Les kept Stratemeyer informed of his success at placing articles in magazines, and Stratemeyer knew of his dream of becoming an established writer of adult fiction. Stratemeyer was also aware, however, of the young writer's growing family and of his occasional requests for advances. Most important to Stratemeyer, though, was the fact that McFarlane was the author of a popular and fast-growing new series; getting another ghostwriter to pen it could possibly hurt and certainly not help its success. So Stratemeyer tolerated Les's peccadilloes. In 1928, the syndicate head wrote a letter gently reminding Les that he had a Hardy Boys book due in a few weeks: "I am writing to learn how you are making out with your writing and if the story will be forwarded as scheduled," he wrote. "I have no desire to break in on your successful work on the magazine and hope it will continue. But, as you can readily understand, we have to get our manuscripts in shape for our various publishers."

About six months after he and Amy moved to the small village of Coteau Landing, Quebec, Les acquired a habit that he would maintain much of his life: the extensive recording of his daily activities in a diary, beginning January 1, 1929. The diaries reflected his daily activities, his thoughts, and his views on many current events and, most important, provided an internal sounding board. His first foray into diary writing was, by most standards, an odd one. Ever the third-person observer in his newspaper reporting and his fiction writing, he began a journal writing not as himself but as his wife Amy. Early on in the diary (which consisted of three or four sentences a day), it is evident that it is written in the voice of Amy, yet the handwriting has the clear, unadorned style of Les and can be easily matched to his later diaries, written in his own voice. Les and Amy's daughter Norah believes the diaries were written by her father as her mother—although the reason for this is unclear.

The first diary begins with an account of the final six weeks of Amy's pregnancy. Daughter Elaine Patricia (known throughout her life as Patricia, or Pat) was born on February 17, 1929. This journal records the way the McFarlanes lived during the first year of their marriage and the challenges they faced. The diaries paint a picture of a man and woman who enjoy socializing with their family and friends (both Amy and Les came from large families), who enjoy a warm, comfortable home and good meals, and who also take great pleasure in reading and in going to plays and movies. The passages portray a mother and father who derive great joy from their new baby, a welcome addition to the family, but they also describe the brutal and unforgiving cold weather that for much of the year brought the perennial misery of colds and flus; the difficult life of a freelance writer who waits anxiously for the mail each day to determine if he can pay the bills that month; and the beginnings of a long battle Amy would have with depression.

A typical entry is this one from January 9, which spells out how the arrival of the mail brightened the couple's day considerably: "Both feeling under the weather today but immensely cheered by word from *Maclean's* that 'Breed of Pioneers' is to be published at last." Of course, fortunes have a way of changing, as evidenced by this passage the next day: "Les and I sick in bed today and our ill luck seems to have reached a climax. It certainly couldn't be much worse. Les invited to lunch by Keith Crowbir [an executive of an advertising firm]." The anxiety generated over the uncertainty of sales of Les's stories is virtually nonstop. On January 26, "Another day of disappointment; No mail of any kind. We were both feeling pretty blue. Our bad luck seems to be at its very worst." Two days later, January 28: "Three letters from [Les's agent Bob] Hardy. Les sold [series] 'Streets of Shadow' to *Munsey's* for $1,000 and we celebrated by dinner at the Martin and to the movies." And, on January 29, ""Both feeling much more cheerful today about the novel. Les banked the money and our financial worries are over for the time being at any rate."

By late January, Amy's—or Les's—journal entries show that Amy was growing increasingly uncomfortable waiting for the baby. She was having trouble sleeping and felt ill much of the time. "Am feeling pretty tough," she wrote on January 30. Or, on February 2, "Started to make a dress but didn't get along very well. Had a wretched night. The waiting is tiresome." Amy and Les went about their daily business, with Les making the rounds to friends, editors, and members of a group of writers called the

Authors League, and both having dinner with friends and family. On February 16, Amy went to the hospital after a sleepless night. "Doctor says baby should be here sometime during the day but not much progress so far." The entry on February 17, the day Pat was born in Coteau Landing, is oddly tranquil, considering it alludes to the fact that the labor was a long and difficult one: "Baby born shortly after 7 o'clock tonight. A fine girl, weighs 7 lbs., 13 oz. If it hadn't been for Dr. Gray, the outcome would not have been so favorable; 48 long hours."

The mystery of the diary authorship continues with the baby's birth. This entry on the day of the baby's birth indicates that perhaps Amy did dictate the passages to Les, but the fact that other entries were recorded when Les was out of town casts doubt on that scenario. It is also possible that Amy wrote journal entries in her own handwriting and Les transferred them to a more formal format of a journal. Les emerges—as himself—on February 18, one day after Pat was born: "Went to see Amy and the baby today. Both are doing well. The baby is plump and pretty and of course we are very much in love with her."

Amy and Pat would not leave the hospital until March 7, nearly three weeks after Pat's birth. Amy had not felt well since the baby's birth, and the McFarlanes' hectic lifestyle and uncertainty about jobs and money was taking its toll. She was still having trouble sleeping, and as Les notes in a journal entry, the hospital finally gave her sleeping pills. Further, as he notes, the baby was having trouble nursing, "and Amy felt blue" (March 1). To add to the troubles, both mother and daughter contracted colds while in the hospital. Amy, meanwhile, was also suffering from chronic headaches.

The proud father's professional career took an upswing in the time his family was in the hospital. He received word that one of his stories had been sold to *Detective Fiction Weekly*, he was making good progress on several others, and the local Women's Art Society asked him to give a reading of one of his stories. "Saturday Evening Post 'almost' bought 'Power of the Word' but it is still homeless. Paid hospital bill of $263 and am preparing to bring the family back home at last tomorrow," he wrote on March 6. Les was finally able to bring his new family home the next day on the 4 p.m. train. But it was a stressful day: "Amy still very weak and tired. Baby cried half the night and we got about 6 hours of sleep," he wrote. And he was a bit more direct in the entry the next day, March 8: "Beginning to find that a baby can be one helluva a lot of trouble. Suppose we'll get used to it in time."

The journal for 1929 indicates that Les flirted with taking regular jobs and abandoning his career as a full-time writer. On January 14, for instance, the entry reads, "Les in Montreal. Mr. Crowbir of McKim advertising agency offered him a job. It will bring at least $200 a month and we will live in Montreal." (He never took the job.) Or, on March 15: "Les went to Montreal today and was offered editorship of *Goblin* and two other magazines" (a job he did take, but apparently left after a short time); September 7: "Les has a chance for a job in the Department of Mines in Ottawa, but we hate to move."

One job offer Les did accept was an associate editorship of *Maclean's* magazine, which prompted the couple to move with their baby to Toronto early in 1929. At the time, Les's brother Frank and his wife, Flora, lived in Toronto, and they helped with the move. Within several months, however, Les and Amy moved yet again, this time back to Haileybury. The reason for leaving Toronto was never explained in the diaries, but moving back to Haileybury appeared to be a relief for all them—Les and Amy would be much closer to their family and old friends, and they were of course familiar with the Haileybury–New Liskeard area, where they had been raised.

Like many new parents, Les and Amy were overwhelmed by the baby and how she affected their daily lives. But nearly all the mentions of Pat in the diaries refer to her in terms of great affection: they were in awe at her first words, noted how cute she looked in various outfits, and were proud to show her to neighbors and friends. They took great joy in watching Pat grow that first year, charting her weight, her new teeth, and her emerging personality. Over the years, their three children would be very important to the McFarlanes and they would devote their lives to them. But their existence would also exacerbate the family's perennial financial worries.

When Pat was nearly a month old, the voice in the 1929 journals becomes once again Amy's. In these passages, Amy offers a glimpse of the beginnings of a chronic sadness and lethargy that would plague her much of the rest of her life as she attempted to keep house, complete domestic chores, and raise an active family: "Feeling awfully tired and depressed today, somehow," she wrote on March 16. "Made an apple pie. Baby was angelic today. . . . Went to bed early."

Of course the physical illnesses brought about in part by the dismal weather may have been responsible to some degree for Amy's lack of energy. Despite some beautiful weather in the summer and early fall, extreme temperatures, rain, and snowstorms seemed to be the norm in northern Ontario. The couple was sometimes forced to build fires in their hearth as early as June 28: "A very cold, rainy day. Kept the fireplace going to keep the chill out of the house. . . . Pat not so well today," Amy wrote on that day. Or, on August 4, "so cold we kept the fireplace going all day and we sat around reading." The McFarlanes spent many of their evenings and weekends involved in social activities with Les's and Amy's siblings, and with their parents. They got together for dinners, Parcheesi, bridge, and poker, and often went out with them to plays and movies, which both Amy and Les particularly enjoyed. Les had once reviewed them for the newspaper, and the journals are sprinkled with references to films like *The Jazz Singer, Abie's Irish Rose,* and *Sins of the Fathers.* Amy frequently mentioned the menus of the elaborate family dinners the couple had: roast beef and Yorkshire pudding, venison, pork tenderloin, chicken, Christmas turkey. As the year wore on, though, it was becoming increasingly obvious that Amy preferred to stay home, or to limit her socializing to being with family or longtime friends only. Yet she still felt lonely staying home without Les, who frequently visited Toronto or Montreal on business or to conduct research for his work. The day after he left by train for Toronto on April 26, "I would be very lonesome today if it weren't for Pat," she wrote. In early July, the family planned a weekend visit to the summer home of some longtime friends: "Mr. and Mrs. Arnott want us to come down to their camp at Kippawa and have decided to altho I do not feel much like it," she wrote on July 3. "We'll leave by boat tomorrow afternoon. It should be a nice holiday." By the next day, however, Amy had changed her mind: "Decided not to go on account of the flies, but Les went anyway. Boat left at 4 p.m. and Pat and I were down to see them off. Came back home, feeling very lonely."

Even socializing with family and attending plays did not bring the pleasure to Amy that it once had. As she wrote on May 10, "Went to see 'Alibi' with Frank and Flora [McFarlane] but did not care for it altho the others liked it. Don't enjoy shows as much as I used to."

Les, however, never tired of socializing, and in addition to some out-of-town trips, he frequently went out with friends without Amy, although he was always the attentive husband and father who often bought gifts and clothes for his wife and daughter. Although he sometimes brought Amy conventional gifts like chocolates and books—and in one case, an original French etching—Les particularly enjoyed buying clothes for Amy, and would do so throughout their marriage, particularly in the few years when Amy was bedridden because of her illness. Amy was an expert seamstress who sometimes made clothes for herself, but more often for Les and others.

Although Les jokingly mentions in his autobiography that he was surrounded by hard-drinking reporters and miners when he worked on newspapers, he notes only briefly that he, too, enjoyed beer. His drinking was nothing to joke about, however, in the 1930s, when he developed a severe alcohol problem—one that required hospitalization. Although his drinking was no longer a problem after he received treatment for it, it would for many years be a sensitive topic to his family—especially for his children after they had grown.

Life back in Haileybury had its advantages and disadvantages. Amy and Les took great comfort in being surrounded by their family and longtime friends. They held teas and parties for special events and particularly enjoyed celebrating holidays with family and friends. Their parents and siblings occasionally provided babysitting for them. Les loved bowling and playing cards and became active in civic organizations such as the library board and hockey club. He frequently gave readings and speeches to civic groups, many of which were written up in the hometown newspaper, the *Haileyburian,* and his success as a freelance writer did give him some measure of fame in his hometown. In addition, he was able to work occasionally for the paper during special events, such as elections, when more manpower was needed. But as Les would learn in the next five or six years, it was easy for the hometown boy to live in the charming and welcoming town of Haileybury, but the region was, unfortunately, far away from Toronto and Montreal, the big literary markets, a major disadvantage to a serious writer. Also, his fictional stories occasionally required him to do research, most of which necessitated travel to the nearest big city, taking him away from his family for days.

Despite their money worries and their frequent moves, it was important to the McFarlanes that they look presentable and live in a well-furnished and comfortable home. Amy's emotional state became increasingly fragile in 1929, but she clearly enjoyed buying furnishings to make her home a warm and inviting place, and news of these purchases made its way into the journal. "Bought an Irish lace tea cloth today and it looks lovely," she wrote on August 20. On September 14, Les ordered a dining room suite and a console table and mirror, which, as Amy noted, "is expensive but good." On October 3, "The big event of the day was the arrival of the dining room suite which arrived at six o'clock. It is beautiful and we are proud of it. Mr. and Mrs. McF [Les's parents] over in the evening to see it. Makes the dining room look very grand." The next day, she notes, Les bought lamps for the living room. Even during the months when money was short, the family's home and clothes were never shabby.

Although Amy was not able to give Les the unexpected gifts he sometimes gave her, she did note the celebration of his birthday: "Hubby is 27 years old today," she wrote on October 27. She bought him some handkerchiefs, and the couple returned a novelty lamp they had purchased so Les could buy a new hat. The McFarlanes' youngest child, Norah, said her father loved celebrating birthdays and throughout his life—even when he was ill—never overlooked them. As the family grew, Les's birthday was a big event for everyone for at least one reason, she recalled: he gave his children presents on his own birthday.

Weeks after Les's twenty-seventh birthday, the couple's money problems intensified, and they had to ask his agent for a fifty-dollar advance on sales of his articles. "Still no cheque although we had been counting on it today," Amy wrote on Nov. 8. "Les wired Hardy to send him $50 as we are down to our last cent. It's very annoying and it worries me a lot." When the check from Hardy arrived the next day, they "paid the grocery bill," Amy wrote. "Les got his new coat and it looks fine, also a pair of spats." When the long-awaited check from the publisher arrived, the couple repaid the loan, paid some debts in New Liskeard, "cleaned up other debts and bought a ton of coal. Feel very relieved," Amy wrote on November 15. The arrival of the money so relieved Amy that she asked the McFarlanes to babysit Pat while she played bridge with friends and went into town to buy a new dress, shoes, and stockings—activities uncharacteristic of Amy, who rarely spent money on herself. The relief was short lived, however. "Spent nearly all the cheque and still not all paid up," she wrote two days later.

During this period Les was having some luck selling long, multipart stories, usually mysteries, that were published first in magazines in serial form and later as short paperback novels. These 20,000- to 35,000-word stories, which Les referred to as "novellas," were often the family's bread and butter: Les could get as much as $600 for one, as he did for "The Laughing Cat Mystery," sold to a magazine called *All Star,* or as little as $425—which was still a healthy payment. Although the word-count of these serials was five or six times that of the average story he sold to the more prestigious *Toronto Star Weekly* magazine, the pay was usually more than five or six times the $75 he received for those smaller articles. Les was also finding through them that success breeds success. Unlike smaller articles and his Hardy Boys books, the novellas were reprinted and generated continual royalties. And once *All Star* purchased one of his articles, it began purchasing more.

Les earned money in other ways as well. "The Root-House," the short story for which he won the *Maclean's* writing award, was reprinted in the British magazine *Argosy*, and he received $70 for that—a special boost considering he had written the stories a few years previously. In addition, the *Haileyburian* reprinted many of Les's serial stories.

* * *

Les completed two Hardy Boys books in 1929—*The Mystery of Cabin Island* and the *Great Airport Mystery*—keeping up the tentative schedule of two books per year that Stratemeyer had arranged. Sales for the series were growing steadily, although it was still outpaced dramatically by the Ted Scott Flying series. The Hardy Boys books sold about 75,000 copies in 1929, compared to about 200,000 for Ted Scott during the same year; average sales per volume of the Hardy Boys that year were about 10,000, compared to about twice that for the Ted Scott series.

Each time Les received good news from another publisher, he considered abandoning his alter ego, Franklin W. Dixon. "Had an 'Uncle Absolom' story accepted and an order for two books from Stratemeyer, but is afraid he can't accept," Amy wrote on March 27, 1929. (Uncle Absolom was the protagonist in a series of stories Les wrote for several magazines including the *Toronto Star Weekly*.) Les evidently changed his mind, as evidenced by a letter dated March 12 from Stratemeyer, who confirmed that Les would write *The Mystery of Cabin Island*. Apparently Les had requested a raise in pay—from $125 to $150 for that book. The clever Stratemeyer did give him a raise for that book, but with a stipulation: "Regarding the price of this story, I have been paying you our regular rates on these yarns, but I will make the price on this particular manuscript one hundred and fifty dollars," he wrote. "It being understood between us that the extra twenty-five dollars is to go to the new young lady in your family whose name you forgot to mention. I certainly wish the young lady and her mother and yourself the best of luck." Also in that letter, Stratemeyer addressed the issue of pay, explaining that the economics of the syndicate prohibited a pay raise for syndicate authors: "You may perhaps think that the price paid on these books is rather small; but you must remember that in issuing these volumes to retail at fifty cents we are giving the public a whole lot for their money and the profit for volume is very small and we have to get quite a sale before we can get the cost of the plant back," he wrote. "These books . . . are the equal of many that are sold at a dollar and fifty cents and two dollars per volume."

Les persevered with the Hardy Boys and accepted the payment rate. But Stratemeyer, too, was forced to make sacrifices. He had to be patient with the Canadian ghostwriter, who was up to his old tricks of turning in manuscripts that were slightly short. Stratemeyer, as usual, was unfailingly polite when he told him, "We have gone over the manuscript [*Mystery of Cabin Island*] carefully and find that it is at least twelve typewritten pages too short." Stratemeyer returned to Les pages 85–87 of the manuscript, with suggestions on where to add the missing pages. "As I wrote you, the publishers are anxious for this manuscript, so I trust that you will send in the additional pages without delay," he concluded.

In addition to providing him with a relatively steady paycheck, Edward Stratemeyer also gave Les the occasional advances he needed to pay his living expenses. Shortly after he received the newly lengthened *Mystery of Cabin Island,* Stratemeyer sent Les the outline for the next Hardy Boys book, *The Great Airport Mystery,* reminding him gently to make the book long enough. He also enclosed an advance payment of $50 that Les had requested, noting that Les would be paid $150 for this latest book, reflecting a raise of $25. Perhaps Les was ambivalent about the raise in pay per book: certainly it came in handy for family expenses, but it also deepened his commitment to staying with the syndicate. As Les would learn over and over in the next fifteen years, he was chained to the Stratemeyer Syndicate by a pair of golden handcuffs.

Edward Stratemeyer's ability to tune into societal trends and to understand the mind of adolescents was certainly paying off by the middle and end of the 1920s. By 1926, the syndicate was near peak production, publishing thirty-one series. Between 1925 and 1927, in addition to the Ted Scott and Hardy Boys series, the syndicate began publishing the Bomba the Jungle Boy series; the exploits of explorer/adventurer Don Sturdy; the Garry Grayson football series; the western adventure series X Bar X Boys, and the Nat Ridley Rapid Fire Detective stories. The Hardy Boys series would ultimately be the most successful of the group, although both the Ted Scott and the Bomba series ran to twenty titles. As one chronicler of the syndicate wrote, "In this midtwenties burst of Syndicate energy, the method was that of a gardener: a variety of new series was sown, and then the syndicate waited to see which ones took root."

Stratemeyer, meanwhile, kept a particularly low profile for someone so successful. He gave very few interviews, so little was known about the man or his business by this time, and of course he asked his ghostwriters not to reveal publicly that they wrote for the syndicate. (No one in Haileybury knew that Les was "Franklin W. Dixon," and as he noted in his autobiography, he was afraid to tell anyone but Amy.) Stratemeyer was known to be a conservative family man who enjoyed lawn bowling and baseball, and who shunned tobacco and alcohol. Much of his life revolved around his job and his wife and two daughters, one of whom was married and had four children of her own by the mid-1920s. Stratemeyer's insistence on keeping both his personal and his professional life private apparently rubbed off on his heirs. Decades after his death, family members who took over Edward Stratemeyer's syndicate had managed to reveal little about it, despite its continual and phenomenal success.

Magazines in North America were rapidly growing by this time. Magazine publishing in the United States first got a shot in the arm in 1879 when the government passed legislation resulting in lower mailing rates; this came on the heels of a spirit of expansion in the country and technological advances in printing. The number and types of national magazines began to grow. In the latter part of the nineteenth century, a privileged class of educated readers could afford highbrow magazines such as *Harper's, Scribner's,* and *Century,* leaving open the market for a less genteel reader. As Stratemeyer helped fulfill a need for less expensive juvenile books, several pioneers in magazine publishing recognized and helped fill the need for magazines that had wider appeal.

Like most successful entrepreneurs, these men—Frank Munsey, S. S. McClure, John Brisben Walker, and George Horace Lorimer, for example—took advantage of the times. Improvements in technology led to the growth in output of goods, which coincided with equally rapid improvements of railway and transportation systems. These events, in turn, allowed local products to be distributed to national markets. As McClure, Munsey, and other publishers realized, advertising and promotion of these products also changed. Retailers needed national rather than local markets to promote and advertise their goods. The local orientation of newspapers would no longer get the job done.

Magazines were vehicles ready made to take advantage of the explosion of retail goods at the turn of the century. Coincidentally, improved printing technology allowed presses to work faster and to turn out magazines with higher-quality graphics at a lower price per copy; enterprising magazine publishers suddenly found themselves in a very lucrative position. In 1893, S. S. McClure published the first copy of *McClure's* and planned to sell it for fifteen cents—ten to twenty cents cheaper than magazines currently on the market. This prompted other clever publishers like *Cosmopolitan* publisher John Brisben Walker and (in the early twentieth century) *Munsey's Magazine's* Frank Munsey to cut the cost of their magazines even more. The formula was epic in its simplicity, as one historian noted: "One could achieve a large circulation by selling his magazine for much less than its cost of production and could take his profits from the high volume of advertising that a large circulation attracted." In this way, everyone was happy: a large, untapped audience of readers could afford the magazines, and more advertisers could advertise at lower rates, since circulation was larger.

Men like Stratemeyer, Walker, Munsey, McClure, and others were clever enough to understand changing cultural values and phenomena and take advantage of them. Many of the magazine-publishing pioneers designed products that would endure for most or all of the new century. For instance, when Cyrus Curtis, publisher of *Ladies' Home Journal*, bought the dying *Saturday Evening Post* in 1897, it had a circulation of 2,231 readers and advertising revenue of $6,933. Thanks to several factors—Curtis's faith that he could revive the declining magazine, his willingness to sink money into it, and the hiring of a talented editor—the magazine gradually recovered. By 1912, circulation was 1.9 million readers and advertising sales were $7.1 million. By 1922, circulation grew to nearly 2.2 million, and advertising revenue was $28.2 million. So the magazine market was ripe in the mid 1920s when Leslie McFarlane became a full-time writer of fiction. Unlike most of the large general-interest magazines of today, fiction was the bread and butter of many of these magazines. And it was an absorbing story—rather than the writing itself—that publishers and editors sought. Theodore Peterson quotes Munsey, certainly an authority on the public's taste in magazines, on the importance of a well-told tale: "We want stories. That is what we mean—stories, not dialect sketches, not washed out studies of effete human nature, not weak tales of sickly sentimentality, not 'pretty' writing. . . . We do want fiction in which there is a story, a force, a tale that means something—in short a story. Good writing is as common as clam shells, while good stories are as rare as statesmanship." By the 1920s, some magazines were also gaining a sophistication they had not had earlier—and editors were taking advantage of an increasingly cosmopolitan population in

North America that had migrated from farms to bigger cities. Les's role model, H. L. Mencken, had joined the staff of *Smart Set* in 1914 as an editor in chief with George Jean Nathan. By 1924, the two men founded the *American Mercury*, a magazine of opinion and ideas that went beyond storytelling and discussions of art and fashion.

It was this lucrative and creative magazine market that Les entered in the mid-1920s. His early success suggested that, with hard and disciplined work, he could take advantage of this need for good storytellers. But, as Les must have known, he needed more than just talent and luck to make it on his own as a fiction writer; he also needed faith in himself. Based on the first few years of his diaries, it is evident that Les wrestled with his ability to believe in himself and to maintain the discipline necessary to make a living as a freelance writer. He must have considered himself reasonably talented, or he would not have made the agonizing decision to leave his full-time jobs to embark on a freelance career. On the other hand, he had self-doubts that made him vulnerable, particularly when finances were low. Like many writers and creative artists, Les's faith in himself was at times contradictory and easily shaken: he believed in his heart that he was talented, but was prone to letting setbacks shake this confidence.

He enjoyed two advantages: he was willing to take suggestions from editors, agents, and others whom he respected; and he always turned out the best product possible. He was not personally insulted by professional criticism, and simply disregarded it if he thought it had no merit. In that way, he had the mental constitution of a successful writer. As his career progressed, he consulted other writers and kept current on the market and what was being written. And while his thoughts on writers' organizations could be ambivalent—as were his views on unions and other professional groups—he thought it crucial to associate with others in his field.

Also, he viewed himself as a professional who never skimped on quality, or denigrated the market or audience for which he wrote—a key quality of a successful freelance writer. Most important, however, was his pride in the fact that his writing gave pleasure to readers.

In his autobiography, Les's reflections on his own ability and talent are telling and candid. He notes that as more and more magazines began accepting his work, he, perhaps unconsciously, adopted a professional attitude: "The professional attitude was difficult to define," he wrote. If one is willing to accept money for writing a certain kind of material, he should do his best. The young, the uncultured or unsophisticated reader is not to blame for his condition and should not be despised—certainly not by the writer who lives by that readers' nickels and dimes. Les said he tried to maintain this attitude even in writing the sensational Dave Fearless books, which he readily admitted were "outrageous fantasies, bordering on burlesque." According to Les, "They were written swiftly, but not carelessly. I gave thought to grammar, sentence structure, choice of words, pace, the techniques of suspense, all within the limits of the medium which was in this case mass-produced, assembly-line fiction for boys. Every kind of writing, from the ancient morality plays to a modern television series, has its own boundaries, and the writer who seeks to earn a living learns the boundaries and works within them."

This philosophy—that the writer should never underestimate or dislike the reader—may explain, indirectly, the great appeal of the Hardy Boy books and why youngsters were so eager to read them. They were written by someone who respected them as readers.

More complicated, however, were Les's views of his own talent and abilities, and his opinions of what can and cannot be cultivated. He acknowledged that he considered himself not a great writer, but a good storyteller: "I probably had the knack for story telling, the entertainer's gift which can always be polished to the glow of art. . . . I enjoyed using it and there was double enjoyment in the thought that it might give some pleasure to others. One had to guard against self-deception, in mistaking the gift for talent which was somehow deserving of esteem."

He concluded that natural ability simply cannot be acquired—a view, he implied, that he learned the hard way: "I knew I was not a genius and moreover that genius cannot be achieved by effort. I also knew that I was not a writer of great talent, although even a small talent can be improved and developed by diligence." After that first year or so of his marriage, Les would learn many hard lessons about the career of a freelance writer. As his business began to pick up in late 1929 and his home life in Haileybury gradually took on a predictable and comforting pattern, he would experience the first of many personal and professional vicissitudes, beginning with the U.S. stock market crash in October 1929 and the sudden death several months later of his patron, Edward Stratemeyer. Once again, his life would change.

7

·······

TOUGH TIMES

By the fall of 1929, Leslie McFarlane had begun to establish a foothold in his career as a full-time freelance writer. And despite the financial uncertainty that came with his profession, his life had achieved some regularity. But much of that would change in late 1929, with the stock market crash in the United States in October and the resulting decline of economic markets throughout North America.

Starting in 1930, Les's diaries clearly were written by him and in his own voice. Throughout the 1930s, the entries grew longer and increasingly introspective. In 1930 the McFarlanes' financial straits became more dire as many magazine markets dried up and others cut back on payments. A current of anxiety runs through the diary entries from this period, as the family was forced to take loans that they prayed they could repay, and their reliance on the mails for checks and word of article acceptance grew increasingly desperate. The stress from this unpredictable existence took its toll on Les, who began drinking more by the 1930s.

Of course, the McFarlane family was not alone in its uncertainty. By 1930, the jobless rate in North America topped 4 million, thousands of businesses were going bankrupt, and little relief was in sight. Still, Les's name was increasingly becoming a fixed byline in some Canadian and American magazines, including the *Toronto Star Weekly, Maclean's,* and the humor magazine *Goblin.* Some of his serialized fiction was reprinted as short "novellas," as he called them. The 75,000-word mystery *Streets of Shadow,* initially serialized in *Munsey's* magazine in 1929, was published by Dutton in early 1930 and, as Les notes in his journal entry on March 25, 1930, it had three printings and the biggest advance sale of any Dutton mystery for the spring of 1930.

The journals indicate that the McFarlanes lived, literally, day to day—with spectacular highs and crushing lows. After Les learned of the success of *Streets of Shadow,* for instance, the couple celebrated. Amy bought a new hat and went to play bridge at the Knights of Columbus hall, and Les met a friend for a "few" drinks, as he noted on March 25.

As was increasingly the case, however, a "few" grew to many more: "Caught hell when Amy got home," he wrote.

The highs they experienced could come crashing down. The more Les worried about money, the more he suffered writer's block that kept him from finishing a good day's work. Further, the daily grind of maintaining a home and family often kept him from his writing, as he indicates in his diary. "Must . . . pick out some material for some new suits. My wardrobe is in bad shape. Hope I can raise some money soon. It is discouraging to be so broke, with so much stuff [work] out. Have only a few dollars left," he wrote on September 21. The next day: "Wasted a whole morning going down to Cobalt to see [the tailor] but he didn't arrive. . . . Tried to work in the afternoon but it was like pulling teeth. . . . If I could only get a break, it wouldn't be as discouraging. . . . Pat fell off the cupboard tonight but luckily escaped without bruises." And, on the next day, September 22, "Thought I would do wonders today, as I felt in the mood. The chimney sweep came around. Our furnace pipes are busted." Still, Les was, normally, a consistent worker who occasionally experienced bursts of intense productivity. Entries in his diary indicate he could usually write from 3,000 to 5,000 words a day. If he was not productive for several consecutive days, he could usually catch up and still turn out 16,000 words in a week.

Unlike Amy, Les was able to derive great happiness from the small pleasures in his life. He writes cheerfully how the new clothes he buys give him a morale boost, and notes how much he enjoys taking part in such activities as an Amos 'n Andy act at a local carnival, a bowling league, and an autograph signing at a local store. He also went camping with friends, and wrote happily in his diary about fishing and boating outings. Clearly, these activities helped sustain Les through hard times. An inveterate reader, he refers frequently to reading modern classics such as *Look Homeward Angel, Wallingford,* works of George Bernard Shaw, Mansfield's poetry, and many more. Ever the arts reviewer, he offers in his diaries brief commentary on the many movies he and Amy saw.

Their unstable financial situation and the resulting tension were increasingly wearing on Amy. Although she did continue to meet with her family and play cards with her family and close friends, Amy became more worried in 1930 about Les's drinking, and she was frequently bedridden with colds, headaches, muscular aches like lumbago, and other illnesses. Some of Les's favorite activities—including trout fishing and playing cards—involved drinking beer, much to Amy's dismay. But

Les was blunt about it in the diaries of 1930: "[A friend, Danny Hogan] stayed with us tonight," he wrote on March 26. "Am pretty well pickled as I write this." Other times, Amy apparently left the house to look for her errant husband, as he notes in at least one passage, on October 27, 1930. After spending a few hours at the home of two friends, he returned home to find that "Amy had been patrolling the streets for me. Good joke on her." In 1930, the markets for magazine fiction fluctuated wildly, and it is probably not coincidental that as his article sales flagged, his drinking increased. In October of that year, Les wrote a letter to the syndicate—which by this time was run by the Stratemeyer daughters—explaining that due to a poor magazine market, he was more than willing to write even more Hardy Boys books. "The magazine game is in terrible shape these days and I'm cutting down on output until conditions are more settled, so I'll be able to give more time to the new story," he wrote on October 15. (Within four months, however, Les would tell the syndicate that he wanted to cut back on writing serial fiction).

References to drinking in his diaries end in late 1930, and he even notes in mid-1931 that he had his first drink in a long time. The end of the year was usually a happy time for Les because it brought with it the Thanksgiving and Christmas holidays, which were major events for the McFarlanes and their family. By early November of 1930, however, the family had apparently taken out a loan on an insurance policy. He wrote on November 1, "Feeling very tired today. Disappointed when the Stratemeyer letter came with outline for new story but no advanced cheque. Absolutely broke now. Not a nickel in the house. Both very tired and went to bed early. . . . Insurance loan should be in tomorrow."

Christmas that year was special for Les and Amy because it was Pat's first real Christmas, as he noted in his diary. She was thrilled with her gifts of a stuffed dog and a carriage, although the excitement of the holiday made her ill by the end of the day. Their daughter was the center of the world for Amy and Les, although she could be a fussy baby who frequently kept them up at night and who was prone to minor illnesses such as colds. The year 1931 would be another difficult one for the family, but it would also bring with it in late summer the arrival of a baby brother for Pat—the McFarlane's second child, Brian.

As Les's freelance career took off, he had hoped to give up his work for Stratemeyer. So he was extremely disappointed that the poor economic times forced him to keep writing the Hardy Boys books—or the "juveniles," as he referred to them—strictly for the paycheck. He found them boring and yet no small task to write. He had to conform precisely to the plot outlines and length the syndicate established, and he still felt compelled to add his own brand of wry humor and sophistication to the books. Most important, however, was the task of maintaining consistency in characters and actions within and among books in the series. Each of the principal characters had distinct personality traits that must be sustained throughout the series, and frequently previous activities and mysteries were referred to in the books (in addition to the formulaic plot summaries of previous books that were a staple of the Stratemeyer series books). Through all the Hardy Boys' accidents, adventures, chases, and tricks, Les had to make sure he was consistent—but not repetitive—within each book. As Les would learn nearly half a century after he started writing the books, Hardy Boys fans through the decades charted the boys' activities and could point out even minor flaws or discrepancies in character, geography, and plot. So writing about the exploits of Frank and Joe Hardy was a time-consuming task. On December 27, Les's diary entry sounds a note that would become a recurring theme in his life: "Did some work on the juvenile and will make a New Year resolution never to do another if I can help it. Won't finish until Monday as it is dull stuff."

Les's disenchantment with the Hardy Boys series—or at least his resolve to abandon his work for the syndicate—may have deepened in the spring of 1930 when he learned of the sudden death of his employer and sometime patron, Edward Stratemeyer. Stratemeyer died on May 10 after a few months of illness. He developed thrombosis of the leg in February, which cleared up, but after two heart attacks in early spring, pneumonia, and a third attack, he passed away. His passing no doubt came as a shock to everyone associated with him, including Les, who was informed by letter two days later by Stratemeyer's younger daughter, Edna Stratemeyer: "It is with great sorrow that I announce to you the death of Mr. Stratemeyer last Saturday at his home in Newark, New Jersey, after a week's illness of pneumonia and heart complications," she wrote, adding that "copies of 'The Hardy Boys: The Great Airport Mystery' have been received in this office. Later I will see that you receive a copy of the book."

The relationship between Les and the Stratemeyer Syndicate changed forever. For six months after Edward's death, syndicate business, including the writing of several book outlines, was handled by his assistant, Harriet Otis Smith. Stratemeyer's daughters, Harriet Stratemeyer Adams and Edna Stratemeyer, considered several prospective buyers, but by late 1930 decided to take over the syndicate themselves.

They moved the headquarters back from Manhattan to East Orange, a
few miles from Harriet Adams's New Jersey home. Novices at business
and creative activities, they would ultimately prove to be nearly as adept
at handling matters as their father. The family-owned business would
continue to churn out books for another fifty years. And they were also
as polite and professional in dealings with writers as their father had
been. Still, while Les and Edward Stratemeyer were hardly friends, they
maintained a warm relationship that in some ways transcended business.
Stratemeyer was there when Les needed an advance, provided an ear
(by letter) when Les told him about his latest literary accomplishments,
and was unfailingly cordial even in his criticisms of manuscripts. The
kind-hearted Stratemeyer had stipulated in his will that each of the syndicate's ghostwriters receive a payment equal to one-fifth of their earnings upon his death. It was a shot in the arm for the McFarlanes in 1931,
when they received it.

Les certainly realized the role Stratemeyer played in his life, as illustrated by the letter of condolence he wrote to Edna Stratemeyer. It said,
in part:

> In Mr. Stratemeyer's last letter to me he mentioned
> that he had been ill but it was a shock to learn that his in-
> disposition had terminated fatally. Although I had never
> had the pleasure of meeting him personally I felt that I
> knew him as a real friend by reason of my five years' as-
> sociation with him in the writing of the books he as-
> signed to me. His kindness to Mrs. McFarlane and myself
> at the time of our marriage and on the occasion of the
> birth of our daughter betokened a personal interest that
> we appreciated more than he possibly imagined. I think
> he must have been a very kindly and warm-hearted man,
> and although pressure of other work had prevented me
> from continuing with the books of late, I missed the con-
> tact of his letters and feel his death very deeply. . . . My
> work for Mr. Stratemeyer helped me so much in days of
> my literary apprenticeship that you may be sure this let-
> ter is no hollow and conventional expression.

By the time of Stratemeyer's death, Harriet Adams had been away
from the syndicate for nearly fifteen years and had four children. She

began editing manuscripts and then moved to writing some stories, while Edna assumed some of the business-related tasks. Like their father, the Stratemeyer sisters kept very low profiles publicly and disdained publicity. One syndicate historian noted that, in a book entry prepared for her twenty-fifth class reunion at Wellesley College, Harriet mentions only a few words about her role as a Stratemeyer Syndicate owner, saying instead that she is involved with her marriage, the raising of four children, and "a good bit of club work."

Although the Stratemeyer Syndicate was, physically, a single office with only a few full-time employees, Stratemeyer's daughters took on a tremendous job when they assumed responsibility after their father's death. Even aside from the fact that neither had ever worked full-time in the publishing industry, the current economic depression affected all aspects of the business, from the publishers they used to the ghostwriters they employed, to their readership. The Stratemeyer daughters were forced to take over at a pivotal point. In fact, the syndicate was, in many ways, in its infancy when Stratemeyer's daughters took control. Edward Stratemeyer's obituaries referred to him as the creator of the Rover Boys, which was his most successful series to date. The phenomenally successful Nancy Drew series had been launched in 1930, literally a few weeks before his death, but by 1932, Mildred Wirt, who had been writing the series, left the syndicate. Another key syndicate writer, Howard Garis, left in 1935. (Wirt, however, returned to write the Nancy Drew stories several years later.) The Stratemeyer Syndicate was forced to reduce the number of series it created as well as cut back on pay. But it endured these tough times and prevailed.

After Stratemeyer's death, his daughters Harriet and Edna would also be forced to deal with Les's ambivalent attitude about his work for the syndicate, and letters between the daughters and Les show that it may have been frustrating for them. In October 1930, less than six months after Edward Stratemeyer's death, Les had told the new syndicate owners that because some of his freelance markets had dried up due to tough economic times, he was glad to write for the syndicate. A mere ten weeks later, however, things must have brightened for Les. Days after he confided to his diary his New Year's resolution to abandon his work for the syndicate, he wrote a letter to the syndicate to that effect, telling Harriet that he did not have the time, at least in January, to write for them. He paints a rosy picture of his prospects: "I hate to disappoint anyone and I do not wish to upset the Syndicate's arrangements but really I can't see where I could possibly find time to do another juvenile just now," he wrote. "I have promised a monthly short story to each of two Canadian magazines, I do a monthly novelette for an American magazine, I have started a new mystery novel and this year I have determined to put in a certain amount of work on a serious book. At a minimum of 2 cents a word I have more work than I can handle as it is. Things took a sudden turn for the better toward the end of the year. . . . I'm awfully sorry if it inconveniences you and I feel badly about turning it down but I'm afraid I'll have to do it."

The Stratemeyer daughters were no doubt disappointed by the letter. While the syndicate had reduced slightly the volume of books it published in the early 1930s, it was still creating new series in 1930, 1931, and 1934. One, the Perry Pierce mysteries, was launched in 1931, and, based on correspondence between Les and the syndicate, it is evident that he wrote the first book in the series, as Clinton W. Locke, and was scheduled to write at least the second. A letter from Harriet Adams notes on December 31, 1930, that she had received from Les the manuscript for *Who Closed the Door, or Perry Pierce and the Old Storehouse Mystery* and was enclosing a check for it. (Les's sales notes indicate that he received $125 for the book in late 1930.) She noted that she was pleased with it: "I am so glad that you caught the humor—it has seemed to me that the modern mystery story has had too little humor in it." Later in that letter, she notes diplomatically and politely that if Les does not do the second volume in the fledgling Perry Pierce series, it could put the syndicate in a bind, and asks if he would reconsider his decision not to do it: "We realize that in times like these one does not want to take the chance of turning down any work, and we do not want to say anything more about our good fortune in being crowded with other stuff, except that it of necessity causes us to rearrange our plans rather suddenly."

Les did not reconsider. After writing the first Perry Pierce book, he never did another one. The series had a familiar ring: it revolved around Perry Pierce, the leader of the Skull Mystery Club, who solves mysteries with his chums, much like their syndicate brothers Joe and Frank Hardy. Like Joe and Frank, Pierce and his buddies tracked down counterfeiters in one volume (*Who Hid the Key, or Perry Pierce Tracing the Counterfeit Money*), and their penchant for searching abandoned buildings and deciphering hidden messages on notes sounds familiar. The syndicate produced four volumes of the Perry Pierce mystery books (published by Henry Altemus

Company) before discontinuing the series in 1934. Stratemeyer ghost-writer Howard Garis wrote the outline for the first Perry Pierce series; the remaining books in the series were written by ghostwriter Walter Karig, who had written three Nancy Drew books in Wirt's absence. Like their father, the Stratemeyer daughters did not let personal disagreements interfere with their business. They and Les remained on good terms, and, as the tide turned, it was not long before Les once again needed the reliable paycheck the Stratemeyer Syndicate had provided him.

Judging by the new series the syndicate launched in the early 1930s, the Stratemeyers were playing it safe: most of the new series mimicked the characters and scenarios of successful existing series. In addition to the Perry Pierce series, the syndicate launched three others in 1931: Doris Force, a mystery series for girls; another aviation series, Sky Flyers; and another adventure series for boys called the Jerry Ford Wonder series. No new series were launched in 1932 and 1933, but two new mystery series for girls began in 1934 (including the Dana Girls, which Les would write.) No series were launched from 1935 to 1947, marking the end of the syndicate's creative period. By 1935, the syndicate had dropped all its publishers except the ones it used most, Grosset & Dunlap and Cupples & Leon. This was due, in part, to poor economic times that forced the closing of several of its publishers and the absorption of others into larger companies. In 1935, however, it was still publishing fourteen series.

***

The first part of 1931 was relatively prosperous for the McFarlanes. Les felt secure enough to tell the Stratemeyers that he would at least temporarily stop writing for the syndicate. He was receiving royalties for some of his novellas and writing regularly for the *Toronto Star Weekly*. Many of his articles were short ones that earned less than $100, but he was becoming ensconced as a regular writer for the publication. *Maclean's*, too, began publishing his stories regularly, including four in 1931. The big event of the year, though, for the McFarlanes was the birth of their son, Brian, on August 10. Brian was a big, strapping, amiable baby who, like his sister, Pat, would charm his parents. The McFarlanes learned that two children can require twice the care of one, and Les notes in his diaries that caring for one or the other of his children sometimes interrupted his writing. He was amazed at how fast Brian was growing, and amused by his antics. Within three weeks of his birth, "everyone is amazed at the size of him," Les wrote on August 31. When he was six months old, "Brian has distinguished himself by achieving another lower tooth, which is contrary to all the records and averages, according to Amy," he wrote on February 29, 1932. "But then again he is an extraordinary child and probably will sprout a mustache without warning." As soon as he could walk, the adventurous Brian became something of an escape artist. Les notes periodically in his diaries how Brian would surreptitiously leave his crib, or even the house, and Les or Amy would find him outdoors. One time he made his way to the banks of Lake Temiskaming, where he was apprehended by a small search party.

The McFarlanes evidently had trouble deciding what to name two of their three children—they had finally decided on a name for Pat about two months after she was born; and Brian was known as "Sonny" or "wee lad" for the first few months of his life, before Amy and Les decided on Arnold Brian. In his autobiography, Brian writes jokingly that by the time his parents decided what to name him—seven weeks after he was born—he was nearly old enough and, at nearly fifteen pounds, big enough, to name himself. Even then, he writes, his parents thought the spelling would be Bryan. He never determined how or why it was changed. Amy and Les had him baptized in St. Paul's Anglican Church in Haileybury on a cold, rainy day in November, three months after his birth. In his diary, Les noted that the baptism began after a minor disturbance in the rear pew by Pat, who sat there with her paternal grandmother. Pat insisted on coming to the front and taking part in the ceremony.

Despite his busy schedule, Les found time to participate in community events and enjoyed the activity. For many years, he was a member of the library board in Haileybury and occasionally he wrote in his diary of the battles the board would wage over what he called censorship of some books. Les already had an inkling that the Stratemeyer Syndicate books had generated their share of controversy among librarians and teachers (as he was told by the *Springfield Republican*'s book editor when he left the paper and began to write the Dave Fearless series), but little did he know the scope of the controversy the syndicate books would create over the decades. The library board position was perfect for a book lover like Les. He read for pleasure, and he read to be a better writer. At various times in his diaries, he offered brief commentary about the books he was reading. On November 16, 1931, for instance, he "went over to the library and got 'Hatter's Castle' by [A. J.] Cronin, one of those morbid, gloomy, somber yarns with powerful writing but quite humorless." The next day, he notes he read Cronin again, and quoted him in the diary: "'Gobs of gloom are lathered on so lavishly the whole thing becomes a nightmare.' Quite incredible."

His writing also required him to read nonfiction—particularly works about mining, the timber industry, and other subjects that often formed the backdrop of his fiction and some nonfiction. His love and knowledge of sports, particularly hockey and boxing, were vast, and he used that knowledge in his many fictional sports stories. But, as his children noted after his death, Les was a voracious reader, and the McFarlane homes were always overflowing with books, mostly borrowed from the library— Les could not afford to buy the quantity of books he and his family read.

The year 1931 brought relative comfort for Les. His short novels were getting good reviews, and Amy and Les, able to relax somewhat, were showing off Brian to friends and relatives and enjoying having people in for dinners and bridge. But, as was always the case, the brief period of prosperity did not last. Within a month of Brian's birth in early August, the passages in the diary begin taking on an ominous and worried tone. Les's agent, Bob Hardy, was once again having trouble finding markets for his work, and money was once again short. Les was able to look at the family's periodic lack of funds as a sporadic problem. Amy, though, chronically worried about the lack of money, and the humiliation that resulted brought on additional stress: "A bad day," Les wrote on Sept. 25, 1931. "Had to meet an overdraft at the bank . . . [Amy] couldn't understand how our finances got so low and feels badly. . . . Amy is feeling wretched tonight and almost fainted." The next day, the McFarlanes were forced to dismiss the maid who occasionally came in to help Amy with the housework, and Les contemplated giving up his tiny office in downtown Haileybury for financial reasons. (It is unknown whether Les did give up the office at this time.)

The Christmas season always brought happiness to the McFarlanes, and 1931 was no exception. Les's brother Frank came to visit from Toronto, and Les and Amy always visited their family in Haileybury and New Liskeard. This Christmas, though, brought its share of misery. Pat was seriously ill for weeks before and after Christmas, and kept Amy and Les up much of the night for several days, which made Amy ill in turn. In addition, Les's uncle Tom, his father's brother, died six days before Christmas, further dampening the family's holiday spirit. And, despite the year's promising beginning and the fact that editors were now getting to know him and to consider him a reliable and talented writer, Les's sales for 1931—including the $500 legacy from Edward Stratemeyer's estate—totaled $2,454, slightly more than half of the $4,085 he earned the previous year. The Depression had taken its toll on the magazine and book industry, and its ripples affected the many freelance writers who earned their living in that business.

***

By 1932, Les was kept busy with his writing, his growing family and, by the middle of the year, with a move to a house on 580 Brewster Street in Haileybury. The Brewster Street house, built in 1907, was a larger home than the one they lived in for two years at 435 Broadway. The family rented it from a Haileybury attorney.

Les was an active participant in civic affairs in Haileybury, and had an interest in what happened in his hometown and around the world. But little is mentioned of politics in his early diaries, and his writings would never have a vein of political activism or take a political bent, even though his interest and concern with world events would be described in much more detail in later years. Decades after his death, Les's two surviving children described him as politically conservative, although that description may be too limiting. Many of Les's views on social issues were not "conservative" in the modern sense, nor did they necessarily jibe with the prevailing views of the era in which he lived. As he noted in his autobiography and in several interviews, he strongly believed that children should not blindly accept authority, and should indeed question it at times. In his lifetime, most of the successful and famous writers were men, but that did not stop Les from recognizing the writing talent of his younger daughter, Norah, and strongly encouraging her throughout his life to nurture that talent, even in an era when women were expected to invest most of their energies into marrying and raising families.

Even more striking, however, was Les's view of capital punishment. He abhorred it, and did not hesitate to write about it early in his career. Norah Perez was aware of her father's opposition to capital punishment, although the source of these strong feelings is unclear. Capital punishment—death by hanging—was legal in Canada while he was a young adult. He wrote a subtle but biting commentary against it in the form of a "news" story in his hometown paper, the *Haileyburian,* in June 1933. Some of Les's fiction also appeared in that newspaper, and he was hailed as a minor celebrity in his hometown by the early 1930s, giving him creative license to write about a variety of topics in that newspaper. Evidently, he took advantage of that license when he wrote a scathing account of the hanging of a convicted murderer early one summer morning. The thousand-word story appears at first to be a conventional news story despite the somewhat unconventional headline ("Haileybury Hanging a Creditable Affair"). Dryly and with a straight face, Les writes a congratulatory story granting kudos to both the town and the convicted murderer, William Antinowicz, for executing, so to speak, a flawless and quick hanging. He writes sarcastically in the lead that perhaps Haileybury can be a role model for other cities when it comes to hangings: "I rejoice in being able to report that Antinowicz was killed so quietly, so unobtrusively and so efficiently that the executing may well stand as a model of its kind." Antinowicz—who was convicted of killing his former girlfriend and her husband—went quietly and without fanfare, Les notes: "[He] is entitled to his share of the credit for he made no outcry, did not struggle and showed such lamblike obedience that his conduct made everything easier for the people who were obliged to kill him. It is upsetting and awkward when a man objects to being hanged."

In addition to mocking the barbaric manner in which he was killed, Les writes briefly of Antinowicz's background, implying that it cultivated murder. He was a peasant in "some Central European country" when war broke out, the article says: "He was conscripted, a gun was thrust into his hands and he was told to go out and kill . . . in . . . the noblest tradition of patriotism." In the last paragraph of the story, Les calmly compares the "civilized" Canadian government to savages: "We have guarded ourselves against this dangerous fellow very thoroughly. He can harm none of us now. We have, too, endorsed the wisdom of those savage tribes who hold that spilt blood must match spilt blood."

With its dry tone and somewhat formal language, this story is a tongue-and-cheek editorial about where Les stands on the issue of capital punishment. And, as he noted in his diary, several readers wrote to the paper praising the story. But the Antinowicz article is a rare piece of political commentary on his part; Les did not have the stomach for the controversy political and cultural critiques generate.

***

As Les would eventually learn in the 1930s, the road between Haileybury and Toronto was a long three hundred miles. He soon found out that the small town's isolated location and its distance from Canada's large urban areas would keep him out of touch with key figures in the literary markets. Until he moved his family closer to Toronto in 1936, however, he took advantage of his hometown's obscurity in at least one way: he periodically wrote about the interesting people and events of the mining industry in northern Ontario, since few other writers who wrote for major magazines had the intimate knowledge he did of the region and the industry. As he learned when he was a very young child—almost as soon as his family moved to Haileybury in 1910—the region's character was dramatically shaped by the miners and prospectors who joined the rush near the turn of the nineteenth century when silver was discovered in the tiny town of Cobalt. As an adult, Les realized that a clever and knowledgeable writer could also mine the region—for fascinating and unique stories that were off limits to those who lived far away in urban settings.

Some of his nonfiction focused on the spectacular scale of mining in terms of its economic impact and the unfathomable grandeur of the mines. One of his two-part nonfiction stories, "How Deep Is Down?" describes the larger-than-life physical world of mining and the jobs of miners. Adequately representing this world to the lay reader, however, was no easy task, because large numbers alone could not convey its scale. Instead, Les put it in terms readers could understand. The deepest Canadian mines, he wrote, plunged 6,142 feet into the ground: "The Bank of Commerce Building rears its bulk 473 feet above a Toronto street," he wrote. "The Empire State Building towers 1,250 feet into the clouds over New York. Imagine twelve more Bank of Commerce buildings atop the original, imagine the Empire State extended to five times its present height. Then you will have, in reverse, a notion of the depths achieved by the deepest Canadian mine."

Les wrote several large, multipart stories for *Maclean's* on the mining industry and the hardy—sometimes foolhardy—souls who risked their lives to make new discoveries. One particularly gripping two-part series, "A Canadian Eldorado," describes the journey of two veteran prospectors (one from Haileybury) who traveled in the middle of winter to sub-Arctic territory in far northern Ontario on a hunch that they would discover untapped silver veins in this uncharted wilderness. What they found, Les writes, exceeded their wildest dreams: thick veins of silver and pitchblende, a source of radium and uranium, that they knew would trigger another mining rush and make them rich men. Les's description of their trip sounds fictional—not unlike an outrageously dangerous trip Frank and Joe Hardy would take in wild pursuit of a treasure. Like Frank and Joe's antics, this journey had an improbably happy ending.

The men, temporarily blinded by the glare of the snow, almost froze to death in the unrelenting cold and icy wind even though decades of prospecting in Canada had made them "inured to hardship." At one point, they were forced to harness the brutal wind and literally "sail" on a sea of ice: "Shod with steel creepers to hold their footing on the glare ice, they hauled a sled loaded with 1,500 pounds of supplies. Their sled was provided with a sail, so that at times the wind became a third partner."

As Les points out throughout the piece, only experienced prospectors would even know what they were looking for. Few people would have the knowledge and experience to identify these large veins of minerals, even if they were standing on them. But the "hero" of the story, with his strength, motivation, and knowledge, figuratively struck gold; literally, he struck something even more valuable. After his partner bowed out from exhaustion not far from their destination, Haileybury native Gilbert LaBine made the final trek across the ice to a nearby island where he found a few veins of high-grade silver—certainly a cause for celebration. As he traveled a bit farther, however, a second discovery rendered the first nearly irrelevant. "A streak of a dark, greenish-black substance, like a narrow ribbon of some deeply colored lava, coursed irregularly down the side of the rock to the ice," Les wrote. In finding the fat vein of pitchblende, "LaBine was alone, so no witness is available to testify that he danced a jig, flung his hat in the air, turned cartwheels or performed any of the antics that commonly signify a delirium of joy . . ." LaBine was aware that radium sold for $70,000 a gram.

To Les, though, the LaBine story was more than just a true adventure tale. It had at its core all the qualities that he loved in fiction: it revolved around the fickle and wild Northern Ontario country, focused on a hapless hero who toiled for years and finally got the fortune he deserved, and, best of all, showed that success in life was a combination of luck, determination, and hard work. He even spelled out these themes in the second part of the series: "'Gold is where you find it.' That is the prospector's creed, significant of the prospector's philosophy—a philosophy which contends that success is a matter of one part knowledge, two parts hard work and seven parts luck." Yet, as Les notes later in the story, LaBine's thorough knowledge of minerals allowed him to identify his find. It was a knowledge nine out of ten miners did not have, he wrote.

The heroes of many of Les's fictional stories shared many of the same characteristics: they were hapless but honest men, frequently newspapermen, office workers, or affiliated either as an owner or a referee with a hockey team. Most of Les's freelance writing in the 1930s consisted of mysteries or light comic pieces that often took place in a small town. With his adult fiction, of course, he was not burdened by the need to follow a strict plot outline, complete with names of characters, nor was he constrained by precise length requirements. Ironically, though, many of his characters shared the same Dickensian names as his Hardy Boys villains— or they had Irish surnames, names full of alliteration, or names with a hard consonant sound (Arthur Chadwick, P. K. Perigoe, Waldo MacNish). Others had descriptive nicknames (for instance, Two-Fingered Finnegan, Baldy McGonigal, One-Wallop Willie) or, for his Quebec readers, French names (Baptiste François d'Artagnan Poupet or Lucien Dumais). Interestingly, contemporary studies of humor that probe the reasons some words instantly draw a laugh show that readers and listeners instinctively feel that names and words with the hard "k" and "g" sounds are humorous. (For example, the names Gladys and Chuck are funny.) Perhaps Les sensed this.

Some of Les's stories were written in the first person. But most of his fictional pieces—especially for *Maclean's*—were domestic comedies, featuring a likable hero for whom the path of true love is not smooth. The hero invariably desires a beautiful young woman whom he cannot have for complicated reasons usually involving mistaken identity or longtime squabbles between relatives, friends, or business partners. As was the case in the Hardy Boys books, though, the protagonist always triumphs in the end. For instance, one of his light short stories featured a bumbling but honest hockey referee who suddenly finds himself pursued by two beautiful women—including one who impulsively grabs him and kisses him after he makes a controversial call in the favor of her team. Two-Fingered Finnegan is the name of the star player in that story. But the real hero is the narrator who can't seem to understand why two beautiful women would fall for him.

In his stories for *Maclean's* the same characters and towns often reappear from story to story, and many of the stories are lengthy, multipart series. One of his most prominent pieces was the four-part "Wakeville, Awake!" which features some characters who appear in another form in others of Les's works. This series is typical of much of Les's fiction of the 1930s and '40s—it is set in a small Canadian town and is full of eccentric characters, all of whom are related in some way. Many of these odd characters nurse longtime grudges against each other, triggering the chain of misunderstandings and squabbles that forms the backbone of the narrative. The main character, George Claybourne, is a hard-working, noble, but bumbling young man who is almost too nice to get what he wants. George is dating and in love with Penny Foster, the daughter of the grumpy but good-hearted police chief, Obadiah "Flannelfoot" Foster. As he begins the first day of his new job as mayor, one would assume George would be happy: he has a prestigious new job and the heart of the woman he loves. But this is also the day he has been dreading. It marks the arrival of his Aunt Gertrude Duxbury. Because her nephew is now mayor, she has come to help him make "civic" improvements to the sleepy town.

The character of Aunt Gertrude in "Wakeville, Awake!" is a modified version of the aunt of the same name in the Hardy Boys books. Because Les was now writing for an adult audience, she is developed further—physically and in the narrative: "She was a massive woman, mostly bust and bustle, and she had been having her own way for a long time. . . . 'Quaint place,' said Aunt Gertrude, in a manner implying that she considered Wakeville a terrible hole."

The brusque, no-nonsense Aunt Gertrude throws the sleepy town of Wakeville into chaos, insisting that in the name of progress it lure factories to the city, clean up the streets, and install a legitimate police force that is more serious about eradicating crime than the laconic Flannelfoot Foster. (The name of the story is taken from a new civic slogan that Aunt Gertrude insists the city adopt.) For three more installments, Gertrude and Foster engage in a dispute so bitter that it threatens the very existence of the town as well as the romance between George and Penny. At the arrival of Aunt Gertrude, George's life and the complacent lives of those in Wakeville start to collapse.

Although Les had an active imagination and was a voracious reader, much of his fiction was based on his own experiences of life in a small town and its peculiarities. He described Wakeville:

> George looked at Main Street. . . . He didn't see anything wrong with it. Wakeville had a quite sleepy charm that suited George right down to the ground. Main Street looked as it always looked at this hour of the day. Vrooman's hound dog asleep on the Four Corners,

three loafers on the post office steps, a clerk stacking baskets in front of the chain store, cars parked all over the place at all angles. Butch Prout sprawled under a truck in front of the Elite Garage. The wealthy and eccentric Mr. Johnson was emerging from the Continental House for his morning walk; Flannelfoot Foster shuffling majestically around the pool room corner. A peaceful scene.

By the late 1930s, *Maclean's* was promoting Les's work heavily, usually running a small thumbnail photo of him with his work and referring to it in an editor's column at the front of the magazine. It devoted pages and pages of space to his fiction and published large and elaborate drawings with it. Numerous photos ran with his nonfiction work. Into the 1930s, then, Les was beginning to reap rewards for his work that were far more than financial, even while the monetary rewards were shrinking further.

John Henry McFarlane, father of Charles Leslie McFarlane, in 1911.
(Unless otherwise credited, all photographs are from family collections)

Leslie McFarlane with his parents, John Henry and Rebecca McFarlane

Leslie McFarlane in Haileybury, 1919

The McFarlane home at 105 Marcella Street, Haileybury, Ontario. John Henry McFarlane bought the house in 1913 and rebuilt it in 1922 after it was destroyed in the fire that roared through Haileybury.

The McFarlane brothers, 1923. *Top row:* Graham and Wilmot (Dick); *bottom row:* Leslie and Frank

Leslie McFarlane as a newspaperman in the 1920s

Edward Statemeyer, ca. 1930. Courtesy Stratemeyer Syndicate Records, Manuscripts, Archives & Rare Books Division, The New York Public Library, Astor, Lenox and Tilden Foundations

Leslie McFarlane on his honeymoon, 1928

Leslie and Amy
McFarlane's honey-
moon cottage in Coteau
Landing near Montreal

Devil's Rock in Haileybury,
Ontario, possibly the model
for Leslie McFarlane's
description of the cliff in
The House on the Cliff, the
second Hardy Boys mystery.
Photo credit: Richard
Steward

Leslie McFarlane with daughters Patricia *(left)* and Norah in Whitby, 1937

Book cover from *The House on the Cliff* by Franklin W. Dixon. Copyright © 1927, 1959 by Simon and Schuster, Inc. Reproduced by permission of Pocket Books, an imprint of Simon and Schuster. HARDY BOYS and all related characters and images are © and registered trademarks of Simon and Schuster, Inc. All rights reserved. The classic hardcover editions of these Hardy Boys titles are available from Grosset & Dunlap, an imprint of Penguin Books for Young Readers.

Leslie and Norah McFarlane in
Toronto, 1939

Patricia, Brian, and Norah McFarlane in Ottawa, 1944

Leslie, Patricia, Norah, and Brian McFarlane in Ottawa, 1944

Amy and Leslie McFarlane in Ottawa, early 1950s

Amy Arnold McFarlane, late 1940s or early 1950s

Leslie McFarlane *(kneeling at lower left)* directs the National Film Board of Canada's *The Boy Who Stopped Niagara* in Ottawa in 1945. Appearing in the film was Norah McFarlane *(lower left)*.

Leslie McFarlane *(second from right)* as a director for the National Film Board of Canada, late 1940s or early 1950s

Leslie McFarlane *(far right)* directs a National Film Board production, early 1950s

Leslie McFarlane on a National Film Board set, 1950s

Leslie McFarlane as a writer for the Canadian Broadcasting Corporation in the late 1950s or early 1960s

Brian McFarlane as a college athlete, early 1950s

Leslie and Amy McFarlane with grandson Matthew McCauley, 1955

Norah McFarlane's wedding, 1955. *From left:* Leslie
McFarlane, Norah, husband Lou Perez, and his parents,
Meta and Louis Perez

Leslie and Beatrice McFarlane in Toronto, 1960s

Leslie McFarlane's children celebrate his sixty-fifth birthday in Toronto. *From left:* Patricia, Brian, Norah, Les

8

· · · · · · ·

THE CIRCLE GROWS

As Les's stature as a freelance writer grew, his financial situation, ironically, became increasingly desperate. As he notes in his diary throughout the early 1930s, the market for magazine fiction was drying up, pay was declining, and editors sought shorter and thus less expensive stories. *Maclean's* continued to publish his stories because they were crowd pleasers. By 1932, though, this may have been cold comfort to Les. Even *Maclean's* was cutting its pay to freelance writers by 15 percent, and the family's finances, as he noted in an entry on February 29, "[were] damned near desperate."

Summer brought little relief: temperatures in Haileybury skyrocketed that year, causing dangerous brush fires. "Not a cent in the house and won't be until the dividend cheque comes in," Les wrote on June 15, 1932. The worry made it difficult to concentrate and write, although Les was always able to churn out material, even if it was not necessarily to his liking. ("Worked hard all day and finished the story but it lacks something and I can't seem to hit the weakness," he wrote one day in June.) Mid-month, he finished an article, but found he had no money to purchase stamps to mail it (June 17, 1932).

The remainder of 1932 brought only slight relief. Amy and Pat—and to a lesser extent, Les and Brian—suffered chronic colds and respiratory illnesses due to temperature extremes. Winter only exacerbated the family's dire financial straits, as it brought with it the need for more heating fuel and more medical care. The weather was taking its toll on even the sturdy baby Brian, who, Les notes, got frostbite on a finger as Les was carrying him home one icy evening.

The diary entries during the years of 1932 and 1933 took on an added desperation, and Les seemed to have abandoned some of the hope he had in the earlier few years: "Blue. Banknote came due and they'll only give me another month," he wrote on November 12, 1932. "Not a nickel in the world and nothing in sight. Am simply desperate with anxiety." He routinely took out some of his frustration on the Hardy Boys, who seemed to bear the brunt of his periodic writer's blocks. As he wrote on January 23, 1933, "I worked at the juvenile book. The plot is so ridiculous that I am constantly held up trying to work a little logic into it. Even fairy tales should be logical." Based on the diary entries for this period, Les apparently drank little in those days, but Amy's health was increasingly poor and she was still plagued by illnesses that forced her to withdraw and stay in bed for days at a time.

By the early 1930s, Les began making periodic trips to Toronto to talk personally to editors and to attempt to sell some of his stories. But the trips may have been more than just practical necessities. As he gained a small measure of success as a writer, and as he grew older, Les may have found he needed the companionship of other writers—others who experienced the same successes and frustrations as he did, and men and women who would understand the ins and outs of his profession. Although Amy was a supportive wife, the practical necessity of making ends meet dominated her thoughts when it came to Les's career. As his diary indicates, Les met occasionally with writers and former newspaper colleagues in and around Haileybury, but he had no one in whom to confide on a regular basis. Edward Stratemeyer had filled that role to a limited degree, but whereas Stratemeyer always encouraged Les—even to the potential detriment of his syndicate—they never seriously discussed the craft of writing adult fiction.

So the periodic trips served many functions for Les aside from allowing him to personally hawk his wares and conduct research for some stories. He was able to meet and talk at length to other writers and to take part—at least temporarily—in the literary milieu of Toronto literary critic William Arthur Deacon, who would become a confidant and sounding board for Les.

***

William Arthur Deacon had been a longtime literary critic and editor for several Toronto-based magazines and newspapers when he died in 1977 at the age of eighty-seven. Deacon was a literary critic early in his career for the magazine *Saturday Night*, but was known for his three decades as literary editor for the *Mail and Empire*, which later became the *Globe and Mail*. While most literary critics have an influence and notoriety among writers, Deacon's fame during the era in which he worked exceeded that of most people in his position. A former attorney, his love for writing, particularly by Canadian writers, made him a fixture in

Canadian literary circles, and his role as a reviewer for newspaper readers did not begin to describe his true job as a booster and mentor of writers. A founder of a group known as the Canadian Authors' Association, Deacon believed that writers needed continual nurturing, encouragement, and promotion if they were to succeed, and that it was the responsibility of Canadian writers of his era to blaze the trail for future generations of writers in that country. And this encouragement needed to come not just from the public, but from other writers. The CAA, as it was known, was a fraternal association of writers across Canada whose purpose was to nurture the growth of Canadian writers. As his biographers John Lennox and Michelle Lacombe note, Deacon "became a reader's reviewer and a writer's critic, directing his reviews to the general readership he was trying to create and addressing the writers' concerns more directly in his private correspondence."

Deacon's newspaper columns encouraged spirited discussion, debate, and disagreements among authors regarding such topics as the role of literature in society, the challenges facing Canadian authors, and legal issues affecting writers. Most important, however, was Deacon's genuine love for Canada and its literature; he left behind a cache of thousands of letters to many authors, offering opinions about their books, views on their personal lives, and invitations to stay at his home. Deacon was a Canadian nationalist who strongly believed that what he saw as the country's collective inferiority complex could keep it from spawning great writers. The only thing the idealistic Deacon may have loved more than writers was Canada itself. A book he wrote at the age of forty, *My Vision of Canada*, touches on his nationalistic philosophy. But he had always planned to write more—including, after a forced retirement at the age of seventy, his memoirs, for which he had a contract. They were never written.

It was natural that Les would cross paths with Deacon. In addition to reading his column, Les was familiar with the critic's philosophy of Canada and its writers. Les began an extensive correspondence with Deacon, confiding to him his dreams of writing the Great Canadian Novel, his ambivalent feelings about living in small-town Haileybury with his family, and his philosophy about the role of the writer. Like Deacon, Les was a prolific and nearly manic letter writer, although most of the letters he would write came much later in his life. Like Deacon, the former attorney, Les could have made a better living in a more mundane job. Whether to leave a life of literature was never a matter of real conflict for either man, though—both felt compelled to devote their lives to writing.

Les's correspondence with Deacon began in 1925 but intensified in 1931 as the result of a disagreement and spirited argument over Deacon's pet project, the Canadian Authors' Association. The CAA was founded in 1921 by a group of Canadian authors including B. K. Sandwell and Stephen Leacock. It was formed initially to improve copyright legislation, but the organization took on a life of its own, growing dramatically from its first year and serving as a social and professional club for Canadian writers who longed for the camaraderie of a writers' circle. Membership in the CAA increased rapidly, and within a few years the group had an official house organ, national conventions, branch activities, and, ultimately, lobbying power. It served as a forum for both established and novice writers who previously had been overshadowed in their homeland by the publicity and respect given to writers from the United States and England. By the early 1930s, the CAA would seem to have had in Leslie McFarlane an ideal supporter. In his late twenties at the time, starting to achieve success as a writer after nearly a decade of hard work and sacrifice, he could relate to the established professionals in the group as well as to the young would-be writers who were still trying to get a foothold in the profession. But such support was not to come from the young author from Haileybury. In fact, his harsh and vocal condemnation of the CAA was to be heard across Canada, thanks to Deacon.

Like many Canadian authors, Les had written a few personal letters to Deacon in the late 1920s, commenting on and praising columns the literary editor wrote for *Saturday Night*. Apparently Deacon had mentioned Les's mystery novel, *Streets of Shadow*, in one column, as Les thanked him for the mention in a personal letter. Deacon had "introduced" Les to readers in the late 1920s, in Deacon's literary column for *Saturday Night*, "Saved from the Waste-Basket." Les, he wrote, "is a young man worth watching" and a regular contributor to several magazines. "First thing we know he'll be imposing a novel on us." In a response in 1925 to a letter from Les praising an article by Deacon, the critic wrote Les that "from what [another writer] tells me, you are already very much on the map [as a freelance writer]." The twenty-three-year-old Les had to be pleased that none other than William Deacon recognized him in this way, and in his second letter to Deacon, Les told him that he prided himself on being a writer without "literary pretensions," and one who realized he needed to mature before he tackled a big, artistic project:

"Rather than write immature, bad 'literary' novels, I do none at all," he wrote. "When this commercial tripe has earned some freedom from financial worries, when I know more about my trade than I do now, when my outlook is not quite so hazy I shall tackle some big things I have in mind. I have too much respect for the job to go at it with undeveloped talent and unripe judgment."

This slight familiarity with Deacon apparently gave Les the nerve to write a scathing letter to him the following year criticizing the CAA. To Les, the CAA's relaxed rules for membership (its only requirement was that members enjoy writing and pay the five-dollar yearly dues) turned the group into a haven for novices who never had a word published. Les's definition of a "writer"—one who makes a living at the craft—differed greatly from that of the CAA's relaxed version. Further, Les thought the group served primarily writers who lived in big cities, where the organization had more established activities. It overlooked the many writers who lived in small towns throughout Canada, he believed.

It is a credit to Deacon that instead of being infuriated by this young writer's comments, he delighted in them. He wrote about Les's opinion in one of his columns, and immediately responded to Les personally. Deacon was impressed by Les's articulate arguments, and even more important, he saw his comments as a way to trigger a needed debate about the function and purpose of the CAA. In turn, Les responded by letter to Deacon, pulling no punches. As a journeyman writer who must support a family, Les wrote ironically, he evidently has "committed the crime" of not producing a masterpiece "for the great glory of Canadian literature." Further, his affinity to Haileybury, he wrote, is based on "a weakness for fresh air which probably atrophies the critical faculties," even though, he notes, Deacon views him as "a mercenary yokel of abysmal ignorance."

Despite the sarcastic tone of the letter at the beginning, Les invited Deacon to visit: "I would promise to discuss nothing more explosive than trout-fishing. But I would enjoy showing you around town, having you meet some of our people and proving to you that there can be a degree of culture and background even in Haileybury. You might recognize a perspective lacking in Toronto." Les was clearly flattered that Deacon acknowledged his unorthodox point of view about the CAA. He closed the letter, "amused, dumbfounded and highly honored by the attention paid my irreverent remarks, assuring you of my highest personal and professional admiration."

Deacon responded within two days to Les, and while the critic did not visit him, the exchange triggered a close correspondence that would last much of the decade. The two touched on topics including the problems of writers in small towns and the challenge of making a living while still maintaining artistic integrity. Indeed, while Les was certainly a practical man who was forced to concentrate on making a living, he was oddly ambivalent about the realities of copyright and protecting his rights as a writer—two topics the CAA considered important. As a young man, Les did not seem to worry about overseas copyright matters, an issue taken very seriously by the CAA, which had the goal of encouraging writers to take control of the financial aspects of their vocation. And, despite his amiable and social nature, Les was not a joiner.

To make the debate about the CAA public, Deacon encouraged Les to put his views in the form of a column that Deacon would publish in the pages of the *Mail and Empire,* and Les obliged. The column was a spirited and articulate denunciation of the CAA. The tone of the letter, while not bitter, was hardly light, although it was clever and biting. Les said his main complaint about the CAA was that its membership included too many dilettantes—supposed "writers" who never published a word and absorbed most of what the CAA had to offer: "The solemn idiots who take the Canadian Authors' Association as seriously as they do themselves, those literary Babbitts whose stupidity, lack of humor and general stodginess hamper your sincere efforts." Further, he said, the CAA is not serious about helping writers, but instead focuses on conventions that are "seven-tenths social activity to three-tenths hot air." Les, hardly sentimental about his job as a writer, compared his vocation to that of a bricklayer—and took pride in it. "I regard [the CAA] with the same dubious regret that would consume any honest bricklayer if he saw the Bricklayer's Union admitting all applicants with no greater qualification than a fondness for the odor of mortar."

Deacon's airing of Les's criticism of the CAA is a testament to the critic's good nature and illustrates his philosophy that some disagreement among authors was healthy. His generosity impressed Les, who himself was open to criticism when it came to his career. Further, Les's expression of his thoughts and opinions to Deacon may have made them clearer in his own mind. What may have impressed Les more, however, was Deacon's revelation that the cosmopolitan literary critic who seemed to shun small-town life was originally a small-town boy from the Ottawa Valley. The fact that they had similar backgrounds no doubt touched Les and gave Deacon legitimacy in his eyes. In one of his first letters to Les, Deacon described his boyhood in the Ottawa Valley: "As a kid I often summered in Mattawa; and while still in dresses I remember sitting all day in the prow of a little steamboat on Lake Temisaming, while two husky members of the crew . . . walked out front and shoved the logs away to either side so our boat could get through."

So, for Les, Deacon was not some pretentious pundit sitting in an ivory tower in Toronto criticizing authors who lived in small towns. He was someone who had once been in the same position as Les. Further, Les learned, Deacon's sympathy for unpublished writers did not mean he ignored hard-working journeymen like Les. For practical reasons, he told Les, it was important that he periodically leave Haileybury for bigger cities: "A fellow needs fairly frequent contacts with those facing the same problems," he wrote, adding that if Les had talked to the two hundred or so delegates at the CAA convention, he would have learned that they had the same problems he did, and that he should not underestimate the value of this camaraderie: "You'd feel less lonely . . . there are hundreds of us, plugging away at the same game . . . and we've got to stand together just as trainmen do, and lawyers and doctors and carpenters." In this three-page letter, Deacon gently chides Les, telling him that he is naïve to ignore practical concerns such as copyright legislation, and that even if he does, others will fight those battles for him and Les will ultimately benefit.

This letter from Deacon—which would be the third of dozens he would send Les over the next decade or so—did stir Les. He immediately wrote back a long and confessional letter, confiding his frustrations about his job and acknowledging that some of his harsh criticism of CAA were based on negative comments about it from friends who were members. (Indeed, in 1932 Les was still applying for newspaper jobs, although with the idea that he could write part-time on the side; either he got no job offers or he turned them down.) But he reiterated that writers are in a unique position regarding professional "competition": "The professional writer is the only professional man who must face not only the competition of his fellows, but the competition of every janitor, schoolboy, society woman, hired girl, stenographer, etc., etc. who would like to be a writer," he replied. "We never complain about that, about the cheap autobiographies by retired cops, night nurses and chauffeurs, that cut down the sales of honest books." Les described how his life—like the life of other journeyman writers, he surmised—was full of disappointments: "You know well the struggles we undergo to build up even a meagre reputation as story-tellers," he wrote. "The hard work, the bitter disappointments, the drudgery—even to reach the status of a hack." As for Deacon's advice to Les that either a move to Toronto or frequent visits there would help his career, "if you only knew how often I plan these trips and look forward to them and never get them, you would be surprised. . . . Work, domestic arrangements, finances—something has always cropped up. I know I need the contacts but it has just been impossible in these particular two years of furnishing a house and establishing a family and trying to get up another rung of the ladder."

Les once indicated to Deacon that family responsibilities left him torn: by the mid-1930s he began to realize that he might not be able to sustain his life dream of being a full-time writer while at the same time raising a family. On the other hand, he writes, he hated to abandon that dream and take a full-time job outside the home. In any case, Les was between a rock and a hard place. "I could keep on writing magazine thrillers and the better stuff on the side," he wrote Deacon in 1931. "It can't be done. To make a living at pulp fiction the big thing is output. Low pay and heavy wordage. . . . Not much time for respectable work after that sort of prostitution." Les felt that, as a writer, he would improve dramatically if he could focus solely on "quality" fiction, abandoning his hack work. But with his domestic state, that was an impossibility. "Living for one's Art and [writing] nothing but what one feels is good is impractical, and I'm not using wife and baby and home as an alibi either." His only alternative was to get a full-time job and hope to write during his time off.

Deacon may not have persuaded Les to join the CAA, but he did persuade him to join a smaller Toronto-based group called the Writer's Club, which provided some office space and quarters for out-of-town writers who visited that city. He explained the need for Les to visit Toronto more frequently, and was probably instrumental in Les's decision to move his family to Whitby, Ontario, outside Toronto, in 1936. It should be noted that Les was not isolated professionally at this point in his career and that he had some contact with other writers, many of whom he worked with on newspapers. But his communication with Deacon instilled in him the necessity of establishing links with others in his field, and drove home to him the importance of getting to know and supporting other writers. In one particularly confessional letter, Les tells Deacon that he has had few if any professional role models in his life.

One was a man named Hoffman, an editor at the pulp magazine *Adventure*, whom Les refers to in a letter to Deacon, noting that Hoffman gave him some writing coaching "as he has coached many others who are big names." Another mentor of sorts was Joseph Cranston, the editor who published his first story in the *Toronto Star Weekly* in 1919, one of the rare Canadian editors at the time who believed it important to publish the work of Canadians.

***

The abysmal economic conditions of the early 1930s made the job of a writer even more uncertain than it had been earlier. Les's diaries in the first few years of the decade indicate that the financial crisis had been more severe than ever. He would not again see a yearly income of $4,085—which he earned in 1930—for many years. His income was slightly above half that in 1931 and only $1,135 in 1932. Before things looked up for him by the end of 1932, he was forced to write the Stratemeyer Syndicate asking for more work. The request came out of desperation. In a letter of June 18, 1932, Les told Edna Stratemeyer that even Depression conditions had not seriously affected his work until recently. "This year, like every other writer I know, I have experienced a disastrous setback. My markets have been wrecked. Having lost my old newspaper contacts it is impossible to get a job. It is a straight bread-and-butter struggle. Please don't regard this as a play for sympathy. . . . What I do ask . . . as one who has written about a score of books for the Syndicate is that you give me your best consideration when any assignment comes available." Not even the tremendously successful Stratemeyer Syndicate was able to avoid the effects of the Depression, and assignments from them were few and far between for Les in the first two years of the 1930s, when only two Hardy Boys books were published: *The Great Airport Mystery* in 1930 and *What Happened at Midnight* the following year. Worse, syndicate payment had dropped to a low of $85 per book at this time. Sales of the Hardy Boys books and of the popular Ted Scott Flying series began dropping by 1932, and 1933 was a particularly bad year for sales of both series. By 1932, total annual sales of the Hardy Boys books and the Ted Scott series were about equal at around 75,000 per year—an interesting phenomenon, since up until the Scott series had far outpaced the Hardy Boys in total sales. After taking a dip to about 40,000 each in 1933, sales of both series were in the 50,000-per-year range in 1934 and 1935, although the sharp drop in Ted Scott sales must have been disappointing for the syndicate. Annual sales of the Hardy Boys books remained stable at about 70,000 or 80,000 from 1929 to 1932, so the slight drop during those middle years of the 1930s was not catastrophic to the syndicate.

As had been the case for six years, though, the syndicate in 1933 came to the rescue for Les. Within a few months of his letter came a request to write the three "breeder" books to launch a new series.

After the death of founder Edward Stratemeyer, the Stratemeyer daughters played it safe when devising new series. So it was natural for them to design a new series based, indirectly, on two of their most successful series: the Hardy Boys and the Nancy Drew series. The Nancy Drew books, which over the twentieth century became the syndicate's most successful series financially, featured the teenaged detective Nancy Drew and her circle of friends, including Bess Marvin and George Fayne. Like Frank and Joe Hardy, Nancy had a strong role model in her father, Carson, an attorney, and she was influenced not by a mother but by housekeeper Hannah Gruen, who, like Aunt Gertrude, played a maternal role in the books even though she was not the mother in the family. Like the Nancy Drew series (which was written in its infancy by several authors, including Mildred Wirt, Harriet Stratemeyer, and others), the official name of the "author" of the new series would be Carolyn Keene.

Les might have experienced *déjà vu* when he read the syndicate's description of the new series. It would feature two teenaged girls, Louise and Jean Dana, who have "a natural ability to solve mysteries." Louise, sixteen years old, is dark-haired, and is the more serious of the two. Jean, a blond one year younger, is "humorous and gay." Unlike Nancy Drew, the Dana girls are orphans who attend boarding school. Though this might undercut their independence somewhat, the scholastic venue could provide plot opportunities not available in Nancy's scenic home of River Heights.

For the first Dana Girls book, *By the Light of the Study Lamp*, the Stratemeyers sent Les an exhaustive, seven-page, single-spaced plot and character outline, a typographically crowded document with only minuscule margins. The first book in the series is populated by an army of characters, including Aunt Harriet Dana ("Maiden lady—attractive—45 years old, keeps house for her nieces and brother") and Uncle Ned Dana, "Sea captain of large passenger boat, the 'Balaska.' Is about 50 years old." Other characters include a stuttering hired man, Ben Harrow; the buxom maid Cora Appel (cleverly nicknamed "apple core" by Jean Dana); and a host of young and older characters who live in and around Starhurst, the boarding school.

According to the outline, the plot of the first Dana Girls book would revolve around a beautiful antique study lamp, which, in chapter 1, the two sisters delight in receiving via the mail from their uncle, the sea captain. Although all seems happy and carefree in the first chapter, a hint of evil materializes immediately. While the clumsy maid is washing a wall upstairs in their home, a mirror tips over and smashes to bits on the floor. After the pieces of the mirror are swept away, the sisters return downstairs only to discover their new lamp has been stolen—in an act that the superstitious maid is sure signals the start of several years of bad luck.

Like most syndicate protagonists, the Dana sisters defy both bad fortune and evildoers. *By the Light of the Study Lamp* quickly launches into the car chases, missing person searches, and near-death escapades that characterize the syndicate's adventure books. By the beginning of chapter 4, the Dana sisters have already saved a man and a dog after the two fall off a cliff into a raging river. The mysterious stranger bashes his head against the rocks below. Thanks to a daring rescue by the girls involving ropes and knots, both man and dog survive, only slightly injured and disoriented. Even the dog seems to sense the girls' bravery. "[The dog] lay on the rocks panting, feebly trying to wag its tail to show some gratitude," Les wrote. The girls are forced to carry the unconscious man to their home to recuperate. But this is just the first of many harrowing experiences that all end happily, culminating in the retrieval of the missing study lamp.

The first Dana Girls book lacked the practical joking and joshing of the Hardy Boys books, but Les was not hesitant to comment indirectly on the class system inherent in a private girls' school. He does this in the form of the "tall anaemic" Lettie Briggs, a frequent critic of the girls. Lettie, whose father was a rich oilman, consistently reminded her classmates of her wealth. "Her breeding was not such that she could permit the circumstance to go unmentioned," Les wrote dryly. "She lost no opportunity of grandly informing her schoolmates that her father made his money in oil, and that he 'could buy the whole place and use it for a garage if he so wished.'"

These details were not included in the plot outline, although this first outline for *By the Light of the Study Lamp*, written by Edna Stratemeyer, was far more detailed and complex than those early Hardy Boys summaries. It was the outlines, of course, that provided the backbone of series fiction plots. Edward Stratemeyer's outlines for the first nine Hardy Boys books were two to three pages in length and did not break the outlines down into specific chapters, as the Dana Girls outlines did. After his death in 1930, Stratemeyer Syndicate assistant Harriet Otis Smith wrote the outline for Les's next Hardy Boys book, *What Happened at Midnight,* and Howard Garis wrote the outline for *While the Clock Ticked,* published a year after Stratemeyer's death. Edna Stratemeyer and Harriet Stratemeyer Adams took over the job of writing many of the outlines. The Stratemeyer daughters' long, elaborate, and detailed outlines were meant to simplify the author's job, but they actually posed more of a challenge to the author, who was now required to follow and fill in the model for each specific chapter.

Les was candid in his letters to the Stratemeyers about the fact that his top priority was not writing juvenile fiction, but his polite letters did not reveal the depths of his unhappiness about writing the syndicate books. After he finished the first Dana Girls book, he began writing the second, as he had promised. And, as the Stratemeyers had pledged, they sent him an advance for the second book. Still, as he noted in his diary on June 8, 1933, it was not a pleasant job—especially since the syndicate wanted some dramatic changes: "They certainly found plenty wrong with it," he wrote. "Started on the juvenile from the beginning again and dread the long grind ahead." The next day, "Tried to get at the juvenile again today but the ghastly job appalls me."

Les also found himself in the unenviable position of juggling the work he wanted to do—magazine articles and short stories—with the writing of the Stratemeyer books. By mid-1933, a sudden influx of work coupled with the syndicate's request that Les write the first three "breeder" Dana Girls books in a period of only a few months created an awkward situation for him. As he was working on the second Dana Girls book, *The Secret at Lone Tree Cottage,* he was called to Toronto suddenly by an editor who wanted to see some of his work. Although he had not yet completed the Dana Girls book, he needed the balance of the fee from the Dana Girls work to make the trip to Toronto. He was forced to write an awkward letter to Edna Stratemeyer, seeking full payment for a book that was missing a final chapter: "[The final chapter] will follow tomorrow," he wrote. "I have worked day and night this past week hoping to get the story into the mail by Thursday but it is an hour from train time and the last chapter is still unwritten." He asked if the Stratemeyers could send or wire his payment immediately so he could make the trip.

Les was on thin ice with the Stratemeyers as it was—in addition to the on-again, off-again relationship with them that was based on the status of his other work, Edna Stratemeyer had criticized portions of his work in some drafts of the Dana Girls books. For example, in a draft of *The Secret at Lone Tree Cottage,* she urged him to "correct your work carefully before mailing it to us. . . . We found it necessary to do a great deal of correcting . . . in the 'Lone Tree Cottage' story. . . . Please do not repeat words, phrases or ideas unless the object is to strengthen the meaning." The Stratemeyer daughters, like their father, were realists. They knew that Les was spending most of his time and effort on serious adult fiction. Still, Edna Stratemeyer tried to tell Les in the letter that better times were ahead for the syndicate regarding pay levels and amount of work, and she noted that she had heard that there was an "upturn" in business, and "we are hoping we will get back to the heights on which we were living three years ago." Les was experiencing this same upturn in his other work—so much so that he almost left the syndicate hanging in regard to the Dana Girls breeders. He missed his deadline for sending in the third book of the series, *In the Shadow of the Tower,* prompting a polite but biting letter from Edna Stratemeyer, observing that he had sent in only seventy pages of the book by its due date: "We are pleased with the handling of the plot so far, but are concerned because you have failed to mail us the rest," she wrote. "Apparently other work has taken your attention, which we realize you need to assist you with your income. Nevertheless, due to the fact that we have given you a substantial advance on this story and we are in need of it, we wish that you would go ahead with this work promptly." The syndicate was in a bind, of course, because the Stratemeyers had promised their publisher, Grosset & Dunlap, three Dana Girls books to launch the series in 1934.

Les was always clearsighted about his work with the syndicate, even though he disliked doing it. He told Miss Stratemeyer that his actions were the cause of "justifiable annoyance" on her part, and promised to finish the manuscript within a week. The cause of his tardiness, he said, was a "writer's slump" that kept him from turning out good work. "[It was] one of those dreadful slumps into which any professional falls from time to time. . . . I made good progress in the early chapters . . . and then had to cut in to do some work for a pulp editor. . . . I got back at the book again and was going at my usual gait until the hot weather hit us and now it is like pulling teeth to get a single chapter done. Some of it, on reading it over, I have been so ashamed of that I threw it away and rewrote. I don't think I have ever made slower progress with any story. There is no excuse."

Although writing the Hardy Boys was tedious for him, Les had the formula down for the two teenaged detectives, and he enjoyed throwing in a bit of humor and some literary references. But devising a readable and engaging narrative style for a new set of books, particularly one that featured girls, clearly took extra time. The first Dana Girls book, *By the Light of the Study Lamp,* had the same style as the Hardy Boys books, minus some of the practical jokes and literary references that Les would weave into the Hardy Boys. It was a book written by the numbers, although the characters were engaging and there was plenty of action.

Further, the combination of a slightly improving economy, a growing family—their third child, Norah, had been born on February 4, 1933, as he was writing the Dana Girls books—and the increasing malaise he felt about writing series fiction was making it more difficult for Les to work for the Stratemeyers. But the syndicate, and the Hardy Boys, would, yet again, be his salvation. By the end of the year, he was asking the Stratemeyers if he could write about the boys again, while privately damning the books in his diaries.

Les abandoned his Carolyn Keene identity after completing the three Dana Girls breeders and the fourth in the series but, like Nancy Drew, the Dana sisters would live on for much of the twentieth century. For thirty-four volumes, until 1979, the sisters continued to spend their spring breaks solving mysteries and chasing criminals and kidnappers, in a few cases traveling all the way to Europe. The Carolyn Keene *nom de plume* was clearly a winner for the Stratemeyer Syndicate. As the syndicate proclaimed (somewhat erroneously) on the first Dana Girls book, "by the author of the Nancy Drew books."

As his workload began to increase, Les was learning about the effort and time that a family required. Baby Norah was born in early 1933, when Brian was nearly two years old and Pat was four. The children were still too little to go out and play by themselves, so Les and Amy had to keep a close eye on them. During this time, the entries in his diary were full of references to taking Pat and Brian fishing and to the lake—activities that were not a chore to Les, who loved trout fishing. While the winters in Haileybury were brutal (and the summers sometimes unbearably hot), it was difficult for Les to ignore the distractions that came along with the warm weather of the spring and summer. In addition to the outdoor activities that he loved, he bowled in a league that began in June, and frequently saw his brothers Frank, who visited from Toronto, and Dick, who lived nearby.

By 1933, when he was nearly thirty-one, the thought that his children would not remain toddlers was disheartening to Les. When Brian got his first haircut at age two, Les sounded heartbroken in his diary: "Brian left his golden curls in a barber shop today and I feel sad because we have lost the little baby boy . . . he seemed almost a stranger when he came home. A boy now, a baby no longer. Nearly everyone approves but I can't be enthusiastic" (August 30).

When it came to his children, Les could get sentimental—a trait that intensified as he grew older. After his children had grown, Les wrote them voluminous letters about his thoughts and activities. In many letters, he would describe the day of their birth. Birthdays always triggered nostalgia in Les; in a letter to Norah written in 1965, a month or so after Norah's birthday, he reminisced: "I can recall how delighted we were when you arrived; you were a very dainty, tiny baby whom we loved at first sight." Les wrote that after Norah had developed jaundice days after she was born, he and his two small children went to visit their new sister on a freezing day in February: "I remember going over to the hospital to see you and your mother a few days afterward, with Brian in a sleigh, warmly bundled up against bitter weather and Pat trudging beside me in the snow on a very cold, windy winter afternoon and occasionally pushing the sleigh through drifts." He remembered vividly the fear he felt when he had no money to pay the hospital bill. "I said . . . 'I'll have a cheque for you tomorrow,' with no prospect of any cheque.'" Again, a mighty rescue: "When I returned home that afternoon, there was a cheque for $75 waiting . . . for a story I never expected to sell. So the Lord provided." When she was forty-five years old, Pat recounted in a letter to her father her warm recollections of the first Christmas she could remember, in Haileybury. She recalls a trip the family made to her grandfather's home by sleigh, "stopping en route to visit some friends. Brian or Norah was in the little sleigh with the back on it—all bundled up and I can remember the magic sparkle of the sun on snow and the attempt to hitch a ride on the little sleigh at the risk of squashing the baby. I remember some details of the house we visited, but not of the people— but it seemed a happy and exciting time." Pat went on to recall happy memories of the family's Christmases in their various homes, and of the tree and elaborately decorated homes: "I could go on for pages—recalling the smells, the sounds, the glimpses of people, rooms, colours, weather and good times of the past . . . they were good and happy Christmases that we shared—a very real part of what life is all about." As they grew into adulthood, all three remained close to their father, although Les's relationship with the tempestuous Pat was not always smooth.

In those early years, he delighted in watching his children play games—particularly those that dealt with writing and storytelling. As he notes early in 1934, "Told the children stories in bed and they told me one in return, with Pat providing plot and action and Brian interspersing details" (February 13). As a parent, Les was hardly a disciplinarian, his children remember. In fact, they can barely remember him ever getting angry at them and cannot recall him raising his voice at them.

As he was helping to launch a new series in mid-1933 and trying to balance his work with his family life, it may have been easy for Les to blame the Stratemeyer Syndicate for his declining finances, although he realized in rational moments that the syndicate rescued him in the leanest of times. In 1933, as he was writing the second or third Dana Girls book, "Stratemeyers want their damned book so I had to pick it up again today," he wrote on June 29. "If only I didn't have that juvenile to do I'd be able to make some money now. It's a cursed nightmare. I'll never do another." Six months later, however, Les was thanking the Stratemeyers for asking him to resume writing the Hardy Boys series, even though the payment per book remained at $85. Les asked the Stratemeyers politely if he could be paid more per book, but he was not as diplomatic in his own diary: "Stratemeyers want me to do another book—the Hardys," he wrote on January 13, 1934. "I always said I would never do another of the cursed things but the offer always seems to come when we need cash. I said I would do it, but asked for more than the $85, a disgraceful price for 45,000 words." Les had tried another ploy for a raise in pay—he explained to the Stratemeyers that he was feeling the adverse effect of the exchange rate between American and Canadian currency. Unfortunately, the astute Stratemeyer sisters noted in a letter to him that they had checked the exchange rate, and it was 99 3/4 to the dollar: "We are delighted that there is not such a difference between the value of the dollar in Canada and that in the United States, a fact that would seem to point to better times ahead for all of us."

In his diary at the end of 1933, Les was typically upbeat, as he usually was at the end of each year: "The year has been fairly good to us. We have Norah and good health and happiness. I sold every story I wrote last year and seem to be well established with [pulp publisher] Street and Smith." (December 31). By early 1934, however, Amy was getting ill and confined to bed ("Amy sick in bed and I had a sample of what it means to do housework for three youngsters," Les wrote on January 14. "By 6 o'clock I was ready to drop.") Worse, Les's mother, Rebecca, who was sixty-one, became ill and, after a very brief improvement in her condition in February, died on March 10, 1934.

After only a brief respite, Les once again had severe money worries— at one point an advance from the Stratemeyers allowed the family to pay their grocery bill. By February 14, "Finances are low but I refuse to worry about these things anymore," he wrote once again. By October, a downbeat Les sounded uncharacteristically depressed and distracted. On his birthday, October 25, he wrote, "Thirty-two years of age today. They go swiftly now. And again I pass the milestone forced to admit I have done nothing." Les wrote that Amy and his children gave him pajamas and a shirt and tie and his father gave him socks and tobacco. It may not have been unusual for a young man like Les with a growing family to have unsettled thoughts about his accomplishments on his birthday, a day that could prompt reflection. More ominous, though, was the following day's diary entry: "Clint [a friend] over first thing this morning, and I made the mistake of breakfasting on beer. The rest of the day was pretty bad. We all went to bed early tonight." Les apparently began drinking again, and it was becoming more evident from his diaries that the extensive drinking began when his fortunes were at their lowest.

As usual, though, by the very end of the year, he was upbeat again, noting, ironically, that 1934 had actually been a good year, salvaged in part by a last-minute sale of a story to the slick publication *The Country Gentleman,* a sister publication of the *Saturday Evening Post.* Les called the sale a windfall that allowed him to pay many of his bills at the end of the year. (His sales records indicate that he was paid $400 for the story.) A jubilant Les celebrated on that last day of 1934: "Went to a party . . . played poker and had a few drinks but I watched my step this time and stayed sober," he wrote. "Got my new suit and wore it to the party." On that last day of the year, life looked good to him, despite the death earlier in the year of his mother, and the focus was the future, a time when he felt he might accomplish his goals. "So much for which we are thankful. Financially we are pulling our way out of the troubles that threatened to swamp us completely. I sold all my stories and am getting into the better magazines, although I have not got down to any important works *yet.*"

9

. . . .

GOOD OR BAD BOOKS?

While Les's diaries give an indication of the fluctuations of his fortunes and state of mind, some of his later letters to William Deacon in the mid-1930s reveal even more vividly his dire financial situation. In one, he asks Deacon for permission to use his name as a reference for employment, noting that he must get a full-time job if he is to make ends meet—and at one point even telling him that he was considering working full-time in a logging camp. (The idea, which Deacon endorsed in a letter, was that Les could write in the evening after work, unencumbered by family.) Whether he could not obtain employment or simply turned down job offers he received is unknown, but Les continued as a full-time freelance writer.

Despite his growing reputation in Canadian and U.S. markets as a respected freelance writer, he was unable to make a living at it. Les notes this irony to Deacon and in his diaries and points out that even though in some years he sold everything he wrote, his family was nearly destitute.

By mid-1934, however, Les found himself in an advantageous position with the Stratemeyer sisters, whose launching of the three Dana Girls books had been enough of a success that the series would continue. They virtually begged Les to write the fourth Dana Girls book for them, and they persisted even after he refused: "The reason we are so eager for you particularly to undertake this volume is because the series is so new we do not like to switch to another writer. . . . It is hardly fair to the readers or to the publishers, for no two authors are exactly alike." A reluctant Les agreed, in part because realized he was holding all the cards. He told the syndicate that he would do his best to turn out the book, although it would mean "a great deal of extra work" at a lower rate than what he made on other projects: "Can't you raise the price to $100? . . . I'm simply forced to shelve some two-cents-a-word fiction to get the book out. . . . Don't think for a minute that I'm going high-hat on the Stratemeyer Syndicate just because work is rolling in again." In the same letter, he asked for yet another $50 advance. The Stratemeyer sisters bought his argument: Les's sales records for that year show he earned $100—not the going rate of $85—for *A Three-Cornered Mystery*, the fourth book in the Dana Girls series, and a letter from the syndicate shows that it honored his request for an advance. The Stratemeyer sisters acknowledged that they knew he was paid much more for his other freelance work, but they also pointed out that his other work was entirely his creation, for which he was not provided with story outline, title, and plot, apparently implying that it was more difficult and more time-consuming work. Further, they told him, their more complex story outlines made the writing of the series books faster than it ever had been (claims that no doubt amused Les). As Les noted forty years later, the ubiquitous advance was part of the reason that writing for the syndicate became addictive: the advance was usually spent immediately. He later called it, half jokingly, a form of "bondage."

But the Dana Girls made Les uncomfortable, as did his identity as Carolyn Keene. After the fourth book, he remembered, "I begged off. Starvation seemed preferable." Les also noted in his autobiography that although Jean and Louise Dana survived for many more decades, they never offered much competition for the immensely popular Nancy Drew. He may have been partly to blame, he acknowledges: "Perhaps the virgins who followed the adventures of Jean and Louise sensed a lack of empathy. . . . I never felt comfortable as Carolyn Keene, and I was glad to don Franklin W. Dixon's cap again." Les could afford to reject that fifth Dana Girls book; by 1933 he was writing quite a few stories a year for sports publications such as *Field and Stream* and had become a regular contributor to *Sports Story*, a magazine featuring sports fiction put out by the pulp publisher Street & Smith, for which he wrote a boxing serial each summer and a hockey serial each winter.

When Les told William Deacon of his activities and his writing, he rarely mentioned his work for the Stratemeyer Syndicate. But Deacon disdained some of the work Les did for the sports magazines as well as *Adventure* and the other pulps. Their correspondence focused on a larger project Les had in mind—an epic work of fiction on the Canadian North—and on his writing for slicker, respectable publications such as *Maclean's*.

In his diaries, Les referred to all the writing he did for the Stratemeyers as "the juveniles" or the "yarns." But by the mid-1930s, after writing about a dozen or so Hardy Boys books, he clearly preferred those to any of the others the Stratemeyers asked him to do. He had no interest in writing more Dana Girls books, and had truly disliked writing the early Dave Fearless and Perry Pierce stories. As he implied many decades later in his autobiography, he assumed a certain ownership of the Hardy Boys books and took pride in writing them. And, indeed, the formulaic outlines dictated by the Stratemeyers were not too different from the plot structure of the sports and mystery stories Les wrote for adults. The adult fiction was of course more sophisticated, but relied on a smooth narrative, plenty of action, and colorful but down-to-earth characters to whom readers could relate. Les's pulp work, his writing for the slick magazines, and his writing for the "juveniles" all had in common the fact that the narrative moves along seamlessly, and the stories are crisp and easy to read. In the Hardy Boys books, as in the stories he did for the better magazines like *Maclean's,* the writing is tight and clear, and full of specific detail. Whether he wrote about the ice rink or about the cliffs and waterfalls of fictional Bayport, he captured the rhythms of the environment; the reader sensed, consciously or subconsciously, that he knew what he was talking about.

Les's mastery of narrative, combined with a flair for developing sympathetic and likable characters, is what gave his Hardy Boys books a distinctive personality. The characters' personalities in the series books did not change much throughout the early years, yet they were not boring, but comforting to readers in their regularity. Readers knew, for instance, that the author would get much mileage out of Chet Morton's voracious appetite. In one scene in the *Hidden Harbor Mystery,* Chet Morton enters, munching nonchalantly on an apple until he realizes the dreaded Aunt Gertrude is in the room. Frank and Joe's "maiden aunt" reminds him sternly that he was eating an apple when saw him three months ago: "Is it the same apple, or does your father buy them by the barrel?" she asks. The sight of Chet reminds Aunt Gertrude that he was the one who stole a homemade apple pie from her window. But the quick-thinking Chet saves his own skin: "Chet gulped and blushed . . . 'When I had taken a little bite I knew it was the best pie I had ever tasted and before I knew it, why, the whole pie was gone.'" The compliment melts stern Aunt Gertrude, and all is forgiven. Thirty pages later, Chet buys three candy bars, six oranges, a bottle of soda and a bag of peanuts "to fight off famine until lunch time" as the boys board a train one morning. Worried that the boys' sleuthing could land them in jail, he was stocking up in case of incarceration. "I have it on good authority that jailers don't believe in over-feeding their prisoners," he says. "They believe in wholesome food in small quantities, which means porridge, prunes, cabbage soup, dry bread and water." Chet's penchant for puns and practical jokes, along with his love of a good meal, makes one wonder if he was based on the author himself.

The Stratemeyer series books were a genre with many rules devised by the syndicate. The author could write them in a formulaic way with little embellishment, or, as Les did with the Hardy Boys, add his or her own branding. The cliffhangers created at the end of many chapters were no easy task to create—Les, like the other authors, had to make them tantalizing enough to lure readers into the next chapter. Many middle-aged men and women who have written decades later about their love for the Hardy Boys books discuss what drove them to read them; nearly all mention an identification they had with the characters, the ability of the books to engage the senses, and the quirks that made the characters sympathetic and not wooden (such as Chet Morton's clumsiness, the boys' puns, the literary references, the boys' irreverent attitude toward some authority figures). Edward Stratemeyer's outlines were a blessing and a curse for Les. On one hand, they made the writing go faster, required little imagination or creativity on his part when it came to plot, and allowed him to focus on the writing and characters. On the other hand, they relieved him of true ownership, distanced him from the final product, and forced him to travel a route he might not have selected and, indeed, found ludicrous at times.

Perhaps because he was the original "father" of the Hardy Boys, Les took the series and made it his own. Several researchers who have studied series fiction have noted that the series (at least during the first half of the twentieth century) had a specific structure that varied only slightly from book to book. Arthur Prager believes that most of the books follow a four-part plot outline that can be described simply: Fenton Hardy "hands down" a case; the boys take it on, usually because of some kind of coincidence; the boys follow a trail left by the evil-doers and get into trouble, although they are rescued at the last minute; and the criminals confess and good triumphs. In her analysis of the books, however, Carol Billman notes that the structure is more complex: many of the Hardy Boys books follow that basic format, she observes, but the books usually lay out multiple and more circuitous plotlines that are connected by the end. What keeps the reader guessing, she writes, is not the outcome of a single plot as much as "the interconnection that will inevitably tie together the disparate threads." Billman also notes that the focus on the many caves, rivers, and fields of Bayport and the outdoor environment turns the Hardy Boys into a form of adventure book as well as mystery—not surprising since Les made his living writing adventure stories for adults.

Certainly Les realized that Bayport and environs had to be one of the most crime-riddled regions in the country—a fact that he ridiculed in his memoir. He noted that after he finished his last Dana Girls book, he wanted to lock the Dana Girls and the Hardy Boys "in one of Bayport's numerous abandoned buildings . . . just to see what would happen. It might have done the four of them no end of good." The lack of even a hint of sex in any of the series books, of course, ensured that would never happen. Yet, as readers were no doubt comforted to know, the crooks were *always* brought to justice and goodness prevailed. Not, as Les knew, the way it was in real life.

***

By the age of twenty-nine, Les was optimistic that his best days as a writer were immediately ahead of him. Deacon warned him in a letter, however, not to get complacent. Most successful writers write their most enduring pieces when they were in their early and mid-thirties, he said. The critic had a profound effect on the way Les thought, and it was Deacon who first suggested to Les that he begin planning an epic novel about the history of northern Ontario. The book, Deacon said, could put Les on the map as a writer. He urged Les to put a lower priority on his writing for pulp magazines and for the Stratemeyers, and to take a chance and write the "big" novel. Here's how he envisioned it: "What the hell is the use of living in Haileybury if you are blind to the epic of your locality—the great story of Northern Ontario. . . . Go back to the logging days, follow with the mining days, then on to the farm and the town and power. Not the adventure stuff, the epic."

Deacon had been sharply critical of Les's mystery novella *The Murder Tree*, a serial magazine story that had been turned into a short novel. He minced no words in a letter to Les, who sent him a copy of the book. "By the standards of hocus-pocus of the detective story I believe it will advance you in the esteem of the great army of fans. . . . You have written the standardized, mechanized, guff. . . . I can't believe it has any more relation to literature than the cross-word puzzle or Tom Thumb golf. . . . Further, I feel it's so wholly unreal that the craze will pass like appendicitis, cigarette lighters and greased hair." In reality, though, Les's adult mys-

· 128 ·

tery stories received strong reviews in 1931. *The Murder Tree* was praised by the *New York Herald Tribune* and the *Saturday Review of Literature*. The former called it "an intelligent, well written and properly exciting goose-flesher," and the latter, "a good story." The *New York Times Book Review* said, "In style and substance. . . . far above average." Of course, the fact that respected and widely read publications such as those chose to review it at all was a feather in his cap. Still, Les took no umbrage at the letter from Deacon. After all, Deacon was a friend and respected literary critic—and someone in whom he could confide.

Despite the friendship and candor that he offered Les, Deacon had his own ax to grind. A strong Canadian nationalist, he reminded Les frequently that he was one of a generation of Canadian writers who was obligated to blaze the trail for future generations of Canadian writers—and that this pioneering role might require sacrifice. It was from Deacon's suggestion that Les fleshed out an idea for an epic Canadian novel that would revolve around the romantic and brutal history of northern Ontario—a history with which Les was thoroughly familiar and one that he had, to some degree, lived. This involved a fictional account of the silver rush days of Cobalt, the dashing characters who populated the mines, and the pioneers who helped civilize the wild frontier. To Les, the history of the region had all the elements of drama—it was glamorous, it was exciting, and it was, ultimately, tragic. By the early 1930s, much of its mystique was gone. "I've often thought of the story of Cobalt," he wrote Deacon. "The bush, the railway, the silver find, the roaring camp days, the mines, business driving out the picturesque, then the withdrawal of the men who seek new frontiers, and now that faded, drab town that depresses me. . . . The days when poker games ran along with a couple of thousand dollars in the pot, when a man could be cadging a drink on Tuesday and swinging a fifty thousand dollar deal on Wednesday, the gaudy rip-roaring Cobalt of memory, could be conjured up again." Certainly fodder for a best-selling and respected novel, if only Les had the opportunity to write it. As Deacon advised, this epic would not be plot-driven, but would instead concentrate on character, history, and the beauty of the writing: "Stick to the major and basic human emotions and passions. You can make a big powerful story better out of the simple, elemental factors of existence than out of too detailed a plot," he wrote. "Get a theme . . . and then develop it in terms of a developing character. Follow it through, expand on it." As far as the talent required to write the novel, Les would probably be up to the task. But, on a practical level, it may have been impossible, even though Deacon did not acknowledge this. In this way, he may have played on Les's guilt—or at least on Les's belief about the important mission of a writer. Deacon's views on the power of the writer were nearly evangelical: "There is a great attractive force in desire," he wrote Les. "Christians call it the power of prayer. What you want with your whole soul very often comes our way. . . . People do not so much realize their ambitions by work as by yearning powerfully, and the desired thing comes almost by itself." (Deacon dismissed Les's arguments that he had to write pulp and syndicate novels to support his family, and he denigrated Les's role as a husband and father: "By God, the race can grow ten thousand good, reliable husbands, who are good providers, to one first-rate novelist," he said.)

On one hand, Deacon was an encouraging force who continually reminded Les of his talent and the importance and value of his work. On the other, he may have led him to believe that even though he was still young, time was wasting, and that Les should not fritter away his talent. "If, with your ability you don't try the big thing, and go on just being a good husband and father, the time is going to come, when it is too late, when you'll be soured on life, when you'll feel yourself a failure, when you'll envy the boys who have written good books and remained poor. Then, when you are a sour old man of 50 do you suppose you're going to be a pleasant person to live with? . . . You'll take to drink or women to help you forget what you might have been—how will your wife like that?"

It is true that Les worried through much of his young adult life that he would not achieve his goal of becoming a well-known and well-respected writer of adult fiction. And it is true that he never did write the Great Canadian Novel, or anything like it. But his closeness to his family, his upbeat and amiable personality, and his ability and willingness to change with the times saved him from the fate Deacon had predicted. And, late in his life, he did achieve a measure of fame as a writer, although it was in a way he could never have imagined.

***

Although he did not accurately predict Les's future, William Deacon was familiar with the lifestyles and psyches of writers, having devoted most of his life to writing about, reading about, and spending time with authors. He persuaded Les of the importance of mingling with other writers, and was probably responsible for introducing Les to many Canadian writers of the 1930s and '40s, several of whom visited Haileybury and stayed with Les. In several of his letters to Deacon, Les asked the critic to describe his visitors' personalities and quirks so he could be prepared for their visit. And the picture Deacon painted was not always a pretty one.

Deacon wrote voluminous letters throughout his life to many Canadian poets and writers, and was, at various times, an officer in both the Canadian Authors' Association and the Toronto Writer's Club, groups whose programs drew hundreds of Canadian authors. A handful of writers spent several decades in the early and middle part of the twentieth century traveling through Canada giving readings and speaking to authors in some of the country's smaller cities and communities. These included poets Wilson MacDonald and Charles G. D. Roberts, both award-winning writers who shared Deacon's feelings of Canadian nationalism. Both came through Haileybury to speak, and Les served as host to MacDonald for a week in 1933. In Deacon's biography, MacDonald is painted as a somewhat self-centered artist who often was envious of other writers he felt were more successful than he. (A magician, MacDonald sometimes charmed the small children of writers whose homes he visited, as Les's daughter Norah remembers, although others recall that his magic tricks could not make up for his sour nature.)

Of course, one of the many bonds that joined Les and Deacon—and Deacon with many other writers—was their love of books. For most of his adult years in Haileybury, Les served on the city's library board, a voluntary position that he took very seriously. The library was formed in 1931, as Les noted in a letter to Deacon, and survived on minimum funding from the government and through one-dollar membership charges. In early 1935, the library was hurting financially and relied heavily on donated books from city residents. As Les told Deacon, however, it was vital that the library buy new titles and keep up-to-date. Les sheepishly asked Deacon if he could provide the library, free of charge, with some of the review copies of books that the literary critic received.

Because of its limited funding and staff, the supervision provided by the board was particularly vital in determining such issues as what books the library should buy with its money. By the middle of 1935, though, another issue had emerged: a practice that Les deemed censorship. It was the topic of several letters between Les and Deacon, who planned to write about it in his column until Les stopped him.

Haileybury library officials were providing a special shelf (behind the main check-out desk) for a few books the librarians deemed objectionable or in poor taste. The idea of a special shelf for certain books was in theory objectionable to Les, who nonetheless was willing to allow the hiding of a few books, including Hemingway's *A Farewell to Arms* and Pearl Buck's *The Good Earth*. But he grew livid when he learned that the number of books on the "reserve shelf" was gradually expanding and included such works as Thomas Wolfe's *Look Homeward, Angel;* some books by Dashiell Hammett and by James Branch Cabell; and others that Les felt were well written and harmless. As he wrote Deacon, most of these books were on the list not because of questionable content, but because some board members did not like them for any number of reasons. What had started as a little-practiced library policy based on the opinions of one or two people had flared into a full-blown controversy. Les threatened to leave the library board over the issue, and was angry enough to write about it to Deacon.

The critic, too, was outraged by what he viewed as censorship, and wanted to write about it in his column—an idea that horrified Les. Les had great respect and admiration for the founder of the library, who, he told Deacon, had built the facility almost single-handedly from nothing to an institution with 2,500 books and a juvenile section, a rarity in that era. "Any sort of publicity to the row would be utterly abhorrent to the founder . . . a quiet reserved Englishman and a damned good fellow," he wrote Deacon, pleading with him not to write about it. "He has not favored extreme censorship but has been trying to avoid the inevitable clash. Publicity would mean a flare-up and a hell of a lot of unpleasantness." Les's plea came not a moment too soon; Deacon had included in a letter to Les a four-hundred-word essay about the matter that he planned to run in his column. He called the special shelf "an isolation ward," and noted that throughout history, sanctimonious librarians have tried to control the circulation of many great books, always with disastrous results.

The censorship incident may have been a tempest in a teapot, since it was mentioned in about half a dozen letters between Les and Deacon and not brought up again. It is perhaps ironic, then, that the works of Les himself would also be targets for suspicious librarians for decades to come.

***

Almost from the day it was formed, the books distributed by the Stratemeyer Syndicate were lightning rods of debate for librarians, children's book critics, parents, teachers, and even business writers. The debate about the "quality" of Stratemeyer's series fiction would rage more than half a century after he died—and it continues decades after the syndicate was sold in the early 1980s to a mainstream publishing house. It is almost laughable that the staid, religious Edward Stratemeyer, who prohibited even a hint of sex in his syndicate's books, would stir such heated debates. But former readers, librarians, and educators have lined up on either side of the argument about the value of the books; and, even into the twenty-first century, the Hardy Boys and other series books are banned in some libraries.

Les learned about the controversial nature of series fiction shortly after he began writing for the syndicate in 1926. The first battle against the syndicate books, waged in 1914 by Franklin Mathiews, then chief librarian for the Boy Scouts (see chapter 3), caused some temporary problems for Edward Stratemeyer and the syndicate simply because it received support from some teachers and librarians, who advocated reading by youngsters of more "respectable" books. In the end, however, the melee was just a blip on the radar screen for Stratemeyer: it did not, in the long run, affect sales of books.

In 1934, however, four years after the death of Stratemeyer and shortly after his daughters took over the syndicate, the business magazine *Fortune* fired another salvo. This time, the syndicate was accused in a more subtle way of contributing to the decline of the era's youth. More important, however, was the fact that the author (who was unnamed in the article) revealed for the first time the workings of the syndicate and the fact that authors Roy Rockwood, Victor Appleton, Laura Lee Hope, et al. were no more real than the characters they supposedly created.

The *Fortune* article, under the ominous title "For Indeed It Was He," became notorious among fans of series fiction throughout the twentieth century, and it is probably safe to say that most true aficionados of the Hardy Boys, Tom Swift, Nancy Drew, the Bobbsey Twins, and the syndicate's other enduring series are aware of its existence. Written in elaborate—and sometimes purple—prose, the article implies that the syndicate is making phenomenal sums of money from the naivete of innocent juvenile readers who are being misled about just who is writing and producing the books they are devouring. Further, it implies, while some of the syndicate's success stems from Edward Stratemeyer's creativity and cleverness, much of it comes from lies and deceitful marketing.

"The fifty-cent juvenile," as the *Fortune* reporter calls it (although some sold for more and some for less than that), "has few literary pretensions: it is a flat-footed account of the superhuman exploits of adolescent

Ubermenschen—and if it is successful it may have sequels that ramble on for as many as thirty-six volumes . . . The Rover Boys is its [the series book's] quintessence: a substantial profit for author and publisher is its only, and unblushing purpose." While a Stratemeyer book may not blow out boys' brains as Mathiews suggested, it is hardly a work of literature: "If not exactly literary, it makes up by action for what it lacks in art." The writer briefly mentions a criticism that some educators and librarians throughout the century would have of much series fiction—that it focuses on well-to-do, upper-middle-class young heroes who can fly planes, own boats, and solve mysteries because they have privileged lives. (Few children's books at the time did focus on lower-middle-class protagonists.)

The ostensible purpose of the article is to illustrate that the death of Edward Stratemeyer in 1930 did not mean death to the syndicate. It continued to thrive and spawned one of its most successful progeny: the Nancy Drew series, which, in its four years of existence, had become the highest-selling Stratemeyer series of all time. "Nancy is the greatest phenomenon among the fifty-centers," *Fortune* writes. "How she crashed a Valhalla that had been rigidly restricted to the male of her species is a mystery even to her publishers." (The fact is that the Nancy Drew series was not the first girls' series that Edward Stratemeyer created, although he might have been surprised at its great success.)

The Stratemeyer Syndicate is nothing if not successful, the writer notes, comparing it to one of the great industrial monopolies of the era. "Oil had its Rockefeller, literature had its Stratemeyer," he writes. The *Fortune* article discusses in detail many of the business and marketing operations of the syndicate, facts that were not known at the time—and facts that the syndicate wanted to keep under wraps. It notes, for instance, several factors that distinguished the marketing of series fiction from that of other juvenile books of the times: most notably the "breeder" concept, whereby the syndicate published the first three books in a series simultaneously, and the fact that the books were sold by about thirty energetic traveling salesmen who tried to place them in newsstands, drugstores, notion stores, lunch counters and just about anywhere else. "They are over the country like a plague of locusts," according to the article. Here, the writer notes, Stratemeyer's ingenuity entered the picture—he knew that most readers "were too busy shooting marbles" to pay attention to conventional book advertisements. (Actually, it was the publisher that employed the salesmen, not the syndicate. The Stratemeyer Syndicate, if it were around in modern times, would probably be called a book packager. It would work with publishers, whose job it is to distribute the books.)

What seems to intrigue the writer most, though, is what he or she refers to as the odd literary foster parenthood arrangement that series authors have with the syndicate. The arrangement forced writers like Les to relinquish all rights to the books while receiving a flat fee—anywhere from $85 to $150—for writing them. Their real names are not used, a ruse that can be considered deceitful to readers, the article implies: "What, the [Stratemeyer] sisters demand in amazement, would their clients think if they knew that the great gallery of juvenile authors . . . was nothing but a waxworks invented by their father?" Not only are the books "manufactured" by phony authors, the article notes, they are produced by what is, literally, an assembly line: "At the end of the chute stands a representative of the publisher who, acting like a U.S. Government meat inspector in a packing plant, certifies that manuscript is factually fit for consumption." (As noted above, the publishers of the Stratemeyer books acted primarily as distributors, since the syndicate also often owned the electroplates on which the stories were typeset.)

The *Fortune* article revealing the inner workings of the syndicate must have been a scoop for the magazine at the time. It is unlikely to have hurt sales of the books, at least in a direct way, but it has long been fodder for critics of series books, who have been persistent over the decades in their attempts to rid libraries of the books. The *Fortune* article has been widely quoted ever since it was written. John T. Dizer, a researcher of series books, wrote in 1982 that nearly every criticism of series books has at its root the *Fortune* article, including articles in many small state library journals that were written shortly after the *Fortune* article. The early articles in some of these small journals have been continually reprinted or cited in later articles, sustaining the life of the *Fortune* story. Further, he noted, the fact that the article appeared in a slick and well-respected publication made it eminently quotable: "The article has the air of exposing dark secrets, long suspected by the virtuous but now actually brought to light," he wrote.

The debate about the value of series fiction stirs deep passions in many adults associated with children's literature. The children who read the books, however, do not have the forum to speak. But their power is greater than that of the adults in one way: they are the ones who decide what they read.

***

The debate about the suitability of series fiction takes a turn from the conventional arguments about what type of literature is proper for children. Traditionally, these arguments about young adult literature center around sexuality or perceived sexuality, offensive language, and, in the latter twentieth century, the issue of diversity or inclusiveness in the literature. (The Stratemeyer books were, in midcentury, targets of those who thought their content was xenophobic.) But Stratemeyer insisted his series books be squeaky clean as far as sexual content and offensive language—Joe and Frank Hardy, for instance, were not even allowed to kiss their girlfriends, and nary a "damn" could escape their lips. Even the "violence" consists of little more than pratfalls in which only minor injuries are ever sustained. Edward Stratemeyer did not permit bloody and gory violence in the pages of his syndicate's books. And few literary characters could match Stratemeyer's creations in civility and decorum. During the first three decades of their existence, for instance, Joe and Frank Hardy were impeccably polite in public, wore hats much of the time, and referred to their friends and acquaintances as "fellow." Nancy Drew, Tom Swift, and the others were equally decorous. The issue of the suitability of series fiction, then, revolves around none of these issues. Instead it focuses on the nebulous and indefinable "literary value" of the books.

Dizer, an unabashed fan of series fiction, is quick to note that the subject stirs deep emotions in proponents and critics of series fiction alike. The layman, he suggests, would never understand the nature of the conflict and the deep divisions in literary philosophy. "Gentle readers who are outside the librarians vs. serious books combat arena may wonder at the persistence and intensity of the critics' attack," he wrote in 1982. Like other emotionally laden social and cultural issues, the disagreements run so deep that reasoned arguments on either side are usually wasted. To Dizer, many of the same arguments against series fiction in the 1920s endured for the length of the twentieth century—the books are poorly written by "hack" writers; they are repetitive and superficial in plot and character; they contain no valuable social themes or messages; and they are produced in a cheap, assembly-line manner. Some critics have said the decidedly middle-class characters make the books classist; that is, they do not reflect the lives of lower- and lower-middle-class readers.

As the century progressed and the subject of children's literature became more complex—more publishers began publishing it, more librarians and teachers studied it, and more parents became aware of what was available—the debate took dramatic turns. And as television, radio, and other forms of entertainment grew, educators became more concerned with ways to keep youngsters reading.

In 1969, journalist and children's author E. B. White weighed in on the debate over selection of children's books, arguing that an elitist approach to picking what children read—one that focuses on the "classics"—not only alienates children but patronizes them, to him a fatal error. He said most juvenile readers are sophisticated, demanding, and observant when it comes to reading, and select their reading material for many complicated reasons. This is particularly true, he believed, in matters of vocabulary: "Some writers deliberately avoid using words they think a child doesn't know. This emasculates the prose and, I suspect, bores the reader."

The selection and publishing of books is much more complicated for young readers than for adults, many in the field believe, because of the emotions attached to reading selection. While subject matter and style are key elements in the success of adult and children's fiction, children's thought processes when selecting reading material are much more sensory and emotional. According to one author and professor who has taught a class on the culture of childhood, the books children select to read "slip[s] under our intellectual radar screen, remaining resistant to analysis." Children get attached to certain books because "their reading experience is inextricable from powerful memories of discovering a secret new world. . . . Often they have crossed this threshold on their own."

This explanation is borne out by the many writers, professors, and other professionals who have written glowingly about their childhood experiences with the Hardy Boys, Nancy Drew, and other series books. Usually these essays and articles focus on the idea that these accomplished adults knew as children that the series fiction was not "acceptable" reading; but for many reasons they kept reading it. English professor Tim Morris, for example, remembers that when he was a nine-year-old in Chicago, his teacher had a contest to see who could read the most books. After slogging through some "recommended" book list, he tentatively approached his teacher: "Does the [Hardy Boys] *Tower Treasure* count?" Relieved, he learned it did.

Indeed, it may be the forbidden nature of these books that made them so attractive. In many cases, the adults who reminisce about reading series fiction said that it was series fiction that introduced them to reading as a pleasure and not a chore to be endured. Alison Lurie believes that

many children are drawn to the "subversive" nature of books—the qualities that allow them to separate themselves from their parents' life and
values and to escape. As she wrote in *Don't Tell the Grown-ups: Subversive
Children's Literature*, some children's literature "overturned adult pretensions and made fun of adult institutions, including school and family. . . .
They were subversive." Hence, the appeal of Nancy Drew's and Frank
and Joe Hardy's nonstop adventures—and the fact that parents, though
respected, played a small role in their activities. And this accounts for the
appeal of the Keystone Kop police figures in the early Hardy Boys books.
As children's author and educator Selma Lanes notes, the series relies on
airplanes, boats, and fast cars that serve as symbols of power for young
readers, allowing them unlimited mobility to roam the world.

Some former readers imbue the books with the same literary characteristics as some classics—recollections that may have amused Les and
other syndicate authors like Nancy Drew writer Mildred Wirt Benson
and Howard Garis, who wrote many of the early Tom Swift books. Les
took pride in his work, although one has to wonder if he would compare
himself to Charles Dickens or James Joyce. Tim Morris writes, "The
Hardy Boys archetype is a fair schematic rendering of what happens in
Joyce's Ulysses, and therefore the Odyssey as well—give or take a few
chapters. And Bayport, that bustling city on Barmet Bay, is just as fully realized a chronotope as Trollope's Barsetshire or Dickens's London, or
Simenon's Paris."

Still, those adults whose recollections have found their way into print
also ask another common question: Can millions of young readers be
wrong? (Although sales figures vary, it is estimated by most sources that
by the time the syndicate was sold in the early 1980s, it sold about 6 million copies a year; sales leaders were the Nancy Drew series, with more
than 2 million copies a year, and the Hardy Boys, with between 1 and 2
million copies a year. It is estimated that the Stratemeyer Syndicate ac-
counted for about 90 percent of series book sales by the time it went out
of existence.) Try as they may, it has been impossible for adults to stop
children from reading series fiction. Throughout the twentieth century,
and as late as 1999, the books were banned in some libraries across
North America. Some critics of the banning have long accused librarians of succumbing to various "fashions" in children's fiction over the
years, or of barring works that do not meet their definitions of "social
significance." Others have said that librarians, who are usually women,
do not understand the reading needs of boys, and have thus not under-

stood the appeal and value of books like the Hardy Boys series. Library director Ervin J. Gaines has even questioned what he calls the cozy relationship between children's librarians and publishers. He maintains that because the majority of children's book sales are to libraries, publishers are willing to let librarians maintain an "elitist monopoly" of acceptable books. Selma Lanes believes that the power of librarians in selecting what children read is so strong that publishing houses "play it safe" with well-established authors when selecting what to print, in hopes of pleasing librarians. And no less an authority than Leslie McFarlane himself believed that too many children's authors write to please adults, resulting in work children shun. "You can't force kids to read what they don't like," he wrote in the early 1970s. "A good deal of juvenile literature today is actually written for adults—librarians, teachers, etc., because they do the buying and they buy what they think the youngster should read."

In 1999, librarians in Essex County, Ontario, removed Hardy Boys and Nancy Drew books from the shelves of that library system's sixteen branches. "There are more literary, less repetitious books out there," one librarian said. But library officials returned the books to the shelves after newspaper stories prompted angry calls to the library from patrons. A 1975 *Wall Street Journal* article about the syndicate noted that the New York Public Library decided that year to put a few series books on its shelves after several decades of banning their circulation. But many other library systems still did not allow the books, the article continued, quoting the executive secretary of the American Library Association's children's services division as calling the Nancy Drew series "the same books written over and over again." Ironically, the series fiction books were pulled from library shelves in East Orange, New Jersey, a city that had long housed the headquarters of the Stratemeyer Syndicate. If children want syndicate books, they could get them elsewhere, one librarian there told an interviewer. In their widely read textbook, *Children and Books*, Zena Sutherland and May Hill Arbuthnot imply, on one page, that series books, like comic books and paperback romance novels, are part of the "errors" in the trial-and-error process of publication and selection of children's literature. Yet, in the same book, the authors quote the opinion of an educator, Fred Inglis, that it is very difficult to limit the assessment of most children's books to either "good" or "bad." He writes, "Certain books are good, others are bad, and a very large number have something of both. The books are good because they comment on experience with profundity and intelligence and occasionally with genius; and these qualities lead us to some glimpse of the truth about human experience."

There is no concrete answer to whether the Stratemeyer children's books are legitimate "literature," whether they encourage children to read or waste their time or pollute their minds. But their existence throughout most of the twentieth century has triggered debate and ambivalent feelings among the adults who have come in contact with them—including Leslie McFarlane, who wrote one of the syndicate's most popular series. Les himself bemoaned in his diary that he had to waste his valuable time on sometimes trite and repetitive stories that he knew would never be considered great literature.

But no less a critic than author George Orwell claimed that it is not only the great works that hold a place in readers' hearts, and that readable but less-accomplished works often have a longevity that their artistic counterparts do not. In an essay titled "Good Bad Books," Orwell defines such a book as "the kind . . . that has no literary pretensions but which remains readable when more serious productions have perished." He used as an example the Sherlock Holmes series and several other less famous works, including Guy Boothby's *Dr Kikola* and Ernest Bramah's *Max Carrados*. His classic example of the genre is *Uncle Tom's Cabin,* which, he notes, is full of "preposterous and melodramatic events" but also "deeply moving and essentially true."

Although he was speaking of writing for adults, Orwell's descriptions in 1945 of this "genre" of good-bad books sounds very much like the description adult fans have given over the years of series fiction. It is "escape literature," he wrote, that "form[s] pleasant patches in one's memory, quiet corners where the mind can browse at odd moments, but they hardly pretend to have anything to do with real life." He notes that not all art need be intellectual in nature. "The existence of good bad literature—the fact that one can be amused or excited or even moved by a book that one's intellect simply refuses to take seriously—is a reminder that art is not the same thing as celebration." One wonders if Leslie McFarlane, who was probably writing his last Hardy Boys book when Orwell wrote these words, would have taken comfort in them.

Throughout much of the twentieth century, one thing is clear: to many adults, the seemingly benign exploits of young series fiction heroes like Joe and Frank Hardy, Nancy Drew, and Tom Swift are far from innocent. As one librarian in Oregon noted, "You would be amazed at how much heat you can generate by bringing up Nancy Drew."

10

. . . .

THE BEST AND WORST OF TIMES

By the mid- and late 1930s, Les's career as a freelance writer began to gel; with experience, and through his contact with other writers and editors, including William Deacon, he had become more sophisticated about identifying suitable markets, pursuing reprint and copyright issues, and developing salable story ideas. He began looking at the far-reaching marketing potential of each story.

The late 1930s, however, would be the best of times and the worst of times for the McFarlanes. Les's stock as a writer was rising, and in a limited market he was becoming a known byline. In one week in 1937, Les had stories in seven magazines on the newsstands. An editor for *Argosy* told him in 1938 that if the magazine published his story, it would want to promote his name on the cover of the magazine because he had "cover value." His stories and name were sometimes promoted on the covers of other magazines like *Maclean's,* and he was becoming involved in writing for the nascent medium of radio. Based on entries in his diary, money, while tight, was not quite the severe problem it had been earlier in the decade.

But all was not well with the family. Les's drinking was increasingly a problem, and, by 1936 his family had evidently thought it had grown out of control. And, by the end of the decade, Amy's depression had worsened.

***

Although he does not mention a drinking problem overtly in his diary, hints that alcohol was affecting his career and life can be found throughout Les's entries in 1935 and parts of 1936. He indicates during this time that he is having trouble coming up with story ideas, and that his usual pattern of writing regularly for several hours a day had been interrupted. Les, who developed disciplined work patterns early in his career as a freelance writer, could by now write three thousand to four thousand words on a productive day (the equivalent of about twelve to fifteen typewritten pages). Keeping a diary was important to Les, and he had been faithful about it for seven years by 1936. Most of the entries were one-quarter to one-half page in length, and carefully written every day in his crisp vertical handwriting. By early 1936, however, the handwriting grew wilder, becoming nearly illegible in parts, with passages occasionally drifting from assigned spaces on the page and wandering into slots for other entries. And, even more unusual, entire days went by with no entries, and sometimes entries were limited to only one or two sentences. What he did write seemed to reflect a daily life that was grinding to a near halt. "Loafed all day," read many entries, a phrase never used before that begins to pop up with ominous regularity. On November 17, 1935, two days after staying up much of the night playing poker—sometimes an expensive hobby when he was inebriated—the entry consisted of three succinct sentences: "Loafed around all day. Jim Murray [a friend] came over for a chat. Went to bed feeling jittery and exhausted." By the next day, "Desperately trying to get away on another short [article] but could not get a plot."

Perhaps it was Frank and Joe Hardy, however, who bore the brunt of these desperate days in 1935 and early 1936. In November 1935, he reluctantly agreed to write *The Sinister Signpost* after initially turning down the job. The prime reason? After completing fourteen Hardy Boys books, he ultimately did not want anyone else to write about the boys' exploits. "When it occurred to me that it would be the first Hardy boys book to be turned over to someone else I decided I would have to squeeze it in somehow," he told Edna Stratemeyer. Although he occasionally groused in his diary about having to write the "juveniles" for money, his complaints about writing for the syndicate were particularly virulent in this period. On January 8, 1936, after bemoaning the fact that he had made no entries in his diary for a week or two, "as usual, however, when I am writing one of those cursed juvenile books everything else goes by the board. . . . Day after day has been a solid sweat at the damnable boys book, usually 4,000 words a day when I have been in a good working streak, some days so fed up that I have been able to do nothing at all." Then Les goes on to savage the plot of his latest Hardy Boys book, *The Sinister Signpost*. "Full of mad inventors, secret chambers, etc. and a kidnapped racehorse as well as the obnoxious Hardy brats." Although the Stratemeyers kept his fee at $100 rather than $85, Les muses that he lost money doing the book because it kept him from more lucrative, fee-per-word work.

This entry is particularly revealing in its negative emotion and bitterness; even during the early years of the Depression, when Les was selling nearly all his work but making next to nothing, the frustration and shame reflected in his diaries did not reach this level of contempt. By January 28, "I worked very hard and finished up the boys' book at 5 o'clock [in the morning], sent it out by express at once and feel as if I have just climbed the Matterhorn."

Based on entries in his diaries, Les's drinking began to intensify in early 1935, and worsened as that year progressed. After "making a night of it" in nearby New Liskeard one cold February day in 1935, "I'm in bad shape today and badly in disfavor. No wonder," he wrote the next day. But Les was a realist and knew the toll his lifestyle was taking. Two days later, "Still enfeebled . . . my health can't stand this nonsense much longer. Got back to work and am now over the worst of the book, into the home stretch. Ten days overdue and a bad job . . ." By October, things had not looked up. "Tired today and in no shape for work," he wrote on October 1. He apparently thought he could recuperate with the hair of the dog that bit him: "Revived myself with a Bass."

According to the entries in the diary and recollections of Les's children, his increased drinking was, naturally, affecting more than just his work. Norah Perez said her father's actions would exasperate her mother, who often went out looking for her husband on the nights he was holed up on drinking binges. On some desperate evenings, she would hide his clothes in the oven as a preemptory strike—no clothes, no drinking, particularly for someone like Les who made sure he was always neatly attired. And her husband's activities no doubt exacerbated the family's financial problems as well as her own battle with depression.

Finally, in the spring of 1936, Les's father, John Henry, stepped in and took him away for "the cure." Les's children, who were very young at the time, barely remember this era and believe that Les went to a sanitarium for a month or so in Hamilton, Ontario. Norah Perez believes this drying out consisted of a treatment like Antabuse, which is designed to instill a strong distaste for liquor or the thought of it. Norah said the only time she remembers seeing her father drink after that was in 1955, on the day of her mother's funeral. Some correspondence between Les and his two daughters after the death of Amy indicate that they were concerned about their father and alcohol. But nothing indicates that Les ever had a problem with alcohol for the remainder of his life, although he was a social drinker much later in his life.

When Les emerges again in early 1937, his diary entries return to their previous disciplined—and legible—style although work sporadically kept him from making entries. (The fact that he was too busy to keep the diary religiously each day in 1937 bothered Les; one of his New Year's resolutions in 1938 was to keep up the journal.) Les's diary was always important to him—even the volumes' physical appearance conveyed seriousness. The journals themselves, consistent from year to year, looked like attractive bound books, with thick, lined pages, each with the date and year, and a hardbound, multicolored cover with "Daily Journal" (and the year) embossed on the cover. When it came to writing daily passages, he would do the opposite of what many writers do: he would sometimes type the entries and then transcribe them by longhand into the diaries themselves. By 1937, he obtained journals that permitted full-page instead of half-page entries. He was prone to chastising himself when he neglected his diary entries, evidently because he believed a fulfilling life is reflected in interesting passages: "The full-page journal seems to be a mistake and it seems I seldom fill a page," he lamented on March 2, 1937, "which confesses a dull life and a destitute mind." He sometimes wrote up to 20,000 words a year, he noted in an entry, but reminded himself that "quantity, though, is nothing; quality is the thing. And this is not a good journal by any standard." He blamed his own personality for that: "Actually a good journal should be the expression of an interesting personality against the background of his environment and times. This falls down on all counts" (March 4, 1940).

The fact that the contents of his diary declined in both quantity and quality in 1935 and 1936, then, was an indication that his drinking did get out of hand in that period. Even after his recovery, however, Les was not fully convinced that alcohol hampered his work. When he was having difficulty writing early in 1937, he speculated on the cause: "I do seem to have lost my punch this past year and the change of personality due to cutting out the liquor may have a great deal to do with it. Lay awake for a long time mulling over ideas for another story but none of them were especially bright." But this passage may just been an expression of frustration at his lack of ideas at the time. His life and that of his family appeared to normalize after he stopped drinking.

The hard-drinking writer has long been a stereotype in North American literary culture, and when it came to the freelance writers of the 1920s and 1930s, that image may have had a basis in reality. Indeed, his affection for liquor may have been one of the few behaviors that linked Les with other pulp writers of the era, many, like him, former newspaper reporters. In his biography of author and pulp writer John D. MacDonald,

Hugh Merrill said that only about three hundred writers—most of whom lived in New York—filled the pages of America's many pulp magazines in the 1920s. And most of those did not have families to support. They lived in cheap hotels, ate in cheap restaurants, and were prone to spending what little money they had on liquor. During that era, Merrill estimated that American pulp magazines published about eight hundred pieces of fiction a month. So Les was an anomaly, both socially and geographically, in terms of his fellow pulp writers.

Life for the McFarlane family brought not only frustrations but simple pleasures. In spite of frequent colds and flus caused by the climate, the children were healthy and, with the exception of some frequent dental work in the late 1930s and occasional eye strain, so was Les. Amy was getting to a point where she was frequently bedridden with unspecified ailments and began to fear leaving the house. But she still enjoyed seeing friends and family and occasionally playing bridge. She also derived pleasure from maintaining a comfortable home and periodically acquiring new furniture for it, events that sometimes merited mention in Les's diary.

Despite his troubles, Les still maintained his lifelong enthusiasm for holidays, birthdays, and anniversaries, celebrating all with gusto and gifts. On their wedding anniversary in 1936, he gave Amy flowers and chocolates. "Conventional, but she asked me not to give her anything," he wrote. (The prospect of not receiving an anniversary gift from Les was unlikely.) His children's birthdays were almost always noted in his diaries, complete with a summary of the celebration and the food served. Even in the depths of his money worries and Amy's illness, Les recorded the happy reaction of the children to their gifts, and birthdays were celebrated even when Amy's illness was at its most severe. The day before Norah's fifth birthday, Les went to the store to buy her some handkerchiefs as a gift. "Her excitement over the impending event is quite delightful," Les wrote on February 3, 1938. The next day, he wrote of Norah's reaction to aging a year: "Norah did not think her slippers would fit her this morning, as she assumed that her arrival at the age of five would be accompanied by a sudden gain in growth," he wrote.

As he had written William Deacon, he was torn between the desire to please Amy and his family, and his writing career. It would be unthinkable, for instance, that a wedding anniversary or family birthday would go unnoticed by Les, and despite his volume of work, he always wrote and sent the family Christmas cards. And he tried to win Amy's approval in many ways other than his gifts to her, gifts which his daughter Norah remembers, were always lovely and considerate. His diary entries indicate that he sometimes gave Amy and his brother Dick drafts of his articles to read. He was particularly pleased when Amy complimented his work.

Les always observed anniversaries of deaths; he noted in his diary for several years the anniversary date of his mother's death, and in March 1935 even forced himself to go to church on the one-year anniversary, something that was anathema to him. ("Going to church was not quite the ordeal I had expected—nevertheless it all seems very childish to a rational mind," he said in his diary.) Anniversaries of deaths were sentimental rather than spiritual occasions for him. Much later in his life, even after he remarried, Les frequently included in his letters nostalgic references to Amy on the anniversary of her death.

Amy sang in the church choir, played bridge, and met frequently with her sisters. Les preferred poker, but also played bridge with Amy's family, and was active in a bowling league. Most of all, however, he spent much of his free time reading. Perhaps the one positive result of Les's increased drinking in 1935 and 1936 was that he apparently spent the time away from his typewriter to read even more. He notes during those two years that he particularly enjoyed Thomas Wolfe's new book, as well as autobiographies of H. G. Wells and Trollope. He also enjoyed the newly released *Gone with the Wind*—"with its fine climax"—and said he could understand why it was so popular (March 1, 1937). In his late thirties, however, Les became a much more discriminating reader, offering longer critiques of books in his diary entries. He also became more critical, noting if books were derivative and comparing writing styles of authors. In 1939, for instance, he offered in his diary a relatively long critique of Willa Cather's *Lost Lady*, which he thought was overrated. The style of writing, he noted, is "fine, words are beautifully used and the compression is skillful." But overall, Les thought, the book is too obscure. "I have a dumb idea that no writer should be intentionally obscure. Her subtlety is carried to such an extent that opinion would certainly differ to what Cather was trying to say." He acknowledged that different readers bring different experiences to their interpretation of narratives, but "I'm not in agreement with that notion as a foundation for writing fiction" (March 5). Of John Steinbeck's *The Grapes of Wrath*, he observed, "In spite of the obvious propaganda, it is a very powerful book with bite to it. Some of the characterizations are very thin but a few are excellent" (February 2, 1940).

Although he preferred fiction to nonfiction, he did not limit himself to fiction, praising at length, for example, an exposé of the food industry by Consumers' Research, "Eat Drink and Be Wary" (July 6, 1936). And, because of his job, he found he had to read nonfiction for plot details in his fiction. For instance, he noted in an entry that he read an informative article in the *Saturday Evening Post* about prizefighting, the subject of some of his fiction. "[Gave] a lot of good dope about prizefighting technique," he noted (March 30, 1937).

Always a movie lover, he went to more films by the late 1930s, at a time when it cost 25 or 30 cents to see a movie. His critiques of them in his diaries became more frequent and detailed. His diary not only noted whether he liked them, but also commented on their technical and artistic merits. Les was not always kind to the actors and filmmakers: "Saw a mystery movie tonight," he said in one entry in May 1935. "I could write a better one in five minutes on the back of an envelope." Or, of *Alexander's Ragtime Band,* "A good picture despite Tyrone Power and Don Ameche," he wrote on November 16, 1938. "Two hams if I ever saw them—but the Berlin tunes were catchy. Of them all, 'Alexander's Ragtime Band' had the most vitality." Despite the occasional criticism of what he saw on the screen, as he wrote on a depressing day in early March 1937, he maintained "my boyhood enthusiasm for the movies."

When he stopped drinking, Les became much more introspective and self-critical, whether as a result of his sobriety or of approaching middle age. Many of the diary entries take on a grave and sometimes defeated tone, despite the fact that money problems were easing for the family and at one point Les notes that he even had a few hundred dollars in the bank.

Even more important, though, was that Les's career was starting to take a different direction. During these latter years of the 1930s, radio entered Les's life—it became a part of the family's day-to-day existence and provided a new career direction for Les. In addition, he began editing and rewriting other people's work, and was able to take small breaks from his own writing.

Most important, though, was the fact that the family moved out of Haileybury in 1936 to a home in Whitby, outside of Toronto. Brian Mc-Farlane remembers that his father wanted to move because his expanding and diverse job duties made it necessary to be closer to major markets. By 1936, the family no doubt wanted to establish roots, and if

THE SECRET OF THE HARDY BOYS 10

Les believed that if he were to move, this would be the time. Pat was seven, Brian five, and Norah three. They rented a home in Whitby, but the move had to be a tough one for Les. In Haileybury, he was a big fish in a small pond, and he had his family and in-laws surrounding him. But beyond this, his love for Haileybury and the Temiskaming Lake region never diminished, even as he approached middle age. Les wrote about its beauty whenever he had the chance. As he left Toronto one November day in 1937 on a business trip to northern Ontario, he described the view as he looked out of the train window onto the Temiskaming Valley: "Looked out the window after the train passed North Bay, saw the familiar Northern terrain . . . under a frosty dusting of snow in the moonlight . . . saw Haileybury, asleep and silent, from the coach window."

The McFarlanes' departure did not go unnoticed by the Haileybury community. At a farewell celebration at the Odd Fellows Hall, the mayor, the high school principal and many other city dignitaries presented him with a silver tray. The mayor "expressed his regret, together with that of other citizens, at his departure," a newspaper story said. The women of Haileybury feted Amy and presented her with a silver service that matched the tray.

***

The move to Whitby marked a new chapter in Les's life and signaled career and personal changes. His last Hardy Boys book of the 1930s, *A Figure in Hiding*, published in 1937, was written right after his move to Whitby. But the move signified, for all practical purposes, a separation from the syndicate that was all but permanent. He returned to syndicate work in 1943 to write four more Hardy Boys books, but his dedication (such as it was) to the syndicate was never the same. After the move from Haileybury, he wrote the Hardy Boys books in his spare time and frequently when he was away from home and concentrating on other projects.

Despite their nitpicking about Les's failure to follow outlines precisely, his habit of turning in books that were a few pages short, and his admitted tendency at times to give the syndicate short shrift, the Stratemeyers valued him as an author. When they asked him to write *A Figure in Hiding*, a confident Les drove a hard bargain, telling the Stratemeyers that because of his move, he needed money immediately. He requested and received the entire $100 fee for the book in advance. Otherwise, he noted, he would have to write instead an article for a pulp magazine. In the letter to the Stratemeyers, Les made an unusual, fleeting reference to his alcohol rehabilitation. "Had a very good summer, after being hospitalized for a month last Spring." This rare hint of intimacy is unusual, since little else is ever mentioned about his illness, either in his diaries or in his correspondence, and he was not particularly close to the Stratemeyer daughters.

The Stratemeyers were astute enough to recognize that in Les they had a professional who insisted on turning in high-quality work despite occasional deadline problems and requests for advances. And they may have learned the hard way that consistency of authorship was the key to the success and accuracy of series fiction. Harriet Stratemeyer Adams and Andrew Svenson, who would become her chief assistant in the late 1940s, said in interviews that they were meticulous about all facts within the Hardy Boys books, and that they put the details of all people, places, events, and the like on index cards to ensure accuracy and consistency. After studying the content of the Hardy Boys series in detail, fans such as Robert L. Crawford believe that this system could not have been put into effect until after numerous errors and inconsistencies had been uncovered over the years. As Crawford points out, it is astounding that some of the errors in the Hardy Boys books 17–21—ones that were written by Dr. John Button, a physician—ever made their way to print. (Some mistakes are so obvious that they are downright mysterious, themselves worthy of investigation by the Hardy Boys.) For instance, in the *Mystery of the Flying Express,* Laura Hardy's first name becomes Mildred; the Hardy home is located on Elm Street instead of High Street, and Chief Ezra Collig, a favorite character of Les, becomes Chief Finch. Crawford contends, too, that in addition to discrepancies in obvious facts, the writing quality in these books declined dramatically. Crawford attempts to base his definition of quality on objective measures, and, in each of these five books, he charted, among other things, the number of accidents, falls, and the like and the number of relatively insignificant characters who are mentioned briefly and then abandoned in the narrative. He found that in these five books, rational plot development is all but abandoned, and the writer takes the easy way out by focusing on meaningless characters and an overabundance of action and accidents. "A poor writer would just run a car off a cliff or bring in Mr. Jones," Crawford writes. He also quotes several Hardy Boys researchers who, he said, refer to this era from 1938 to 1942 as "the weird period."

Crawford maintains that of the Hardy Boys books that appeared during this five-year period, *The Disappearing Floor,* published in 1940, has the greatest number of mistakes and the most convoluted plot. "It is the worst of the lot, with writing and plot construction shoddy and preposterous, jarringly episodic, and having an odd, disturbing surreal quality. Important events or persons happen or appear without reason or context, and are often not mentioned or explained thereafter," he wrote. He compared the plot to "that nadir of B Movies, 'Plan 9 from Outer Space.'" Crawford goes on to describe dozens of plot errors, character redundancies, contrivances, meaningless narrative turns, and silly happenstances that would no doubt have angered Leslie McFarlane had he bothered to read them. These include the introduction of characters who are never heard from again; a sinister cabdriver who drives his car off a cliff for reasons never explained; characters forgetting what they previously knew or said; and, curiously, Frank and Joe dressing up as women.

Other than the major problems found in volumes 17 to 21, fans who dissected the Hardy Boys books during the first twenty years of their existence found that they were relatively free of error. Typographical errors were rare, and plot and character discrepancies in the other books were usually relatively minor, according to Crawford. (For example, Fenton Hardy has an elaborate office in his home in most of the books, although he has an office away from his home in two books; in *Footprints under the Window*, size six footprints are found early on, yet it turns out they belong to Fenton Hardy, who is a big man.) About a dozen or so of these errors are found, but none is nearly as severe as the ones in volumes 17 to 21. Some series book researchers credit meticulous syndicate worker Harriet Otis Smith with ensuring that the facts in the books were uniform and error-free. She left the syndicate, however, in late 1930.

The muddy writing, carelessness, and factual problems associated with these five "interim" Hardy Boys books underline how important it was for the series books to be written in a consistent way by an author who cared about his work. Different levels of inventiveness, creativity, and care were displayed by different authors. Les's tight and crisp writing style as "Franklin W. Dixon" contrasts sharply with the flaws of the "weird period" volumes. In his books, every action and bit of dialogue has a connection to what happened before or what comes next, making for seamless writing.

Whether the Stratemeyers were aware at the time of the errors in the books is unknown. It is highly unlikely that Les learned of the problems of these books even as they were published. Almost certainly he never read them. Even when his own Hardy Boys books were published, Les simply took his free copies and put them on his bookshelf without reading them.

In fact, Brian McFarlane in his autobiography describes how he learned purely by accident at the age of ten or eleven of his father's authorship of the Hardy Boys books. He happened to notice them on his father's bookshelves, and asked his father if he had read the books as a boy. The response was startling to Brian. Les not only had read them, he told his son, he had written them. Brian, whose friends at the time had read the series, asked why his father had never told him that before. "I guess it didn't occur to me," he said. Les told his son to keep the information a secret.

* * *

The move to Whitby did not solve all of Les's writing problems. By 1937, he was getting bored and depressed by his writing career—even apart from this work for the Stratemeyer syndicate—and he was starting to slow down. He did not pull punches in his diary. "Had a bad morning trying to get down to write," he wrote on March 20, 1937. "Had no plot in hand, had plenty of orders but didn't know just what to tackle." He noted that he did manage to eke out 1,800 words of a prizefighting story, but continued: "I feel burnt-out and discouraged about this writing game, however. My old vigor seems to have left me. It is all drudgery now and I can't bring myself to even make a beginning of the good work I must do if I am to justify myself. Psychologists explain this procrastination as sheer lack of confidence, fear that one won't make good." Early the next year, things had not changed much. In one entry, he was enormously self-critical, noting with odd irony that he was "heartened" that, after rereading his early fiction, he found it "terrible." Although he is still mediocre, he said, he is, at least, moving forward. He wrote on January 23:

> Read over some of my old pulp stories and they cheered me up a good deal. They were terrible. It seems impossible that I should have been able to make a living from that sort of rot at all. So there has been progress because at least my present pulp stuff is better done. So often I've felt that I have been going back, that I was at my best when writing prodigiously for All-Star and other pulps. Now I can see that I have always been a very mediocre writer and that I am really very

lucky to have sold as much as I have. This makes for a
proper humility and a better perspective.

A year later, he had not emerged completely from this funk. His diary
entries are sad, even on holidays, which usually served to cheer him. In
1938, on New Year's Day, usually a positive time for Les, who had always
counted his blessings at the beginning of a new year, things looked grim.
While noting that he finally had paid his bills on time and had regular
work, "nothing but lowered vigor and flagging inspiration to prevent me
from making a fortune in 1938," he wrote.

On his thirty-sixth birthday in October of that year, Les said that for
the first time, the family had money in the bank—four hundred dollars.
Still, he was uncharacteristically morose:

> My birthday . . . finds me a quiet, dull, respectable small-
> town citizen, with waning ambitions, energies and en-
> thusiasms, making the inevitable compromises but on
> even poorer terms than I expected. Getting very little
> fun out of life, making no new friends, with all novelty
> and excitement apparently behind me rather than
> ahead. Pipe and slippers and radio every evening, three
> healthy, noisy youngsters at the meal table, my work a
> prosaic business of trying to write stories that will be
> even good enough to split up the advertisements in the
> magazines. Held back from writing the novels I planned
> by two things—lack of money, which is a reasonable
> alibi, and perhaps a subconscious fear of failure.

Despite the gloomy tone of the entry, Les is quick to note the birthday
gifts he received as the family had a birthday dinner in a hut under a
cedar tree in their garden: a chocolate cake, cigars, and handkerchiefs.
The evening ended with a treasure hunt for the children, who sought
trinkets Les had hidden in the house. A month later, as he awaited word
about the acceptance of one of his stories, he acknowledged that he was
caught in a vicious cycle: when he was in a negative state of mind, he
could not write, but when he became frustrated at trying to write, he became unhappy: "I am never so wretched as when I am not working and
this was another of those days spent staring at the typewriter," he wrote
on November 17.

By the time he moved to Whitby, Les was able to identify with other writers and appreciate that many of their challenges were the same as his. During this era, his reading increasingly included autobiographies of writers. The advent of radio, with its vast array of programming, opened up new worlds for him regarding interviews and information about authors. In one diary entry, he noted that he had heard Sinclair Lewis on the radio. The timing of that particular radio program was fortuitous because Les had begun thinking again of giving up writing and taking a full-time job with the Postal Service or another government agency. He filled out a civil service form to this end. But he heeded the words of Lewis: "He said writers should 'keep on writing' and pointed out that there isn't very much room in the Hall of Fame. Also that a writer can 'know' places in his imagination. Maybe now that I've come this far along the straight fiction path, I'd be a fool to quit and get onto a sidetrack" (February 28, 1939).

It was in those late years of the 1930s that Les acquired one of his most prized possessions—a letter from F. Scott Fitzgerald. In 1938, Les apparently wrote a letter to Fitzgerald, offering criticism of his work, *Tender Is the Night*, and making reference to some recent articles Fitzgerald had in *Esquire* magazine. A beleaguered but grateful Fitzgerald responded in a scribbled note from Baltimore, echoing the emotions of many writers who do not mind criticism, and are just pleased that someone was reading their work:

> Dear Mr. McFarlane:
>
> There is a 3rd piece to come in Esquire in which the writer emerges somewhat from his abyss. I am glad I wrote the article, or rather the three short articles, not because they furnished any special catharsis but because they evoked such letters as yours from various literary men and women. One of the ghastly aspects of my gloom was a horrible feeling that I wasn't being read. And I'd rather have a sharp criticism of my pet child Tender is the Night such as yours was, than the feeling of pouring out endless words to fall upon as ears as I had had.
>
> I rather think I am done as a writer—maybe not, of course. The fact that I can still write a vivid metaphor or solve a technical problem with some suavity wouldn't be an indicator one way or another.

However time will tell. And in the meanwhile I appreciate the goodness of heart that prompted your letter.

F. Scott Fitzgerald

Les had to be heartened that a writer of Fitzgerald's stature would choose to respond to him—and encouraged that a writer of Fitzgerald's stature would have the same insecurities as he did. In the case of Fitzgerald, time did "tell"—he was to become one of the most widely read and well-known authors of the twentieth century. By 1938, he was a successful writer in the mass-circulation "slicks," particularly the *Saturday Evening Post*. In the 1920s and '30s, he earned more than $100,000 for his magazine work, an amount far greater than that earned by his novels. But even that was not enough for Fitzgerald, a legendary drinker and big spender. Of course, Fitzgerald was not the typical writer of the era, nor was the *Saturday Evening Post* the typical slick magazine. It was the most attractive of all the slick magazines, due in part to its image as highbrow yet readable. As one researcher noted, "To appear regularly in its pages as [an] author . . . was to reach a point of well-paid professional success midway between the syndicates, Sunday newspapers, and pulp magazines on the one hand and the sober literary and intellectual journals on the other." By the time he wrote Les in 1938, Fitzgerald was recuperating from one of his many downward spirals; the letter came shortly after the two-year period that he himself labeled in an essay "The Crackup," when he was deeply in debt, frequently drunk, and suffering writer's block. Fitzgerald, who was six years older than Les, died in 1940 at the age of forty-four, two years after Les received his letter. But Les remained a life-long fan; twenty-five years later, in a letter to his daughter, Norah, he discussed the careers of Fitzgerald and Hemingway, noting that although magazine publishers of the 1930s seemed to prefer Hemingway, by the 1970s, editors of magazines like *Esquire* seemed to understand, finally, that Fitzgerald was the superior writer. Les wrote, "And writing aside I think Fitzgerald the better man, more sensitive, more human, more generous. Hemingway wound up as a vain bitter pompous old drunk playing the role he thought people expected of him. Fitzgerald died still trying although harassed by lack of money and personal worries."

Contributing to Les's flagging spirits by the late 1930s was no doubt Amy's wobbly emotional state. She was not happy in Whitby and a year and a half after the move was not adapting well. Whitby was a far cry from Haileybury, New Liskeard, and the "North Country" in more ways than just distance. Toronto and its surrounding urban area had little in common with the more rural undeveloped north country; the differences in geography, climate, and style of living were profound. Amy's sister Else remembered that when she visited her shortly after the move, Amy seemed very unhappy.

In several diary entries, Les refers briefly to the fact that Amy was increasingly reluctant to leave the house and remained in bed. This was not just worrisome for Les—it was inconvenient, because it meant it was he who was responsible for the daily upkeep of the house and care of the children (although he alludes to the fact that a housekeeper came in occasionally). If Amy was sometimes averse to leaving the house, Les tried to make sure that did not stop her from enjoying herself. On a spring day in 1938, he went to the store to buy ham, bologna, soda pop, and biscuits—"And we all had a picnic on the lawn" (May 31, 1938). Later that year, on a warm Thanksgiving day on October 19, 1938, he wrote in his diary that he was pleased that she walked downtown with a friend: "This is definitely a turn for the better. I have been worried by her lack of confidence in her ability to venture away from the house."

Amy's daughter Norah remembers that her mother's illness hit its peak around the late 1930s or early 1940s, when Amy was bedridden for much of the time. Although she was a little girl during this time and certainly did not understand the nature of depression, Norah remembers that her mother would occasionally say things to her to indicate her misery. Norah recalled specifically one comment from her mother: "You know what you do when you get to the end of your rope? You hang on." The comment was a strange one for a mother to make to a six- or seven-year-old, Norah thought.

Amy's condition deteriorated by 1939, and Les indicated that he felt oddly ill at ease on the first day of that year. As he writes, he was annoyed that he did not go out and have a more spirited celebration of the New Year than he did. "I went to the movies [on New Year's Eve] . . . and enjoyed it very much. We hadn't been asked anywhere, but when I came home I learned that two invitations had been given us while I was out. Welcomed the year, accordingly, by listening to other people having a hell of a good time by radio. I would have liked to go to a real bang-up New Year's Eve party, just once." Still, he writes, Amy prepared a delicious New Year's meal of roast beef and Yorkshire pudding—departing from their traditional New Year's meal of goose or turkey.

Les usually grew sentimental or philosophical around New Year's Day, but he could not muster up the enthusiasm to do so that year. Ironically, he had always thought as a very young man that having a bit of a financial cushion could cure many ills for him and his family. Even though he was finally at a point in his life where he no longer felt the shame of being broke almost constantly, that evidently did not ensure happiness: "A good diarist would fill this page with profound philosophical epigrams, but I'm not up to it," he wrote. "We've been this year out of debt, with a little money in the bank, more comfortable than many, with fewer worries than most. As to happiness, that's relative. If Amy's health were better I suppose we might feel that we may look back upon this someday and feel that we were never happier."

Two days after he wrote that passage, he experienced the shock of the sudden death of his father, John Henry McFarlane, on January 3, 1939. Les immediately packed and traveled alone to Haileybury to help his three brothers who were there make arrangements. His diary entries for the next five or six days show how stunned, confused, and choked up he was by the event. He recorded exactly what he was doing when he heard the news:

> This is a memorable day—sadly memorable. I was working at the radio script at noon, trying to finish the second episode to make tonight's mail when the telephone rang. The telegraph operator read me a message from Frank. Dad died suddenly this morning. It was a crushing, terrific shock. [In another call, Frank told Les that their father had dropped dead while walking home from a friend's house.] Of course, we knew it would come some day and probably very suddenly, but it was difficult to realize that it had actually happened at last. I suppose every man tastes a little from the cup of his own death at such a time.

Les's diary entries for the next few days have a descriptive and almost surreal narrative quality, and he acknowledges the fictional aspects of the activities. Even the train ride home takes on an unreal dimension to him. "I reached the old town at half-past four of a clear frosty Northern night with a bright moon and the mercury at twenty below," he wrote. "Walked down the familiar hill and the familiar street to the familiar house. The crepe hanging beside the door chilled me. It was like a somber exclamation point clinching and emphasizing a terrible fact" (January 4, 1939).

Les's brothers told him that on the day of his death, their father had gone downtown to buy flowers to put by their mother's framed photo— it had been their wedding anniversary. Shortly after he arrived in Haileybury, Les went upstairs to sleep, in his father's bed, and slept until noon. He wrote his father's obituary and an account of his life for the local paper, the *Haileyburian*. Strangely, Les, the creative and versatile writer, was so numb that he could not muster emotion, he wrote in his diary. The newspaper article "was lifeless, stiff, quite without feeling, but perhaps better that way." The next few days were a whirlwind of activity for Les and his three brothers as they planned for the funeral and hosted visitors offering condolences.

The trip to Haileybury for his father's funeral did give Les and his brothers an opportunity to get together. Dick and Graham at this time lived in northern Ontario in the Temiskaming region, and Frank lived in Toronto. Although the four had gone in a variety of directions geographically and vocationally, none had conventional nine-to-five jobs. But, like Les, they did not have the luxury for much of their lives of counting on a regular paycheck. Dick, the only one of Les's brothers who enjoyed writing, was described by Dick's wife as the most like Les in temperament—both were natural storytellers and practical jokers. Dick joined the air force during World War II and was by trade a watchmaker, although prospecting was his first love.

Les was, in fact, the only one of the four McFarlane brothers who did not make money from mining. Frank, also, was in mining exploration, and Graham, the youngest, worked in gold mines. Graham became a radio technician in the early days of radio and then went overseas with the air force. He spent most of his later adult life in the small town of Larder Lake in northern Ontario. Normally, when the brothers met as adults, the four had a raucous time, although this cold day in January of 1939 was naturally a somber time for them. Les also noted that the trip gave him an opportunity to see Graham's new baby, Rebecca.

The church was full of mourners on the day of the funeral, Les noted. As the funeral procession wound through downtown Haileybury, it passed the school where John Henry had been principal for many years. The scene of the flag at half-mast, with the children quietly standing by their desks, deeply moved Les: "I felt the sharpest stabs of emotion I had ever known," he wrote. The burial was on the Haileybury hillside over-looking the city, "where the view of the lake has such grandeur," he wrote.

Les and his brothers were to experience another blow that week of their father's death—one that sounds like a twist out of a Hardy Boys mystery. They discovered that John Henry's only will was one he made in 1934, five years before his death, and the family could find no cash assets. They all believed a more current will was missing, and that their father's assets were in some undisclosed location. They searched his home to no avail. That news was disturbing and unexpected to the McFarlane brothers—and somewhat of a cliché, Les noted in his journal: "To think that only a few days ago I was objecting to use of the 'missing will' idea fictionally as too improbable and hackneyed. Perhaps hackneyed because it is not uncommon at all" (January 7). After he returned to Whitby a day or so later, the plot thickened: Amy told Les that his father, fearful of losing his assets in case a war broke out, told her the previous summer that he was selling many of his belongings and converting them into cash. Les called his brothers to tell them of this, but apparently nothing came of it. All his brothers found in the next few weeks was six hundred dollars' worth of power company bonds in a safe deposit box. It dawned on the brothers that the cost of the funeral and related expanses could eat up what little was left. Dick McFarlane and his family moved into his father's home.

Even after he returned to Haileybury after the funeral, the death of his father dogged Les beyond the complications of the estate—he had trouble returning to work immediately because he took the responsibility of arranging for the thank-you cards, acknowledgments of gifts, and other matters associated with the funeral and burial. And he could not help but think about his father: "At half past eleven this morning, while working at the short story I glanced at my watch and realized that it was exactly two weeks to the minute from the time of Dad's passing," he wrote on January 17. "There is such a feeling of emptiness and loss."

11

. . . .

NEW OPPORTUNITIES

The McFarlanes' move to Whitby changed their lives in more ways than they could have imagined. In Les's case, it allowed him to travel frequently to Toronto, thirty miles west of Whitby. Proximity to Toronto, the main center of Canada's literary and publishing scene, allowed him to meet frequently with editors and radio programming officials and to network with others in his field. His new location also gave him easy access to the United States, particularly New York City.

The geographic location of their new home opened up doors for the McFarlane children as well. Brian, who started playing hockey at a young age, could now go to professional hockey games as well. All the children enjoyed proximity to libraries, schools, and more social and cultural resources than were available in small, isolated Haileybury.

The only one in the family who did not seem to benefit from the move was Amy, whose depression was deepening as the 1930s ended and the 1940s began. Les did not write about it at length in his diaries, although he expressed concern in many passages and hope whenever it appeared that she might be breaking out of her illness. In one entry (January 20, 1940), he referred to her breakdown bluntly as "the crack-up," a term he had never used before in the diary.

The move to Whitby brought at least one disadvantage for Les. For many of his years in Haileybury, he was able to rent an office outside his home. His "office" in their Whitby home was barely bigger than a closet and had no door—allowing him to hear the antics of his three children when they were home. Brian and Norah remembered years later how their father would hole up with his typewriter in the tiny office in their Whitby home as they and their sister Pat played, did homework, and ran around in the house. As they recall it, however, the noise they generated barely affected their father and his work; indeed, he seemed immune to it. Les, hardly a disciplinarian, rarely if ever mentioned in his diary that he was distracted by his children. Of course, during the school year, they were away much of the day. In the summer, they spent time outside. Nonetheless, in one entry on a cold winter's day, he did say that their presence hurt his concentration. They had been sick with colds, and home for a few days, he wrote. "I have got to do something right away about this place-to-write situation. It is costing me money with every passing day. It isn't the youngsters' fault that they annoy me—they are lively kids and being cooped up is no fun for them—and I feel so ashamed when I get angry at them" (December 3, 1940). If Les did get angry at them, evidently he never let on—his children barely remember his ever losing his temper about anything. When he did, they recall, it was easy to sidetrack him with a joke or antic to get him to smile.

Being able to visit New York more frequently perhaps made him realize what he was had missed by living so far from large metropolitan areas. Les was far from unsophisticated, and his work on newspapers in Canada and the United States had instilled in him a certain worldliness. But he had spent the last ten years working and raising a family in a small town, and a visit to Manhattan in the summer of 1939 was an eye-opening experience that allowed him to witness vital events in America's cultural history. He toured Radio City Music Hall, saw championship boxing at the Polo Grounds, ate at an elaborate Fifth Avenue restaurant courtesy of one of his editors, and visited the 1939 New York World's Fair. He found the latter event an awesome experience that nearly defied description— quite an admission from someone who made his living writing fiction.

The boxing match between Tony Galento and Joe Louis was thrilling despite its brevity. Galento, a New Jersey bartender turned heavyweight boxer, was the underdog from the start, but he stunned his opponent in the first round and knocked him down in the third. The legendary Louis came back in the fourth to win the fight. As Les noted in his diary, the outcome may ultimately have been predictable ("Galento, tubby, baldish, with short pudgy arms, looked like a big turtle against a panther") but the contest was exciting nonetheless (June 28, 1939).

The futuristic World's Fair made a convert out of the skeptical Les, who admitted in his diary that he had not expected to be impressed by it: "It is extraordinary. It is lavish, luxurious, beautiful, gargantuan, etc., etc. and at night the lighting effects are amazing. I could go on throwing adjectives but they express nothing" (July 1, 1939).

By the time the family moved to Whitby, the periodic bouts of writer's block that Les suffered were getting longer. So it was a godsend when *Maclean's* asked him in the summer of 1939 to edit stories in their office full-time for about three months. In addition to getting a change of scenery, he acknowledged that the circumstances worked better than his editing from home, due in part because he became part of the Toronto scene. "It was a better experience this time—perhaps because I was more accustomed to the work and because I caught something of the tempo and spirit of the city by living there." He wrote that the job had taken him out of a rut and given him a new vitality (December 2, 1939).

By the late 1930s, the relatively new medium of radio was becoming a fixture in North American homes, and its popularity gave Les a new outlet for his writing. Advertisers saw it as a way to pipe their message into millions of homes. After all, to listeners, radio was "free" entertainment and provided an outlet to escape their lives of worry and sacrifice. The number of radios in American househoulds was growing at a phenomenal rate, from about one in every two households in 1930 to nearly two in every three households ten years later. By the mid-1930s and 1940s, the Golden Age of Radio had been born; nearly every household in North America had at least one radio, and diversity in progamming exploded. Listeners heard drama, comedies, musicals, variety shows, and news. Canadian National Radio opened its first station in 1927 and soon developed service to about 15 stations. By 1932, the Canadian Broadcasting Act created the Canadian Radio Broadcasting Commission (CRBC), the forerunner to the national Canadian Broadcasting Corporation (CBC). As was the case in the United States, the number of Canadian households with radios took off—by 1937, three-fourths of the nation's diverse and scattered population was able to get radio coverage. By 1939, the CBC reported the war overseas and began special wartime broadcasts.

Radio was a natural form of communication for Les. In addition to his experience as a news reporter, he loved theater and movies, and the new medium was a perfect setting for his gift for narrative and storytelling. For Les, radio had "arrived" at the perfect time. By the late 1930s, he began to write scripts for radio dramas, and, at the beginning of the 1940s, he wrote many plays for the Canadian Theater of the Air, a radio drama program. By the end of the decade he contributed several scripts to an American radio serial *Meet Mr. Meek*.

By 1940, the Stratemeyer Syndicate and the Hardy Boys had receded far into the background of Les's life. He was becoming even more versatile as a writer—in addition to writing radio drama scripts, he had fiction and nonfiction in "slick" magazines; sports stories, mysteries, and adventure tales in pulp magazines and books; children's fiction for the

Stratemeyers; and even some poetry in *Maclean's*. Les had long dabbled in poetry, although much of what he had written was humorous. A holiday poem published in *Maclean's* in 1940, "Canadian Christmas 1940," was far from light. The five-stanza, seventy-seven-line free-verse poem describes the physical beauty of the Canadian winter contrasted against the background of the destruction, fear, and terror of World War II. The magazine devoted an entire page to the poem, publishing it in the center of two narrow drawings—one a gentle outdoor winter scene, and the other a scene of airplanes bombing a village. The poem read, in part:

> Snow falls on our land
> Snow falls in the Rockies and drifts on the prairies,
> Blankets the roofs of the homesteads,
> Frosts the green trees by the Lake of the Woods,
> Skirls white on Superior,
> Falls silent and soft on the woodlands and farmlands. . . . .

Yet the beauty of the season contrasts sharply with the chaos in Europe, he writes.

> Hate's blizzard sweeps Britain.
> Havoc hurtles on London and blasts at the Midlands,
> Pelts screaming and howling on hedgerows in Sussex,
> On city and shire and on village and moor,
> On Edinburgh, Aberdeen, Plymouth and Bristol and
> Dover.
> Murder skims on the Thames, murder whirls in the fog. . . .

He poses the question of whether Christmas of 1940 can be celebrated:

> Can Christmas be happy under the cloud?
> Can a whisper be heard in the tumult of wrath?
> Can truth be heard clearer than falsehood and folly,
> Hatred and spite, bombast and terror,
> Forecast of ruin, threats of chaos and doom,
> News of destruction and tidings of death?
> Can you hear? . . . . . . on earth peace good will toward
> men.

Les closes with what he calls a prayer for Christmas and gives thanks for freedom and family. The poem was probably a true expression of how Les felt as the war broke out in Europe. On a personal level, he noted in his diary that his brothers Dick and Frank had both joined the air force, and ultimately he felt that he should contribute to the war effort. Although Les had no immediate plans in early 1940 to enlist, he changed his mind by that fall, although he was rejected for military service because of his height. (He recalled in his autobiography spending an entire day "naked in a drafty recruiting hall with a dog tag around my neck" before someone told him he was too short to serve. "It was a humiliating experience, from which I gained only a head cold.") His attitude about the war at the time was not so flippant, however, and his concern and fear about it intensified as the year progressed. Although he had always followed current events, Les was apathetic about politics for most of his life and had a distaste for politicians. Until 1939, only rarely did he write in his diary about politicians and their actions, and his daughter Norah said politics was not a topic frequently discussed in the house. The diary passages take a sharp turn in early 1940, when Les writes about the war nearly every day. It is obvious he is fearful—and angry because he feels his fellow Canadians are too complacent about the war and oblivious to its ramifications for them. This fear, combined with his lifelong love of Christmas and of his country, no doubt moved him to write the poem.

Although the editors with whom he worked did not know the depth of his versatility—that is, they did not know that he was Franklin W. Dixon or that he wrote young-adult fiction—they were aware that Les was comfortable with a variety of writing styles. *Maclean's* editor Napier Moore once wrote in an editor's note that readers were continually surprised at the breadth of Les's abilities, and said jokingly that *Maclean's* editors would be only mildly surprised if he submitted an article with a title as esoteric as "How to Play a Harp." Les evidently took that as a challenge. A few days later, the editor wrote in a note, he submitted his story, "How to Play a Harp." It appeared on pages of *Maclean's* in early 1941. The fey piece is a light satire on the many how-to articles that appear in magazines, and it has many of the stylistic elements of humorist James Thurber, who gained fame for his wry satirical essays and books. The piece is a step-by-step, tongue-in-cheek outline for the novice harpist: First, he wrote, the prospective harpist must rid himself of the common myths surrounding harp playing. The first is that harp playing is only for the privileged class: "That is nonsense. Harps are very democratic." Second is the myth that the ability to play it is innate: "'Born to harp,' as the saying is. This is ridiculous. Some harpists' kids are so dumb when they try to learn the harp that it would amaze you." And last, of course, is the long-held theory that one must die and go to heaven before one can take harp playing seriously: "Obviously, this is a mere rumor."

Some of Les's fictional stories for *Maclean's* and other magazines bear a resemblance to Thurber's fiction. The exploits of some earnest but unlucky lovestruck young man—frequently an office worker of some sort, sometimes henpecked by one of the women in his life—were usually at the heart of Les's humorous short stories of this era. Often, the plot is driven by mistaken identities, misunderstood actions and missed opportunities. But it always ends happily, usually with the bumbling hero getting the girl. Thurber joined the *Saturday Evening Post* as a reporter in 1929, and became a staff member of the *New Yorker* shortly thereafter. He is best known for his wry commentary on daily life, usually featuring a male protagonist to make his point. His short essays were compiled into several books in the 1930s, 1940s, and 1950s. It is unknown, however, if Les took inspiration from the work of Thurber. He is not mentioned in the diaries, nor have Les's children mentioned Thurber as an influence on their father.

A classic example of one of Les's Thurberesque short stories is "The Cat Called Claudius," published by *Maclean's* in 1942. The title character of the story is a strong-willed runaway cat whose escape fuels the tangled plot. Animals were key players in much of Thurber's writing as well as in his comic drawings and cartoons, although they did not often play key roles in Les's fiction. But according to his diaries, animals were frequently members of the McFarlane household. When he and Amy were newlyweds, the diary written in Amy's voice periodically bemoans the fact that they missed their cat, Bozo, after they moved to Quebec, and how happy they were see her again when they visited Haileybury. Les alludes to the various family dogs and cats in his diaries and letters, and he clearly had affection for them. A short young-adult book he wrote much later in his life, *Padgett's Pooch*, tells the story of two children, a hockey team, and a runaway dog. Not surprisingly, it was written at a time when he owned a dog named Pooch.

Although it could be compared loosely to Thurber's work, "The Cat Called Claudius" was in many ways classic Leslie McFarlane, with its plot twists and Dickensian character names. The story starts as the lovestruck Horace Lumkin sits dejectedly in a city-bound train for a hastily called meeting with his boss in the home office. Lumkin, a washing-machine salesman (who, coincidentally, had been rejected for military service because of his height), has just been given the gate by his girlfriend, Elsie Shackleby, and he expects to be fired by his boss. He sits next to a stout bonnet-clad women who is carrying a big basket awkwardly on her lap, which she asks Harold to hold temporarily until she gets downtown. The chivalrous Harold agrees.

Of course, as the reader soon learns, the basket holds a temperamental runaway black cat, Claudius, who was the beloved pet of famous movie star Sonya Monyona. The stout woman had found the cat and was on her way to return it to Miss Monyona, who was staying in a downtown hotel, awaiting Claudius's return. The successful return of the cat would reap several benefits for the train traveler: she would get to meet the movie actress and earn a handsome reward.

Needless to say, in the rush of the crowd, Horace loses the bonnet-clad traveler, but is stuck with Claudius. He has an idea, though: he realizes his beloved Elsie would think him clever and lovable again if circumstances allowed Horace to introduce her to the famed Sonya Monyona.

Plans are never simple for McFarlane protagonists, and the course of true love never runs smoothly for them. Claudius is lost yet again, several more runaway cats enter the scene, and the lobby of a fashionable downtown hotel is ultimately thrown into chaos. By the end of it all, though, Claudius is returned to his rightful owner and Horace gets a promotion. And, of course, the lovely Elsie is back in his arms.

***

Les's career, and to some degree, his personal life, hit a slump in 1940. His magazine and radio sales for that year totaled $1,765, down by $1,085 from the previous year. His sales income totaled $3,072 in 1936, remained stable at $3,080 in 1937, and dropped to $2,402 in 1938. Little mention is made of money shortages in his diaries in 1940, although the passages once again indicate an anxiety on his part regarding the mail. As a novice full-time writer, he had often recorded in his diary the ordeal of waiting for the mail each day and the disappointment he experienced when expected payments did not come, or when he did not hear whether a story had been purchased. These frustrations regarding payment by mail resurfaced again in a limited way in the early 1940s, although it is evident that perhaps Les had bigger worries during this era.

Throughout much of 1940, he suffered a near-paralyzing writer's block that demoralized and nearly incapacitated him; also that year, he became very concerned about the war effort overseas and grew extremely worried about the ramifications of the war for North America. And Amy had her ups and downs—she was still ill after a breakdown, but was able to conduct some normal family activities, such as taking the children to church, celebrating holidays, and even going for a long summer vacation with the family to northern Ontario. Despite their illnesses, Les and Amy seemed to be able to keep their household running smoothly. With very few exceptions, birthdays and holidays were always celebrated with all the trimmings and the children were always well cared for. On one occasion, Les noted in his diary that because of Amy's condition, they had to cancel plans for an eleventh birthday party for Pat, who, he notes, took the disappointment well. Even so, Les, Brian, and Norah dutifully trooped to the store to buy gifts for Pat (February 16). Although they were very young when their parents had their most severe problems, neither Brian nor Norah remembers their lives being seriously disrupted and both recall having a very happy "normal" childhood. "If we were destitute, or close to it, at times, the McFarlane kids never knew it," Brian wrote in his autobiography. "Every day was a happy one. We were rich in friends, blessed with the natural wonders around us and given the freedom to enjoy whatever small-town life thrust in our paths."

But life was particularly tough for Les during those early months of 1940. The weather that year in Toronto was brutally cold, and all three children suffered from a variety of ailments from colds to chickenpox. Although he frequently suffered from writer's block, the bouts were usually short and he was usually able to make up for lost time. This time, however, the attack was pernicious and he was nearly paralyzed for months, even failing to write in his diary for several months at a time. Some of his diary entries give a clear indication of the depth of his troubles. Early in January, he felt so poorly he went to see his doctor, who recommended more exercise.

As the months wore on, he failed to improve. For several days in late January, Les simply stayed in bed. Although he did a limited amount of work, his idleness made him even more tired mentally. For the ambitious and tireless writer who could once pen magazine mysteries in a matter of days, the act of planning an upcoming Rotary Club speech was exhausting: "I got up today and went down for the mail. There wasn't any," he wrote on January 23. "Tried to do some work on the talk for the

Rotary Club next week but couldn't do much. After this I think I'll turn down all these speech bids. Too much trouble and no return for it. An idle day and consequently very tiresome." A week later: "Still loafing, which is as hard as working" (January 30).

The seriousness of Les's condition is indicated by the diary passages that show an actual physical aversion to writing: "Didn't go back to work after all," he wrote on January 29. "Tried it but the very sight of the typewriter made me ill." He did note, though, that he had the energy to flood part of the backyard for an ice rink for the children. As usual, his apathy and fatigue did not extend to the children. References to them abound during this debilitating period: A party complete with gifts for Norah's seventh birthday ("The darling had a grand time!"), pride over the report cards of all three of them (April 4), preparations for a big family Easter egg hunt (March 24), and happiness that friends were taking Brian to Toronto to see his first professional hockey game (March 8).

Despite the comfort he may have derived from his family, Les's slump had not improved by late March, and he returned to blaming his sobriety: "I'm really worried by this long slump," he wrote. "My plot sense seems to have deserted me; the very idea of writing is revolting. I'm stale, stale, stale and burnt out. . . . This has been coming for a long time. Actually I haven't had any imaginative power since I quit drinking" (March 25). Things had not changed six months later: "I woke up this morning at dawn with a conviction that as a writer I am through, burnt out. That I have never been a writer at all. It seems so extraordinary that I can't write a page any more without having to go back and rewrite and rewrite until the thing solidifies in my hands and goes dead" (September 11).

Still, Les was far from completely dysfunctional professionally. He began working on a radio version of his award-winning short story, "The Root-House," and he was working on drama scripts for the Canadian Theater of the Air series. By the summer, things improved temporarily, due to a change in scenery which may have helped Amy's condition, also. The family went to Les's father's old house in Haileybury and then on to a camping vacation at a lake. (A "wretched" month in Haileybury, but a "grand" two weeks at the camp, he wrote.) The vacation did wonders for the family: Pat and Brian learned to swim, and Amy's health improved (August 24). His optimism was short lived, however, after he returned to his typewriter at the end of August: "I muddled away at the story, inching toward the end. Like putting a jigsaw puzzle together. Mechanical, lifeless work" (August 30).

The usually apolitical Les seemed deeply affected by the news of the war—a war that certainly transcended politics. As a young man with a family, Les seemed to disdain the current Canadian government in Ottawa, and noted in 1940 that while he and Amy went to vote, theirs was more a protest vote against the current administration than a vote that would have any effect on the results. And he was right—the incumbents won by a landslide (March 26).

But the war in Europe was far more worrisome to Les than what he believed was a flabby and sometimes inept Canadian government. Despite an admiration for Winston Churchill—and for his eloquent and moving speeches during the war—Les grew more and more morose as the year progressed and the war wore on. He became increasingly irritated with his countrymen, who he believed did not understand the gravity of the situation—a mindset, he believed, they absorbed from Canadian national leadership. Les was part of a local war-relief committee that met periodically, and he found the activity an exercise in frustration. He realized the group could not actually achieve anything that would make a global difference, and he became annoyed with what he felt was the provincial attitude of many of its members. Listening to and reading the news made him even more agitated. He had not written a single diary passage in May and much of April of 1940; by early June, Les had little to say in the diary outside of current events. In those two months, "there have been tremendous historical changes and we have lived through weeks of nerve-wracking anxiety," he wrote. Indeed, much had happened, but none of it was good. "Norway has been invaded, Denmark taken, Holland and Belgium conquered, the British army has been squeezed out of Northern France" (June 5). Within two weeks, he was lamenting the fall of Paris ("Another black day in the news. Paris has fallen. German flags flying over Versailles"); within another week, "it seems to me that the odds against England are so overwhelming that she will be crushed." At this point, Les predicted Canada would soon begin feeling direct effects of the war either physically or, at the least, economically (June 20).

By September, the usually optimistic Les was far from sanguine about the war: "First anniversary of the war. And only to this journal would I admit my feelings that the best we can hope [for] is a stalemate" (September 1). The live nature of radio brought the war home more intensely than newspapers ever could. Within a week, he noted that although little news was coming through to North America, he could hear the explosions in London over a BBC broadcast. It made him so bitter and vengeful that he wished for the destruction of an entire nation: "The bombing of London continues," he wrote on September 8. "There is something fantastic and unreal about it, as when one comes on a stock dramatic situation in real life. The thing belongs in 'Chums' or H. G. Wells—not in the newspapers of the day. Apparently it is tremendous, deliberate . . . destruction on the heart of the Empire, too sickening to bear thinking about while it is going on. May God eternally damn the German people and may we obliterate them from the face of the earth!" The next day, he writes about enlisting: "The terrible news continues, becomes more terrible. We do not talk about it. I go downtown and scarcely hear it mentioned in the streets. But not because of indifference. I tried to work but got little done. I think I shall enlist, if they'll have me, if I could do anything!" (September 9). Of course, he could not enlist, although within a few years Les would find a way to contribute to the war effort. His feelings about the war no doubt contributed to his writer's block that year, although much of his inaction, as he said, probably stemmed from spending too many years writing too many stories at a breakneck pace.

Despite his frustrations over this extended period of writer's block, his concern about the war, and his worries about Amy, Christmas of 1940 did brighten Les's spirits. The holiday drove home to him his versatility and the fact that his talent might be useful for the growing medium of radio, and he and his family had the exciting experience of listening to his poem being read on the radio. A reference in a diary entry indicates that his poem, "A Canadian Christmas 1940," was picked up and read—although in a greatly edited version—over the CBC. As a result of that, a radio station based in Hamilton, Ontario, apparently wanted the poem for broadcast, in its original, longer version (December 27). More important, however, was the pleasure Les derived from celebrating Christmas with his children. In his diary, he reviews at length the gifts the family received (soldiers and a toboggan for Brian; a bicycle for Pat; books and games for Norah; a skirt, sweater, and jacket for Amy). Les received socks and tobacco, as well as his favorite kind of gift, a book. This year it was Ernest Hemingway's *For Whom the Bell Tolls*. Les started reading the book immediately and offered commentary the next day in his diary: "A very clear book and very sincere," he wrote. "And yet somehow a pathological taint seems evident in all Hemingway's work, a preoccupation with virility. . . . It is a very good book, though, with strength and depth. But no magic."

The family ended its Christmas celebration that evening by listening to "A Canadian Christmas 1940" on the radio, and the poet offered his own commentary in his diary. "Very drastically cut but beautifully delivered," he wrote.

12

. . . .

DIRECTING THE PICTURE

By 1941, Les's career was heading in a new direction—he was writing radio scripts almost exclusively and by 1942 he took the full-time job that he had been pondering halfheartedly since he began his career as a free-lance writer. The year 1941 was also unusual in that it was the first full year that he did not keep a diary. This lack of personal communication speaks to the burden of his work, but that was no excuse for Les, and by New Year's Day of 1942, he chastised himself and resumed his diary entries. He bemoaned the fact that the missing diary would leave a gap on the shelf of beloved journals that he had kept since 1929. "I regret that missing book. . . . I'll try to re-establish the journal habit," he wrote. He blamed the missing diary year in part on his cramped writing quarters at home. Evidently, like most writers, he needed a comfortable place in which to write—a room of his own, as it were. But he seemed ashamed to admit even in his diary that the commotion sometimes caused by his three energetic children interfered with the concentration he needed to write.

Les summed up the entire year of 1941 in a brief "1941 memorandum" section at the beginning of his 1942 diary, and it is interesting to see what he selected to record about the year. Most of it is positive. He noted that he began writing for the network program *Canadian Theatre of the Air* by revamping a story called "Dunkel from Dunkelbury" he had published in *Maclean's*, "and it clicked." As a result, the show's producers asked for more scripts, until, Les noted, he became an established scriptwriter in the eyes of the New York agency that produced the show.

As they had for several years, the McFarlanes spent summers at a cottage at a beach called Seabreeze in northern Ontario. That year, the family had an idyllic summer that Les believed would live on in the memories of his children. He was able to spend time with his children and write there, and he also sensed an improvement in Amy's condition that summer. In Les's eyes—at least as he recalled it optimistically at the end of the year—the only sour note of the year was the death of the family's beloved collie, Tony.

As was the case much of his adult life, however, the good times were short lived, according to passages from the first part of 1942. Still, as recordings of feelings and emotions, Les's diary passages might not always reflect the reality of the times. He was usually upbeat and optimistic by the end of the year, perhaps choosing to forget some of the bad times of the year, but frequently morose and dark during the first few months of the new year. By early 1942, the medium of radio—and, ironically, the war—breathed new life into Les's career, but money problems began to dog the family once again. And, as before, financial uncertainty was the source of particular anxiety for Amy and triggered feelings of inadequacy in Les. He continued to ponder the reasons for his near-paralyzing bouts of writer's block. But this time, he wrote in his diary, he feared they could be based on a subconscious fear of failure. On the third day of the year of 1942, he was at his typewriter struggling with scripts for the American radio show *Meet Mr. Meek,* realizing that his entry into radio could mean a major advancement in his career. But negative feelings of *déjà vu* prevailed. "This may really be a big opportunity and yet, as has happened so often in the past, it finds me written out, tired or frozen by a sort of stage fright."

On a subzero February day in 1942, when the rent was paid and more money was on its way, the specter of bad times still prevailed. "There was no mail and I'm in another of those damned terrible periods that I've sworn a hundred times would never happen again," he wrote on February 2. "Not a copper in my pockets." He was frank in his diary when describing how the thought of poverty darkened the household. "These times do terrible things to my confidence and self-respect. It's so degrading and humiliating, the atmosphere around the house is so full of reproach and gloom that I can't concentrate on work for an hour at a time." The prospect of Norah's birthday in the next few days—usually a happy event for him—did little to brighten his mood. "Birthdays are a jinx on this household," he wrote the next day. " I don't think we've ever had a spare dollar to celebrate a birthday." Actually, the children's birthdays were usually cause for celebration and cheer in the house, although Les's state of mind was so low now that he evidently forgot this. The war, too, still had him shaken: "Tonight's headlines are all bad, retreat in Libya, bombing of Singapore . . . retreat, retreat, retreat until we're sick of the word and pray for one honest attack that could even be rated a third-degree victory."

Les and Amy tried hard to shield their children from their problems. Les feared that his children would absorb a negative atmosphere in the house: "As the children grow older, the one thing I try to do, to shield them from any feeling of insecurity, is beyond me now for they know; they feel it in the air" (February 2, 1942).

Les's relationship with his children was always a warm and loving one, and it remained so throughout his life. In addition to routinely noting in his diary their birthdays and their social and scholastic activities, he periodically commented on their personalities and talents—always in a positive way. And in rare personal notes to both Edward Stratemeyer and, later, his daughter Harriet, Les proudly told them about his children.

In Brian, he saw a cheerful, athletic, and enthusiastic child who was devoted to sports and to his sisters; in Norah, a budding writer who continually surprised him with her creativity and intellect. His relationship with Pat, however, was slightly more problematic. Les was proud of her artistic ability and her beauty. As she grew older, though, Pat could be temperamental and argumentative, qualities that may have been triggered by insecurity she felt because she married young and did not go to college, and thus felt that she had disappointed her parents. Her tempestuous nature was of course at odds with that of her mild-mannered father, who disliked confrontation and usually worked hard to avoid it. Yet letters between Pat and her father over the years show that they had a deep love and affection for each other.

By the time he was eleven or twelve, Brian was already a gifted athlete, and he was old enough to become a sophisticated sports fan. As he noted in his own autobiography, he was on ice skates by the time he was four and played hockey in makeshift arenas in Whitby when he was only a few years older, oblivious to the often-brutal weather and occasional injuries. His father was an extremely knowledgeable and avid fan of a variety of sports, particularly hockey and baseball. Brian was in awe of his father's knowledge of sports, and he remembers very clearly going to professional hockey games with him.

Norah, too, has vivid memories of her father's discussions with her as a little girl about writing and getting published. A successful author of young-adult fiction as an adult, she recalled that her introduction to the Whitby Public Library came at a very young age. Limited by a rule that allowed her to borrow only three books at a time, she would borrow the books, run home and read them that day, and return the next day to get more. Equally vivid was her father's graphic example of the power of print; little Norah would write stories in pencil, and her father would type them up on his old Underwood to show her firsthand the magic of the printed word. And then he would urge her to consider markets that would buy her creations. Occasionally, she did sell them—indeed, she was a prodigy of sorts. At the age of eight, she had two poems published in *Maclean's*. "Sometimes they [her works] would be published and often they wouldn't be," she said. "But I remember how exciting it was when I received a dollar—or a couple of dollars—for what I had put to paper." Even more important, she believes, were early lessons taught to her by her father: that rejection is a part of life for all writers and it should not be taken personally, and that a talented storyteller can make the most mundane events come alive on the written page. As was the case with Brian, Les's encouragement paid off for her even more as she grew older. At age sixteen, she won five hundred dollars in a short-story contest sponsored by *Seventeen* magazine for "Time of Casting Stone," which tells the thoughts of an unpopular girl who goes to a dance with a boy she does not like.

Some of Les's comments about his children were eerily prescient. For instance, after he walked downtown with the twelve-year-old Brian, Les described the pleasant trip in his diary: "A grand youngster, Brian, very cheerful, friendly, ingratiating with the sort of personality that will carry him a long way and help him over a lot of rough places. And with an odd small boy dignity that you have to respect" (January 6). In his own memoir, Brian McFarlane writes at length about the challenges of navigating the tough and competitive world of sports broadcasting—a feat no doubt that required much mental and emotional agility.

In 1944, in an uncharacteristically intimate letter to Harriet Stratemeyer Adams, Les described his family in detail. His relationship with Adams had always been cordial, but was strictly business. The letter was sent after he and Adams came to terms about the fee for *A Short Wave Mystery*, the twenty-fourth of the Hardy Boys series, and was evidently prompted by Les's realization that he had by this time worked for the syndicate for eighteen years. In a burst of sentimentality, he described to Adams the warm note her father had written him in 1929 to congratulate him on the birth of his first child, Pat, and seemed to feel compelled to tell Adams more about his family: "It does seem strange that . . . I haven't told you very much about the McFarlane family," he wrote.

> We have three children; Patricia, just turned 15, in second grade at High School. Patricia is rather dazzling in looks and will probably shatter a few hearts; then we

have Brian, age 12, a good-looking, good-natured ras-
cal who seems to have the ability to get along well with
everyone, who spends his winters with a hockey stick in
his hand and his summers in a bathing suit or on a
baseball diamond and managed to do pretty well at
school without any visible attention to homework. Then
there is Norah, who is 10 and was born with more personality than anyone has a right to have. She is about
the size of a minute and twenty seconds, with an elfin
face and an imagination completely out of this world.
Norah has an ear—the most precious asset in a writer—
and I'll lay bets with anyone living that she will eventually be the finest writer in Canada. It has been a bit of a
problem to restrain myself in guidance of Norah but
her writing gift is so spontaneous, so natural, that I'm
afraid to risk cramping her style by any sort of instruction at all. Right now she is a much better writer than
her father will ever be. At present she specializes in poetry, writes herself a poem every day or whenever a subject occurs to her.

Les told Adams that he was sending along some examples of Norah's poetry, including one called "Heaven" that she wrote when one of her
friends from school died. "She turns instinctively to writing for release
when anything worries or puzzles her," he added.

As for Amy, he continued, "she's one of those grand people you meet
about once in a hundred years, serene, lovely, neat, marvellous housekeeper, with a sense of humor. She needs it. We're a very happy family
and I am a very lucky guy."

Surprisingly, the staid Adams responded with a personal note of her
own in an uncharacteristic spurt of familial pride. A dam seemed to
break in Adams, who rarely if ever gave interviews and offered little personal information even to her college alumni magazine. Adams, it
seems, had been touched dramatically by the war and told Les that she
wished her family story was "as happy as yours." Tragically, the oldest of
her four children, a naval aviator, was killed in the war, she wrote, and
another of her sons, who was eighteen, had just joined the navy and was
stationed at Pearl Harbor (in 1944, after the attack there). The son,
named Edward after her father, "is six feet, two inches tall, and very

blond. According to his sisters, he is 'smooth,'" she wrote. She continued at length and with pride about her other children, a brunette daughter who bore a strong resemblance to actress Margaret Sullavan and a platinum blonde who had been a dancer before she married a navy ensign. She even confided to Les that the Margaret Sullavan lookalike was doing "secret" work for the navy. Her husband, she noted at the end, was "in stocks and bonds" and considered one of the top authorities in New Jersey on municipal bonds.

The response from the usually reserved Adams was no doubt surprising to Les, although his enthusiasm and pride about his career and family had also struck a chord with Edward Stratemeyer, and their relationship, too, transcended pure business. It was without question the warmest exchange between Les and Adams, although it came very near the end of Les's relationship with the syndicate.

During the first seven years of the 1940s, the war took a toll on syndicate activities, as it did on many European and North American businesses. Chlorine, used in paper making, was rationed, and metal, used as plates for printing, was in short supply. The syndicate by 1941 was publishing only its most successful series: Nancy Drew, the Hardy Boys, Honey Bunch and Norman, and the Bobbsey Twins. By the late 1940s—shortly after Les wrote his last book for the syndicate—it would enter a new phase. Edna Stratemeyer had married by this time and became Edna Squier; she and her new husband moved to Florida and she became an inactive partner in the syndicate. At least two of the Stratemeyer series would become ingrained in North American culture even further by the end of the 1940s, though. Four movies with teenage sleuth Nancy Drew came out in 1938 and 1939, and beginning in 1949, twelve movies based on the Bomba the Jungle Boy series were released in three years. Three of the four Nancy Drew films, which starred actress Bonita Granville, were not based directly on individual series books. They were titled *Nancy Drew, Detective; Nancy Drew, Reporter;* and *Nancy Drew, Troubleshooter.* A fourth, *Nancy Drew and the Hidden Staircase,* bore the same title as the second book in the series. These would be the first in a long series of film, television, and other adaptations of Stratemeyer series.

By 1948, Harriet Adams gained a new writer and editor who would be a key player in the syndicate for nearly thirty years—Andrew Svenson. Svenson would help Harriet Adams bring the syndicate into the "modern" age of the 1960s and 1970s, and, among other duties, would write many of the Hardy Boys books after Les. He became a partner in the syndicate in 1961.

In 1942, Les had just completed *The Flickering Torch Mystery,* his first Hardy Boys book in about five years. Correspondence between Les and the syndicate indicates that he drove a hard bargain before agreeing to write the book. He initially asked for $200, and Adams offered $125, but Les said he would compromise and write the book for $165, with a $75 advance.

When he finished *The Flickering Torch Mystery,* Les tried his hand at one more series: the X Bar X Boys series, a western adventure/mystery series that had been in existence since 1926. Grosset & Dunlap, the publisher, described the series as "Thrilling tales of the great west told primarily for boys but which will be read by all who love mystery, rapid action, and adventures in the great open spaces." The books featured Roy and Teddy Manley, the sons of a rancher. They are experts in riding and shooting and, like other Stratemeyer adventure heroes, are particularly adept at getting in and out of jams.

Based on letters between Les and the syndicate, it is unclear why he took the job as X Bar X Boys author James Cody Ferris, although he decided to do so around the Christmas season of 1942 and might have needed the money. Adams sent him an advance for the book, but after he wrote the first eight chapters of the *X Bar X Boys with the Border Patrol,* he asked for the balance of payment. It was not unusual for Les to ask for advances, but it was odd that he would seek the balance of payment before the book was completed. Even stranger, though, was the manner in which he asked for the remainder of the fee. He apparently wrote the letter as James Cody Ferris himself, complete with Texas drawl: "When you were so gracious to send me an advance on this book unasked I *shore* feel *it ain't right mannerly* for me to come *sashayin' up* for more but *dog-gone it, ma'am,* the foreman just broke me the sad news *we don't get no paycheck* before Christmas this year. And *me plannin' to ride out to the depot next week* and go train-*ridin' back home to see my Lulu Belle and the young 'uns. I'm plumb upset"* (emphasis added). At the end of the letter, he abandons the dialect, telling Adams that "I haven't taken to wearing a ten-gallon hat yet." The letter is uncharacteristically familiar, perhaps even overly familiar, although by this time Les had worked with Harriet Adams for nearly twelve years. Whether Les got the second advance or not is unknown, although he did ultimately get paid for his work on the book. He never officially "became" James Cody Ferris, however. The series was abruptly discontinued and *X Bar X Boys with the Border Patrol* was never published.

***

By mid-1942, writing for radio was becoming a major source of Les's income, and the diary passages begin referring to the challenges of translating short stories to scripts and the difficulties of creating characters and dialogue that would "fit" radio. As he worked on a script early in 1942, the writing suddenly clicked. "Got an opening scene that finally seems like real radio," he wrote. "I'm gradually catching onto this medium, I hope" (January 16). As he listened carefully to the finished product, Les realized that the cadences and production of the spoken words differed from that of written dialogue and text, a phenomenon that helped and hurt him. At times, he assumed he could easily convert a magazine story to a script, and other times he found the conversion was not as easy as it seemed. The result, though, was often surprising. "I thought the [Mr. Meeks] show would be terrible," he wrote about one script. "But it played beautifully and smoothly with all kinds of kick" (January 30).

Les was not alone in his discovery that writing for the medium of radio was a matter of trial and error. Not only was this a new art form, it was one that allowed an unheard-of diversity in programming. In his book *Great American Broadcast,* Leonard Maltin describes the phenomenal influence of radio in bringing a variety of art and entertainment forms into the living rooms of homes all over the United States. "Radio made this country smaller, and smarter," he writes. "It brought the finest dramatic and musical performances to the farmhouses of Iowa and the Kansas Plains." And, of course, to the wilderness and cities of Canada.

The medium of radio was in many ways ideal for a versatile storyteller like Les, and its growth could not have come at a better time. Not only did magazine markets dry up at the start of the Depression, but he was getting, as he noted so many times in his diary, "burnt out" as a writer of magazine fiction. Radio mysteries and light comedies—his specialties— were in demand. Maltin quotes a 1932 essay describing the requirements for aspiring radio writers: "The radio audience for detective and mystery fiction wants stories dramatized—not read, to them. You have to translate thinking into action." Such dramatization was an art. An effective writer could convey the action without relying heavily on narrative crutches such as dialogue that describes the events to the audience.

Despite the many changes in Les's life in 1942, the war was still foremost on his mind, and Les was disappointed that he could do little more for the war effort than join a community war-relief committee. So it is not surprising that, ultimately, he contacted Canada's Department of Munitions and Supply in Ottawa and began a government job as speechwriter in its public relations department. Although he had to abandon the autonomy he had as a freelance writer, he was well suited for the job, and he enjoyed it. Les had plenty of experience writing for a variety of media, and, perhaps more important, he felt he could indirectly contribute to the war effort through the job. He moved from Whitby to Ottawa in February 1942 while his family remained in Whitby for at least a year or so. (It appears from his diary that Les moved to Ottawa early in 1942 and that the family followed in 1943, although Norah Perez recalls that it was a full two years before she and her family moved to Ottawa.)

The sudden move to Ottawa and the new job meant an end to his magazine writing career. His extensive traveling also made it difficult to keep his diary on a consistent basis, although he kept it sporadically from 1944 to 1951. His belief in the importance of a diary endured, though, and as always he still took pains to buy diaries each year that were uniform in appearance. At the beginning of 1946, he wrote his first entry a week into the new year because he had trouble finding a volume to match the previous year's copy. He continued to chastise himself for his mundane entries: "I have never been satisfied with these journals—they are very prosaic, mere records of unimportant data, bits of family trivia, but the diary in the grand manner is probably beyond me, like a good many other things" (entered as January 1, 1946). But the journal clearly fulfilled needs in Les and it would be years before he abandoned it completely. It satisfied the need to record his thoughts and emotions, and fulfilled the strongest need of all—to write. In addition to leaving a record for posterity, the journals obviously provided an important outlet of expression for him. His need to express his personal thoughts and activities later manifested itself in the form of letters to his wife and children. As his family grew up and left home and as he grew older, he would write hundreds of such letters.

***

In 1943, Amy, Pat, Brian, and Norah moved to a rented home on 8 Christie Street in Ottawa, where they would live for twelve years. In a letter to Amy before the move, Les mentions hesitantly that it would be cost-effective for the family to live with his Aunt Eva and her son, Barnett. The arrangement, he wrote, would cost them only $100 a month, and with three bedrooms would still allow enough room for the family. Further, he added, the home was near schools for the children and shopping for her. Les may have realized that his wife would not be thrilled at the prospect of sharing a home with another family, a distressing thought because he did try hard to please her. He ended the letter to her half-jokingly: "By for now, darling. I know I'm just a husband and not a very likeable or successful one at that, but even if you don't care a hell of a lot for me and think I'm a heel, for what it's worth you have, All my love, Les." Evidently, the cramped conditions didn't cramp the style of Pat, Brian, and Norah, who by this time were fourteen, twelve, and ten. The Christie Street house would be the family home that the children remembered most vividly, and the one they considered their childhood home. Norah and Brian remember a happy childhood in Ottawa, but one in which their father was frequently absent. Being on the road many weeks of the year was a major lifestyle change for Les after his years as a stay-at-home freelance writer. Still, despite missing his family when he was gone, Les enjoyed the travel. For the first time in many years, he worked for an immediate supervisor, but, strangely, his job would ultimately give him the freedom to be his own boss. And although he always believed that an office job could be stifling, he may have found his jobs over the next ten years less stressful and even easier than what he was accustomed to. The outgoing Les did not mind the socializing that came with the job. In one passage in his diary, he described how he finished a speech with little trouble. "An easy morning at the office," he wrote. "Did my passage of Shril's speech and hit on a couple of happy phrases that pleased Thomson." Afterward, he notes, he had a pleasant lunch with three other men in the office.

Les's work in speechwriting for the Department of Munitions and Supply lasted only a short time before leading to bigger and better things. Because of the hectic pace of his life at this time, his diary was nearly untouched in 1943, so it is difficult to gauge his feelings about this new job and lifestyle.

The move to Ottawa benefited Amy greatly. Her condition gradually improved in the early 1940s, due in part to the fact that she liked Ottawa and felt more at home there than she ever had in Whitby. The people, climate, and overall atmosphere of the city were more similar to those of New Liskeard, where she grew up. Also, by the time she moved to Ottawa, her three children were getting older and required less daily care and her husband had a steady paycheck for the first time in their marriage.

Les's affection for Canada made traveling throughout the country a pleasure. At times his travels would stir memories, as was the case when he was heading from Ottawa toward Montreal by train and passed the home he and Amy had rented when they were first married. The sight touched him, and he wrote about it in his diary, although the ultimate meaning of the passage is unclear: "I saw the long straight road on which Amy and I began our journey," he wrote metaphorically. "A small car was scurrying toward the lake in a dust cloud. At St. Ann's the bridge where we used to walk on Sundays, a fleeting glimpse of the little house where we lived 15 years ago. So many memories. My great regret is that I clouded them so at the time" (Monday, 1943, undated).

In his autobiography, Brian recalled that although the McFarlane home in Ottawa was crowded, to him its proximity to a park and a hockey and skating rink compensated for its shortcomings. It was here that he first met serious competition as a skater and hockey player— there were as many as three games in progress at any time, he wrote. The competition made him a better player. (He noted that one boy with whom he played, Larry Regan, went on to play for the Boston Bruins and became an NHL rookie of the year.) In 1943, twelve-year-old Brian was on the airwaves for the first time. Like his father when he was a boy, Brian won a citywide essay contest. Part of the prize was the opportunity to read his essay about growing up in Ottawa over the radio.

***

Les's resourcefulness and his willingness to bend with the times led to one of the pivotal events in his life: a position with the newly formed National Film Board of Canada, a documentary-making arm of the Canadian government. The new job would change the direction of Les's life and open doors for him for many years to come. The National Film Board (NFB), formed in 1939 by the Canadian National Film Act, was initially designed to supervise government film and distribution in Canada. As noted by historian Bruce Taylor, the board produced primarily newsreels during World War II, believing these provided the best and most cost-effective way to reach millions of Canadians. It produced documentary films from newsreels, armed forces footage, and spot news stories. Later, it expanded and made many different types of films to promote the government and the country.

His work as a speechwriter for the federal government made the step to another aspect of government public relations a natural one for Les. Ultimately, though, the films produced by the board transcended mere propaganda. Under the direction of respected British filmmaker John Grierson, films by the NFB soon became known for their creativity and technical excellence, and because of their high quality were seen outside Canada and all over the world. The NFB, which remains in existence in the twenty-first century, is a well-respected agency worldwide whose films have over the years received several Academy Awards and other international awards. In 1999, the Academy of Motion Picture Arts and Sciences in Los Angeles marked the sixtieth anniversary of the film board with a celebration in Beverly Hills. Eleven years earlier, the academy presented the film board with an honorary Academy Award for its "dedicated commitment to originate artistic, creative and technological activity and excellence in every aspect of filmmaking."

Almost as soon as he joined the film board, Leslie McFarlane became a key player in it. The former newspaperman and magazine writer thrived as a writer, director, and producer of films. Les's versatility as a writer and his willingness to work hard led to success in his new career, but it was also sheer good luck that guided him during this phase of his life. The event that launched this chain of good fortune was an invitation in 1943 from the board's commissioner, Grierson, after Les directed a script he had written about aircraft production for the Department of Munitions and Supply. Les wrote in his autobiography that he never figured out why the respected Grierson had hired a mere writer like himself: "I could never understand why I was hired because Grierson didn't think writers belonged in documentary film work and never hesitated to express his low opinion of them," he wrote. "You didn't write films; you directed and edited films." Les no doubt felt the relief that writers-turned-directors have felt since the beginning of the twentieth century—that he had ultimate control over the words he wrote, and did not have to see his work dramatically altered or edited.

Many print writers of the era entered the emerging broadcast media with trepidation. Magazine writers like Les had always had their work edited, but their "productions" were generally the result of the work of two people—the writer and the editor. What was broadcast on radio or appeared in films, however, was the result of the efforts of many, and the writers ultimately played only a small role in it. Often their words were savaged beyond recognition. The idea of completely controlling a production was appealing to a perfectionist like Les. He took to his new job immediately and soon became head of the Dominion-Provincial Films unit, one of the film board's twelve divisions, with responsibility for travel and outdoor films.

The bureau facilities in the early years were bare-bone and ragtag—qualities that attracted rather than alienated Les, who must have been reminded of the shabby newsrooms he inhabited as a young man: "They toiled in an abandoned sawmill and I thought they were all demented, with the exception of the Great Grierson and a weedy disciple named Norman MacLaren." If Les thought that working at a conventional job out of the house would be less time-consuming than his freelance writing career, he was wrong. This job was hardly nine-to-five; even when he was in Ottawa, he frequently spent many of his evenings as well as most of his days at the film board office. When he was out of town—which was often—his job as a scriptwriter and/or director consumed most of his time, day and night. As he noted in his memoir, his family soon became accustomed to his frequent absences: "I . . . spent the next fifteen years roaming from the coast of Gaspé to the lush valleys of the Caribou country in British Columbia with camera and sound crews," he wrote thirty years later. "My wife, who had just become nicely adjusted to an underfoot husband, was now obliged to adjust to a husband who was seldom at home at all. She managed the one just as she had survived the other."

The versatility of the film board and the diversity of its films is staggering. During Les's years there, he either directed or wrote twenty-nine films ranging from training films for servicemen to films about labor relations, community life, social issues, Canadian industry, and Native people. The films ranged in length from fifteen minutes to nearly an hour, but the production of each required a massive amount of time and the work of a crew of dozens. Some required paid actors, including fourteen-year-old Norah McFarlane, who acted in one of Les's favorite NFB films, *The Boy Who Stopped Niagara,* a fantasy about two children who halt the falls.

His script for *Herring Hunt,* a documentary about the operations of a herring boat, earned him an Academy Award nomination for documentary short. The short film followed the trawler *Western Girl* along the coastal waters of British Columbia and documented the crew's strenuous and risky trip. *Royal Journey,* an account of the British royal family's five-week trip through Canada in 1951, earned him a British

Film Academy award and was a first in many respects for the NFB: it was the first feature film of the film board, the first of its films to reach 2 million viewers in two months, and the first to recoup its production costs. The film follows then Princess Elizabeth and the Duke of Edinburgh on their train trip across Canada and into parts of the United States. *Here's Hockey,* a documentary short about the wide scope of hockey in Canada, was entered in a film festival in Vienna.

Les's first few films at the film board focused on the war effort. *Ships and Men,* one of the first he directed for the bureau, was a tribute to the men who built Canada's merchant ships during the war, alternating footage of Canada's shipyards with scenes at a merchant seamen's school and the actual launch of *Hull 39.* The same year, the bureau released *Target Berlin,* a documentary Les wrote about the Lancaster airplane, the first large bomber built in Canada. The bureau also released training films, such as *Spotting with Radar,* a twenty-three-minute film about the use of radar on battleships, which Les produced.

But the National Film Board was able to demonstrate its true versatility after the war, when it expanded into short features. Several were conventional travel films, such as the tourism short *Toronto Boom Town,* but many celebrated the diversity and richness of Canada and its citizens. Despite being an agency of the federal government, the NFB did not put a happy face on everything it did. For instance, the 1949 documentary *Welcome, Neighbour!* written and directed by Les, sings the praises of the country's tourism industry and the diversity of its offerings. But as the film candidly points out, rapid growth had also caused some problems with roads and social institutions in Canada.

Capturing the infinite variety of a country that had some of the most cosmopolitan cities in the world as well as some of its most rugged and wild terrain was difficult, but the bureau evidently was up to the challenge. It was also clear that its goal was not simply to please the residents of the nation's largest population centers such as Montreal, Toronto, or Vancouver. Films were made outlining the problems of the nation's native Indians, the need for providing diphtheria vaccinations in largely undeveloped territories, and the controversy of unionization in a small manufacturing town. *White Fortress,* a ten-minute short released in 1949 and coproduced by Les, was aimed at the country's rural population in an attempt to explain the services of the National Health Program and the need to seek medical attention when needed. (This film was narrated by Canadian native Lorne Greene, who would later achieve fame in Hollywood as Ben Cartwright in the popular television series *Bonanza*. He and Les would cross paths again many years later in Los Angeles.)

Still, Les's favorite films were no doubt the ones that featured in one way or another the outdoors and the rugged Canadian countryside. These were probably the toughest to produce, direct, and write, but the ones that gave him the most satisfaction. He wrote or directed documentaries on such diverse regions as Jasper National Park and Banff in western Alberta and the beautiful Gaspé Peninsula in eastern Quebec.

Les's work with the film board was never really done. The travel and the extensive output of the bureau with its skeletal staff required Les to be on the go most of the time. Scriptwriting required much attention to detail, but his role as a director was even more time-consuming. As he noted in his diary, in addition to the filming and selection of locations and topics, he was constantly working with budgets, music, lighting, narration, and other details. And he was almost always working on more than one film at a time. A diary entry he made on June 27, 1945, described a typical day: "Had a hectic day keeping control of four productions at once . . . but the 931 job [his training film about use of radar] seems well in hand." Other entries indicate that in one day, he would work on the writing of one script, review footage of another film, and discuss arrangements for shooting yet a third film.

Despite the hectic schedule, the work appealed to him. His diary entries in 1945 and 1946 show little of the gloom and pessimism of the previous few years. The work alone, though, may not have been responsible for this new optimism. He now had a steady paycheck—and in fact earned $3,900 in 1944.

The spring of 1945 brought an end to the war in Europe and was a time of celebration for everyone. On May 2, Les noted in his diary that the headlines indicated that German surrender was near. In a few days, news of it was in the air, and by the end of the day on May 7, there was chaos in the streets. He could write of little else in his diary. "The early broadcasts were full of immediate expectations of peace," Les wrote that day. "As I waited for the streetcar at 9:30 a girl told me the [news] flash had just been announced. Downtown it was quiet but girls were already waving flags as they crowded in office windows above the street." Three hours later, "Downtown was bedlam in the sunshine. A vast litter of paper, a vast smiling crowd. Brought Amy down to see it, went back to work in the afternoon, took Pat down in the evening. We went up to the Parliament Buildings, floodlit for the first time in years."

Les knew that he and others were experiencing history. The next day, he, Amy, and Norah went to Parliament Hill in Ottawa to participate in the celebration. Les, always the writer, described the scene in magnificent detail in his diary: "A grand spectacle with the bright uniforms, the bands, the green lawns and the sombre stone backdrop. The realization is difficult to grasp. My second peace day. I never wish to see another."

By 1945, Les's children were growing up and becoming accomplished in their own right. By the time she was a teenager, the willowy Pat had become a part-time model of military uniforms, and at the urging of her brother Brian, she entered and won the Miss Ottawa beauty pageant. She also enrolled in Ottawa Tech to study art. (All three children were creative. Pat used her ability in art to design, among other things, jewelry and hats; Brian was an accomplished painter as well as a writer, like Norah.)

In 1945, Brian was fourteen and a student at Glebe Collegiate high school in Ottawa, where he played hockey and coached the girls' hockey team. As he writes in his own memoir, hockey became an obsession with him in his teenage years. Not content to practice or play once a week or so, he would practice with teams from other schools. From this time until he graduated from college, the McFarlane family routinely attended his hockey games and became avid fans of whatever team he played for. Before college, Brain became a star hockey player for several city teams, and for years, Les's diary passages were filled with detailed accounts of Brian's games and his performances.

Norah, even by age twelve, had established quite an extensive writing career and was already a published writer and poet, thanks in part to her father's encouragement. By that time, she had also written a book called *Farm Boy* and was seeking a publisher.

On his birthday in 1945, Les, as usual, gave presents to his children in honor of the occasion, and the family celebrated the day with a special dinner. As was frequently the case on his birthday, he briefly reviewed his life in his diary. This year, the prognosis was mixed. "Today I enter my 44th year," he wrote. "And so little done, so little result from so much promise." Still, he was unusually upbeat: "I take heart from the record of those who wrote good stuff and achieved fame after 40" (October 25, 1945).

Even during his work for the film board, Les apparently had not abandoned his ambition of writing a novel. There was little further mention of it in his diary after the mid-1930s, when he was seized by the impulse to write an epic novel about the development of northern Ontario, an idea that grew out of conversations with literary critic William Deacon. Eventually Les may have realized the novel would never materialize because of the practical considerations of working and raising a family. Still, in early 1946, several events prompted him to reconsider: "I should make a beginning at least on a novel with some purpose," he wrote on January 2. Characteristically, the New Year was a time of reflection for him and he notes that his role as an editor and scriptwriter may be hurting his natural bent for writing. He feared it hindered his spontaneity. "Writing comes very hard to me now—the critical sense has outrun the creative," he wrote. The Department of Munitions and Supply asked Les to write a book on the wartime history of the department, but the project did not appeal to him, in part because of his natural disdain for authority: "It is not a task which would give me any special pleasure," he wrote. "Besides, as a subsidized work, it would have to be respectful to the 'fat boys.'"

Late in the year, Les was reading stories by the writer MacKinlay Kantor, a former newspaperman who had written much historical fiction in the 1930s. Like Les, he had been a writer for pulp magazines, and the two had similar backgrounds, a fact Les learned from a biographical note accompanying Kantor's work. Les noted in his diary that the two were both in Montreal as young men writing for *Real Detective Tales*. Kantor's success was depressing to Les, although he was normally not prone to envy. "Our careers paralleled strangely until he wrote his novel and landed in the big time, and I didn't write my novel and stayed in the small time," Les wrote (December 9, 1945). Kantor's most famous novel, the Pulitzer Prize–winning *Andersonville*, would not be published for another eleven years. And, ironically, he and Les would become close friends late in their lives.

13

. . . .

ON THE AIR

As he coped with two new jobs in two years, a move to a new region of the country, raising three children, and worries about the war in Europe, in the late 1930s and early 1940s Les all but ignored one longtime aspect of his life—his writing for the Stratemeyer Syndicate. He abandoned writing Hardy Boys books from 1938 to 1941. Volumes 17 through 21 were written by another Franklin W. Dixon, and when Les picked up the series again in 1942, it is evident from his diary and letters that his heart was not in it. Writing for the syndicate was a very low priority for him.

Judging by his letters to the syndicate during the writing of these last four Hardy Boys books—*The Flickering Torch Mystery, The Melted Coins, The Short-Wave Mystery,* and *The Phantom Freighter*—it is obvious that his travel schedule and workload made it all but impossible to complete them. From 1942 to 1946 apology letters from Les to the syndicate abound, and it is clear that Les wrote the books in his rare spare time. And it is somewhat uncertain whether he even wrote the last one, *The Phantom Freighter.*

His decision to write *The Flickering Torch Mystery* coincided with his move to Ottawa in 1942, and a letter to Harriet Adams in August of that year reflects the chaotic conditions in which he had to write the book. He told Adams that he was sending her the first ten chapters of the book to rid himself of it rather than carry it in his luggage; the remainder would be sent within a few weeks, he said. This was contrary to syndicate preferences; Adams had mentioned to Les a few years earlier that she preferred that he send the completed books all at once. Sending books in several parts complicated the editing process and tended to lead to errors in the manuscript, she said. Within two months, Les may have discovered how difficult it was to write while on the road with a full-time job. A letter to Adams alludes to the fact that Adams required extensive rewriting and had implied that he wrote the book in a hurry. "'The Flickering Torch' wasn't hurriedly written—that itself isn't fatal as I think I remember doing one of the Hardy books in about six days and it turned out pretty well—but it was written under very awkward circumstances which made it almost impossible to maintain an even flow," he wrote her. "I was getting settled in a strange city, under crowded conditions, getting installed quickly in a new type of work. This isn't offered as an alibi." Les went on to say that the hurried effect of the book "may have been due to trying to compress a good deal of outline incident into chapter lengths." He assured Adams in this letter that he would gladly do any rewriting on the book that she requested, and that she could rest assured that his life had settled down since he had last corresponded with her.

Whether he was trying to placate Adams or whether his life did indeed calm down six months after his move to Ottawa, Les's life quickly became complicated once again. In the summer of 1943, when he apparently was writing *The Melted Coins,* she once again received an apologetic letter from Les about the tardiness of the manuscript. "If you knew some of the difficulties I'm up against you would understand," he wrote. "My job here is getting more and more complex, demanding frequent absences from Ottawa and it isn't always possible to bring a fresh mind to the [manu]script work when one goes at it in the evenings."

By 1944, Adams began to get letters typed on letterhead from hotels all over Canada as Les now worked for the film board and barely had a moment to himself, let alone time to write about Frank and Joe Hardy. Most of these letters apologized for tardiness of manuscripts. In one, written on stationery from the Mount Royal Hotel in Montreal, Les gets to the point in the first line: "Dear Mrs. Adams: I've let you down badly— very badly—and no one knows it better than I do." Apparently Les had been sent unexpectedly to several locations to conduct research for his film *Ships and Men* about the men who built Canada's merchant ships during World War II. He foolishly thought he could write *The Short-Wave Mystery* after hours, he wrote. After fourteen- and sixteen-hour workdays, he told her, "I collapsed on the set and was in bed for two days."

As would become customary, Les traveled across Canada, sending Adams forwarding addresses but realizing that visits to multiple locations for short periods made him hard to reach. By late August, he had apparently sent Adams the last part of the manuscript for *The Short-Wave Mystery,* realizing it might be too little and too late. "Regrets are useless," he opened his letter to her in August. "You have probably gone ahead and assigned someone else to finishing the script by now but I have had to travel far and wide in the past six weeks." He was in Halifax and Newfoundland, he wrote, and could not find a typewriter in either location. But Les was nothing if not candid. He admitted that the awkward circumstances of the book's completion may have hurt its narrative flow. "Doubtless it is very uneven, some of it perhaps downright bad," he wrote. "It has had to be written in half-hours here, a full night session there, a Sunday elsewhere. I'm dreadfully sorry."

During these first few months at the film board, Les clearly did not understand the extent of the work required to direct films. As he noted after a few years on the job, the amount of detail work involved in producing even short films was staggering. In addition, he and the staff were at the mercy of factors like the weather, public transportation schedules, and the availability and whims of personnel who worked under temporary contracts.

Still, Adams was not deterred. She eventually did get her manuscripts during this time, and she knew that Les would provide any revisions she requested. Perhaps he was surprised when, after all the complications and apologies, she asked him to write another book, *The Secret Panel*. Les knew by then, though, that his personal circumstances would make the task impossible. He turned her down, telling her that if he took on the obligation of another Hardy Boys book, "I can't see anything else but a repetition of last summer's struggle and I wouldn't embark lightly on that again."

The twenty-fifth Hardy Boys book, *The Secret Panel*, apparently was written by Harriet Adams, although some who have studied the Hardy Boys books are divided over its authorship, and some believe Les wrote it. Based on his letter rejecting the offer to write the book, his diary entries, and his own sales records, which do not list it, he was almost certainly not the author of *The Secret Panel*. It is more likely that Adams wrote the book, and it may not have been a positive experience for her. She asked Les to write the next Hardy Boys book, *The Phantom Freighter*, and he, for some reason, agreed to do it. Les's workload for the film board was still enormous when he took it on, and the process by which it was written remains a mystery; indeed, the tale of *The Phantom Freighter* itself could be called *The Mystery of the Writing of the Phantom Freighter*. Nobody seems to know for sure if the ghostwriter had his own ghostwriter.

The plot of *The Phantom Freighter* revolves around a mysterious boat and the evil Harry Piper's attempts to forge documents and smuggle engine parts using it. Joe and Frank's cracking of a secret code leads to the capture of Piper and his gang. By May 1946, Les told Adams that the book was "under way," but he did not think it could be completed by the June 1 deadline, and that he was entering his busy season at the film bureau. The summer of 1946 may indeed have been one of the busiest of

Les's career, and it was certainly the busiest of his career at the film board. As he told Adams, he had three big films in production: one in the Canadian Rockies in Banff, *Holiday at School,* which focused on a summer school there; at least one and perhaps more films in Jasper National Park, also in the Rockies; and a feature film at Niagara Falls, *The Boy Who Stopped Niagara.*

He then made a startling proposal—that Amy write *The Phantom Freighter* while he was busy in the summer: "As Amy is taking over some of my outside work will you be good enough to regard this manuscript as written by her, with payment to be made to her on delivery and acceptance, addressing correspondence regarding it to her at the above address [his Ottawa home address]," he wrote. "Quality of Ms. guaranteed. She will send you the first ten chapters next week."

This confession that Amy was "taking over" some of Les's freelance work is baffling, as is the fact that Les would undertake another Hardy Boys project while he was so busy with the NFB. According to her children, Amy was not a writer and in fact was embarrassed about her lack of erudition. It is true that she read and commented on much of Les's work—his magazine material rather than his syndicate writings—but periodic letters to her children when they were in college indicate that writing may not have come naturally for her. It is highly unlikely that Les would "turn over" writing of the Hardy Boys to the inexperienced Amy. But correspondence between the syndicate and Amy indicates that the manuscripts were indeed on time and met the skeptical Adams's expectations. In fact, Harriet Adams was so pleasantly surprised by the first seven chapters of the manuscript that she received that she wrote her sister Edna in Florida about it: "I was surprised by it [the fact that Amy wrote it] but pleased with the first seven chapters." Even if Amy had attempted to write the book—extremely unlikely, according to her daughter, Norah—it would be nearly impossible for her, the first time out, to write a book that would so please Adams and fit the conventional syndicate parameters. Further, the humor in the book, particularly regarding Les's favorite characters Chet Morton and Aunt Gertrude, has Les's stamp all over it. On the other hand, it would be very difficult for him to have written the book and written it on time, considering his obligations to the film board.

Norah Perez believes that Les may have asked the syndicate to consider Amy the "official" author of the book for tax purposes. Occasionally in his diary, Les did grumble about the amount of taxes he paid after he joined the film board. Les's comments about the writing of the book many decades later shed little light on what happened, although he does say he wrote the book. In his autobiography, he notes briefly the circumstances in which his last few Hardy Boys books were written, but goes into little detail. In fact, he erroneously recalls that he wrote *The Secret Panel.* "After the *Short Wave Mystery* . . . and the *Secret Panel,* I bowed out with *The Phantom Freighter* which was written in 1946 in motel rooms at night on location in Nova Scotia when I was directing a film." On the record, though, the author of the twenty-sixth Hardy Boys book was, of course, Franklin W. Dixon.

Syndicate researchers, including Robert Crawford, James Keeline, and others, have conducted textual studies on many of the books. They believe—and Les's letters and diaries bear this out—that he wrote the first sixteen Hardy Boys books, and, depending on the authorship of *The Phantom Freighter,* either three or four others, for a total of nineteen or twenty. He definitely did not write volumes 17 to 21, nor did he write volume 25, *The Secret Panel.*

As Les notes in his autobiography, his relationship with the Stratemeyer Syndicate and the Hardy Boys ended not with a bang but a whimper. He seemed to think that all parties involved were simply tired and ambivalent after twenty years and two million words. "I merely sent in the [*Phantom Freighter*] manuscript with a note to the effect that I was too busy to take on any further assignments," he wrote. "The Syndicate didn't plead with me to continue. In fact, the Syndicate didn't seem to care much one way or the other. Other spooks were always available." He felt a curious lack of emotion, he said, although he did experience relief, "as if a couple of relatives who came for the weekend had finally moved on after sticking around for years."

***

Les's family was always his top priority, and by the time the McFarlanes had lived in Ottawa for several years, Pat, Brian, and Norah were becoming wrapped up in school, part-time jobs, and other activities. Birthdays were still grand occasions in the home. Les's travel schedule did not interfere with the celebrations—he still sent them presents when he was away, and they mailed birthday gifts to him. Les still brought Amy gifts on their wedding anniversaries, Valentine's Day, and other special occasions, and he frequently shopped for her when he was out of town. Overall, things were harmonious in the household, and Norah and Brian both recall that all three children were supportive of one another and got along well.

By the late 1940s, Les's numerous letters written home to his family in some ways replaced his diary as a way of expressing his thoughts and emotions and conveying the activities of his life. They also were vital to him for keeping close contact with his family. And writing was the perfect vehicle for him to express some of these personal thoughts. Les was never demonstrative, and probably could say things in the letters that he would not be able to tell his children in conversation.

Les maintained his diary on a limited basis, however. He sometimes took Norah and Amy with him for location work and he noted one time in particular when an excited Norah traveled by train with him and Amy to the Canadian Rockies for the film project *Holiday at School*, filmed at a summer school in Banff. During the ride there, the twelve-year-old Norah kept a diary of the activities, he noted, making entries every half hour (July 21, 1945). It is evident from his diary and his letters that he took immense pleasure in his travels throughout Canada; they allowed him the opportunity to see the landmarks, people, and lifestyles he had only read about. Les had a deep intellectual curiosity about the world around him, and letters home to his children describing his trips indicate he was never happier than when viewing sights that were beyond even his imagination. As he wrote Pat on a trip to Halifax during one of his first years at the film board, "You don't learn much about Canada out of geography books. You have to see it for yourself. I've enjoyed this trip a great deal and I have learned a lot from it." And during his busy visit to Banff: "There is so much to see and do here that the days pass like lightning and no day seems long enough."

By the time Les was heavily involved in his film bureau work, all three of his children were teenagers, and like most parents, Les was finding their independence startling. He noted with pride that fifteen-year-old Brian had just started a job at a local drugstore after school. But that was just one of Brian's many jobs. He also worked one summer as a copy boy at the local newspaper, and was adept at a job requiring him to sell magazines to young women in offices, a job where his good looks and amiable personality no doubt came in handy. Most of Brian's life, however, revolved around playing hockey, and, consequently, going to his games and talking about them afterward became major preoccupations of both his parents. Hockey was a dangerous sport, though, and at least once during his high school years he sustained serious injury when he was hit in the mouth with a hockey stick. He required extensive dental work for some broken teeth and needed stitches to his tongue.

The onset of middle age may have triggered bouts of nostalgia in Les, although when it came to his family, he always was prone to sentimentality and reflection with little prompting. He noted in his diary that he had heard about the death of his father's sister—the last of his father's siblings. "And so passes the last member of Dad's family—all of those who were born on the homestead near Prestonvale." Les recalled the visit he made the previous summer to an aunt in nearby Lanark, where he used to visit as a child. And he was saddened at the deterioration of a beloved childhood landmark. "I went out to the farm, cheerless and shabby against the warm memories of forty years ago, now occupied by strangers" (February 13, 1948).

By the late 1940s, though, Amy and Les had more practical concerns. Pat, who was only eighteen, had fallen in love with one of her high school teachers, Bill McCauley, who was twelve years her senior. The relationship did not please Amy and Les, who believed their daughter was too young to be involved in a serious romance. Worse, though, was the fact that she wanted to be a homemaker and would not go to college if she married him. Amy and Les had hoped that all three of their children would be able to attain something they lacked: a college diploma.

But it appeared that the relationship between Pat and Bill McCauley was serious, much to Amy's chagrin. In his memoir, Brian alludes to the fact that his parents were concerned about the twelve-year age difference between the two, although "scandalized" is too strong a word, he said. But based on letters Les wrote to Pat while he was traveling, "scandalized" may have summed up the situation perfectly, at least for Amy, who was heartbroken when she learned Pat and Bill were seriously involved. Les was not as concerned about the relationship as he was about Amy's reaction to it. Les had apparently learned the hard way not to interfere with the relationships of others, even his children's, and he trod lightly: "I don't like this affair but haven't made up my mind what to do about it, if anything," he wrote in his diary. "If there is one thing I have learned, it is the danger of interfering on other people's affairs, the danger of hasty action, the danger of making up one's mind without complete information and understanding. But this thing I do not like" (February 29, 1948). Several letters to Pat written during this period indicated that her relationship with Bill caused bitter arguments between

Amy and Pat—arguments that seemed to worry Les, who was uncomfortable in his role as middleman.

The letters Les wrote to his children after they were grown were usually long and detailed. As was the case with his diaries, Les took the format of the letters very seriously—most were written either on hotel stationery if he was out of town, or on plain white paper on which he carefully typed his address. Later in his life, he would be sure to have his own embossed stationery. The letters were almost always typewritten, and rarely if ever did they contain typographical errors and never misspellings. Occasionally, if he felt his sentence structure was weak or rambling, or his imagery trite, he apologized for it with a few words jotted at the end of the letters.

As his children grew older, Les's letters frequently gave them paternal advice about a variety of subjects. He advised Brian on such topics as the importance of dressing well, the importance of good grades and a college education, his love life, and career matters. Les could be philosophical as well as practical with his advice to his children. Shortly before Brian's twentieth birthday, his father wrote him a sympathetic letter, noting that he realized his son had his share of worries, despite the prevailing myth that youth should be the happiest time of one's life. "Most people think a teen-age boy hasn't a care in the world and should be at the happiest time of his life but it isn't always that good," he told him. "You've probably had plenty of worries and troubles of your own . . . but as you get more confidence and experience they're easier handled."

His advice to Norah focused on her writing and how to get it published. Even when she was very young, Les praised Norah's writing and encouraged her to keep at it. When she was sixteen, for instance, she received an encouraging letter about an article she submitted to *Seventeen* magazine. Les stressed that she had to be confident about her abilities at the current stage of her career: "You are well on your way to being a writer and you will be a good writer," he said in a letter. "Don't ever feel that you are too young now to be writing professionally because there are many stages in a writer's life and every stage has its own qualities. Just now you have a viewpoint and imagination that you will never have again in the same way, the viewpoint of your own age, and it is just as interesting to readers and just as valid artistically as the viewpoint of an old writer of seventy. Both of you would write about a subject in an entirely different way but one can be just as good as the other." Most important, he said, she should always feel free to write: "Don't be self-conscious, write a story as it comes to you and write it as well as you know how, and always remember that a writer is seldom a good critic of his or her own stuff." Les's letters to Norah also covered topics such as the importance of self-confidence and the evils of smoking—interesting advice, since Les smoked most of his life. His advice about smoking is far from heavy handed and, typically for Les, implies that he is hypocritical to criticize smoking ("I've been smoking tobacco in every form since the age of twelve"); he tells Norah that if she must smoke, she should at least be delicate about it ("If you must smoke, for God's sake be neat and feminine about it and never smoke more than one cigarette at a time").

The letters to all his children were warm and encouraging, frequently congratulating them on their grades and other personal, professional, and scholastic accomplishments. Most contained some elements of humor and painted a picture: "I . . . see you cutting out dolls, or see Norah curled up somewhere with a book, or Brian galloping in to ask if he could go somewhere or Ma coming in from the kitchen," he wrote Pat during one of his trips. "Forgive me for all the times I was grouchy this summer; if you knew how much I miss you all you would know my bark is worse than my bite." The letters to all his children were hardly perfunctory attempts at keeping in touch. Most were a single-spaced, typewritten page or so, and some were longer.

Les's letters to Pat, however, were more complex. Pat's sometimes volatile personality may have frightened him a bit—she never hesitated to speak her mind and could be brutally frank with him. A letter Les wrote from Vancouver to Pat about her affair with Bill was revealing and poignant, particularly when he tried to explain the complexities of marriage and the depth of his love for Amy: "We are both anxious for your happiness, believe it or not, but of course we see marriage from a long-term viewpoint with knowledge of its disillusionments and disappointments as well as its richness," he wrote her. He touched on the subject of his and Amy's marriage: "Because while we're not very demonstrative I think our marriage has been a success. For my part it has been anyhow because I am more in love with my wife now than at the beginning, but it's different, much deeper and based on things we have shared. The romantic side does wear off and there is a sort of bridge to cross before one achieves the deeper affection which is really based on respect and admiration." One wonders if the reserved Les could have told Pat in person what he wrote in the letter: "I fell in love with [Amy] because she was herself, because she was beautiful and attractive and—oh well, just because. We had a few stormy times but now I love her deeply because she is kind, because she is generous, because she is a good woman in all the ways a woman can be good, because she is hard-working and neat and a good housewife and sensible." Les was clearly distressed about the rift in Amy and Pat's relationship. "I want you to try to see your mother's point of view here because I know she is thinking primarily of your own happiness. She has always placed other people before her own wishes and she has had many disappointments. Perhaps my own lack of success has been one of them—success in the sense that we have never had very much money. . . . Her life and career is in her children."

Unfortunately, the age difference between Pat and Bill was not the only concern of Amy and Les. He is diplomatic, though, when he tiptoes around the issue of Bill's personality: "[Amy] has felt from the beginning that Bill's age and personality—reserved and quiet—would make adjustment pretty difficult after the first year or so of marriage, and I have had to respect her intuition in that regard." But the nonconfrontational Les could never end a letter on a negative note: "In the meantime, be cheerful, have a good time, don't worry too much about the situation and remember that to us your happiness comes first but we're trying to look at it in the light of happiness over a good many years rather than just the moment."

The couple did decide to marry, and a congratulatory letter Les wrote to her after the decision was announced is typical of his warm nature. He wishes her well and tells her how he values her as a daughter: "If you are sure, the decision is of your own making and you know that if this is what you want of life, that is what counts, and I wish you all the joy in the world. You have been a good daughter and we have tried to give you a good childhood with happy memories. I hope you have a good marriage and I'm sure you will." Les continued that he is very fond of Bill and "even if he weren't your choice, I would like him." Pat and Bill married in 1950, and after living briefly with Les and Amy, they moved into their own home. The first few years of their marriage went better than Amy or Les had anticipated. On New Year's Day of 1951, Amy and Les celebrated the New Year with a dinner of roast goose at the McCauley home. Pat enjoyed having her own home, Les wrote in his diary, and she and her new husband seemed very happy. "Amy has adapted herself to this marriage," Les wrote. "She is a good sport. As I told Pat several months ago, she would find that her mother would adjust as soon as she knew Pat herself was happy." Bill later earned a doctoral degree and became musical director of the O'Keefe Performing Arts Center in Toronto, and went on to compose film scores. The couple had three children and stayed married until Pat's death in 1980.

***

The frenetic pace of Les's life when he worked for the film board evidently made him happy—gone were the diary references to the lethargy and writer's block that had periodically plagued him for several years. Although he could not write in his journal each day, the passages were more detailed than ever, and rarely did he write terse passages like "loafed all day," as he had during those days of paralyzing writer's block. In fact, on one Sunday, he noted that not much happened, which wasn't unusual for a Sunday. The now-energetic Les bemoaned the fact that Sundays were, in fact, quite a waste of time for him: "Sundays difficult to cover in my journal for the simple and painful reason that Sundays are usually wasted and spent in complete idleness. I can rationalize a little and say that they provide much needed rest but the truth is that I could write a book a year in the time I waste on Sundays" (February 15, 1948). In truth, though, Les spent many of his Sundays reading, an activity he enjoyed immensely, and also one that was required in his line of work.

The film bureau, founded because of the war, expanded its scope and reach after the armistice. In addition to the constant travel, the job forced Les to be a jack-of-all-trades. As he wrote to Harriet Adams, as a unit producer, he not only wrote and directed films, he was responsible for handling the entire unit staff. He was inexperienced in some aspects of the job, such as working on a strict budget, dealing with dwindling funds and department politics and, of course, being ultimately responsible for the work of others.

A film usually took about six months to make and most were done at an exhausting pace, or as one article about him noted, the filmmaking was "far from the romantic conception fostered by stout, easy-living Hollywood millionaires." The director first had to spend about two months interviewing sources and reading material on the subject to become familiar with the material so he could write a script. The director then made a determination about how much time it would take to complete the project and each scene, the equipment needs, and the cost. Then two months were spent shooting the film—the most "terrifying" aspect of the process because so much hangs in the balance. "One false move in the entire schedule, one day of bad work, one missed train, could cost a fortune." Finally, two months were spent cutting, editing, and adding music or commentary. Most important, though, was his job of making sure that the dozens of people on the production work together as a unit—quite a change for a freelance writer who had to be concerned only with writing a manuscript and mailing it to an editor.

Les was committed to his job, in part because he believed deeply that the work he did for the film bureau provided many people with their only image of Canada, and in part because he knew Canadian citizens were footing the bill for the films. Even the shortest film cost about $10,000, a sum paid by taxpayers. He believed the purpose of the NFB films was not escapism or entertainment, but to inform, make viewers think, and ultimately help solve problems.

In 1945, he began two film projects that would consume much of his time for several years. One, the twenty-minute *Holiday at School,* was the story of the prestigious Banff Center summer school, offering instruction in music, art, theater, and French. The summer culminated in a grand exhibit of student work. Les's diaries indicate that the project, which he produced, wrote, and directed, required many months of work and trips to Banff—far more than the usual NFB film. His entries also indicated that he enjoyed the work and was proud of the result.

The other film, *The Boy Who Stopped Niagara,* had a profound effect on him personally and professionally, and differed somewhat from the usual film board fare. The project originated with a proposal by Les to the J. Arthur Rank Children's Film unit in London, a nonprofit group that produced children's films for distribution around the world. When the organization first contacted the film board about possibly producing a film for children, the board routinely passed on the inquiry to Les. Neither the NFB nor the British film agency realized they had just contacted someone with extensive experience in writing for children. (Les had never publicized his experience with the syndicate, and a rare mention of it was made in 1946 in a feature story about the film in a magazine called *National Home Monthly.* The article noted vaguely that Les had written "more than 30 books for boys and girls, published under various pen-names.") But getting approval for a film from the Arthur Rank agency was no easy task—all project proposals had to go through an exhaustive review process of educators and government and film officials, who examined their creativity, marketability, and appropriateness for children. The project eventually received the green light, and Les was on his own to write, direct, and produce one of the biggest film projects of his career.

By the film board's own description, *The Boy Who Stopped Niagara* was the story of a brother and sister who get lost in the falls' power plant and accidentally stop Niagara Falls. The film, billed as a fantasy for children, has Les's stamp. The two protagonists had distinctly Dickensian names: Tommy and Penny Twidgett. The film featured only actors and crew members from Canada. The leads were the fourteen-year-old Norah Mc-Farlane, who made her debut as an actor, and Hamilton, Ontario, native Jeff Martin. Although most of it was filmed at Niagara Falls, not even Les could persuade the helpful Ontario Hydro-Electric Power Commission to completely stop the falls, as the script required. Instead, the crew traveled eight hundred miles to far northern Ontario to have a smaller falls there double for Niagara Falls: Les arranged for those falls to stop on camera.

The reaction to *The Boy Who Stopped Niagara* was phenomenal. Shortly after it was made, it was previewed in Canada, Britain, New Zealand, and Australia, and the positive reaction in those countries prompted bookings in Denmark, Ceylon, Holland, and Egypt. It was officially released in late 1947 to excellent reviews, both in publications and by the children who saw it. Les was told that at showings in London, "the reception was so spontaneous that the lights had to be turned up after every showing so that the audience would settle down and let the show go on," he wrote in his diary. Les also noted that published reviews were "brief but good" in British newspapers, which called it "a lovely Canadian fantasy" and "delightful whimsy." Les was amused at one negative review from the *Daily Worker*, which called it "didactic." "Apparently the pace baffles adults but pleases children," he wrote in his diary (January 15, 1948).

By the time *The Boy Who Stopped Niagara* was released, Les was becoming a minor celebrity of sorts. Newspapers in the locations he visited frequently wrote stories about him and his film bureau role, frequently referring to him as a well-known writer of fiction. By the late 1940s, Les had several careers—newspaper reporter, writer of magazine articles, author of short novels, radio scriptwriter, and now, film director and producer. Missing from the official resume, however, was the label of young-adult author, although with the great success of the Niagara film, he was beginning to rethink his role in that capacity. His years as a newspaperman were far behind him, although he accepted an invitation in late 1948 to join Ottawa's Press Club. Les himself mused about why he agreed to join. After all, he no longer worked on newspapers and had generally opposed the idea of most professional associations. "Why I took it, I don't know," he wrote in his diary. "Sentimental reasons, no doubt. 'I used to be a newspaperman myself'" (March 2, 1948).

14

. . . .

A TRAGIC TIME

In 1948, Leslie McFarlane was asked by officials at Carleton College (now Carleton University) in Ottawa to consider establishing and teaching a fiction-writing course as a part-time faculty member. Les had critiqued the novel of one of the department heads, Wilfred Eggleston, who approached him with the idea. Les thought it was all kismet: "I must confess that such a possibility [teaching a class] was in my mind when I wrote the critique of his novel several months ago with some feeling that this was all part of a predetermined pattern," he wrote in his diary (February 12, 1948). Within a year or so, Les became a devoted teacher at Carleton, and periodically wrote in his diary and in letters of the challenges, frustrations, and satisfaction he derived from the job. His letters indicate that despite his film bureau work, he always prepared meticulous lecture notes and never gave the teaching job short shrift. As is the case with most teachers, Les's challenge was teaching students of widely varying ability. After much soul searching, he decided to target his most gifted students: "It's a little tricky fixing the level of approach but this year I decided to say to hell with the misfits . . . and go on the assumption that if only one person in the class has some talent and imagination I must talk to that one person," he wrote Norah. "If I lower the sights and try to talk to the untalented or the unimaginative then I'll be harming the one person who really counts." He would teach the class for several years, until he moved out of Ottawa in 1956.

Also during this time, Les assumed another role that he would soon become adept at—the role of grandfather. The first of Pat's three children, Matthew Brian, was born on April 1, 1955, in Ottawa. Pat's father was not in town, but he would not dream of letting the event go unnoticed. He sent her a telegram from Chicago: "If this is April Fool prank must say you went to lot of trouble to make it convincing . . . Am delighted and excited. Love to you both and a kiss for Matthew B, Grandpaw." Matthew (who for a short time was known as "Brian") immediately became a favorite of his grandfather, who wrote excited letters to his other children about his growth, his personality, and his antics. Ultimately, Les would be the "grandpaw" to many children—his own children had nine children among them, and, later, he would be stepgrandfather to even more.

The birth of Matthew was no doubt a blessing for Amy, who, by the early 1950s, was suffering from what would later be known as empty nest syndrome. Brian entered college in 1951, shortly after Pat married, and Amy clearly missed the noisy and once-active household. During his first two years of college, Amy wrote Brian many newsy letters—uncharacteristic of her—most of which focused on the activities of townspeople and his former classmates. In one early letter, her true feelings come out at the end. After commenting early in the letter that she believed Norah missed her sister, she admitted she felt the same way: "I miss Pat so much I don't think I'll ever get used to her being married." But Pat and her husband lived in Ottawa, and Amy and Pat frequently saw each other and undertook social and domestic projects together.

Brian McFarlane notes in his memoir, tongue-in-cheek, that while he was not exactly at the top of his class in high school, he was delighted to get the scholarship to St. Lawrence University in Canton, New York, since that was his first choice for college. Brian called himself a late bloomer. At St. Lawrence, he became a star collegiate hockey player, captain of the team, a member of the All-America hockey team, and president of his class. It would be the first time in his life that he would receive national exposure; as a college hockey player, his picture was published in *Sports Illustrated* and appeared on the cover of the NCAA Guide. In addition, it was at St. Lawrence that he began his long career in broadcasting as a play-by-play announcer for football and baseball. He also met his future wife, Joan Pellett of New Jersey. Joan became a flight attendant after graduation, and she and Brian married several years later. The two would have three children, two girls and a boy.

Norah also enrolled at St. Lawrence, a year after her brother. Her high school scholastic record may have been a bit more distinguished than her brother's, and she, too, excelled at St. Lawrence. Where Brian was president of his class, Norah was vice president of hers. That Norah also attended St. Lawrence speaks to the close relationship between the two siblings. All three of the McFarlane children were close growing up, and would remain so during their adult lives, although they sometimes lived in different cities. Like Brian, Norah met her future spouse at St. Lawrence. Brian introduced Norah to his friend Louis Perez, another

St. Lawrence student. In 1955, after they graduated, they were married, and Lou Perez attended law school and later became an attorney. They eventually had three sons.

As Les noted in a letter to Norah during her first month of college, the house was unusually silent with all three children gone: "Everything is very quiet here but not unpleasant in that your parents are getting acquainted with each other again in the strange, peaceful atmosphere which has suddenly descended upon the usually tumultuous abode." The sociable Les evidently advocated more entertaining, an idea that was vetoed by Amy. "I have suggested that we begin a little program of Having People In, which would logically result in a few Invitations Out but for the moment this suggestion has met with little favor and of course the local theatres have picked this week to play the most formidable list of stinkers in a dog's age," he told Norah.

While Les earned a regular paycheck through his jobs at the Department of Munitions and the film board, the McFarlanes were far from wealthy during this period, though they were probably more comfortable financially than they had ever been. Still, sending two children to college was not easy, and both Brian and Norah worked at part-time jobs through their college years.

The fact that Brian and Norah were away from home gave their father an opportunity to write them letters in which he expressed many of his feelings and thoughts, much as he had done in his diaries. Les had sent many letters home to them as he traveled with the film bureau, but by the early 1950s, his children were young adults, and he no longer communicated to them as youngsters. Both, in fact, were embarking on successful careers—Norah as a writer and Brian as a sports broadcaster—and Les could offer advice and encouragement as well as interesting, humorous, and often candid observations about their lives and activities. The letters to Norah, in particular, were long and sometimes complex; in Norah, he may have found a kindred spirit—she was almost as avid a writer as he, and she valued his letters, sometimes reading her father's wry commentary to her friends and roommates. But he did not give short shrift to Brian. Les wrote many letters to Brian during his college years, although with his role on the hockey team, his jobs, and his outside activities at school, Brian was not the enthusiastic correspondent his sister was. Les's letters to Brian focused on his sports performances, job possibilities, and more practical matters.

The relationship between Les and Norah was particularly close, though, as evidenced by the content and tone of his letters to her. He occasionally referred to her in them as "my pet," a rare term of endearment even though the tone of his letters to all three of his children was affectionate. In one letter written to her in college, he spells out his feelings: "We've always been very close together and I value that as one of the very best things of my whole life," he wrote. Or, in another, he apologized at the end of what he feared was a depressing letter to her. "I have always felt you understand me better than anyone else in the world and you realize I'm trying to think things through by writing them down." While he wrote about books, movies, and magazine articles to all three of his children, the critiques he gave to Norah were usually longer and more detailed.

After she had attended college a year or two, though, Les feared he might have a problem with the usually reliable and steady Norah. She had written to tell him she was in love with a man who would soon go off to war. The prospect of the relationship troubled Les—not because he did not trust Norah, but because he feared that a marriage before she graduated from college would be devastating to Amy. The fallout from Pat's marriage was still fresh in his mind and he did not want a repeat of the incident. In a long hand-written letter, he urged restraint: "First love is a very beautiful and memorable experience but it is also a bit treacherous because its very beauty lies like a mist over realities. . . . So I want to warn you against doing anything foolish or irreparable at this time." Les was candid, and admitted that he feared Amy' s reaction if Norah were married: "If you married Eddie *now*, it would kill your mother—not because she has anything against Eddie—but for other reasons. It would be a disappointment she could not take at this time. . . . The greatest thing in her life has been seeing you and Brian going to university and it has offset some of her disappointment over Pat's marriage." While Amy had recovered by this time from her breakdown fifteen years earlier, Les was still quite protective of her.

As it turned out, the McFarlanes had nothing to worry about—Norah did not marry during college, and instead concentrated on her studies and her writing. Like Brian, she excelled in college, and received several awards, much to the delight of her father. She also was succeeding as a fiction writer. While in college, one of her short stories was adapted into a half-hour play that aired on the CBC, and another script aired on CBS on the popular Alfred Hitchcock show. Her father was delighted, and he fielded calls back in Ottawa from friends who saw Norah's name on television. He kiddingly wrote to Norah that each time her name appeared in the local paper or on television for her accomplishments—for being elected to the dean's list and for being named to "Who's Who" of college students—she was called the daughter of "Charles Leslie McFarlane." Les never went by the name Charles, and it had never seemed to bother him until now. "I'm going to apply . . . to get rid of that Charles in my name," he wrote her. "Being father of a clever daughter makes Charles L. McFarlane a Man of Distinction but doesn't do a thing for ole Les McFarlane, undoubtedly a poor relation of some kind who happens to live at the same address."

Les's letters to Norah were full of dry humor, puns, and other wordplay, and in Norah he had an enthusiastic audience. When she was twenty years old, Norah decided to teach Sunday school—a decision that surprised and amused her father, who has always been skeptical of organized religion. He feigned shock, using the appropriate Biblical metaphors: "When you left for college I realized that there were certain risks and perils involved; American universities are notoriously depraved and America in general, as compared with the pure ascetic life of Canada, is as Gomorrah to Zion," he wrote her. "I must confess . . . that this development is something I had not foreseen and the fault is mine. Blindly I let you go to the U.S. immunized against practically everything except the Methodist Church and now look what happened." He offered nearly a page of mock "advice." For example, " Be wary as a hummingbird if the pastor suggests that you will be better equipped to explain the Song of Solomon to your little group if he discusses it with you after Wednesday Night prayer meeting . . ." "Be wary as a hummingbird of practically any male member of the congregation who wants to be helpful—with the possible exception of the leader of the boys' choir or the Scoutmaster . . ." Finally, he offered some helpful advice about what she should do if she was asked a question to which she did not know the answer: "'Look at [the questioner] reprovingly and say in a hushed voice: 'It is not for us to question Holy Writ. The Scriptures are not always meant to be understood but they are always meant to be believed. Faith is everything. It's in the book.'"

Les's letters to all his children were light and often amusing, but when it came to advice about writing, he was entirely serious. Les gave Norah advice about the craft of writing and many more practical matters as well, including ways to get funding, how to find an agent, and the challenges of working with editors. The continuing theme of his advice, however, had always been the importance of maintaining confidence in herself and her talent. During one semester she evidently wrote to her father that she was discouraged about her grades in a creative writing class. Les did not immediately condemn the instructor, but told his daughter, gently, that subjective editors were a fact of life: "Take it in your stride, kid," he wrote. "Being a successful short story writer is partly due to ability to write but largely due to finding editors who like your stories and as editors are human beings—some deny this—they have prejudices, likes, dislikes and all kinds of notions. The professor who reads your stories is in the position of an editor."

Les's advice to all three of his children was generally pragmatic and unsentimental and never moralistic. Often its seriousness was cloaked in a joke or a lighthearted anecdote. He also indicated that much of it came from hard experience—lessons he had learned the hard way. It is interesting, then, as Norah entered college and left home for the first time, that he would give her advice about drinking. Les's drinking as a young man grew worse as the Depression deepened, his magazine markets vanished, and his family grew. After he was taken away for several weeks for what was known as "the cure," he never drank again in the family's home, and ended his binge drinking forever. But he never viewed his treatment as a "cure" because he never saw himself as an alcoholic. Instead, he said later, it was the realization that his heavy drinking was hurting others that made him quit. Les considered himself a social drinker whose period of heavy and destructive drinking came about because of tough times. Evidently his two daughters did not consider him a mere social drinker, though, and periodically Norah and Pat as young women feared that their father would lapse into a pattern of heavy drinking.

Shortly after Norah entered college, he warned her in a humorous way about the dangers of alcohol: "An awful lot of drinking is done just because people want to be like everyone else and I would say that you're better off without it—it certainly won't do you any good and at your age one doesn't need a cocktail to have high spirits." He then offered a tongue-in-cheek "guide" to turning down a drink when it is offered: "Sorry. I'm allergic. It makes me break out in big purple spots like a Christmas necktie." Or, "My old man owns a distillery and if you ever saw them making that stuff you'd never take another drink." Two years after he offered Norah that humorous warning about drinking, some event triggered in Pat and Norah a fear that their father was returning to drink. In a long letter to Norah, Les reassured her that he was not returning to heavy drinking, nor did he even get satisfaction from alcohol.

His period of heavy drinking years before, he explained in the letter, came from his circumstances at the time: "The psychological causes at bottom of my occasional wrestling bouts with the demon no longer exist," he told her. "They sprang largely from a reluctance to face up to responsibilities of marriage, reluctance to make the compromises necessary if I were to remain a writer, a good provider and a good husband all in one, and . . . possibly a reluctance to face up to the realization that as a writer I fell just a little short of top bracket." He went on to say that he never truly enjoyed the taste of liquor itself. "Nothing on earth would induce me to revert to the juvenile patterns of other years. So get this— even the smell of hard liquor nauseates me today."

But Les told Norah in the letter that because of his job and the socializing that went with it, a refusal to drink socially would be noticed. "Among the people with whom I move, I can't go around advertising myself as pious dry or a reformed drunk," he wrote. Instead, he had become adept at accepting cocktails and discreetly leaving them in kitchens or on pianos, or pouring himself ginger ale and letting others think it was scotch, he said.

Although Les could be his own worst critic at times, he was always self-aware—he certainly did not abstain from alcohol later in his life, and no doubt drank occasionally during his travels with the film board. He was devoted to Amy, and he spelled out repeatedly to his children that he did not drink because of his love and respect for her. But he did not hide from his children that he had an occasional drink after Amy's death in 1955. He referred in a letter the next year to several beers he had on Christmas, and he did drink occasionally after his remarriage. But, as he had promised his children, his years as a problem drinker were over.

***

By the mid-1950s, Les was becoming known as a veteran director and writer of documentaries. His work for the film bureau introduced him to a visual mode of communication, and by this time he knew that any writer who limited himself to the printed word was missing out on new outlets for expression. Acutely aware of cultural changes around him, he could see that the relatively new medium of television could provide unlimited opportunities for writers. While still working full-time for the film bureau in 1952, he began writing scripts on a freelance basis for newly formed CBC television, basing some of these scripts on plays and short stories he had written earlier. He acknowledged in letters to Norah and Brian that he found adapting his own stories into television scripts an arduous task.

For the rest of his life, Les would have a love-hate relationship with television, or, as he called it in the 1950s, "teevy." The medium opened many doors for him later in his life and led to some of the national recognition that he had sought much earlier in his life. But Les also found television to be a frustrating and highly commercial world in which the system of internal politics often rewarded the most untalented players and penalized those who turned out high-quality work.

Although television began to gain wide acceptance in North America in the 1950s, it was certainly not a new medium in that decade. Television was spawned during the same era as radio, in the late 1930s, but the Depression and World War II stunted its development and delayed its growth by several decades. After the war, however, a booming economy, a demand for consumer goods, and a growth in science and technology gave television a shot in the arm. By the early 1950s, the golden age of radio was over: many of the top radio stars in the United States were turning to television, news had become a staple of the new medium, and the number of television sets sold was skyrocketing. As was the case in radio, comedy and variety shows dominated and were performed live on television. During the golden age of television drama, from 1948 to 1958, dramatic anthology series such as the *Hallmark Hall of Fame, Kraft Television Theater, U.S. Steel Hour,* and others gained wide popularity, both with viewers and with ambitious writers, who delighted at these new markets for their material. In 1946, fewer than 2 million households in the United States had television sets; by 1950, the number had grown to about 7 million; by 1955, televisions could be found in more than 30 million homes in the United States.

In Canada, growth of the medium was a bit slower. On September 8, 1952, the English language CBC-TV went on the air; a year later, CKSO-TV in Sudbury became the first private television station in Canada and the CBC's first affiliate. CBOT in Ottawa followed that year, joining with Montreal and Toronto via microwave links to establish a three-station network.

In Les's eyes Canada was woefully behind the United States when it came to development of that medium, and he may have been right. By 1954, only a million television sets had been sold in Canada, and Les clearly wished that he could own one of that million. His optimism was fueled when he and Amy found a large crowd gathered in front of the window of their local appliance store in 1953 to watch the Bruins-Canadiens hockey game on television. Amy's enthusiasm about watching the game indicated that the arrival of a television set could be imminent in the McFarlane home, Les wrote Norah. Still, he noted, restrictions on television in Canada in 1953—including the fact that most programs originated from Montreal and were thus aired in French, and that one must obtain a permit to install an outside aerial—did dampen his desire for one. Television may have been late in taking off in Canada, but when it did, its growth was fast and furious. Network affiliates sprang up from 1954 to 1958, and by 1955, CBC transmissions reached 66 percent of Canada's population. By 1958, CBC television was accessible to 91 percent of Canadians.

Les's sporadic writing for television gave him more than just extra money and the opportunity to practice new writing skills. As he continued to do freelance writing for the CBC, he began to cultivate a network of sources in the industry that would ultimately pay off for him. The early years of television provided a fertile training ground for young actors, directors, and writers. In addition to Lorne Greene, who later became the star of the successful NBC television show *Bonanza,* Les also worked with Arthur Hiller, who would become well known in the United States as a film director. But most of these contacts were in Toronto—somewhat ironically for Les, who as a young man had moved to Whitby, near Toronto, to be closer to magazine markets, only to relocate to Ottawa.

By 1955, Les had been with the film board for more than ten years— far longer than he had planned. Early that year, he had embarked on what he thought would be a major film about two young Canadians, Frederick Banting and Charles Best, who discovered insulin in 1921 in their tiny laboratory at the University of Toronto. Les's letters home and to all his children indicate that he conducted extensive research and interviews for *The Quest* for three years. He clearly envisioned it as one of the best and most extensive works he would do for the bureau— and perhaps one of the biggest efforts of his career. As he grew older, Les read more biographies and was also intrigued by biographies in the form of movies and plays, providing extensive commentary on them in letters to his children. Les respected the writers who did not merely recount events in their subjects' lives, but who attempted to find the reason for behavior or actions. The biographies he enjoyed were multidimensional and attempted to put their subjects' lives into the context of the times. The Banting/Best film was proving a challenge on many fronts: not only did he want to write an interesting and thought-provoking script, he had to walk a tightrope to provide equal information about both men so neither would feel slighted. Les also found that a full understanding of their discovery required extensive interviews and archival research. As Les would ultimately learn, though, the biggest obstacle came from the film board itself, which kept reducing the scope and size of the film.

The controversy involving the film led indirectly to Les's resignation from the NFB in 1957, although it is likely that his contacts and success in television scriptwriting would have prompted his departure anyway. In 1956, however, the writing was on the wall. Les wrote Norah that it was unlikely he would stay at the bureau much longer. Writing the insulin script was becoming increasingly frustrating as time went on, he wrote: "I am merely staying on at the Board long enough to see the [insulin film] job through and have pretty well decided to leave NFB next spring. In and around Toronto the people I work with in TV seem friends but here they are merely associates." In early 1958, he was still working on *The Quest*. By this time, it was scheduled to run only about thirty minutes, a length the film bureau only grudgingly allowed. Les wrote to Norah that the bureau evidently wanted to scrap the project but "after spending two years and $20,000 on research and story . . . the idea now is to knock out a little half-hour short cheaply to get it off the books. I couldn't care less by now." *The Quest* was finally released in 1958, after Les left the film bureau; it ran thirty-eight minutes. In its credits, Les is listed as the "Script and Text" writer, but not the director. The NFB apparently reworked that film because three years later, another film on the same subject called *The Discovery of Insulin* was produced by the film bureau. Les was also listed in the credits as writer on this film.

***

As he entered his fifties, Les still had the energy and determination to work more than one job, but his writing for the CBC, his teaching at Carleton College, and his film board job left him little spare time. Still, by the time Brian and Norah were in their final years of college and Pat had her first child, Les and Amy were getting used to their new life without their children at home. Amy stayed busy keeping up her own home and helping Pat and her growing family, and she occasionally traveled with Les on his film bureau business. By early 1955, however, Amy was getting pains in her back and neck that doctors eventually diagnosed as a slipped disc. Although the pain did not incapacitate her, letters from Les to his two children in college indicate that it did sometimes keep her from housekeeping chores. And it seemed to be ongoing.

The family soon learned, however, that Amy's health problems did not stem from a slipped disc. As her condition worsened, she was diagnosed with cancer of the esophagus, which had spread to other parts of her body. After several months of illness and hospitalization, Amy Arnold McFarlane died on September 13, 1955, in Ottawa. Funeral services were in St. Luke's Anglican Church in Ottawa. She and Les had been married twenty-seven years.

***

The death of Amy was naturally devastating for Les and the rest of the family. Amy died within a year before both Norah's and Brian's weddings, and she and Les had a bit of extra money for one of the first times in their lives. They were busily remodeling some of their home, visiting with their grandson, and generally beginning a new pattern of family life. Immediately after her death, Les was numbed by both the shock of it and the activities associated with it—making funeral arrangements, meeting visitors, and writing thank-you cards. The numbness soon wore off, however, and was replaced by an overwhelming sadness. "I don't know what is going to happen to my life," he wrote Norah three weeks after Amy's death. "It now seems to have lost focus, to have no further objective or meaning but I suppose that in time it will assume some kind of pattern. . . . As the shock subsided I had to realize the incredible vastness of my loss and this is the stage through which I have been going." He admitted to Norah that although he could work and socialize, he was just going through the motions: "There is no overall purpose to my life anymore so I am just going on a day-to-day basis and trying to be with people as much as possible because otherwise the deep loneliness is almost frightening at times."

Within a few months of Amy's death, Les once again began writing many letters to his children. The letters, portions of which were sentimental, nearly always mentioned Amy, and they indicate that he was probably happier when he was traveling; he had trouble living in an eerily quiet and empty house, and housekeeping chores were clearly challenging to him. As he admitted in letters, he could never keep the home in the same meticulous shape as Amy had. Les noted that he might be better off if he did not live in the house which, as he said shortly after her death, "was still warm from her touch from basement to attic." During the first few years after her death, their wedding anniversary, the anniversary of her death, holidays, and other events consistently triggered nostalgic recollections in Les.

Brian and Norah both received consistent updates about their father's state of mind, which, he told them, was helped considerably by Pat, who helped him run the house and invited him to her home frequently. Throughout his life, Les believed firmly that one should not overburden family and friends with complaints about illnesses, unhappiness, or unpleasant events, and it may have been difficult for him to discuss his feelings about Amy's death with his children, since they, too, mourned her loss. Still, Les used Norah, particularly, as a sounding board for his reflections about Amy in the months after her death: "My bad days are mental and not physical and they come so strangely, without warning and without apparent cause when I am overwhelmed by the awful realization of loss and the memories of her gentleness and courage and happy disposition," he wrote. "It would help a little if I could remember any good things I ever did to bring her happiness or to make her life easier but I can't seem to do that and all I can recall are the selfish things and my offensive assumption of superiority to one who was so far above me in all aspects and the little hurts and the many absences and the dodging of responsibility and the lack of response to her innocent efforts to make conversation." This complete candor about what he felt were his own shortcomings emotionally was uncharacteristic of Les, although the guilt one spouse feels over the death of another may be normal. He now wished he had another chance to display his feelings toward her: "I suppose there was something perverse in me that made me undemonstrative and formal and cold when I should have met her warmth with warmth, her kindness with appreciation and yet I always loved her but it is not enough to love it must be shown, and while I never believed in heaven or hell now I know they exist and are of one's own creation."

Despite the sorrowful tone of some of the letters to his children, Les was not seeking sympathy—each time he wrote of his sadness, he also mentioned his traveling, the parties he attended, and, frequently, anecdotes about his beloved grandson. In one letter, in fact, he cheerfully describes the bookshelves he bought for his new apartment and how carpeting made the place homey. And he clearly looked forward to the impending birth of his second grandchild, as he wrote Norah: "As you know I think the world of Brian Matthew as a person and a character in his own right but I'll have a very special place in my heart for your baby."

His first grandchild lived in Ottawa, so he was able to see him frequently. The child was a source of awe to Les. When Brian Matthew McCauley (called Matthew) was two years old, Norah's son, Patrick, was born. The months before Patrick's arrival triggered in Les a bout of nostalgia regarding the birth of Pat, when he and Amy were living in Quebec, far from their families. "Well my dear," he wrote to Norah, "I think of you very often and wonder how you are enduring the waiting and I live over again the late months of 1928 when your mother was waiting, with none of her own people near her, and a lot of financial worries to disturb her. And I know you have her courage and common sense." Such reminiscing about milestones in his life—such as the birth of his children—required little prompting, particularly as Les grew older.

* * *

If work had always been a comfort to Les, he must have taken great solace from the fact that his workload for the film bureau as well as the CBC continued to grow by late 1955. He enjoyed the challenge and hard work required to write the script for the "insulin" film, as he called it, although he was not aware at this point that the project would be all but abandoned. As was the case throughout his life, nothing compared to the exhilaration of a good day of writing. "Gosh, I've got a long way to go yet," he told Norah about the script. "But what has been done reads very well and should play nicely I think. I love writing drama. The more I know of its difficulties and problems, the more I enjoy it. How to keep the dialogue terse and yet natural, how to keep the tensions going, how to make people reveal themselves by what they do and say."

Whether it was a result of the stress associated with Amy's death or his immersion even deeper into his work, Les suffered a physical setback in early 1956, about six months or so after Amy's death. He was diagnosed with gallstones and needed to go into the hospital for an operation. Les seemed unusually blasé about the diagnosis and relatively unworried by the hospitalization of about a week. But neither the illness nor the operation kept Les from his compulsion to write, even from the hospital. He wrote out, longhand, a letter to Pat outlining the locations of various bank accounts and funds. Any fear he had before the operation apparently evaporated afterward, and the observant writer found the hospital to be a rich source of material. To keep from getting bored, he wrote doggerel, and later presented some of the results to Norah:

> "Departure"
> Ways of escape are numerous.
> Some people, to be humorous,
> Recommend liquor
> As cheaper and quicker
> Than bus or train
> Or streamlined plane
> But if you really want to get away from it all
> You simply can't beat pentathol.

> "Relativity"
> The patient in 94
> Is making a greater uproar
> About the loss of his specs
> Than the patient in 93
> Who is learning that he
> Has completely lost interest in sex.

Les was fortunate to have had good health most of his life, and, at age fifty-three, this was his first extended hospital stay. By this time in his life, he had put on a little weight, though, and he began mentioning in letters attempts to diet. Although he never weighed more than about 150 or 160 pounds, he felt that was substantial for his five-foot-three height. Within a year of Amy's death, however, his state of mind improved a bit, due to several factors: the news from Norah that he would become a grandfather again, the wedding of Brian, which brought the entire family together again for the event, and, perhaps most important, the entry into his life of Beatrice Greenaway Kenney.

***

Despite a growing restlessness about his job at the NFB, Les moved to Montreal in 1956 when the film agency moved its headquarters there. Factors other than the job, however, may have prompted the move. Shortly after her death, Amy's "presence" in his Ottawa home on Christie Street brought him some comfort, but he soon felt that living in the house did him more harm than good. As he packed up the home to move, the excruciating loneliness he had felt earlier was reignited: "I thought I was over the worst of it but the days and evenings of going through old letters, papers and photographs left me very depressed," he wrote Norah and Lou.

The move to Montreal allowed Les to begin a new life of sorts, but it did take him away from his immediate family—his daughter Pat, her husband, Bill, and his beloved grandson, Brian Matthew. As he told Norah, Pat had been a great comfort to him after Amy's death. In addition to offering moral support and companionship, she helped him cope with the practical issues of keeping a home. But the relationship between Pat and Les had always been a little troubled. The two were very different in temperament—Pat could be confrontational and brutally candid and at times intentionally hurtful, while her father was just the opposite. The feeling that she was a disappointment to her parents seemed to haunt her and color her relationship with her father.

Still, Pat loved her father and a few letters she wrote him late in his life reminiscing about their years in Haileybury and Ottawa indicate that she considered her childhood happy. Les certainly adored and respected Pat for her intelligence, her energy, and her skill in maintaining a home and family. He was fully aware that her temperamental demeanor toward him was simply a reflection of her personality (she would never succeed in a career with the diplomatic corps, he once wrote Norah, diplomatically). But that didn't take the sting from Pat's criticisms of him. For instance, in a letter to Norah shortly after Amy's death, he said that Pat had been sharply critical of his housekeeping skills. Les had been somewhat proud of the fact that he took on the new task of keeping house after his wife's death, and was surprised and hurt by Pat's claim (even though, as his two other children acknowledge, his forte was never housekeeping). Much more hurtful, though, was her accusation much later in his life that Les was not an attentive grandfather. By the time Pat leveled this accusation, Les had more than a dozen grandchildren, including several stepgrandchildren, and he was careful to note the birthdays of all with special gifts and to acknowledge their accomplishments. In fact, he thought long and hard about what would be the perfect gifts for his children and grandchildren. That criticism truly hurt Les, who had always prided himself on the fact that he remained close to his family and welcomed the many additions to his family as his own children grew older. As he wrote to Pat shortly after she married, the marriage of his own children made him think about the grand scale of life: "I have a very strong sense of the continuity of existence—people are born, they have suffering and happiness, they give life to others and the cycle is repeated, so this is all in the normal way of things."

He and Amy had always been close to their own siblings and parents, but the death of Amy drove home to Les even more the importance of family. Shortly after her death, when he learned that he would have a second grandchild, he began taking comfort in the idea that Amy would live on through her grandchildren. "A long and terrible year [the year of Amy's death] has been made tolerable only by the changes that took place in our lives," he wrote Norah and Lou. "I hope there will be much of her in the grandchildren; I could wish them nothing better than to have something of her beauty, something of her kindness and of her disposition as I knew it at its best." And, as he told his daughters, his greatest fear in life was that his family would gradually drift apart and communicate only through Christmas and birthday cards. Fortunately for him, Les's fear was never realized. Little did he know at that time that rather than diminish, his familial relations were about to grow.

***

Les had relocated for professional reasons many times in his life, but the move to Montreal in 1956 may have been one of the most difficult. It was the first time in more than twenty-five years that he moved without his wife or family. As such, the physical act of moving was simpler, but he discovered that it is much easier for a man in his twenties and thirties to pull up roots than it is for a man in his mid-fifties. As he told Brian in a long, confessional letter, he was lonely, missed the familiar routine and people of his life in Ottawa, and lived a rather mundane existence. In November 1956, six months after he moved there and slightly more than a year after Amy's death, he blamed his loneliness in part on himself and the emptiness he still felt about her death: "I shall never be really reconciled to her loss," he wrote. "I have managed to make a sort of life without her but it is a relatively empty, barren existence and dreadfully lonely. I do not make friends readily, of course, but Montreal has been even worse than I expected. . . . A big city is impersonal and one has to make one's own social life which I haven't taken the trouble to do."

The uncharacteristically intimate and confessional tone of the letter was, however, setting the stage for a big revelation to Brian: that Les was involved in a serious relationship that he implied could lead to marriage.

Les had met the forty-year-old widow Beatrice Greenaway Kenney in the spring of 1955 when he was in Hanover, Ontario, shooting *Strike in Town,* a film board project about collective bargaining. Les was introduced to Bea, who told him her three little girls would like to be extras in the filming. He was also told that she had lost her husband, a steelworker, in an industrial accident in Hamilton, Ontario. Although he admitted he thought her attractive at the time, nothing came of their conversation until eight or nine months later, after Amy's death. Les was visiting Toronto on business and happened to see Bea again; the two chatted and began a correspondence that soon led to a serious romantic relationship.

Les said nothing to any of his children about the relationship for nearly a year, apparently fearing that they would not approve. In this long letter to Brian, he hesitantly describes Bea and is very careful to state that his feelings for her in no way detract from his great love for Amy. The letter may reveal more than Les intended as he discusses his heartbreak at not having a family and wife to come home to. "I am thinking of giving up this solo existence in favor of a return to family and domestic life with all its responsibilities and—possibly—annoyances and cares and yet with all its compensations in companionship and the feeling that one is again part of a family, a social unit."

Following was a detailed description of Bea, who, he acknowledges, "is very different from Amy in many ways [but] she has many of the same qualities I respected so much in Amy." Her family was English—like Amy's—and she was a swimmer and softball player in high school ("although there is nothing of the tough female athlete about her"). Les described her as slim and attractive with a good sense of humor, yet he admitted to Brian that words failed him when he tried to convey her true nature: "As a writer I am supposed to be able to describe people but I know that in all this I have not given you any impression of Beatrice's personality at all but she is the sort of nice pretty little woman whom every one likes at first sight." He added, modestly, "I am quite fond of her and although I can't imagine anyone being in love with me she assures me she is and certainly she has a most flattering reverence for my intellectual capacities. We find a great deal to laugh about when we are together and I would say that we are very happy when we are with each other."

Les's letter is poignant in that it understates the elation he felt at meeting and falling in love with Bea. He was fearful that his children would resent the relationship, and he took great pains to tell Brian that Bea had a home and money of her own (her late husband had owned a business). Bea had three little girls living at home and, as he learned later, two older boys who were already out of the house. He very much liked Kathy (eight), Anne (ten), and Claire (twelve). But he naturally feared that his own grown children would bristle at the prospect of a new family for their father.

Les wrote Brian that he had not yet told Pat or Norah about Bea and asked in a postscript if either of them had mentioned anything to Brian about the prospect of Les remarrying. At the end of the letter, he also repeats that he would give up his now lucrative career, his home in Montreal, and his relationship with Bea "to be back in the kitchen at Christie St. at dinner with everyone squabbling and my Amy serving up dinner. Because there was life there . . . if I can't go back maybe I can go forward, realize that people need other people, find some happiness and companionship in what time is left." The closeness and cohesiveness family provided was vital to his well-being. Les was not the type to live in solitude.

Within a few days, Les wrote Norah and Pat about his situation, describing Bea in terms similar to those in his letter to Brian. Les was a realist and acknowledged briefly to Norah that Bea and Amy were unlike in many ways: Bea was an outgoing and social creature who definitely "like[d] a drink," as Les put it, had coffee and cigarettes for breakfast, and loved going out. Having met Les after he had achieved a bit of success, she welcomed the idea of being linked to a recognized writer and enjoyed the perks of his job regarding travel and socializing. Bea had her own affectionate nickname for Les. She called him "Charlie," based on the first name he never used. Bea Kenney was very different from Amy, although it might be said that she and Les were in many ways kindred souls. His marriage to her in 1957 changed his life.

15

. . . .

A GHOST EMERGES

By the late 1950s, perhaps when he least expected it, things began falling into place for Les personally and professionally. He remarried, attended the weddings of two of his children, and, by the end of the decade, had three grandsons. Professionally, he was embarking on a new career and obtaining a small measure of the recognition he had long sought. And, for one of the first periods of his life, he was relatively comfortable financially, so he was able to indulge in his favorite hobbies—reading, traveling, and seeing plays and movies.

In the summer of 1956, Brian's marriage to Joan Pellet outside New York City drew the McFarlane family together, and also allowed Les to spend a few days in Manhattan. It had been nearly a year since Amy's death, and Les was still grieving. Brian's wedding choked him up, as he wrote Norah later: "It was a lovely wedding and they are surely a handsome couple. I couldn't help but think, just as I did at your wedding, how sad it was that Amy missed it and of course she would have been in her glory at her Bri's wedding." The usually stoic Les said he nearly broke down. "During the ceremony I came within an inch of disgracing myself by tears and I'm afraid I wasn't very jolly company over the weekend." Les had always enjoyed the rare gatherings of all three of his children, but indicated in letters to them that the reunions were often so short and packed with activity that he rarely had an opportunity to talk in any depth to any of his children during such visits. And while he occasionally talked on the phone with them—particularly on holidays and birthdays—it was letters that he appreciated and valued the most. As he once wrote Norah, "It was so good to receive a real letter from you. Telephone conversations are all very well—there is an immediacy to them—but letters give more time for reflection."

Life was finally returning to normal for Les. He told Norah that after the festivities associated with Brian and Joan's wedding, he spent a full day in New York City, seeing two movies and exploring the city. Always a critic of sorts, Les's experience as a filmmaker now made it difficult for him to view movies as a layman. He gave Norah detailed critiques of the films he saw—*Moby Dick* and the French-made *The Proud and the Beautiful*. *Moby Dick*, he said, "is a tremendous film, production-wise, and yet it is unfortunately a bit of a bore entertainment-wise." *The Proud and the Beautiful* "is unusual and stimulating and has the damnedest music score I've heard in years consisting almost entirely of a juke box marimba number with a singer who keeps shrieking with absolutely maniac laughter—and this thing goes on in the background, at times so inappropriate as to be almost blasphemous, conveying a sense of strange things. . . . It is really weird and yet dramatically very effective."

Many of his letters to his three children were filled with news about activities of their siblings. In the letters, he frequently referred to visits with his children, thanking them effusively for their hospitality and usually remarking how much he enjoyed spending time with their families. Naturally, his letters to his children revealed his own philosophy about life—with Norah, it often centered on writers and writing; with Brian, about career and success; and with Pat, it often centered on family and the importance of confidence. In one letter written to Pat in 1956 on the first anniversary of Amy's death, Les seems troubled that the beautiful and vivacious Pat seemed to be suffering from low self-esteem. His concern was apparently based on a comment she made to Les that she was intimidated by many of the clever and beautiful women she met at parties in Ottawa. (Pat's husband, Bill, was a conductor and music director, and the two socialized frequently.) "So much of the glib talk is compensation for the things they feel they lack themselves," he wrote her.

Pat's comments may have particularly bothered Les because he had sensed the same inferiority complex in Amy. If Pat suffered from low self-esteem, few around her may have been aware of it—through her early adulthood, she was a part-time artist and model, and, despite a rapidly growing family, she was always involved with multiple community and social activities, and barely stopped to take a breath. Her constant motion sometimes worried her father, who commented on it occasionally in letters to both his daughters. He told Pat that the role of wife and mother is not valued fully or understood in society. And he offered her some words of wisdom that he had learned to live by: "Talent is always recognized in time and the opportunists and highly aggressive people don't always last, nor do they find much happiness in life."

***

As a young man, Les was closely attuned to changes in the world around him, and he was willing to adapt to them when it came to his career. That instinct to change with the times is what kept him afloat financially during his decades as a freelance writer and led to his position at the Department of Munitions and Supply, a key role in the newly formed National Film Board of Canada, and a career as a writer in the newly emerging medium of television. Les maintained this flexibility and willingness to change with the times, even though it frequently meant learning new skills and adapting his existing skills to new formats. ("If you can't change with the times, you're a dead duck," he once said in an interview, describing one of the prerequisites for Canadian writers.) While he worked at the film bureau, he could see that television was becoming the wave of the future, and it was probably inevitable that his occasional freelance television scripts for the Canadian Broadcasting Corporation would lead to full-time work as a television scriptwriter and editor.

The so-called golden age of television in the United States in the late 1940s offered diverse programming in a variety of formats. But none was so daring and innovative as the hour-long dramatic productions aired live. In 1948, the Ford Motor Company was one of the first corporations to sponsor an hour-long dramatic program, *The Ford Television Theatre*. The CBS program aired once a month, and usually featured fifty-minute versions of three-act Broadway plays. Max Wilk, who wrote and helped produce some of those early *Ford Television Theatre* shows, described in a memoir how the inexperienced cast, crew, and writers stumbled through the initial shows. The writers soon learned that adapting a stage play to the medium of television was not as easy as it first looked. Those involved with the show earned little money, he wrote, but loved every minute of it. Surprisingly, after all the blunders, Ford wanted to continue into a second season—with two shows each month. *The Ford Television Theatre* ultimately aired such classic plays as *Arsenic and Old Lace*, *The Man Who Came to Dinner*, and *Night Must Fall*, starring the likes of Edward Everett Horton, Zero Mostel, and Boris Karloff. In addition to providing a valuable training ground for writers and actors, that show and several others, including NBC's *Philco Television Playhouse*, pioneered the idea of the corporation as sponsor of live television drama, a concept that would shape the future of television.

It is not surprising that the enterprising and versatile Leslie McFarlane, who by the mid-1950s had nearly three decades of experience in a variety of media, would want to play a role in the emerging world of television. Writing radio plays had introduced him to the art of writing scripts, and his role at the National Film Board had accustomed him to communicating visually. He was a natural.

Almost as soon as the CBC broadcast its first show in English in 1952, Les began taking part in its development. A Canadian version of the U.S. anthology series first aired in the summer of 1953 with the CBC *Playbill* series, a thirty-minute live drama series that featured work by Canadians and non-Canadians. A year later, a series called *On Camera* debuted. Les wrote for both series. Six of his scripts were adapted for broadcast from 1953 to 1955.

As Canadian television coverage expanded in the middle and late 1950s, so did the diversity and number of shows produced by the CBC. Like their counterparts in the United States, Canadian corporations and Canadian divisions of American companies began sponsoring hour and half-hour live dramas. General Motors, for instance, sponsored two different shows: *General Motors Presents* and *General Motors Theatre*. Both focused primarily on the work of Canadian writers and actors, although producers of the former, a one-hour weekly broadcast, found they sometimes had to import scripts simply because they did not get the volume of Canadian scripts needed to air a regularly scheduled show. (Les wrote one script for this series, "Love Story—1910," in the early 1960s.) *General Motors Presents,* which aired from 1954 to 1956, was initially produced by Sydney Newman, who came to the CBC from the National Film Board, along with story editor Nathan Cohen. Both were dynamic and controversial pioneers in Canadian broadcasting.

Central to this landscape, however, were talented and enthusiastic writers who were willing to work hard and take a chance on this new medium. Les already had a foot in the door in the late 1950s and early 1960s because of his scripts for both General Motors shows, but it was a combination of sheer luck, determination, and contacts he made through the film bureau that led to a key role with the CBC.

Before he went into the hospital for his gallbladder operation in 1956, Les had made a commitment to give Nathan Cohen a rough outline for a television script. As he lay in the hospital recovering from his surgery, the compulsive Les scrawled an outline for a TV play on hospital stationery and sent it to Cohen. The resulting last-ditch effort, which Les told Norah he could barely remember, apparently caught the eye of Cohen, much to Les's delight. As he recovered at his daughter Pat's home in Ottawa several weeks later, Cohen tracked him down and called from Toronto to tell him the CBC would pay him $1,000 if he could provide them with a draft for the play in a month. The timing could not have been better: it conveyed to Les that he could, indeed, be a player in this new medium and, on a purely practical note, it would help pay for his operation. The result was "Black of the Moon," which aired in October 1956 on the CBC *First Performance* series, a series commissioned by the Canada Savings Bond promotional campaign. The show was a dramatization of the Riel Rebellion, an uprising in the Northwest Territory of Canada in the late 1800s.

Several of the early CBC series, including *General Motors Theatre,* aired the early work of the British-born Arthur Hailey, who had moved to Canada and held dual citizenship. Hailey would soon write several best-selling novels, including *Airport* and *Hotel.* The producers of *General Motors Theatre* offered the inexperienced writer $600 for his first try at writing—a script called "Flight into Danger" about a novice pilot who must fly a plane from Vancouver to Toronto when the crew becomes ill after eating the in-flight meal. The show was later made into the film *Airport.* Many actors who got their start in the CBC—including Leslie Nielson and William Shatner—later became well known in the United States. The director Norman Jewison also established his career as a director of CBC series dramas during these early years of the network.

Canadian television drama in the 1950s was creative, innovative, and idealistic, focusing on using primarily Canadian talent. But while that goal may have been admirable for a public television outlet, producers for the CBC series were learning quickly that there simply wasn't enough of that talent to go around. The problem may have stemmed partly from pay levels lower than in the United States. Les discovered that story editors were begging for talented and productive Canadian writers like himself. He bluntly told Norah that "apparently the Canadian writers who bemoan the lack of opportunity for native talent just can't deliver." The connection with Nathan Cohen would turn out to be pivotal in his life. The television play Les sketched in his hospital bed, "Black of the Moon," drew kudos from viewers and a CBC producer, who told Les that no one wrote better drama in Canada. As a result of that play, Cohen commissioned him to write more. And, oddly, the link to Cohen and the CBC indirectly led to the reawakening of a sleeping ghost in Les's past: the Hardy Boys.

When his television writing career accelerated in 1957, it had been more than ten years since Les had written for the Stratemeyers. After he ended his affiliation with the syndicate, he never looked back—literally or figuratively. All he had left to remind him of the Stratemeyers was a shelf full of two dozen or so syndicate books that he had written as Franklin W. Dixon. After all, as he noted in his memoir decades later, the work for the Stratemeyer Syndicate offered him a little extra money when he needed it—about $2,500 or so for all his work—but it was nothing he used to promote himself professionally. In the fall of 1957, Les and Bea invited a young writer named Stuart Trueman to their home. Les had just adapted Trueman's book *Cousin Elva* for the CBC series *First Performance*, working with Cohen and Trueman on that project. As he wrote Norah, the subject of Franklin W. Dixon came up during Trueman's visit, and much to Trueman's delight, he learned that he was in the company of the Hardy Boys author: "I have seldom seen anyone so impressed," Les wrote. "I autographed one of the books and sent it home with him as a gift to his eleven-year-old son and a letter today indicated that Mr. Trueman . . . has become a hero to his son and the son has become a lad of distinction at Rothesay Central High."

While this incident may seem trivial, it was not: for perhaps the first time in his life, Les realized his value as Franklin W. Dixon, a role about which he was ambivalent for much of his adult life. This sudden, retroactive fame as the author of the Hardy Boys touched Les, and he no longer kept secret his dual identity as Leslie McFarlane and Franklin W. Dixon.

***

In Bea, Les had found someone who enjoyed travel and the social scene as much as he did. Shortly after their marriage in 1957, the two traveled to Banff and Calgary on film board business. After a whirlwind tour that included a visit to a cousin of Les's in Calgary, Les called the trip a success: "Bea enjoyed every minute of the trip and declared it the high spot of her life. We had a lot of laughs and I surely enjoyed having her with me," he wrote Norah. Luckily, her children, who had stayed home, "hadn't withered away when we got back."

It was no surprise when, in 1958, the CBC offered Les a full-time job: he would replace Nathan Cohen as a network story editor, with responsibility for two key CBC series: the hour-long *General Motors Presents* and a half-hour series called *The Unforeseen*. The job entailed soliciting scripts for the shows and determining whether they were suitable for broadcast, as well as adapting existing plays for television and writing scripts on his own. *The Unforeseen,* in particular, was an important and unique show for the CBC. Each show was to be suspenseful and end with a twist in the manner of O. Henry. According to CBC publicity, some of the shows were futuristic narratives or tales of the supernatural, much like the American show *The Twilight Zone.*

The Unforeseen provided special challenges for the CBC. Years later, a CBC official reflected that the nature of the show excluded most Canadian writers: "We had a fair number of playwrights who could write a story involving a personal situation with which they were familiar, but what we lacked was the sort of skilled craftsman who could be given this sort of assignment, think for a few moments, and then come up with the sort of suspense story or mystery that the series demanded." It was the versatile "skilled craftsman" Leslie McFarlane whose job it was to find and edit provocative scripts for the innovative *The Unforeseen.* As he soon discovered, the job was not an easy one.

***

Les took a leave of absence at the film board to take the CBC job, although it was probably assumed he never would return. The new job came at the perfect time in his life: while he did not dislike living in Montreal, he was now able to relocate with Bea and her three daughters to the Toronto area. The move allowed the couple to start a new life together at a time when Les finally had some disposable income. They first bought a home in Agincourt, outside Toronto, and had lived there for a few years when one day Les decided he wanted to show Bea the home he had owned in Whitby before he went to work for the film board. The two drove there and found a for-sale sign up on the house next door. The same day, the McFarlanes bought the house at 704 King Street, next door to the home where Les and Amy and their three children once lived. Although Les moved frequently in his life, he said in many interviews that his favorite city was Whitby. As a story editor at CBC, Les was indeed a minor celebrity in the town, and, as he had been during his young adulthood in Haileybury, a favorite son of the community. Eventually, he served on the city's library board, as he had done in Haileybury, and on his seventieth birthday, city officials named a street after him—McFarlane Court. (After his death, a school in Whitby was named after him.)

During his first year or so with the CBC, newspapers and television stations throughout the region interviewed him—a startling role reversal for Les, who was usually the one doing the interviewing. He described to Norah the shock of watching himself being interviewed on a television show that was aired in Toronto and Ottawa. "My loyal family assure me that I was sensational and did them great honor," he said. But, he added, "it was a traumatic experience to see this aging, jowlish dignified old party pontificating on CBC script problems. . . . How is it that one always thinks of oneself as being quite young and sprightly. . . . The soul doesn't age; the body does. So I suppose one must be on the alert and see to it that gay, sprightly Soul doesn't betray dignified, ponderous old Body into unbecoming attitudes and antics."

While Les did not "pontificate" in the newspaper stories, he did address the network's script problems with candor. The main problem was, simply, that there were not enough Canadian scriptwriters to provide material for the CBC live shows. As he told a writer for the *Toronto Telegram*, part of the problem was the fault of the CBC, which did not pay its writers well, forcing them to seek jobs in the United States: "Most of the top-flight writers— those who are looking for big money—have turned to Hollywood," he said. Writers like Arthur Hailey, he said, had no reason to accept the $1,000 per script that the CBC paid when they could earn eight to ten times that much in the United States. Les told another reporter that there were only about a dozen professional drama writers in all of Canada.

Les loved his country and his fellow Canadians, but he pulled no punches when he said that, sadly, many Canadian writers simply lacked the ability to write for the relatively new medium of television. Many good fiction writers cannot maintain the tension needed in the visual world of television, he said: "In writing fiction, you're telling a story. But in writing a television play it's more than a story . . . it's a drama, dealing with tensions between people. You may have a very predictable plot, but if the tensions between people in your story are strong enough, this can be a good show." Of the hundreds of scripts he read each month, few were usable, making it necessary for him to write many of the scripts himself—a task which could take from several nights to six or seven months, depending on the subject matter of the show.

In the case of *The Unforeseen*, show officials did adapt stories from writers such as H. G. Wells and Guy de Maupassant. Les sought scripts that dealt with unconventional themes, occult forces, and unexplained phenomena. He was careful, though, not to let the tail wag the dog when it came to plot: "Like a scorpion, the sting is in the tail," he told a reporter, referring to the importance of a surprise ending in the narrative. "But the danger is, you can sting yourself to death. Besides a trick, you've got to deal in tensions between sympathetic human beings."

Les was intrigued by the pervasive—and often invasive—nature of television, which was unlike anything he had ever experienced before. The fact that viewers watch plays in their own living rooms often prompts brutal candor, he said. "You make such devastating remarks. You'd never be so insulting, if you were with company in the theater. Because TV is free, you feel free to exclaim, 'Oh no! Not that ham again! What a corny script! What a lousy singer!'"

Les was always quick to point out that most writers of fiction use incidents and observations from their own lives as the backbone of their work. But as he grew older, he became increasingly interested in reading and writing about the lives and motivations of real people. His reading increasingly leaned to biographies and memoirs, and his work for the CBC frequently centered around the dramatization of true stories and historical events. The people who drew his interest were not always famous, but they were usually complex or unconventional.

An enterprising scriptwriter and avid reader of biographies evidently could find plenty of fascinating people to write about. Les's "Love Story—1910," for instance, which aired as part of the *General Motors Presents* series in 1961, told the story of the sensational murder trial of the physician Dr. Hawley Harvey Crippen, a case that has fascinated the British for nearly a century. Crippen, an American who lived in London, fell in love with his secretary; together they boarded a ship headed to Quebec shortly after Crippen's wife mysteriously disappeared. Crippen's lover was dressed as a boy, and the two traveled as father and son until they were discovered by the authorities, who had found Mrs. Crippen's dismembered body in the couple's home. Crippen maintained his innocence throughout a sensational trial, but was ultimately found guilty and hanged. Les may have been ahead of his time when he came up with the idea to write about Crippen: true-to-life crime stories became fodder for television shows and movies in the late twentieth century.

One of Les's favorite scripts, though, was "Eye-Opener Man," which he developed for the *General Motors Presents* series. It told the story of Bob Edwards, a frontier editor and humorist whose quirky weekly newspaper, the *Calgary Eye-Opener,* was innovative in the early 1900s. Les compared him to Mark Twain and Ambrose Bierce. Les conducted extensive research into the life of Edwards, and he acknowledged he was pleased with the result. "Of all the stuff I've written for TV, this came closest to being what I've been trying to do," he told a reporter. The play was later adapted into a series by the same name for the network.

From his experience as a newspaper reporter, Les had developed a soft spot in his heart for editors and writers who were crusty icono-clasts—including those in his own family. Upon learning that his great-great-grandfather, the Irishman William Tully, had founded the first newspaper published in the Ottawa Valley, he wrote the script for the comedy "Don't Shake Your Family Tree" for the series *Playdate*. Tully em-igrated to Canada by boat with his young daughter in 1818, inspiring Les to write about the descendants of those who made that perilous jour-ney and the importance of their Irish heritage.

Les may not have been paid as well as his American counterparts, but he did have the luxury of working for a noncommercial network. Theo-retically, at least, he did not need to worry about bowing to the pressures of commercial sponsors who wanted to have an impact on program-ming. In 1960, after about two years as a story editor, Les told a reporter that he did not feel pressure from corporate sponsors to alter the con-tent or subject matter of the shows he accepted. In an interview with *Lib-erty* magazine, Les said that neither the network nor sponsors ever restrained him or chastised him for any episode of *The Unforeseen*. "I have yet to receive a directive from a sponsor, asking me to remove a 'damn' or a 'hell,'" he said. Still, he added, his "small-town upbringing," combined with his feeling that vulgarity has no place "in the parlor," had also kept him from accepting scripts that he saw as obscene. Les was em-inently aware that *The Unforeseen* was aired early in the evening and was viewed by families. He acknowledged that he walked a fine line as script editor of that show: while he did not want the scripts to talk down to au-diences, he also knew the shows must be creative and entertaining.

The *Liberty* interview painted a picture of Les as the seasoned veteran writer that he felt he was: "Short and stubby, with pleasant blue-gray eyes, he was attired in black braces and a pink tie on a lemon-yellow shirt. At 56 [although he was probably 57 at the time], he's a writer of the old school." His small Toronto office, the article noted, "is deco-rated with quaint circa-1912 movie stills showing John Barrymore col-lared by a cop and Francis X. Bushman about to be hanged as a cowboy." Later, after a day's work, he is described as sinking, exhausted, into a seat at the Celebrity Club, brooding over a whisky and soda.

As Les soon learned, CBC sponsors' definitions of what they considered "vulgar" could be broad. While the scripts Les selected, wrote, or edited did not use risqué language, at least one sponsor believed they could be politically incorrect. In 1961, General Motors pulled its sponsorship of a comedy called "The Conquest of Cobbletown" that Les wrote for the series *General Motors Presents*, complaining that it satirized Canadian nationalism and appeared to advocate U.S. takeover of Canadian companies. GM of Canada said it could not sanction a show that criticized Canadian patriotism. (The play satirically tells the story of the president of a small Canadian company who makes rash statements about the invasion by the company's new American owners.) The CBC aired the show anyway without GM sponsorship. Les was unfazed by the controversy, which even merited a small story in the *New York Times*. "If this happened in the United States, where the networks are commercial, I wouldn't be backed up," he told the *Montreal Star*. The CBC even went so far as to issue a statement claiming that Sunday evening audiences "will find this light comedy by one of Canada's top writers to be entertaining and amusing." Les added that while he believed the relations between Canada and the United States were a bit "strained" in the spring of 1961, he felt it did no harm to poke fun at Canadian nationalism as well as American patriotism.

Les had earned the network's loyalty—the year before the controversy, in 1960, he was named by *Liberty* magazine as Canada's best television playwright of the year, an honor that brought prestige to him and the network. The series *The Unforeseen* was also honored by the magazine as the best dramatic show on Canadian television. Those honors, the prestige and publicity he received as a top CBC editor and writer, and his new home life made him a happy man in the early 1960s.

***

As Les wrote Norah, he was adapting well to his new life with Bea and her three children. "The children are nice little creatures, exuberant and curious . . . and I like them very much indeed," he wrote. Les enjoyed watching Bea's interaction with her daughters, no doubt because her personality and style of child rearing differed so greatly from Amy's. "Bea alternates between cussing the hell out of them and spoiling them to death," he wrote, although arguments between the girls and their mother inevitably ended with apologies and hugs. His marriage and new family were good for him, he told his children. "I am happy and contented," he said. "Bea has a ready laugh and a considerable wit of her own, waits on me hand and foot and I guess we've each learned a good deal about marriage and how important it is to overlook things that don't really matter much." Les's job with the CBC did not require the extensive travel of his film bureau job, but he and Bea enjoyed taking trips for fun, including one to England and Ireland.

Les inherited a ready-made family with this marriage to Bea. The girls were young enough that as they grew up, the only father figure in their life was Les, and as they said much later in their life, they considered him their father. (Kathy, in particular, the youngest, was four when her father died; the oldest, Claire, was eight.) As they got older, they also grew to respect Les for his dry sense of humor and his kindness to them.

Les had always been conscious of the fact that he needed to change with the times professionally, and he had been successful in doing so. As he grew older, though, he was also very conscious of the fact that he needed to observe social and cultural changes and not let time slip past him. As he wrote Norah about watching himself being interviewed, he wanted to re-main a "young soul." Through all the changes he had seen in literature, radio, films, and now, television, he had never seen anything like the per-missiveness that characterized some of the media in the late 1950s and early 1960s. As he said when he was interviewed about sponsor pressure on programming, Les was ambivalent about the profanity and frankness that he felt was becoming a part of literature and popular culture, and did not necessarily want it beamed into his own living room. But he also knew he could not ignore or criticize changing values without becoming familiar with them. He regarded some aspects of this new wave of culture with skep-ticism and humor. For instance, in a letter to Norah in early 1958, he de-scribed in humorous detail a new play he had seen called *Cat on a Hot Tin Roof*—a play, he believed, whose messages were not exactly subtle. "Act Three has everyone on stage except Big Daddy all shouting and abusing each other like mad and the play comes to a satisfactory conclusion when the blonde locks up all sonny boy's booze and won't give him the key un-less he does come to bed with her," he writes. "As the curtain falls he is crawling reluctantly between the sheets while his wife croons happily, but as he has had a glass in his hand ever since the beginning of Act One and has made at least eighteen trips to the bar for a refill in the course of two hours and a half, I would consider her triumph as hollow."

But his initial dislike of such modern playwriting did not completely alienate him; Les would keep up with popular culture, eventually reading the work of contemporary authors like J.R.R. Tolkien, Stephen King, and others, and even going to see the film *Last Tango in Paris*. As he told a reporter in 1969, what goes around comes around—even when it comes to matters of taste. "He has so far not fallen in with today's trend to sex and violence," the story said. "He thinks the pendulum has swung the other way from the straight-laced and unreal fiction of years ago, and in turn will swing again from equally unreal writing of today."

***

Les was consistently the subject of newspaper and magazine stories during his tenure as CBC drama editor, and nearly all these stories had one thing in common: they noted that he was the author of many of the first Hardy Boys books—a fact that Les rarely mentioned to anyone for most of his career. There were two main reasons for his secrecy about his ghostwriting days: first, he never thought that his work there was important enough to merit mention; and second, he understood that he may still have been under the vow of silence the Stratemeyers asked of their ghostwriters. Until the late 1950s, the only recognition he gained as Franklin W. Dixon came when his son Brian learned accidentally that his father was the author of the Hardy Boys books when he and his two sisters were growing up in Whitby. As a result, he occasionally brought in friends to have his father—aka Franklin W. Dixon—autograph their copies of the Hardy Boys books. ("God forgive me, I started to sign Franklin's name," he recalled thirty years later.) It was then that Les began to realize what would be driven home to him during his CBC years—that while he didn't take his work as Franklin W. Dixon seriously, millions of others did. During those three or four years with the CBC, Les found that people were impressed when he revealed that he had once been Franklin W. Dixon. He knew, vaguely, that the books sold well, but did not know *how* well, so he never gave much thought to the impact they had on readers. A few of the interviews Les gave simply mentioned his past affiliation with the Hardy Boys. Others went into more detail about such topics as his lack of royalties for the work and whether he regretted signing away any future income he might have derived from the best-selling books.

Although the Hardy Boys were old news to Les by this point, he had long accepted the fact that the agreement he signed early on with the Stratemeyer Syndicate was binding, and that he was not and never would be entitled to royalties from the books. By the late 1950s, however, he may have realized just how much those royalties would have amounted to: by that time about 12 million of the copies of the Hardy Boys had been sold. "I went into it with my eyes open," he said in a 1962 interview with the *Toronto Star.* But he noted that even if he had been paid a half cent royalty per book, he could have retired early. The article called Les the most prolific and best-selling author in Canada.

It had been a long time since Les had thought about his work writing the Hardy Boys, but he must have briefly had contact with the syndicate or its representatives shortly after Amy's death. During this time, he did agree to forfeit any further claim he had to profits generated from any future film or television version of the Hardy Boys. Little is known about this episode in his life, although in the mid-1950s, the first televised version of the Hardy Boys aired on the Mickey Mouse Club show, and it is possible that his forfeiture of rights was associated with that show. It is likely, though, that his grief over Amy's sudden illness and death made this a low priority for him at the time

The many references to his authorship of the Hardy Boys books during these days in Whitby prompted children to visit his home. As he had done for some of Brian's friends during his previous residence in Whitby, he autographed their books. The revelation that he was one of several Franklin W. Dixons did not prompt attorneys for the Stratemeyer Syndicate to seek him out for revealing company secrets, but it did reawaken Les's ambivalent feelings about his role with the syndicate.

He must at least have been pleased that people he liked and respected were impressed that he wrote the books they and their children cherished. Yet he was also annoyed that with all his accomplishments and awards, it was his role as Franklin W. Dixon that seemed to garner the most publicity. After ticking off all his accomplishments in magazines, with the film bureau, in radio, and with the CBC, one reporter noted in 1969 that "Mr. McFarlane's most famous writing by far, which has entertained literally millions of young men around the world, is a part of his career he isn't really very happy about." His long-dormant feelings about being the stepfather of the Hardy Boys had always been complex, and now the boys were coming back to haunt him.

16

. . . .

GHOSTS OF THEIR FORMER SELVES

By the early 1960s, Les's life had stabilized—he was happy in his marriage to Bea and he enjoyed his new family. He was also reasonably comfortable financially, and could finally buy a house and travel with Bea.

Living in his favorite town of Whitby, he had become a minor celebrity, a status that meant much to him. In Whitby, which had a population of about 12,000 people, he was active in the community and was a member of the library and school boards. By the time he was in his mid-sixties, though, he may have experienced a sense of *déjà vu* professionally: the markets had changed, he had once again become a freelance writer, and again he experienced the wild ups and downs of that profession.

The fact that the Hardy Boys books had become so popular had eluded Les over the years, in part because most of their sales were in the United States, simply because of the bigger market there. Throughout the latter part of his life, he was asked repeatedly about this issue of royalties, and always had the same answer: "I . . . realize that the interviewer feels I should be regarded as an object of sympathy or contempt—sympathy as a victim of one of the greatest swindles of all time, contempt as the dumbest sucker of the age. It maddens me. It also saddens me." This speaks not just to his honesty, but also to the fact that, ultimately, his goal as a writer was not necessarily to become rich. To Les, writing was more about producing high-quality, respected work than it was about money, although a certain amount of celebrity would not have hurt. Finally, in his sixties, he was getting a taste of that recognition.

Part of his contentment at this point in his life stemmed from the fact that his own children were successful, personally and professionally. Norah and Brian, in addition to raising growing families, were thriving professionally. Norah, like her father, had become a versatile writer for television, for *Ms.* and other publications directed toward women, and of books and stories for juveniles. In 1967, her book *Summer in Stratford* won an award as Canada's best juvenile book for that year. Brian had become a sports broadcaster at several television stations in Canada and the United States, including ones in Schenectady, Montreal, and Toronto, and had also embarked on a career as an author of sports books. By the mid-1960s and early 1970s, he was becoming a well-known face and name in Canada. Les proudly described in a letter to Norah how he was once introduced at a cocktail party as "Brian McFarlane's father." Brian, of course, would go on to become even better known as a commentator for *Hockey Night in Canada,* one of the nation's leading sports broadcasts.

Les, too, was finally getting some of the recognition he had sought for many years. The outgoing and social Bea enjoyed her role as the writer's wife and the many social events to which they received invitations. She loved seeing Les as the center of attention, although it was not a role the reserved Les necessarily sought. After one gathering, he received a note from the hostess: "What a celebrity you have become, Leslie. Your presence simply made our party," she wrote.

Les's demeanor and behavior at these gatherings was far from flamboyant—in fact, his dry humor and discreet manner were his trademark, as his stepdaughters remember. Kathy, the youngest, recalled decades later that her stepfather usually sat back at cocktail gatherings and observed, occasionally making wry and hilarious comments. But his humor was good-natured, and he naturally got along well with people. "He wasn't outgoing," she said. "But he was so eloquent. He would sit back and take it all in."

The town of Whitby was the perfect location for Les. It was a beautiful small town that had the rustic feel that Les had always loved, and, in the 1960s, was far enough away from Toronto that its residents ventured there only on special occasions. For Les, though, the proximity to Toronto allowed him easy access to one of the busiest literary markets in North America. His home in Whitby and his new family gave Les just what he needed. In his letters to his Norah, Brian, and Pat, he frequently talked about his gardening and home upkeep efforts, happily describing the planting, painting, and mowing that are a part of home ownership. (His stepchildren said that his enthusiasm in the realm of home improvement may have been greater than his talent—it was Bea who usually took the initiative in upkeep of the house.) There is little question, though, that Les savored the beauty of the world around him: "Tulips are flourishing gaily, the apple trees are in bud, the beat-up juniper hedge has been grubbed out and replaced by spirea, the mint bed is green with promise of juleps to come and from now on it is going to be difficult to remain at the typewriter."

Their stepfather's biggest weakness may have been, in fact, his inability to deal with things mechanical, despite the best of intentions. Les was proud father of the bride to all three girls, and at Anne's wedding reception, he decided to film the reception. But the former film bureau director had apparently neglected to take the lens cap off the camera—the film did not come out.

Les's stepchildren remember him as a warm and gentle father who never exhibited anger or impatience, and who always provided an ear for them. Unlike their friends' fathers, he worked at home, and did not leave for an office regularly every day. Anne Yarrow and Kathy Palmer, like Norah and Brian, remember his ability to work with great concentration in his home office despite the chaos of three teenaged girls around the house, monopolizing the telephone and the bathroom. On a normal day, his stepdaughters remember, Les would stay in bed reading the paper and drinking orange juice while their mother got them off to school. He would then work much of the day, and he and Bea would have a cocktail at 5 p.m. Then came dinner—always an event for the family. Les not only loved food, he loved the process of dining. "We weren't allowed to wolf down a meal and then leave the table," Kathy Palmer remembers. "We talked about our days, what we did. He loved the conversation."

Like many people who love food and the ceremony surrounding its consumption, Les in his middle age had become quite an accomplished cook. Although he did not cook regularly, he had a collection of complex and offbeat recipes that he occasionally made for the family and for company. His specialty was a sweet white bean dish made with mint, canned tomatoes, paprika, and green peppers—a crowd pleaser at parties. "[Before social gatherings] they'd ask him to please bring his beans," Yarrow remembered.

To the three girls, though, their new father's gourmet tendencies cut both ways. A year or two after the five began living together, Bea was out of town one morning, leaving Les to provide breakfast for the girls, who then were all under the age of fourteen. He decided to make them a dish of whipped frozen orange juice concentrate with raisins, poured like syrup over toast. As Yarrow remembered, she and her sisters appreciated the effort, but were shocked at the result, desperately asking each other when Les left the room what they should do with the concoction.

As was the case when he lived in Haileybury as a young man, he was once again a big fish in a small pond. In Whitby, he was, as one headline writer wrote, "an inter-nationally known literary figure." Indeed, Les was, to a limited degree, internationally known as a television scriptwriter. Several of his plays that aired on the CBC were purchased by British TV, and at least one, "Don't Shake Your Family Tree," the comedy about Irish Canadians, was sold to CBS television in New York and aired on that network.

Small towns with their homey atmosphere, quirky residents, and folksy traditions were always a rich source of humor for Les, and they provided the material for much of his fiction, from his early days as a freelance writer for *Maclean's* to his years as author of the Hardy Boys books (set in the scenic but crime-riddled town of Bayport) and, now, as a television writer and lecturer. A popular speaker, Les frequently gave talks about his career as a television writer and his years as Franklin W. Dixon. Sometimes, his speeches were localized versions of his old short stories. In one tongue-in-cheek talk to the Whitby Rotary Club, for instance, he focused on ways the sleepy town could become more provocative and lure more visitors. For example, he said, the town could liven up its conventional speed-limit postings with something like the following: "This is Dundas Street on Highway Two / Maybe you'd like to go roaring through / But watch it buster, if you do / Our traffic cop has his eye on you." Les's affection for the town of Whitby manifested itself in ways beyond his civic involvement. Even after he and Bea sold their home on King Street in 1973, Les wrote a play for the Whitby Theatre Guild about Peter Perry, the founder of Whitby. The setting was his country store, the first building in the town.

***

Despite his status in Whitby and his comfortable financial situation, Les's career was far from secure in the early 1960s. His full-time job with the CBC—which was never designed to last longer than a few years— ended in 1961 or 1962, and he became a full-time freelance writer once again. He was an established name by this time, and his extensive contacts and experience in television helped him sell his work, but changes at the CBC caused diminishing television markets to dry up even further, and writers like Les were slowly being consigned to the sidelines.

The late 1950s had clearly been the heyday of live drama for the network, but by the early 1960s, that market was being replaced by documentaries and other types of programming. Few if any other venues outside the CBC existed for writers interested in television drama in

Canada. Many accomplished Canadian writers had fled to the United States, where writers were paid much more, and others had abandoned the profession completely because of low pay. The dearth of talented Canadian writers may have hastened the demise of television drama. One 1964 article in the *Toronto Star* noted that of only about twenty-four television drama writers in all of Canada, only two were able to make a living at it (one of those two being Leslie McFarlane). Many of the shows were written by non-Canadians, a phenomenon that worried CBC officials, who tried to offer incentives to Canadians to write for the CBC because they thought it important for the network to feature the work of the nation's citizens.

By 1962 or 1963, Les was in the familiar but uncomfortable position of waiting to hear if work he sent off would yield a paycheck. He told Norah how, if an outline he submitted to the CBC series *Playdate* was rejected, he would simply "look into the file marked 'Ideas—Playdate,' find another notion that seems reasonably promising, and do another outline." Of course, Les was not under the kinds of financial pressure now that he faced as a young man, so it was not imperative that his work be accepted. But, as a seasoned and successful professional, rejection was even harder on his ego, and signs were evident again of the old insecurity that used to dog him. One project in which he was instrumental, a series called *Eye-Opener Man*, had been canceled and, as he wrote Norah, "the atmosphere around the CBC . . . appears increasingly indifferent." But Les did not simply blame the CBC for his problems. He had, he said, "greater difficulty in making words do what I would like them to do and a deepening awareness that my talent has never been very substantial and that it is losing whatever contact it ever may have had with 'the times.'"

***

As the situation at the CBC worsened for Les in the mid- and late 1960s, he realized that his years as a television writer were coming to an end. Hastening this realization, perhaps, was an incident involving a labor union that infuriated the usually unflappable Les. Les had written a play called "The Great Casa Loma Purchase" for a CBC series called *Show of the Week*. The play revolved around some con men who sought to "sell" Toronto's landmark Casa Loma castle, much as previous fictional crooks tried to sell the Brooklyn Bridge. Les requested a last-minute reading from the seven actors in the play to determine if it needed rewriting. Minutes before the 8 p.m. rehearsal was to begin, the steward for the Toronto chapter of the Association of Canadian Television and Radio Actors (ACTRA), the actors' union, entered and demanded the show be canceled because it was written by a non-union writer—Les. The actors left and the show was indefinitely postponed. As the incident was reported in the *Toronto Star* two days later, Les blew up, noting, loudly, that "I'm the author" and that cancellation of the rehearsal was "a contemptible insult" since his four decades as a writer in Canada had created countless jobs for Canadian actors. Union officials said later that before the incident, they had sent Les an application to join the union and even kept the ACTRA office open late that night in anticipation of his joining. Les told the reporter that he was ready to join when he read a troubling statement on the application. It noted that non-union writers were, among other things, people "without backbone" who are "cheap" and "without talent." He decided against joining. Although the incident temporarily halted the broadcast of the show, it did air on the CBC a few months later.

Les's problems with labor unions and writers' associations dated back to his days as a young writer still living in Haileybury. Then he believed that few legitimate writers reaped many benefits from joining such associations and unions, and that only those who ran them benefited. His distaste for unions is also evidence of his iconoclastic and independent nature: politically conservative (he told Norah in 1962 that for the first time in his life, he was casting a Liberal vote in the national elections), he was also anti–labor union.

***

In the 1960s Les began to reconsider his strengths as a writer. Whether because of the attention paid to him as a former Hardy Boys author, the fact that he was once again father to three children, or just soul-searching, he apparently began to reconsider the market for juvenile fiction and to see himself as a writer of stories for young adults. In some ways, the transition was natural—after all, he had extensive experience writing the Hardy Boys books, and as he grew older began to think of himself as a storyteller rather than a "novelist." Late in his life, in a series of interview notes he distributed to reporters writing stories about him, Les noted the difference between "storytellers" and "novelists." "Many first-class storytellers have run aground trying to become novelists," he wrote in those self-deprecating notes, referring, apparently, to himself. "I regard myself as a writer of entertainments. I doubt if I have the capacity for a serious novel," he wrote. "My whole training has been over the short course, the piece written in less than a month's time."

Certainly young readers, then, would appreciate Les's talent for storytelling. In 1965, he signed a contract with the publisher McClelland & Stewart for a four-book deal. The first of the books he wrote was *The Last of the Great Picnics*, a hundred-page, twelve-chapter story for juvenile readers about Sir John A. Macdonald, Canada's first prime minister, and his plan to reach out to the people of Canada through, of all means, picnics. Set on July 1, 1887, in the Ottawa Valley, *Last of the Great Picnics* is typical Leslie McFarlane—written with his fey humor, it was fictional yet based on real historical events. ("The people, with one exception, are imaginary but I am sure they all lived there somewhere in that bygone time," he wrote in a foreword.) *Picnic* came complete with a male version of Aunt Gertrude, Uncle Ogden Pettifer, described by one character as "the contrariest man in Renfrew county."

Within two years, Les published another young-adult book and was at work on a third. The hockey novel *McGonigle Scores!* tells the poignant, funny story of the last game of Skates McGonigle, a former NHL pro and scout for the Blue-Shirts. Although the book sold only several thousand copies, it received positive reviews, including one from Ted Reeve, a popular sportswriter for the *Toronto Telegram*, who praised the book several times in his columns, calling it the best hockey story ever written. According to Reeve, *McGonigle* captured perfectly the Canadian passion for hockey and the unique characters who share the love of the game: "A vivid account . . . of truly Canadian town rivalry, the hold of hockey on most of us who grew up in this land, the scouts . . . the financially pressed team backers in the hardware store, the friendships that endure . . . in mining country." Les, he added, "is as Canadian as a Prairie train whistle at night or the geese going by on high." Clearly, Les's recollections of the wild hockey rivalries he witnessed in Haileybury as a boy, along with his lifelong love for the game, formed the backbone of this book.

Although these were juvenile books, Les was doing what he had always done: writing about what he knew, using bits and pieces of his own life in the narrative. As Norah became an established author, he continued to offer her advice on writing—and he pulled no punches when he told her that she should not feel squeamish if her fiction writing were based on what she had experienced and observed in her own life: "Every good novel emerges, in part at least, from the writer's own life; it has to," he wrote her. "And to write a good novel you cannot allow yourself to be inhibited by fears lest people who know you are going to read self-revelations in it. They simply have to recognize that a novel is a creative and imaginative work which springs from the life and mind of the individual."

And, as he proved, it is sometimes the seemingly mundane aspects of one's life that provide the most interesting material for books, and what were once frightening incidents in one's life can turn later into compelling anecdotes. In 1967, Les wrote a short story for the magazine *Canadian Boy* about a dog named Pooch, a hockey team, and a dog-catcher. Perhaps not so coincidentally, Les owned a beloved poodle-spaniel mixed breed at the time named Pooch. "It is inspired partly by some frantic episodes involving our Pooch and the local dog-catcher— episodes which infuriated us at the time but which, as usual, I have managed to sublimate in fiction," he told Norah. Actually, as his stepdaughter Kathy remembers, the three girls had wanted a dog for a long time but Les had continually vetoed the idea, claiming a dog required too much work. One day, Bea and the girls decided to bring home a puppy despite Les's objections. The result was that Les and little Pooch, as he named him, became inseparable and the dog was a beloved member of the family for many years.

Les's foray into writing for young adults did not mean his career as a broadcast writer was over. In the late 1960s, he was still producing outlines and scripts for Canadian television, and some of his previous work was being performed in regional theater. And, once again, he began writing for radio. Late in his life Les said that writing radio scripts was one of his favorite types of writing because it "frees one from the production strait-jacket that prevails in television and the whims of directors and producers." He also believed that radio allowed writers to use their imaginations fully.

Despite the changes in his personal and professional life, Les was still not ready to give up on the hope he had of one day writing a serious novel. Now, for one of the first times in his life, he had both free time and extra money—circumstances that were perfect for a novelist. He brought up the idea with a few close friends, including those at Carleton University, where he used to teach, and with a book editor he knew. All enthusiastically endorsed it.

His contract with McClelland & Stewart for juvenile books apparently triggered in Les thoughts about bigger writing projects. Not only was he thinking again about an epic novel, by this time he also considered writing a memoir of sorts about his days as a ghostwriter for the Stratemeyer Syndicate. In 1969, he wrote Norah that either an article on that subject, or an outline for a book, was half done with the tentative name, "How I Became Franklin W. Dixon and Carolyn Keene." That project would come to fruition seven years later with the publication of *Ghost of the Hardy Boys* by Methuen, but it would be a long and arduous project for Les. Always a realist, he was concerned early on about the Stratemeyers' reaction to one of their former ghostwriters spilling trade secrets in a book and revealing himself. "I imagine the Stratemeyer people will raise hell about the use of those valuable copyrighted pseudonyms in a book title but I'm ploughing ahead regardless and we'll meet that little bridge when we come to it," he wrote Norah.

***

In 1960, the Stratemeyer literary syndicate was fifty-five years old and still run by Harriet Stratemeyer Adams, who took it over with her sister, Edna, when their father died in 1930. Edna Stratemeyer Squier had become an inactive partner in 1942. By the latter part of the century, the syndicate had not changed too much since the days when it was run by its founder. Like her father, Harriet Adams ran a bare-bones organization from East Orange, New Jersey; and as in her father's day, all the books in the syndicate series were squeaky clean and written in assembly-line fashion by ghostwriters using pseudonyms who signed away rights to the book.

By this time, Adams had as her right-hand man Andrew Svenson, a former newspaperman who joined the syndicate when he started writing Hardy Boys books in the late 1940s, after Leslie McFarlane left the syndicate for good. Svenson became indispensable to Adams, and by 1961 was a syndicate partner.

Adams, now a grandmother, still followed the strict production formula pioneered by her father and still used Grosset & Dunlap as the series' publisher. Until 1959, she seemed happily oblivious to societal and cultural changes that conceivably could have affected the content of the syndicate's books. In fact, when it came to her work, she tended to ignore entire cultural and social movements. And why not—the books still sold in phenomenal numbers: "100 Books—and Not a Hippie in Them," proclaimed the headline of a *New York Times* profile about Adams in 1968—one of the few profiles written about her, since Adams, like her father, did not seek publicity. She began giving a few interviews around 1965. Still, the Stratemeyer sisters may have been a bit more forthcoming than their father about syndicate activities. They gave several interviews in the 1930s, and an extensive one in 1946 to the *New York Herald Tribune,* in which they mentioned the existence of ghostwriters. And the obituaries for both Howard Garis, in 1962, and his wife, Lilian, in 1964, mention their roles as ghostwriters for the syndicate.

But ultimately, not even Adams could justify the many dated terms and practices of the series books. By the late 1950s, few people traveled in "roadsters," although many had sports cars or convertibles; use of the word "chums" may have been relegated to senior citizens who had used that term when they were the age of the Hardy Boys themselves; and the commercial airplane was hardly a new-fangled device.

More important, as Adams was finding out, was the fact that it was no longer considered quaint to refer to characters in books by their racial or ethnic background, and the portrayal of villains as "swarthy" or as having foreign accents was no longer acceptable. As a result, Adams undertook the years-long project of revising three Stratemeyer Syndicate series—the Hardy Boys, Nancy Drew, and the Bobbsey Twins—to make sure they conformed to current expectations of cultural diversity.

Diversity was not a concept unknown to Edward Stratemeyer. He may even have considered his first few plot outlines for the Hardy Boys series multicultural. Two of the Hardy Boys' friends, Phil Cohen and Tony Prito, would not be white Anglo-Saxon Protestants like Joe, Frank, and most of their other friends. The first outline describes Phil as "a Jew"; Tony, an Italian American, initially speaks in an Italian dialect. Indeed, the two boys were known to utter phrases such as "Oy" (in the case of Phil) and "What's the mattah?" (Tony).

As some critics of the rewritten books note, these ethnic stereotypes were not mean-spirited and, indeed, may have been an attempt by Stratemeyer in the late 1920s to be inclusive. As Robert L. Crawford notes in his exhaustive *Lost Hardys: A Concordance,* "while judging these phrases, it is important to keep in mind the era in which they were written; ethnic references were commonplace in the 1920's and 1930's." Nonetheless, phrases like "there's a nigger in the woodpile" (in the second book of the series, *The House on the Cliff*), "been pretty white to me" (in *The Tower Treasure*), and "hasn't a Chinaman's chance" (in *The Secret of the Caves*) may have been hard to defend by 1959. Further, other characters often follow ethnic stereotypes throughout the series: black characters, for instance, frequently speak in dialect. In *The Hidden Harbor*

Mystery, it is a "Negro" who puts his feet up on the seat in front of him on a train, despite polite rebukes by the conductor. "'Luke Jones don't stand for no nonsense from white folks!' he said audibly. 'Ah pays mah fare, an' Ah puts mah shoes where Ah please.'"

Gerald O'Connor, one of the harshest critics of what he perceives as the racism in the original Hardy Boys books, claims that many of the first thirty-eight books were riddled with racist, sexist, and ethnic slurs that made them dangerous for children to read. One of the most notorious books in the series—*The Hidden Harbor Mystery,* written by Les—is particularly virulent, he writes, in its treatment of blacks: "The message [of the book] is as self-evident as it is self-condemning; blacks should be kept in servitude because they are an ignorant, violent, immoral people who are as incapable of understanding freedom as they are of fulfilling the responsibilities concomitant with it." O'Connor implies, though, that the Hardy Boys authors were at least equal opportunity xenophobes: they are not just racist, he says, but anti-Scottish, anti-Irish, and anti-Asian. "Irishmen pound beats, Scotchmen sweep floors, Italians sell bananas," yet the WASPy "Applegates, Websters, Blackstones and Rands—and the Hardys—have the money, the tradition and the brains."

It is true that the thugs in some of the books are Chinese—in *Footprints under the Window,* the menacing Louie Fong has an "evil yellow face." And the bumbling Con Riley, one of Bayport's incompetent policemen, may be of Irish descent, as was Leslie McFarlane, who endowed the policeman with this ineptitude. But whether this is racism may be a matter of debate, as is the leeway today's readers should give those early books based on the norms of society at the time they were written.

But a few memos between Leslie McFarlane and the Stratemeyer Syndicate indicate that Les, too, might have had some problems writing in characters that he thought were stereotypical. Shortly after he completed the manuscript for the Dana Girls mystery *In the Shadow of the Tower,* Harriet Stratemeyer wrote to tell him he did not follow her outline exactly when it came to the portrayal of black characters. After praising the manuscript, she continued, "we noticed that you failed several times to follow the outline. The idea of the colored people in that locality being superstitious, believing in the supernatural and giving the story a ghostly and spooky twist because of them was entirely omitted." She added, "we thought that possibly the reason you neglected this angle was due to your unfamiliarity with Negroes and their peculiar ghostly aberrations." Two years later, after he sent in the manuscript for *The Hidden Harbor Mystery,*

Harriet Adams once again referred to his apparent timidity when writing about black characters. Again, she praised the book while noting that he did not follow all elements of the outline. "Knowing how hard it is for you to portray colored people, we think you did very well."

Les's feelings about these portrayals of ethnic and racial stereotypes are not known. He does not discuss them in his diaries or in letters. Nothing in his personal correspondence indicates any racism on his part.

By 1959, Harriet Adams had apparently decided to update several of the syndicate series books, including the Hardy Boys and Nancy Drew series. Papers from the syndicate reveal detailed plans by Adams and Andrew Svenson in 1959 to overhaul the books to update their language and rid them of stereotypical characters. In a "Report on racial, dialect, etc. aspects," each of the first twenty-four Hardy Boys books was reviewed with brief comments about possible negative racial and ethnic stereotypes—but that wasn't all. Evidently, Bayport's bumbling police officers and anyone who drank alcohol would also be "revised" in new editions. For instance:

· In *Hunting for Hidden Gold:* "Colored porter on train (minor charac.), thick dialect—pp. 67, 68. Two Negroes driving in car—thick dialect—(pp. 78–79)"

· *Footprints under the Window*—"O.K. re racial. Chinese—some good, some bad. 'Pidgin English' spoken, Police stupid."

· *The Great Airport Mystery*—"o.k. re racial. Drunken pilot and others mentioned drinking liquor, p. 64. Boys use guns. Police and sheriff stupid (Chief Collig 'small and fussy')"

· *The Mark on the Door*—"o.k. (re racial). Heavy Scottish dialect, p. 6 Mexican villain throughout—a horrible character, ref. to as 'swarthy stranger,' unscrupulous rogue. 'Half Breed' Mexican Indians helping crooks, 'good' Mexicans also."

· *The Twisted Claw*—"o.k. re racial—French and Irish thick accents, pp. 16, 23, 27, 32 and other pp. Villain seems to be French."

· *The Clue of the Broken Blade*—"Negro servant uses dialect, pp. 194, 199, 200. Minor character, otherwise ok."

Even critics of the rewritten books acknowledge that many of the stereotypes in the original books were, at best, outdated and, at worst, racist and xenophobic.

The revised versions of the Hardy Boys included sweeping changes in the books. The changes began in 1959 with revisions of the first two books, *The Tower Treasure* and *The House on the Cliff*, and continued until 1973 with the thirty-eighth book in the series, *The Mystery at Devil's Paw*. Critics over the years have complained that the Stratemeyers went much too far in their "revisions"—or in some cases, rewrites—of the books. Many longtime Hardy Boys fans believe the Stratemeyer Syndicate threw out the baby with the bath water, robbing most of the books of the humor and detail that made them so readable. Complaining about the revised Hardy Boys books has become a cottage industry for the legions of Hardy Boys fans around the world, who have debated since 1959 the sacred aspects of the text, and how much, if at all, it should have been changed or altered. The revisions, in fact, have become a line of demarcation for many of the fans who now often divide chat on websites into two categories: before the changes and after them.

When the syndicate decided to "update" the books in 1959, it also decided to shorten them; as a result, plot and character were affected, especially in the first twenty or so books. The 214-page books were reduced by about five chapters, or about 34 pages; some characters were eliminated or changed, and many of the details of their appearance, actions, or personalities were eliminated. Inexplicably, Frank and Joe have aged in the revisions—the sixteen-year-old Frank is now eighteen, and Joe, who was fifteen, is now seventeen. And, evidently because the publishers believed the sophistication level of young adults had grown during the twentieth century, the target audience of the books grew younger, from a target age of fourteen to sixteen in the originals to an audience of ages ten to fourteen. (When the syndicate was purchased in 1984, the intended audience grew even younger—from eight to twelve.) As the initial outlines for the changes indicate, the policemen, who had been objects of ridicule as Les wrote them, were cleaned up and became respected authority figures. (Of course, Edward Stratemeyer told Les in the late 1920s that he did not want the police portrayed as fools. While Les may have softened their portrayal a bit, the cops remained boobs while he wrote the books.) But many people believe the updated books themselves were stripped of their identity.

Cullen Murphy, a writer for the *Atlantic*, noted in 1991 that the Hardy

Boys revisions, which he called "The Big Purge," robbed the books of their personality: "Little remained in the books after their revision which could possibly discomfit anyone (such as dialogue rendered in dialect, humor at the expense of policemen, and big words that might have to be looked up)." Like many Hardy Boys fans, Murphy is skeptical that such revisions of the books were an attempt to update them; instead he believes they were an attempt to "write down" to impatient readers who want nothing but quick and simple plot. The original books' "earnest squareness," he writes, also gives away their old age—and old age is anathema to marketers, he believes.

In *The Twilight of American Culture,* Morris Berman claims that the "dumbing down"—that is, the revisions—of the Hardy Boys series is merely a reflection of a television culture that seeks books with simplistic plots and bland narratives, desires instilled in them by advertisers who find it easier to market and brand such simplicity. "The books have been reduced to mental chewing gum," he writes.

The debate about the changes in series fiction heated up in the 1990s, more than thirty years after the changes were initiated. This may be due to the fact that many parents who had read the books as children suddenly saw, upon giving them to *their* children, that they had been changed. Another reason for this renewed interest may be that as communication channels grew and expanded and the Internet was born, it was simply easier to reveal and talk about these changes, albeit several decades after the fact. Articles in popular and scholarly publications throughout North America—usually written by former Hardy Boys readers—bemoan the changes. Many of them note that the revised versions of the series are not your father's Hardy Boys books. As one critic notes, the characters are robbed of their introspection and distinct personalities, and the plots of their richness. The new Hardy Boys, he writes, "are still virtuous, but it is the embalmed virtue of Disneyland."

In the online magazine *Salon,* for instance, columnist Steve Burgess laments the narrative neutering performed on previously colorful characters. "Chet Morton's practical jokes were a regular feature of the original books but much rarer occurrences in the faster-paced successors," he writes. The much-loved Aunt Gertrude is no longer her "peppery, dictatorial, raw-boned" self, as Les described her. "Aunt Gertrude is reduced to making occasional remarks, almost invariably described as 'tart,'" Burgess writes. And the ethnic Tony Prito and Phil Cohen no longer give any verbal indication of their background: they are now simply "lively with a good sense of humor" (Phil) and "quiet and intelligent." (Tony).

Some readers take the changes in the books very seriously. Murphy of the *Atlantic* argues that the omission of at least one notable scene in *The Tower Treasure*—in which Fenton Hardy talks to his sons about the importance of being observant—is akin to the omission of a pivotal passage in the Sherlock Holmes mystery *A Study in Scarlet* in which Holmes demonstrates the nature of his powers. Even sadder, Murphy notes, is the elimination of the wonderful celebratory feast at the end of *The Tower Treasure,* when even the gourmand Chet Morton admits he's full.

And, many of these critics note, sophisticated words used in the originals, like "sibilant," "expostulate," "ostensible" and the like were also victims of the rewrites. These critics approve of the use of complex words that boys would be forced to look up (though they might admit that such phrases as "'So!' she ejaculated" could well be omitted—as they were—from *The Missing Chums).* Many of the rewritten passages are bland, colorless ghosts of their former selves, and gone is the leisurely description and texture of the narrative. For instance, following is a passage in the original *The Tower Treasure* introducing Joe and Frank Hardy:

> While there was a certain resemblance between the two lads, chiefly in the firm yet good natured expression of their mouths, in some respects they differed greatly in appearance. While Frank was dark, with straight, black hair and brown eyes, his brother was pink-cheeked, with fair, curly hair and blue eyes.

Following is the same passage, revised:

> Even though one boy was dark and the other fair, there was a marked resemblance between the two brothers. Eighteen-year-old Frank was tall and dark. Joe, a year younger, was blond with blue eyes.

Gone, too, is the detailed physical description of Chief of Police Ezra Collig that reveals his personality. As Les described him, he

> was a burly, red-faced individual, much given to telling long-winded stories. Usually, Collig was to be found re-

clining in a swivel chair in his office, with his feet on the desk, reading the comic papers or polishing up his numerous badges, but this day something had happened to shake him out of his customary calm.

In the rewritten version, the police chief is simply "a tall, husky man, well known to Fenton Hardy and his two sons."

The ubiquitous villains did not fare much better than the law enforcement officials in the rewrites. In the fourth book of the series, *The Missing Chums,* one thug is described as being among a group of men who were "unsavory looking fellows, unshaven, surly of expression. . . . [He was] bareheaded, revealing a scant thatch of carroty hair so close-cropped that it seemed to stick out at all angles to his cranium." In the revised version, he becomes simply "a huge man with a bald head."

Even some details of what the boys ate were changed. In the original 1946 version of *The Secret Panel* (not written by Les), Laura Hardy is making muffins; in the revised version, they are mysteriously turned into popovers.

As the first several books in the series were revised, they carried a notation at the beginning of the book: "In this new story, based on the original of the same title, Mr. Dixon has incorporated the most up-to-date methods used by police and private detectives." Others that were revised later in the process carry no such disclaimer. But the revised books usually carry several copyright dates on their flyleaf: the date they were first written and the date or dates of revisions.

When the first few Hardy Boys books were revised in 1959 and 1960, it is unlikely Leslie McFarlane knew about the revisions. But in a letter to Norah in 1963, he had apparently gotten word that they had been rewritten to update them, although he did not know then the extent of the rewrites. He told Norah that the original versions of the books he wrote had copyright dates of 1927 to 1947, and that they did not bear the paragraph on the flyleaf explaining that they had been rewritten to incorporate "up-to-date" police methods.

***

Les had lived in several cities in his life, and was not afraid to relocate if he felt it would help his career or improve his life. But it was surprising when, in the fall of 1968, he and Bea moved to Los Angeles. Whether the move was meant to be permanent is unclear; the family did not sell their home in Whitby, and Kathy Palmer remembers that her mother and stepfather saw the move as an "adventure." At the time of the move, she was in nursing school in Kitchener, Ontario, and her two sisters had married, with Anne, her husband, and their toddler living in the Whitby home.

Apparently discouraged by the fading market for television drama in Canada—and encouraged by reports of writers making thousands of dollars per script in Hollywood—Les decided to take his chances in California. Many other Canadian writers and CBC television workers had gone to Los Angeles, so there was a small cadre of Canadians in the entertainment business there. Still, the move to Los Angeles seems like an odd choice for a small-town, unpretentious Canadian who never learned to drive. Moreover, Les had always taken pride in the fact that he was a "Canadian writer," and, of course, he had deep affection for his country. A dozen years before he made the decision to move there, he had written Norah about his negative feelings for California in general, implying that it has no depth. "Everyone goes to California," he said, calling it a region where the oranges look lovely, but are tasteless; where the weather is perfect but monotonous; and where the flowers are beautiful but without fragrance. And, indeed, while his year as a Hollywood writer was educational for him, he was prescient. He quickly learned that the artificial culture of Los Angeles and the often cruel workings of the entertainment industry were not for him.

By early 1969, shortly after he and Bea moved there, he received some promising news from the story editor of the hit NBC show *Bonanza* about some ideas for scripts that Les had sent him. Les had been around too long not to know that kind words do not always translate into signed contracts, but nonetheless he was encouraged. Further, story editor John Hawkins, or "executive story consultant," as he was known—a euphemism that amused Les—had been a writer for pulp magazines at the same time as Les.

By February, Les got more encouraging news from the *Bonanza* staff—a producer had read a sample comic script he had written and was impressed enough ask him to write a comic script for the series. Although he was interested in writing for other shows produced in Hollywood, particularly some half-hour comedies including *Mayberry R.F.D.* (a spin-off of the popular *Andy Griffith Show*), *Bonanza* was the perfect vehicle for Les. First, he knew Lorne Greene, a star of the show, from when both did work for the film board in Ottawa. More important, though, was that *Bonanza* was a serialized "niche" program that featured the same male protagonists in a static setting: the Old West of the mid-1800s. Its scripts were a mixture of comedy and drama—with some shows purely comic—and its main characters had established personalities.

The production facilities at Paramount, where the show was shot, were far more elaborate than those at the CBC, where Les had worked. But in some ways the work was the same. He told Pat that the numerous retakes, flubbed lines by actors, and overall chaos were no different from what he was accustomed to as a director for a CBC series. He also learned, however, that everyone in "TV land," as he called it, lived and died by the Nielsen ratings, which "determine the fortunes of just about everyone," he told Pat. Even production of an established and successful show like *Bonanza*—which was in its tenth season in 1969—was in a holding pattern until it could be established that it still ranked high in the ratings.

Life in Los Angeles was a revelation to Les; a small diary he kept during that era noted briefly that he and Bea saw all the conventional tourist sights and were able to enjoy the warm weather, even though torrential rains soaked the area during the first month or so of their visit. But Les quickly became disillusioned with Hollywood and the West Coast style of doing business. He was at once puzzled, amused, and dumbfounded by, among other things, the city's reliance on credit, its citizens' tendency to drink and drive, and the cavalier attitude residents had toward the city's beautiful environment. Les was a writer, but unlike some in Hollywood, he maintained that he had always been able to tell the difference between reality and a movie set. As he told Brian, Los Angeles was eye-opening to a "barefoot country boy from Whitby, Ontario."

Les watched wide-eyed the goings-on in his new home: "Hollywood! There isn't even any such place," he wrote Brian. "It is a couple of square miles of a vast city. There is no Hollywood city hall, no Hollywood post office—merely a zip code number—and most of the studios are not in this fictitious real estate division at all." Les quickly learned that he wasn't in Whitby any more: "Stores selling booze are open all night and on Sundays and holidays and deliver the stuff—on credit—at any hour. Every seventh driver on the freeway at night is blind drunk, according to the police, and the courts are so jammed with cases that most of them go unsettled for years."

In this letter to Brian, Les seemed to come to the realization that as a writer, he was complicit in furthering this artificial culture. "I wouldn't have missed it for anything," he wrote. "I write about a West that never was for viewers who seek a non-existent world to escape from the unreal world in which they live and get paid off by a computer in fictitious dollars that buy food which turns out to be synthetic and without taste and gorgeous synthetic shirts that will catch fire from a hot grain of cigarette ash." To Les, however, these were not complaints—they were simply observations that led to the conclusion that this was not the place for him. "I'm not beefing about it," he told Brian. "I simply find it unbelievable and fascinating and not for me at my time of life because it is as unreal as a movie set."

That fact was that Les was not impressed by much of the television produced in Hollywood, and he certainly did not care for the tyranny of the Nielsen ratings and their power to dictate what was aired on television. In addition, getting to be a regular on the writing circuit was difficult: some shows, like *Mayberry R.F.D.*, had staff writers who did most of the work; others, like the popular situation comedies *Bewitched* and *The Flying Nun*, were silly, Les thought, and not worth writing for. And he quickly learned that a writer rarely if ever had his work aired the way he wrote it—it was almost always edited beyond recognition or "helped along" by another writer.

Les's year-long tenure in Los Angeles was productive, however. He wrote a few scripts for the *Jane Wyman Show* and the *U.S. Steel Hour,* and, according to Brian, for a few half-hour situation comedies. He was proudest, however, of a *Bonanza* script called "Abner Willoughby's Gold" (later renamed "Abner Willoughby's Return"). The show focused on the sophisticated thief Abner Willoughby and his interaction with Joe and Hoss Cartwright, whom he meets after attempting to steal Joe's horse. But even the success of that script sale was watered down for Les. Shortly after the McFarlanes left Los Angeles, Les learned that his script had been turned over to a writer for the show named Jack B. Sowards, who apparently rewrote it to the extent that he shared the writing credit. Les, however, tried to downplay the hurt he may have felt in a letter to Norah: "This goes on all the time and of course I did a little of that myself when I had the editorial spot at CBC so it's give and take and a cut throat business in general," he told her.

Les was not bitter by nature, but his disillusionment over the trip to Los Angeles—and the state of television in general—was real. He felt particularly depressed that quality itself did not seem to matter much when it came to writing for television. In late 1969, he told Norah bluntly that he was disappointed with television in general and embarrassed to claim ownership of two CBC scripts he wrote. "Direction poor, casting awful and pace abominable. I was ashamed to see my name on them."

Life in Los Angeles left him somewhat battered. In 1973, nearly four years after his year there, the experience was apparently still fresh in his mind. Pat's husband, Bill, a composer and conductor, had apparently considered writing scores for Hollywood films. In a letter, Les warned Pat about working in Los Angeles: "Show business, especially the Hollywood brand, is like nothing else in the world for cruelty, injustice, stupidity, double-crossing, opportunism, nepotism and all the rest of it," he wrote.

But Les was a seasoned veteran and had sufficient experience, contacts, and pride in his work that he could start over again when the family returned to their home on King Street in Whitby. He had gone full circle, though, and was now once again making his living by his wits and by sheer determination.

17

AT HOME AT THE TYPEWRITER

It seems very strange to be living in a place where there is sunshine every day, even though it is mid-winter. Every morning I go for a walk on the beach. One can walk a long way in the sand, which is white as snow and as soft as talcum powder. . . . Sometimes there are pelicans flying overhead, looking for food. They are big, ungainly birds and when one sees a fish in the ocean he will dive right out of the sky, like a big stone dropped into the sea, and he will come up with a fish in his mouth. He has a big pouch under his beak and the baby pelicans will swim up and eat from the mother pelican's mouth.

—*Letter from Leslie McFarlane to his grand-son Jon Perez from Sarasota, Florida*

Bea and Les returned from Los Angeles to Whitby, finding a quiet environment with no children at home. When Bea married Les, she acquired a full-time companion. Not only did he work at home, but, because he did not drive, she accompanied him to many of his appointments and activities. An accomplished curler who played in a curling league, Bea got Les involved in the sport.

Les's life in these early years of the 1970s had in many ways gone full circle. He again became a full-time freelance writer, which required him to live by his wits as well as his talent. And he was also a full-time husband and grandfather. All eight of his children and stepchildren were by then married, and he reveled in his role as grandfather to many babies and small children. He frequently babysat his grandchildren on weekends and always remembered their birthdays. Les devoted much thought to the gifts he gave his children and grandchildren; he never picked out a conventional present to ship off hurriedly. Kathy Palmer remembers that Bea and Les once drove for hours around Toronto to find the right puppet for one of Les's grandchildren. "It was very important that the gifts be perfect," she said. "And he took great joy in watching them being opened." As his grandchildren grew older, Les often sent them subscriptions to magazines he thought they would enjoy, such as the satirical *Mad* for adolescent grandsons and *Seventeen* for several of his teenaged granddaughters. And he also wrote occasional letters to Pat's, Norah's, and Brian's children as they grew older.

Les's personal habits, his love of holidays and family, and his way of life had ultimately changed little over the years. But literary and broadcast markets changed routinely, and he knew he had to change with them. Even at age sixty-eight, Les was prepared to make those changes and probably felt that his most significant work might still be ahead of him.

***

With the exception of a few scripts, Les's affiliation with CBC television was over by the mid-1970s, and he began to concentrate once again on radio scripts. He disdained the politics that came with writing for television, in Los Angeles and Canada, and now he found that what he wrote and what he saw on the screen were often two different things. As he had written to his children, Les was disappointed in the lack of control scriptwriters had over the final product; he had routinely seen his scripts reduced or changed. Furthermore, he never became comfortable with the fact that what aired on television was often controlled by ratings, the whims of mercurial executives, or a fickle public. The money was good, but one had to have a strong ego to take the perpetual rejection. Les was always surprised at the unpredictability of television producers. In the early 1960s, for instance, he was asked to write a script for a prospective children's television series for the CBC to be called "The Ranger Boys." He was handed, as a model, a few volumes of Hardy Boys books—but the creators of the prospective series were not necessarily pleased when they learned they were dealing with Franklin W. Dixon himself. "The people were a bit disconcerted when . . . I told them I had not only read said volumes but had written them to boot," he wrote Norah. Although Les received five hundred dollars for the script, he correctly surmised that his affiliation with the series would end with the pilot.

He was blunt but not bitter when he wrote to Norah in 1974 that he believed his days of contributing to the CBC were over, but in his usual optimistic way, he noted he had once been on the other side of the desk when it came to firing writers: "The CBC has phased me out as a television writer under the new regime but I phased out a few writers myself in my day so there can be no complaint on that score. He who liveth by the sword . . ."

In the 1970s, Les was enthusiastic about radio projects that gave him the license to write about history and biography. He wrote periodically for a series called *Bush and Salon,* which featured events in the history of Canada. One of his plays, "Fire in the North," which he wrote in 1972 for the anniversary of the great Haileybury fire of 1922, was converted to a radio play and performed in Haileybury. Another play told the story of C. C. Farr, who first developed and named Haileybury. Les also spent much time researching a radio play about Charles Dickens's visit to four Canadian cities in 1842. He was not content simply to get the facts, but, as was typical of him, wanted to get a true picture of the writer's personality, even going so far as to writing to England to get a copy of one of the amateur plays Dickens staged in Montreal.

During the early 1970s, Les also had the time to revisit his roots. In addition to the plays about events of the early years of Haileybury, he also wrote a short memoir about his childhood years there. As he wrote Norah in 1974, though, he was still seeking a publisher for his memoir about the Hardy Boys and by now he had been working on it for several years. Further, another novel he had started, which he later would call *You Can't Win Them All,* had stalled.

Amid all this, though, his luck did change rather suddenly. Within a few days in 1974, he received four unexpected calls: one from the educational publisher Gage, informing him it wanted to publish a short story he had sent them nearly a year before; one from CBC radio offering him a contract for a radio play he had written; one from Methuen Publications in Toronto saying it wanted to reprint some mysteries he had written back in the 1920s and '30s; and one from the Ontario Arts Council offering him a grant to write the short book about his early days in Haileybury. "I comforted myself by saying [the trouble placing the Hardy Boys memoir] was all very much like my early days as a writer, especially during the depression, when nothing would sell . . . telling myself if you keep on writing it will all work out somehow," he told Norah.

Methuen told him it would publish six of his novellas as part of a multipart paperback series it called its "Checkmate" series. Included in the series would be three of Les's 126- and 128-page adventure stories and three hockey stories. The publisher also wanted to include some of Les's short stories in each of the six volumes. The books would sell for $1.50, and, of course, could now be read by contemporary audiences, a phenomenon that evoked mixed emotions in Les, who had spent some time editing and revising the stories this second time around. He would now get royalties once again for the books, but, in providing requested publication information about them for the publisher, he was forced to reread his old diaries from the 1930s, a bitter experience that evoked some guilt and regret. As he wrote Norah, "It was really sad to go back to those old days when the harried author of the Hardy Boys would curse his way through another 50,000 words and then turn to a [prize] fight novelette . . . and wait and wait for a cheque for $100, spent before it was arrived." It had been twenty years since Amy died, but Les still fretted over the effect their early days had on her. "It's a wonder your brave mother didn't leave me. . . . I find myself strangely indifferent to the extra money [the books] will bring now. It comes too late."

In contrast, Les took great enjoyment in writing his recollections of growing up in Haileybury. The arts council–funded *A Kid in Haileybury* was written for the Highway Book Shop near Haileybury, which specializes in regional topics. The book is an eloquent, loving, and funny tribute to the northern Ontario city he loved and the people who lived there.

During these early years of the 1970s, Les was not necessarily writing to make a living, since his pensions covered his living expenses. But he was hardly in retirement, a word that was unknown to him. "I know I couldn't abide retirement if it meant sitting around and wondering what to do with myself. There is nothing like a steady program of work." As he had known his entire life, money was not the reason he wrote—nor had it ever been: "What a blessing work is!" he told Norah.

Still, the mid-1970s brought their share of professional disappointment to Les. He wanted to adapt his children's story "Padgett's Pooch" into a short book, but could not get a publisher interested. Worse, he seemed to have trouble finding the right voice and focus for his Hardy Boys memoir that he had started in 1970. He mentioned the book numerous times in letters to his children, and clearly neither he nor the publisher—which was initially McClelland & Stewart—had a clear vision about the book's focus or intended audience. Les seemed to vacillate between telling too much and not enough about his work outside the Hardy Boys, and it was unclear how much of a role his personal life would take in the book. The tentative title of the book in 1970, "How I Became Franklin

W. Dixon," did not seem to satisfy Les, and other rejected titles, "The Hardys of Bayport" and "The Bayport Boys," did not gel either. By the mid-1970s, Les had several versions of the book and no publisher. The problems with the book undermined his confidence: "I have lost all confidence to turn out anything readable," he wrote Norah in what was probably an overstatement. Yet, he added, he still considered himself the professional he always was. "But when I'm behind the typewriter, I feel as professional as ever, enjoy working as much as ever." Once again, though, he was taking the wild ride he took as a young freelance writer, waiting breathlessly for the mail (or now, phone) for good news. "I have a strange this-is-where-I-came-in feeling with a reject following an acceptance and all the waiting for verdicts on scripts," he wrote Norah. There was one big difference, as he told Norah: the waiting was no longer a matter of survival.

Eventually, *Ghost of the Hardy Boys*, as it finally became, did come together for Les, and it was published. The book had become, first and foremost, a story about how the Hardy Boys series was written, with philosophical comments on juvenile books in general and remembrances about his newspaper days. It was published in a joint venture between Methuen in Canada and the U.S. publisher Two Continents. Writing and getting the book published had been a struggle for Les, although he did get some help in his efforts from some new friends.

***

Les had always been blessed with good health. "I don't feel any older," he told Norah, "except for a few bothersome creaks and pains and . . . an aversion to settling down to any prolonged job of work." By the time he reached the age of seventy, though, he was developing a bit of bursitis and finding himself more cognizant of the behavior and language patterns of "senior citizens." In a letter to Norah describing a visit to a senior citizens' home, he dryly noted the euphemism: "Hamilton [Ontario] has very good old folks' homes—pardon, I mean Senior Citizens in line with the modern custom of dressing up unpleasant things in fancy names which don't make them any pleasanter." Les's seventieth birthday was a happy occasion, as Pat, Brian, and Norah had lunch with him in Toronto. "The luncheon . . . was the happiest part of one of the happiest days of my life," he told Norah later. On his return home to Whitby, Bea met him at the train station and announced she had a "few" friends over to see him. About thirty people celebrated his birthday, including the mayor of Whitby, who read a resolution introducing "Mc-Farlane Court" as a street in a new Whitby subdivision.

Les had witnessed many changes in society and culture throughout his life, and he was eager to adapt to the times. But even he, who tried to remain open-minded, was sometimes shocked by what he saw on television and at the movies. He was taken aback by some American medical dramas, which he evidently thought were brutally frank in content. But that was nothing compared to films such as the controversial *I Am Curious (Yellow)* and the X-rated *Last Tango in Paris*. Of the latter, he told Norah, "I can take almost anything in my stride. . . . These new film makers know nothing of the first principle of story telling, which is lucidity. . . . I found the obscene tirade toward the end of the film revolting in terms of being tiresome—foul words just for the sake of shock value."

It seemed to him that when it came to theater, nothing was sacred—not even Shakespeare. Les gave a thumbs-down to a 1971 performance of *Macbeth:* "Shakespeare ceases to be Shakespeare when the poetry goes out of Macbeth to be replaced by ranting and raving and the action seems to take place in some timeless Maoist region and the Scottish soldiers all look like Chinese peasants," he wrote Norah.

Les dreaded being thought of as old-fashioned, but he could not avoid raising his eyebrows at some of what he saw—and he knew the media would get increasingly more permissive. "At age 70 I am beginning to wonder what modern society is going to be like in 30 years, but I'm not sure I want to be around to find out," he told Norah. But Les was serious in his efforts to keep a youthful outlook, and that included not talking incessantly about his aches and pains and complaints about current society. "I have told Bea that if she catches me mentioning diabetes or gall bladder or referring to anything [less] recent than 1970 to give me a damn swift kick," he wrote Brian in 1973. "I'm training myself to think of what I'm going to do rather than anything done in the past."

Les was always open to new writers, and did enjoy some of them despite his earlier skepticism; after much reluctance, he began reading J.R.R. Tolkien ("I tend to resist books that inspire cults") and concluded, "Strange, poetic fanciful stuff." He told Norah that he read and enjoyed an up-and-coming young fiction writer named Stephen King. After acknowledging in a letter to Norah that he did not care for the writing of Kurt Vonnegut, Les praised comments Vonnegut made in a *Playboy* interview in 1973 about the value and virtues of families and small towns. Les's favorite writers seemed to change throughout his life, although he consistently thought that James

Joyce's *Ulysses* influenced twentieth-century writers more than any other work, commenting that he had read the book twenty times and found something new in it each time. Late in his life, he said his favorite contemporary writer was Vladimir Nabokov, whom he called "the true world writer" and master of the language.

***

Les had always taken pride in his heritage as a Canadian, despite periodic impulses to move to the United States for professional reasons. He had worked briefly in Massachusetts as a young newspaper reporter, had lived a year in Los Angeles, and of course traveled periodically to the United States, visiting the New York area in particular. Despite the allegiance he felt to Canada, however, the ambivalence he felt toward his home country deepened as he grew older. During his time with CBC Television, Les resented that the network could not or would not pay scriptwriters as much as American networks were paying, with the result that many of the country's most talented writers left Canada for the States. Furthermore, he felt that most Canadians had a collective inferiority complex and did not promote the accomplishments of their own countrymen, accepting the United States' role as the world leader in arts, business, and culture. Even as a child and young man, he had noted that Canadians had instilled in them the notion that they simply lacked the ambition and drive of their American neighbors. Yet Les took tremendous pride in his nation's cultural identity and in its citizens' strong work ethic and unpretentious nature. And he certainly loved the country's majestic beauty.

So he might have been a bit defensive when he told his family and friends that he and Bea had decided to move to Sarasota, Florida. The couple had visited there during the winter of 1972–73, and found that they enjoyed it. In February 1973, they bought a condominium and made tentative plans to live there much of the year, hoping to rent their house in Whitby. Les was almost apologetic as he told Brian that he and Bea were becoming "more and more fed up with the interminable Canadian winter, mild or severe, because of its unutterable dreariness. . . . At 70 I decided that because every day was so much like another the years were flashing past much too quickly and that we needed to shake ourselves out of it a little." To some of his family, the purchase of the one-story, two-bedroom, Spanish-style condominium in Siesta Key was an impulse buy, and they were a bit concerned about how the couple would finance it. (At this time, Les had retirement benefits from the CBC as well as a pension from the government.) But Les took great pleasure in describing to his children the condominium itself and the forty-unit complex, which was a short drive from shopping and the beach. The complex, Westgate Village, was a colony of sorts to many other Canadians who had moved south.

As he implied in earlier letters, for the first time in their lives, he and Bea were beginning to feel the physical effects of age: Bea, who was about thirteen years younger than Les, had arthritis in one arm, a condition that worsened in extreme cold, and Les by now had diabetes that required insulin treatment. Never one to try to fool his family and friends, he bluntly told Pat in a letter that he resented getting old and that "there is an awful difference between the sixties and seventies."

Ultimately, Les and Bea enjoyed their quiet lives in Florida, and Les could still write and keep in close contact by telephone and mail with markets in Canada and New York. They liked the people they met in Sarasota and they loved the beach and perpetual warmth. As Les wrote wryly in a letter to Pat, they did have some of the benefits of Canadian living as far south as Sarasota. Les noted that he thought he saw a familiar figure one day as he looked out the window of his condominium in early winter: "The robins are here already. They eat juniper and berries and get smashed," he wrote Pat. "One came tottering over toward me the other day, drunk as the proverbial hoot-owl, and I told Bea it was because he recognized me and that I was positive I had seen him under one of the apple trees at 704 King St. a year ago. After a few loud hiccups he flew away and almost collided with a sober seagull."

Les and Bea resumed their hobby of curling (although Les was surprised to find that most people he met in Florida had never heard of the sport), and he went swimming each day in the pool in the complex. The Chicago White Sox did their spring training in Sarasota, so Les, a diehard baseball fan, could frequently be found in the stands of spring training games. Best of all, though, within months of their move, Les reported that his blood-sugar readings had declined, indicating his diabetes had stabilized. As a result, he experienced less dizziness during long walks, and he was more energetic. In addition he had lost weight—he was down to 147 pounds.

As Les had joked in many letters to his children, he had, as a retiree in Florida, officially joined the ranks of "senior citizens"—a euphemism he loathed. But Les always had a great sense of humor when it came to himself, and although he enjoyed his new life in Florida, a humorous article he wrote shows that even Nirvana isn't always what it seems. "A Letter from Paradise," written for *Weekend* magazine in Florida, is a long "letter" from Sam, a Canadian retiree in sunny Florida, to his friend Charlie, who still lived in frigid Canada. The suntanned Sam, who lives in a colony of transplanted Canadians, begins the letter singing the praises of the sand, the sea, and the surf, telling his friend that he must also move south. The weather and environment will make a new man of him, Sam says. As the letter progresses, though, we learn things are not so rosy for Sam. It's difficult to get news about Canada ("Down here, the people think North America stops at Buffalo"), and the group of Canadians huddle around the radio each day to get a minuscule dose of it on the program *Canada Calling*. Floridians are very nice, he notes, but, oddly, they don't give a darn about hockey, so news about that sport is also non-existent. And catching a glimpse of anyone younger than sixty can be a challenge. And while the sun is pleasant, it can cause brutal sunburns . . . and all anyone talks about is their poor health, their surgery, and their aches . . . and an exciting day consists of shuffleboard *and* square dancing on the same day . . .

Les's life in Sarasota, while slower paced than his life in Whitby, was still full. He supplemented his retirement benefits with freelance writing and was still dependent on the mail and telephone. Les's stepdaughters remember vividly that when they lived with him in Whitby, the arrival of the mail each day was a high point for him. Waiting for the mail once again became part of his daily routine, an activity that was temporarily interrupted by a mail strike in Canada in the early 1970s that caused him great frustration. The slow pace of letters between the United States and Canada irked Les for most of the years he lived in Florida.

Shortly after they moved to Florida, the McFarlanes decided they enjoyed it so much that they would sell their home in Whitby. They calculated that the proceeds from the sale, combined with Les's pensions, would allow them to live relatively comfortably for the rest of their lives. After selling the house, though, they learned they would have to return 15 percent of the proceeds as income tax unless they pledged to spend at least six months of the year in Canada or buy another home there. So their indecision over whether to remain in Florida all year was settled—by the tax man. They first rented an apartment in Whibty, and in 1976 they moved to an apartment in Oshawa, a town about forty miles east of Toronto.

The move to Sarasota brought with it an unexpected benefit for Les: entry into a rather exclusive writers' club whose membership included men whose work Les had been reading for nearly fifty years. The little writer's colony in Sarasota was, as one biographer called it, "a mixture of high culture and low." Its members included Joseph Hayes, a writer of paperbacks, including the successful *The Desperate Hours;* mystery author John D. MacDonald, who created the famous detective Travis McGee; Dick Jessup, author of *The Cincinnati Kid;* and the unofficial leader of the group, the unpredictable MacKinlay Kantor. Although Les joined the party late—the group had been meeting since the 1950s—he was accepted immediately by the group, who no doubt appreciated his soft-spoken manner and dry wit.

When Les joined in the early 1970s, the group met on Fridays for lunch. It was a close-knit and occasionally raucous group, due primarily to MacDonald and his mentor, Kantor. McKinlay Kantor was a versatile writer whose novels touched on such diverse subjects as a foxhound and her master (*The Voice of Bugle Ann*); Yankees escaping from a Confederate prison (*Arouse and Beware*); and a passenger pigeon. Kantor's claim to fame, however, came with his 1956 novel *Andersonville,* which won the Pulitzer Prize, and much later, *Valley Forge.* A journeyman writer like Les, who had followed his career long before they met, he too had written detective stories for pulp magazines early in his career and had later become a screenwriter in Hollywood.

Kantor could be loud and overbearing but, like others in the group, he did not romanticize or inflate his own talent and experience. Kantor believed his work in pulp fiction had no value other than as pure entertainment and to earn him a few dollars. But he also believed it honed his narrative abilities and ultimately improved his writing overall.

The gatherings of the writers' group were sometimes marked by loud and hysterical rants by Kantor over any number of topics, according to Les's letters. Kantor was conservative politically, and frequently the targets of his wrath were professional women, liberals, or, as Les described in a letter, Richard Nixon and Watergate.

The group also loved to play spirited games of liar's poker, in which the writers would read aloud either fake or real serial numbers on dollar bills—the trick was to be clever enough to lie convincingly to one's competitors, while at the same time discerning who else was lying. The biggest loser bought the drinks for the day.

The men in the writers' group were kindred spirits for Les. Through-out his life, he enjoyed talking about writing with writers he respected. Les had long had an interest in the debate regarding the authorship of the works of Shakespeare, a subject that happened to be one of the group's favorites. (Les was a traditionalist who believed Shakespeare was who he was widely believed to be.) Most important, though, was that the members of the group were more than happy to help each other profes-sionally when possible. When he was suffering through the writing and re-vising of *Ghost of the Hardy Boys,* Kantor read parts of the manuscript and encouraged Les to continue when he was disheartened. Ultimately, he wrote a short biographical blurb about Les that was used on the back cover of the book, saying the memoirs "have a special romance, lyrical and profound."

Although it had been nearly thirty years since Les had stopped working for the Stratemeyer Syndicate, he still feared that copyright agreements he entered into fifty years before were in effect, and that they could keep him from writing at length about his years with the syndicate. And even though several Canadian newspapers had reported Les's "secret" identity over the years, this information was not widely disseminated, nor had he discussed in any detail his years with the syndicate. An unexpected link to the syndicate ultimately cleared the way for the book. In 1975 Les received a letter via a newspaper columnist from syndicate vice president Andrew Svenson, who had begun writing the Hardy Boys books in the late 1940s after Les had stopped. Fortuitously, Svenson had heard from his daughter, a Sarasota resident, that Les was living in Florida. Svenson generously told Les that he admired his work on the Hardy Boys series, and credited him with establishing its loyal audience and ensuring its longevity. He told Les he could reveal his identity as "Franklin W. Dixon."

Despite Les's troubles writing *Ghost of the Hardy Boys,* Methuen officials had high hopes for the book and thought it could be a big seller. Les, of course, was experienced enough to know that expectations and reality often diverged, but letters he wrote to his children indicate that he was ex-cited about the prospect of a highly successful project. In its publicity for the book, the publisher wrote that Les "recreates the rough-and-ready days of the northern Ontario frontier, remembers the old time city news rooms, when every reporter wore a rumpled trenchcoat and a battered hat, and the Horatio Alger myth of success at every door still lived." The publishers had planned extensive publicity for the book, and its comple-tion now allowed Les to finish some of the other projects he always had underway, including the major work of fiction, *You Can't Win Them All,* that he had been writing for several years, a book that he said began as a "bizarre mystery" but ended as a character study: "I decided to get deeper under the skin of the characters and now it has turned into a rather interesting novel with the questions involving the how and the why rather than the who." After he mailed the manuscript to Methuen in the fall of 1975, he told Pat and Brian that he had done extensive rewrites, was very happy with the book, and had a good "gut feeling" about it. Even more telling, he told Brian it was the "best thing I have ever done." But he added cautiously to Pat, "I hope the title isn't prophetic."

***

By 1975, Les had learned the hard way that the publishing industry had changed dramatically since he earned his living as a full-time writer of magazine fiction and short mystery and sports novels. He acknowledged to his children that he was lucky to have been a full-time writer in the 1920s and 1930s when print markets were plentiful; there was plenty of demand for fiction even in the years following the Depression, after some magazines had gone out of business and others merged or changed their focus. The world was a less complicated place then, and even rejections came quickly with the reasons usually clearly stated. The publishing environment had indeed become hostile, and Les found that sending out books, scripts, and story ideas could be a frustrating exercise that ended frequently in the worst-case scenario of no response at all. Global economic factors, interoffice politics, and general serendipity could destroy one's chances of getting published, and the success or failure of one book often affected the fate of another completely unrelated project. On and off throughout his career, Les worked with an agent to help place his work. He had no agent in 1975, however, when he was trying to sell *You Can't Win Them All,* which he had finished by the fall of that year. He was told that while one publisher was reading the book, he could not send it to another simultaneously, a practice that bewildered him. "It seems a little strange to me, not to say unfair, that the fate of my book . . . be decided by the fate of somebody else's book, which might be very bad, or poorly promoted or badly timed, or subject to the whimsical winds of the publishing world in Canada, and that in the meantime I must cool my heels and wait," he told Norah. Still, Les ended his complaint with his usual note of optimism: "I have a feeling it will all turn out well." He also was discouraged at this point by his failure to sell *Padgett's Pooch*, the children's book he had adapted from a short story.

Les and Bea had their share of ups and downs in the early to mid-1970s. In 1973, Les had a scare when his doctor noted some nodules in his throat and did a biopsy. The nodes were benign, but the incident ended a lifetime of smoking for Les. Bea suffered a minor stroke in 1974, one that doctors said may have been caused by medication she took for high blood pressure. She recovered quickly and began paying more attention to eating habits, though she did not stop smoking. By 1975, Les's health had begun to decline dramatically. His diabetes had worsened, he was getting angina pains, and even the ultimate optimist seemed to stop taking pleasure in some of the activities he once enjoyed.

In October 1974, Les was invited to appear on the popular game show *To Tell the Truth,* hosted by Garry Moore. The show had a regular panel of four celebrities whose job it was to reveal which one of three guests was telling the truth about his identity, and which two were impostors. The three guests were paid five hundred dollars if they could stump the entire panel. In this case, Les was the real thing, while the other two only claimed to be "Leslie McFarlane," author of the first Hardy Boys books.

Les and Bea were given a free trip to New York, courtesy of the show, which included their travel and hotel costs. But Les, who normally enjoyed visiting New York, did not have a good time, as a long letter to Norah reveals. He was shocked by the high prices of everything in the city, disappointed in the overpriced and bad food he had in restaurants, and disturbed by broken fixtures in the room of his noisy hotel. He described in a few paragraphs the experience of being on *To Tell the Truth,* noting that the panel was in a bad mood because they had been stumped twice in two shows that had already been taped that day. As the questioning came to an end and three of the four panelists were fooled, Les said he was "practically spending the $500." Alas, panelist Peggy Cass guessed the truth, dashing the hopes of Les and the impostors. "It will be seen by 50,000,000 slackjawed viewers over 175 stations within the next few months," he told Norah. Meanwhile, he notes, he and Bea were happy to return to Whitby. "As for New York, let's put it this way. It may be a nice place to live but I sure as hell hate to visit it."

Les' uncharacteristically sour view of the visit might have been aggravated by ill health or the fact that, even upon finding an agent for his manuscript, he was still finding it difficult to have it read. He learned that even an agent could not make a writer less vulnerable to what he believed was a cruel and profit-oriented system. "Getting a [manu]script read at all is becoming tougher; getting it accepted when read is getting tougher; getting it printed is tougher; getting it promoted is tougher and getting it sold is damn near impossible," he grumbled to Norah.

His negative attitude about the trip may have been triggered by the fact that it was spawned, once again, not by his fame as a legitimate writer, but by his role as Franklin W. Dixon. His deeply ambivalent feelings about the Hardy Boys re-emerged after publicity was generated for his book, *Ghost of the Hardy Boys,* which had finally come out in late 1975. The timing of its release was, by chance, abysmal.

***

By the summer of 1975, Les's angina pains had worsened and he felt pain even during short walks. As he wrote Pat, he worked hard that summer on writing projects simply because he could not go outside much. His diabetes was also worsening, due in part to the lack of exercise. In the fall of 1975 during a visit to Canada, shortly before *Ghost of the Hardy Boys* was to be published, he was rushed to the hospital because of severe angina pains. Methuen had already started publicizing the book, and Les had begun doing interviews with several media outlets about it.

After spending several days in the hospital—and being given new diabetes medication—he returned briefly to the home of his stepdaughter Kathy Palmer and her family, before he caught his plane back to Sarasota. As he wrote to the Perez family several days after he had returned home, he felt much improved, although he admitted, "I was a great deal sicker than I realized." Les's letter is upbeat but cautious. "The blood sugar readings, etc. are normal again. For how long, who can tell?" He expressed unusual skepticism about an interview he had done with the *Toronto Sunday Star:* "I have a feeling he [the reporter] is going to do me dirt, somehow, because I don't trust reporters." Strange words for Les, who never forgot his early years as a newspaper reporter. Ultimately, he liked the reporter and was happy with the story.

Several months after what may have been a heart attack, in the spring of 1976, he suffered another, just before the start of an extensive publicity tour that included spots on popular American television shows such as the *Merv Griffin Show.* Ultimately, the three-week, six-city publicity tour was dramatically reduced because Les was ill, and the overall response to *Ghost of the Hardy Boys* proved to be a disappointment for Les and for Methuen. Although the book was reviewed favorably overall, its sales were below expectations. Les was disappointed that the *Toronto Star Weekend Magazine* did not pick up serial rights for the book.

Les indicated to Norah that he was disappointed in the publisher's promotion of the book. By late 1976—when he realized that the book would not be as successful as he had hoped—Les seemed pleased that it was widely reviewed during his limited book tour. "Reviews in New York and Boston were really great," he wrote. Singer Debbie Reynolds, whose children were Hardy Boys fans, praised the book on a television show, and a Boston talk show host spent thirty minutes talking about the book on his morning show, Les noted. He added ruefully, however, what might have been the story of his life: that praise and publicity do not equal dollars. "The mail has been gratifying but damn it the mail merely means autograph requests which don't pay off and cost postage money. Such is life on the Big Time Literary Beat."

But *Ghost of the Hardy Boys* was well reviewed in Toronto. The headline in the *Toronto Star*'s book review noted that "The Hardy Boys are at their best in Funny Memoir." The reviewer, Roy MacSkimming, devotes an entire newspaper story to it, calling it "a cheerfully cynical and frequently funny memoir." As he points out, "he's not the first writer to be known by a work he cares least about, and he won't be the last." *Library Journal* called it a "fine" autobiography in which the author writes "engagingly" about his struggles as a freelance writer and his joy at his ability to make a living literally by his wits.

Life was not easy now for Les, whose seventy-fourth birthday had just passed without much fanfare. "I felt no particular elation at reaching 74," he wrote. "I was simply too weary of the whole business to celebrate." Part of his weariness, perhaps, was due to the disappointing performance of his book and to the life lesson it taught him. Perhaps good work does not speak for itself, as he once had told Norah. "The financial rewards of writing nowadays have actually little to do with literary merit," he wrote to Norah. "Salesmanship is everything, so you must take what comfort you can from doing a decent job."

Meanwhile, Les was awaiting word about publication of his book *You Can't Win Them All.* His health declined substantially by the fall of 1976, to the point that he had trouble typing. The hundreds of letters Les had written over the years to his family were almost all typed—and they were typed almost perfectly, with virtually no misspellings, awkward sentences, or typographical errors. Typographical errors began to pop up in his personal letters over the last year or so, and by this time the letters were getting shorter and keyboard strikeovers more plentiful. He related little news about the books and articles he had read, the movies and plays he had seen, or the other daily activities and events that had always characterized his letters.

Les confided to Brian in November 1976 that his poor physical health had made him forgetful, and that he feared it might be affecting his mental health (a fear that might have been warranted, his stepdaughters recall). As he wrote Brian, "Life here is a matter of half a dozen different pills a day, oxygen three times a day, a visit to the doctor every two weeks but he seems satisfied enough."

He was not too ill, though, to congratulate Brian on his latest book, *Hockey '77*, and his entry into the Hockey Hall of Fame, just as he was not too ill during this period in his life to critique and praise Norah's latest work and continue to offer her advice about writing and marketing what she wrote. As he told Brian, though, he did not want to alarm Norah and Pat about his health: "Don't say anything to the girls about this health situation; they will merely worry and I am sure the [situation] will improve, even if slowly."

Les's situation did not improve, though, and by late 1976, shortly after he turned seventy-four, he had another heart attack and was once again in the hospital, this time in Florida. Pat and Norah were sufficiently alarmed that they flew down immediately—Pat from Toronto and Norah from Youngstown, New York, near Buffalo—and Brian visited him there later from Toronto. On Christmas, doctors feared he would not survive the day. This episode was even more worrisome to everyone because Les acknowledged later that he had very little memory of it and the months surrounding it, and even afterward his illness left him temporarily confused. It took him nearly two months to recover.

By the spring of 1977, he was back in Canada at the rented home in Oshawa. By this time, too, Les had received word of the death of his youngest brother Graham, who had spent most of his life in Larder Lake, near Haileybury. Graham had a stroke, and his health deteriorated dramatically afterward. While his death was not unexpected at this point, it saddened the already weakened Les, who could not attend the funeral.

In March, as he was recuperating, Les received devastating news from doctors. In a newsy letter to Pat—one which first discussed the weather, his health, and a speech he was scheduled to give for Canada Day—he revealed that his doctor had told him he had five years at the most to live. He seemed blasé, though, about facing his own mortality, perhaps because he did not believe the prediction. "It is very strange to find one-self in a situation where everything one does is predicated on a limit to one's existence," he wrote Pat. "I don't find that particularly appalling because everything depends on the quality of one's life, not its length, and if I can't write everything loses its meaning." Les added that he had stopped smoking and drinking and was down to 120 pounds, and was willing to prove the doctors wrong. Les the writer of course saw his changing life in terms of a narrative: "From now on, everything assumes a different texture, a sort of 'this-may-be-the-last-time' note which is not very happy. Maybe this is what I should be writing now in a book or arti-cle but I am not up to it yet."

Also troubling Les were the hospital bills he had incurred that winter. He and Bea had to pay the bills up front with hope of insurance reim-bursement, not knowing how much they would get back. This uncer-tainty, combined with the desire to move back to Canada permanently, prompted them to sell their Florida condominium.

After their return to Canada, Les was well enough to take great pleas-ure from the fact that a Baldwinsville, New York, elementary school was declaring the month of April as "Leslie McFarlane" month, the first time it had ever honored a writer. "Man, I'm all puffed up!" he wrote Pat. In the letter, he noted to Pat that he received several calls and letters from read-ers—and academics—who noted the major influence the Hardy Boys had on their lives.

But Les's health was not good. He made little reference to his work in his letters—highly unusual for him—although he did continue to note birthdays and special occasions in the letters. And, unfailingly, he con-tinued to praise his children for their most current accomplishments. Despite his illness, he read in nearly one sitting Norah's latest manuscript, "Staying Up Late," and pounded out a page of praise. "I don't think I could have written anything nearly so good, ever, which of course is the highest praise one writer can bestow on another."

And in September, as he had done for twenty years, Les recognized the anniversary of Amy's death in letters to his children.

But his health was deteriorating by the summer of 1977, and even the upbeat Les was in a weak and negative state of mind. By this time, he had been in and out of the hospital for several short stays, and his energy level was low. In the fall of 1976, as his illness had progressed, Bea and Les had purchased a summer cottage in Minden, about three hours north of Toronto. They had planned to spend summers there, although Les's condition threatened those plans and of course threw into doubt the wisdom of the purchase. As Les's stepdaughter Anne remembers, the home was on a beautiful rustic spot next to a lake, and even when he was ill, Les savored the beauty around him as he tried to write. His children and stepdaughters worried, though, that the cottage was in an isolated area and their father was seriously ill.

A July 1977 letter to Norah from his apartment in Oshawa indicates that Les may have been starting to face his own mortality. As he signed a bank slip, he was shocked at his illegible handwriting, he said: "I am so full of medication that I am acting like an old man of about 95," he wrote. "I don't write—I scrawl. I don't walk—I lurch. As for writing—we'll see about that but I greatly fear I don't think logically any more but merely grasp at concepts as they skim by. Damn it, this is incredible, especially to a man who once prided himself on his accurate memory and his ability to express himself cogently." Ironically, the fact that Les could still be so clear eyed about his own condition may indicate that he was more lucid than he thought, and he is quick to thank Norah for visiting him and to note how difficult it must be for her to see him so weak.

His health continued to go downhill, and in late August another heart attack sent him to the hospital. This one would prove fatal.

***

In his memoir *Ghost of the Hardy Boys*, written when he was in his early seventies, Les quotes his good friend McKinlay Kantor as saying that writers—"real" writers—never retire. As for Les, "I will be freelancing until someone draws the cover over my typewriter for me for the last time," he writes at the end of the book. And, indeed, he was sitting at his typewriter until several months before his death, until he was too weak to write. As he had always said, writing for him was a natural and vital part of life. Ironically, two versatile, prolific, and gifted writers passed away that fall of 1977: Kantor's death came a little more than a month after Les's.

Les died on September 6, 1977, about six weeks before his seventy-fifth birthday. His funeral service was held in the W. C. Town Funeral Chapel in Whitby, followed by cremation. He is buried in Ottawa, next to the grave of Amy McFarlane. At the time of his death, he had twenty-three grandchildren and stepgrandchildren. News of his death was picked up by the Canadian Press wire, so it was marked by stories and obituaries in news outlets throughout Canada and parts of the United States. Most of the stories mentioned prominently that he was the writer of the first group of Hardy Boys books, but many also noted much of his other work and spoke of his versatility as a writer.

Les took steps to ensure that his friends in the Sarasota writers' group would not forget him any time soon: in his will he left funds sufficient to buy the first round of drinks at every meeting of the club.

18

. . . .

THE FINAL CHAPTER

Ghost of the Hardy Boys described in great detail Les's role as one of the authors of the top-selling Hardy Boys series and revealed quite a bit about the workings of the Stratemeyer Syndicate as witnessed by Les. But people unaware of the book still ruminated on the identity of the elusive Franklin W. Dixon. In the fall of 1976—coincidentally, the same year *Ghost of the Hardy Boys* came out—an article in *Rolling Stone* magazine bemoaned the changes in the revised books, and wondered: Where is Franklin W. Dixon now? The article reviewed some details of the changes in the book and compared Harriet Adams and her colleagues to Soviet historians, who routinely rewrote history.

The article caught the eye of the original Franklin W. Dixon at his home in Florida. He was no doubt dismayed to realize that if *Rolling Stone* had known about his *Ghost of the Hardy Boys,* most of the questions the story posed would have been answered. Les immediately wrote a witty letter to the editor that was published in *Rolling Stone* six weeks later. It first mentions briefly the existence of *Ghost of the Hardy Boys,* then goes into a fictional account of what happened to those who used to travel in the Hardy Boys' circle: "Fenton Hardy, who recently celebrated his 90th birthday, lives in a retirement home in Sarasota, Florida, and spends most of his time rejecting publishers' pleas that he write his autobiography. 'Governments would fall,' he explains, 'and besides, my memory isn't what it used to be.'"

Les then offers updates on the other characters' lives:

· In the retirement home in which she lives, Laura Hardy is famous for her sandwiches.

· The peppery and dictatorial Aunt Gertrude died at the ripe old age of 104, "during a lively argument with a supermarket cashier. Apoplexy, not unexpected."

· Frank and Joe now head an investigative agency "so exclusive
that it takes a certified cheque of $250,000 to get you into
their suite of offices." The boys, however, are not pleased
about the advent of computers in detective work: "Not nearly
as much fun as in the old days in Bayport."

Les's good-natured response may have masked his disappointment that
Ghost had not sold more copies or been better publicized. But by the
time he was seventy-four, he had learned to maintain a sense of humor
about his role as Franklin W. Dixon and the ironies associated with it.

***

By the time *Toronto Star Weekend* reporter Bob Stall came to Les's home in
Whitby to interview him in 1973, Les was used to questions about why he
was paid next to nothing as the author of one of the best-selling book series in history. He had a stock answer—and it was the truth: he had not
written the books to become rich, and he had signed a legal agreement at
the time that prohibited him from earning royalties. (When he was first
asked by Stall about the nonexistent royalties, Les replied quickly: "You
can't get under my skin on that one.") Although he had paid little attention to sales or content of the books since he had stopped writing them in
the late 1940s, he was aware that the books had been updated. But Stall,
during an extensive and candid interview with Les that day, told Les something he did not know—and something that shocked and hurt him.

Les's letters to his children during this time show that he liked Stall,
and while he was usually a bit apprehensive about how stories about him
would turn out, he indicated that he was eagerly awaiting this one. (Publication of the article was evidently delayed several weeks for a variety of
reasons, including Stall's illness.) Les, who was reserved by nature around
people he did not know, was particularly frank in this interview, perhaps
because Stall told him that "Franklin W. Dixon" had introduced him as a
child to the pleasures of reading. In the article, Stall puts Les in the same
category as Mark Twain, Louisa May Alcott, and Lewis Carroll, calling
Les's books "beautifully written." He labeled Les's ambivalent feelings
about his relationship to the Hardy Boys series "literary schizophrenia."

Stall's article implies that an intimacy developed between the two
men and that they were willing to share confidences—as much as two
people can do in front of a few hundred thousand newspaper readers.
For example, when discussing the last Hardy Boys book Les wrote, *The*

Phantom Freighter, Stall alludes to the fact that it was submitted to the syndicate as written by Les's wife, Amy, even though he acknowledges, with a wink, that she was not the true author: "I'm not supposed to talk about it," Stall writes cryptically, and says no more about it.

After Les told Stall that he never read the Hardy Boys books after he pulled them from his typewriter, he added, "But don't say anything like that in your article. That's just the cynical, ambivalent writer in me coming out. I don't want to hurt the kids by statements like that."

By this point in his life, as his health started to decline, Les was no doubt thinking about his legacy. On and off during his career as a freelance writer he had nurtured the idea of writing the great Canadian novel, but by this time he viewed himself primarily as a storyteller and master of narrative. By the time he reached his seventies, Les's ambition may have shifted from a desire to be a great author to a desire to be remembered favorably by those who read his work. The reason he resented the continual questions about royalties was that he never considered the amount of money he earned as a measure of his value, yet he felt that others sometimes used that to gauge his success.

Stall had apparently brought with him that day a series of updated Hardy Boys books to show Les, and he apparently asked Les to compare them with the original ones he had written. At first, Les was unfazed: he knew they had been updated, and even agreed with some of the changes. What he did not know—and what Stall showed him that day in his living room—was that the books were drastically reduced in length, entire scenes eliminated, characters' personalities changed, and colorful descriptive passages omitted. The revelation came as a shock to Les, and as he perused the passages Stall showed him, he became angry. "My God, they've been gutted," Les said, later calling the revisions "a literary fraud." Stall writes:

> The more he skimmed, the more upset McFarlane became. "I hadn't realized they'd been so substantially changed," he muttered. "Thought they were just updated, streamlined. Utterly changed. It doesn't bear any resemblance to the original. I'd have felt better if they'd just been cut."

Les had the sinking feeling that he was no longer the author of the first group of Hardy Boys books—he was the author of the *old* series of books. He told Stall that the books a generation of fathers were recommending to their children were not at all the books they thought they were. "They don't know they've been spoiled," Les said. "They don't know that they're now these crappy things under the same titles under that same author's name."

And Les now realized that many of the books he had been autographing as "Franklin W. Dixon" were not his at all. A third and final layer of authorship had all but eliminated Leslie McFarlane from the process. Perhaps, like the two impostors who played him on *To Tell the Truth*, Leslie McFarlane was no longer Franklin W. Dixon, either.

***

By the end of his life, Les had seen the Hardy Boys go through many incarnations. But Harriet Stratemeyer Adams had witnessed even more changes in series fiction in her lifetime. By the time she died in 1982 at age eighty-nine, the boys were using computers, listening to rock 'n roll, and working with the Pentagon. Over the years, the syndicate had managed to avoid extensive publicity and lawsuits from any of its ghostwriters who earned about $75 to $150 per book. Ironically, though, the syndicate did face a lawsuit from its longtime publisher. In 1979 the syndicate ended its seventy-five-year association with Grosset & Dunlap after a bitter lawsuit over hardcover and softcover book rights and announced it would now use Simon & Schuster as its publisher. (Some syndicate followers have said it changed publishers because Grosset & Dunlap failed to make any special plans to celebrate the fiftieth anniversary of the Nancy Drew series in 1980.) Grosset & Dunlap filed a $50 million lawsuit against the syndicate and Simon & Schuster, claiming copyright infringement and unfair competition. A federal judge later divided custody of the syndicate, allowing Simon & Schuster rights to publish hardcover versions of new stories in the Stratemeyer series, and allowing Grosset & Dunlap rights to continue publishing hardcover versions of the books it had published under contracts with the syndicate dating back to 1930. The judge dismissed Grosset & Dunlap's claim of copyright violations, breach of contract, and unfair competition.

In 1984, the syndicate was sold to Simon & Schuster. Shortly after the sale, the format of the Hardy Boys books was changed again—from hardcover to softcover, with a length of about 150 pages. Since that time, Joe and Frank Hardy have solved crime online, fought Soviet spies, and battled terrorists. Unlike Edward Stratemeyer, the current authors and publishers of the series do not hesitate to portray blood or graphic violence, and even major characters were not immune. For instance, Joe's sweetheart Iola Morton was blown up by terrorists in the late 1980s. (Iola, though, had already undergone other transformations over the years. Like her brother, Chet, she was overweight in the unrevised Hardy Boys books. After 1959, though, she had lost enough weight to be described as "slender.")

Simon & Schuster began publishing a spinoff series known as The Hardy Boys Casefiles in 1987, and the boys joined forces with their syndicate cousin Nancy Drew for two years in the early 1980s in a series of books called Super Sleuths. (The three detectives also worked together in that era in an interactive project called "Be a Detective," in which readers could decide the ending of each story.) A short-lived Hardy Boys series called the Clues Brothers was aimed at readers aged nine to twelve.

Sales figures for the syndicate's most popular series—Nancy Drew, the Hardy Boys, and the Bobbsey Twins—vary and are difficult to confirm. By 1975, though, it is estimated that more than 60 million Nancy Drew mysteries had been sold; sales of the Hardy Boys series topped 50 million by that year, and the Bobbsey Twins had sold about 30 million. After that, both Nancy Drew and the Hardy Boys have sold between 1 and 2 million copies each year.

Of course, as the Hardy Boys entered the television age, they earned their fifteen minutes of fame on the small screen—several times. As early as the mid-1950s, Disney studios created two short serials about them that aired on the popular *Mickey Mouse Club* television show. The first was based on the first book in the series, *The Tower Treasure,* and the second was an original story. Disney also released several products tied into the serials, including a board game, comic books, a coloring book, and a record. Such memorabilia were associated with nearly all the televised Hardy Boys efforts.

The Hardy Boys returned to television in 1967 in one pilot show about their escapades starring Tim Matthieson (now Matheson) and Rick Gates, but this first show was not picked up for the season. An animated version of the series aired from 1969 until 1971. In this version, the boys were rock musicians who also solved mysteries. From 1977 to 1979, the Hardy Boys and Nancy Drew were lead characters in the ABC show, *The Hardy Boys/Nancy Drew Mysteries,* starring Pamela Sue Martin, Shaun Cassidy, and Parker Stevenson. In the 1990s, the boys still did not have much luck sustaining a television show: In 1995, Nancy Drew and the Hardy Boys were featured in two half-hour series, *Nancy Drew* and *The Hardy Boys*, airing on Saturday afternoons. The series lasted one season.

For readers who want the integrity of the original texts but do not want to pay dearly for them on the collectors market, a small publisher in Massachusetts, Applewood Books, began reprinting in 1991 many of the original books exactly as they were written, before the 1959 revisions. Both the original and revised versions of the Hardy Boys continue to sell well. Collectors confront nebulous copyright dates in attempting to determine what version they have and its value. Original copies—those written before 1959—and those written by McFarlane are the most valuable, many collectors believe.

Because of their wholesome quality and their link to pleasant childhood memories, the Hardy Boys series has become a natural subject for parody. The series has spawned at least one theatrical spoof and at least two parodies by the humor magazine *National Lampoon*. In the *National Lampoon* 1985 article "The Undiscovered Notebooks of Franklin W. Dixon," the author purports to have stumbled upon some unpublished Hardy Boys manuscripts found after the supposed death of Mr. Dixon. In them, the boys participate in some distinctly un-Hardy-like activities: "The Party Boys in the Case of the Missing Scotch" is one adventure; "The Hardly Boys in the Dark Secret of the Spooky Closet" (in which Frank and Joe Hardy reveal they are gay) is another. In another more sophisticated article in *National Lampoon*, the writers have the boys searching for the reason the popular Franklin W. Dixon has stopped writing. They find, of course, that he has been kidnapped. The article parodies "Dixon's" writing style, complete with redundant and exaggerated verbs and adverbs: "'Afraid not,'" Jerry apologized sheepishly'" or, "'No!' Will ejaculated." The authors also parodied the frequent references in the text to the boys' physical appearance: "'Yes?' the boys questioned, arching their blond and dark eyebrows respectively." Several of the characters seemed to have developed amnesia, including Fenton Hardy and the feisty—and now vulgar—Aunt Gertrude, whose brief appearance in the article is marked by an expletive that without question would have been vetoed by the Stratemeyers.

The humor magazine *Mad* also took aim at Joe and Frank Hardy: the Hardys appear in a parody of the tabloid *National Enquirer.* In the phony newspaper article, other Stratemeyer creations make an appearance: the boys have been "dumped" by the Bobbsey twins and start a romantic relationship with Nancy Drew. "Will Triangle Lead to Heartbreak?" the headline asks.

The musical comedy *The Secret of the Old Queen,* performed in 1999 and 2000 in Chicago and San Francisco, "takes on the beloved Hardy Boys mysteries, in which the infallible teenage detectives outwit villains and still make it home in time for dinner," as one reviewer noted. As the review stated, though, this is an adults-only version of the series.

Seventy-five years after the first book was written, the wit and wisdom of the Hardy Boys were preserved in venues outside of the series. *The Hardy Boys' Guide to Life,* written by "Franklin W. Dixon" and published in 2002 by Simon & Schuster, is a small book of aphorisms collected from Hardy Boys stories. In *The House on the Point: A Tribute to Franklin W. Dixon and the Hardy Boys,* Benjamin Hoff rewrites the second book in the series, *The House on the Cliff,* for a new generation of young readers, according to the book jacket.

***

Despite the many attempts over the years to change their content and keep them off the shelves of libraries, the Hardy Boys series has proved remarkably durable. In 2001, the *New York Times* noted that for the first time since its early years, the series was losing readers. Noting the tremendous longevity of a series that survived enormous changes in society and culture over seventy years, the article attributed much of its appeal to its first author, Leslie McFarlane, whose descriptions of sumptuous meals and "playful detail" breathed life into what might have been a mundane series, the story said. The popularity of the Stratemeyer series books—like that of all children's and adult literature—was subject to the changing whims of a public that was greatly influenced by outside factors. These whims seem to come in cycles, according to one historian. Russel Nye, who did extensive research into popular culture of the twentieth century, noted that turning points in juvenile fiction came in the 1940s, an era marked by improvement in school libraries, better schools, and an interest in child psychology, and in the 1950s, with the growth of television and comic books. All these factors, he noted, made many of the series books virtually obsolete. (The two exceptions were the Hardy Boys and Nancy Drew mysteries.) At the turn of the century, another cycle coinciding with the advent of compact discs, videotapes, and, most of all, the Internet may be, finally, dampening the interest in the Hardy Boys.

But it clearly would be premature to sound a death knell for the series. In addition to becoming a part of the lexicon in this country, the Hardy Boys have become a cultural touchstone all over the world for a vast network of fans of all ages whose love of the series is a common bond. Despite many changes over many years—in the series, in its readers, and in society overall—the Hardy Boys books are in the blood of some of these fans, and they have created their own conferences, journals, websites, and online newsletters to discuss them and other series books. Each day, in chat rooms all over the world, these fans debate topics such as the true location of Bayport, the correct pronunciation of Iola Morton's first name, and—a common theme—their favorite Hardy character and book. They also talk at length about the impact of the books on their lives.

In magazine and newspaper profiles, well-known and accomplished people occasionally mention the Hardy Boys books as a major influence. Before Canadian astronaut Roberta Bondar went into space, for example, an interviewer asked her what books she'd be taking on the flight. Her reply? The Hardy Boys' *A Figure in Hiding.* When mystery writer Carl Hiaasen was asked what three major mystery writers he would take to dinner, his reply was Raymond Chandler, Arthur Conan Doyle, and Franklin W. Dixon—the third because it was he who hooked Hiaasen on mysteries.

Probably no group of people is more loyal to Leslie McFarlane and his work than the residents of Haileybury, Ontario, the town where Les grew up.

On July 18, 1998, Robert Nelson, age thirty-six, who had collected more than six hundred volumes of the Hardy Boys series, made the trek to Haileybury from his home in Marysville, Washington. Like many other fans of the series, he wanted to participate in a two-day celebration honoring Leslie McFarlane that featured a tour of the homes in which he lived, a tea, and the unveiling of a granite lectern at the waterfront honoring his memory. In a Canadian Press wire story about the event, Nelson described his attachment to the series. "I couldn't do what other kids could do," said Nelson, who was born with cerebral palsy. "But once I started reading the Hardy Boys I had my own adventures."

The residents of Haileybury, long proud of the city's rustic beauty and its colorful history, planned the celebration for two years using private donations. In addition to the granite lectern, the city has marked homes where Les lived with small signs on the lawn commemorating "The Ghost of the Hardy Boys" (along with a logo of a "sleuth" peering into a magnifying glass). It also posted a sign at the entrance of the city noting that Haileybury is the home of Leslie McFarlane, author of the Hardy Boys, and it has much McFarlane memorabilia, including the old Underwood typewriter that he used, at its historical center, the Haileybury Heritage Museum. The city also has sponsored other events over the years honoring Les, including a high school writing contest.

***

Several of Les's relatives, including some who still live in and near Haileybury, attended the celebration in his honor. His two surviving children, Norah Perez and Brian McFarlane, attended, as did one of Patricia McFarlane McCauley's sons, Matthew McCauley.

Norah continues her career as a writer, and still writes articles for national magazines and young-adult novels as well as lecturing about her books and about writing. After his many years as a commentator for *Hockey Night in Canada*, Brian McFarlane continues writing sports books and young-adult fiction, and he lectures frequently about his work and his career as a sports broadcaster. Patricia McCauley, Les's oldest child, died in 1980 shortly before she was scheduled to have surgery. All three of Les's children had three children of their own.

Les's three stepdaughters still live in or near Whitby, Ontario. The youngest, Kathy Palmer, has two grown children, as does the middle stepdaughter, Anne Yarrow. The oldest, Claire Campbell, has three children.

Les's second wife, Bea, died in 1998 at the age of eighty-three.

By the end of his life, Les came to peace with his authorship of the Hardy Boys and recognized its value after he came to realize what his work meant to millions of children. Whether it was his closeness to his own children and stepchildren or the vicissitudes in his own career that changed his mind will never be known. As he told writer Bob Stall, he would never denigrate what his work meant to young readers over the decades: "[Children's] admiration was honest. An honest compliment from a youngster is not easy to come by and it is certainly not to be despised by anyone."

REFERENCES

Much of the information for this biography was obtained from three major manuscript collections at the following locations: the Stratemeyer Syndicate Records Collection in the Manuscripts and Archives Division of the New York Public Library, Astor, Lenox and Tilden Foundations (Stratemeyer Syndicate records and correspondence as well as outlines for Stratemeyer Syndicate books and overall summaries of the first ones in each series); the Thomas Fisher Rare Book Library at the University of Toronto (The William Arthur Deacon collection, including correspondence from Deacon); and Mills Memorial Library at McMaster University, Hamilton, Ontario (family scrapbooks, newspaper clippings, and the like).

Leslie McFarlane's two surviving children, Norah and Brian, provided me with access to the thousands of letters, diary entries, genealogies, and magazine articles that tell the story of his career and life.

Much has been written over the years about Stratemeyer Syndicate series books, but I am especially grateful to Deidre Johnson for her *Edward Stratemeyer and the Stratemeyer Syndicate* (New York: Twayne, 1993) and *Stratemeyer Pseudonyms and Series Books* (Westport, CT: Greenwood Press, 1982) and for Carol Billman's *The Secret of the Stratemeyer Syndicate: Nancy Drew, The Hardy Boys, and the Million Dollar Fiction Factory* (New York: Ungar, 1986). I also used much information provided by James Keeline, with whom I corresponded for several years. I accessed his convention papers and his other writings through his website, www.keeline.com. Also of great use was the website of Alana Nash, www.stratemeyer.net, with its exhaustive history of the Stratemeyer Syndicate and series books.

Some of the information about plot details of the Hardy Boys books was obtained from Robert L. Crawford's detailed analysis, *The Lost Hardys: A Concordance* (Rheem Valley and Old Tappan, CA: SynSine Press, 1997). And I learned a great deal about Haileybury in general from Bruce Taylor's *Leslie McFarlane: The Hardy Boys' Haileybury Connection* (New Liskeard, Ont.: Temiskaming Printing, 1996).

Finally, unless otherwise noted, all quotes from the text of the Hardy Boys books were taken from unrevised versions of those books, which were easily accessible thanks to the inexpensive reprinting of these original texts by the Applewood Press of Bedford, Massachusetts.

The following abbreviations have been used:

BM—Brian McFarlane
EDS—Edna Stratemeyer
ES—Edward Stratemeyer
ES—Deidre Johnson, *Edward Stratemeyer and the Stratemeyer Syndicate* (New York: Twayne, 1993)

REFERENCES

GHB—Leslie McFarlane, *Ghost of the Hardy Boys* (Toronto: Methuen; New York: Two Continents, 1976)
HB—Hardy Boys
HSA—Harriet Stratemeyer Adams
KH—Leslie McFarlane, *A Kid in Haileybury* (Cobalt, Ont.: Highway Book Shop, 1975)
LH—Robert L. Crawford, *The Lost Hardys: A Concordance* (Rheem Valley and Old Tappan, CA: SynSine Press, 1997)
LM—Leslie McFarlane
LM—Bruce Taylor, *Leslie McFarlane: The Hardy Boys' Haileybury Connection* (New Liskeard, Ont.: Temiskaming Printing, 1996)
NMP—Norah McFarlane Perez
PMM—Patricia McFarlane McCauley
SS—Stratemeyer Syndicate
SSS—Carol Billman, *The Secret of the Stratemeyer Syndicate: Nancy Drew, The Hardy Boys, and the Million Dollar Fiction Factory* (New York: Ungar, 1986)
WAD—William Arthur Deacon

CHAPTER 1: TWO LIVES INTERSECT

Haileybury early history: *LM*, 10.

LM's childhood recollections of Haileybury: Much of his memoir, *KH*, reflects on his childhood.

ES's early days: *ES*, 2, 18, 26.

Alger's career: James Keeline discusses this in biographical information he includes on his website about series fiction, www.keeline.com. He also discusses it in several papers he has posted online and presented at annual conferences of the Popular Culture Association.

LM's original high school essay is among the personal papers held by his son, Brian McFarlane.

Fortune article about SS: *Fortune*, April 1934, 86. (No author listed.)

LM's opinions about the syndicate: Interview with LM for the Canadian Broadcasting Corp. in 1972, rebroadcast on the CBC July 18, 1998.

LM's memories of his recreation in Haileybury: *GHB*, 13, 150.

LM's fictional characters: Flannelfoot Foster appeared in several of LM's *Maclean's* magazine stories, including "Wakeville, Awake!" March 15, 1940, 5–7, 39–44; Gideon McCrabb appeared in the *Maclean's* short story "Kelsey Skates Again," February 15, 1941, 16–18, 29–31.

LM's physical description of Haileybury appears throughout *KH*, especially 8, 9, 13, and 17.

Discussion of the economic strata of Haileybury: *KH*, 19. Haileybury Heritage Museum Curator Christopher Oslund discussed the number of millionaires in the city with the author on July 30, 2001, in Haileybury.

Haileybury memories: recreation for children: *GHB*, 151; bobsledding: *KH*, 43; food: *KH*, 57; remembrances of Miss Flegg: *KH*, 28–29.

REFERENCES

Rebecca McFarlane's personality: Interview by the author with LM's sister-in-law, Bertha McFarlane, and his niece, Eleanor Huff, July 30, 2001, in Haileybury.

McFarlane family genealogy: A detailed genealogy written by LM's family is among his personal papers held by his children.

John Henry McFarlane: career: *LM*, 2; observations: from LM's personal papers held by his children; sense of humor and devotion to religion: *KH*, 30, 64, 86; as journalist: *LM*, 17.

CHAPTER 2: A WRITER IS BORN

LM winning literary competition: *LM*, 20.

LM on being short: *GHB*, 98.

LM's summer jobs: *GHB*, 87–88.

Boys' interests in the early 1900s: Arthur Prager, "Edward Stratemeyer and His Book Machine," *Saturday Review*, July 10, 1971, 16.

Rover Boys sales: Memo to the author from James Keeline, April 30, 2003.

Incorporation of trends in series fiction: Prager, "Edward Stratemeyer and His Book Machine," 16.

Number of Tom Swift books sold: www.keeline.com.

Howard Garis as innovator: Bruce Weber, *Hired Pens: Professional Writers in America's Golden Age of Print* (Athens: Ohio University Press, 1997), 76.

Howard Garis's life and career: Weber, *Hired Pens*, 98. Roger Garis describes at length his father's relationship with ES and the SS in his memoir, *My Father Was Uncle Wiggily* (New York: McGraw-Hill, 1966).

"Laying the pipes": Weber, *Hired Guns*, 77.

No secrecy clause: Memo to the author from James Keeline, April 30, 2003.

Ghostwriters never meeting: This story was repeated many times in articles about ES, including in Weber, *Hired Pens*, 77.

LM's concern about revealing his pen name: Several personal letters to LM's family members during the early 1970s when he was writing *GHB*.

Information about Mildred Wirt: *ES*, 10.

Expansion of magazines in the U.S.: Weber, *Hired Pens*, 79–81.

Burning down the wrong house: *GHB*, 91.

Cushing's advice: *GHB*, 93.

Fading of Cobalt: *GHB*, 93.

Editor's view of a reporter's job: *GHB*, 97.

Colleague's encouragement: *GHB*, 134–35.

Reporters as fiction writers: Weber, *Hired Pens*, 113, based on several writings by and about Hemingway, Twain, Stein, and others.

Leaving Haileybury: *GHB*, 99.

Sudbury Star newsroom: *GHB*, 131.

Environment in Sudbury: *GHB*, 101.

LM's duties at the *Star*: *GHB*, 105.

LM never in whorehouse: *GHB*, 95.

LM meets Hemingway: *GHB*, 112.
LM on getting published for the first time: *KH*, viii.
Toronto Star Weekly editor: *GHB*, 112.
LM as hockey commentator: *GHB*, 118; Brian McFarlane describes his father's hockey broadcasting stint in *Brian McFarlane's World of Hockey* (Toronto: Stoddart, 2000), 10–11.
LM's difficulty writing plays: *GHB*, 7–8.
Fictionalized version of brushfire victims: LM's "The Root-House," *Maclean's*, November 1, 1927, 1.
Memories of the 1922 Haileybury fire: *GHB*, 120.
Fire story: *Sudbury Star*, October 7, 1922, 1.
Reunited with his family who escaped fire: *GHB*, 121–22.

CHAPTER 3: THE GHOST OF THE HARDY BOYS

Records of article sales: Kept by LM and found among his personal papers.
Best years as a writer: *GHB*, 134.
Leaving the newspaper: *GHB*, 133.
Desired story: *GHB*, 136.
LM on Mencken: *GHB*, 138.
"Respectable" publication: *GHB*, 143.
LM's salary at *Springfield Republican*: *GHB*, 2.
Life in the newsroom: *GHB*, 4. LM talked about his weight loss in a letter to his fiancée, Amy Arnold, March 21, 1926.
Syndicate books of the era: *ES*, 110–15, 98–100.
Plot and language of series books: Russel Nye, *The Unembarrassed Muse: The Popular Arts in America* (New York: Dial Press, 1970), 80–82.
"Bare-bones" syndicate: See *ES*. *Fortune* magazine ran this in an extensive article about the syndicate written four years after ES died. See "For Indeed It Was He," *Fortune*, April 1934, 194.
Staid nature of series books: *GHB*, 178–79.
Dana Girls: *GHB*, 199.
Mathiews's writings are discussed at length in many articles about the syndicate. See, for instance, Arthur Prager, "Edward Stratemeyer and His Fiction Machine," *Saturday Review*, July 10, 1971; and Ken Donelson, "The Stratemeyer Syndicate, Then and Now," *Children's Literature* 7 (1978): 16–44.
Mathiews's article first appeared in *Outlook*, November 18, 1914. It was reprinted in *The Boys' Book Collector* 1, no. 4 (1970): 106–8.
Comstock: Ken Donelson quotes Comstock in his article "The Stratemeyer Syndicate, Then and Now," 35. Comstock's quote is taken from *Traps for the Young* (1883), ed. Robert Bremner (Cambridge: Harvard University Press, 1976), 12.
Boy Scout books: James Keeline, e-mail message to author, April 29, 2003.
Springfield Republican book critic's report to LM: *GHB*, 54–56.

Winnetka book list: See *ES;* Johnson notes the original reading list was published in 1926 in Chicago by the American Library Association.

Children's sections in libraries: Kathleen T. Horning, *From Cover to Cover: Evaluating Children's Books* (New York: HarperCollins Juvenile Division, 1997), 150.

Books of the era: See Cornelia Meigs, Anne Thaxter Eaton, Elizabeth Nesbitt, and Ruth Hill Viguers, eds., *A Critical History of Children's Literature* (New York: Macmillan, 1969), 303–5, 359.

Moore on writing for children: Horning, *From Cover to Cover,* 150.

Newbery Medal: Horning, *From Cover to Cover,* 151.

Children's book reviews: Meigs et al., *Critical History of Children's Literature,* 394.

See Roger Garis's *My Father Was Uncle Wiggily* (New York: McGraw-Hill, 1966).

Ghostwriters' anonymity: *GHB,* 72.

LM's feelings about Roy Rockwood: *GHB,* 12–13.

Imaginary authors: *Fortune,* 204.

LM's views of series fiction: *GHB,* 19.

Summary of Dave Fearless outline: *GHB,* 22.

Start of Dave Fearless book: *GHB,* 23.

LM on sending off his manuscript: *GHB,* 38.

Year's lease on a cabin: *GHB,* 39–40.

Never a reporter again: *GHB,* 47.

"Hill of Gold" rejection: *GHB,* 58–59.

Trouble with mailing and ES's suggestions to LM: ES to LM, July 8, 1928.

ES's deadlines for LM: ES to LM, September 4, 1926.

ES returning manuscript: ES to LM, September 25, 1926.

Additional pages needed in two books: ES to LM, September 30, 1926; and telegram, ES to LM, December 9, 1926.

CHAPTER 4: BIRTH OF A SERIES

On "Hill of Gold": ES to LM, November 26, 1926, and December 2, 1926.

ES on his ghostwriters' careers: ES to LM, November 26, 1926.

LM as one of the youngest ghostwriters: ES to LM, December 14, 1926.

Cloth vs. paper books: ES to LM, December 2, 1926.

Emphasis on uniform length of books: ES to LM, November 26, 1926.

Financial setup of syndicate: James Keeline, www.keeline.com.

These financial calculations were printed in the *Fortune* article, 88–89.

Adult detective novels: *SSS,* 80.

Two brothers as protagonists: The date of this letter is unknown, although it was probably written in 1926 when Stratemeyer was planning to publish the first three Hardy Boys books. The letter is quoted in Carole Kismaric and Marvin Heiferman's *The Mysterious Case of Nancy Drew and the Hardy Boys* (New York: Fireside, Simon & Schuster, 1998), 18.

LM free of Dave Fearless: *GHB*, 12.
Hardy Boys similar to adult mysteries: *GHB*, 61.
Hardy Boys sophisticated: *GHB*, 63–64.
Eventual sales of Hardy Boys: *GHB*, 64.
ES note to Grosset & Dunlap: SS papers.
Unpublished HB book summaries and HB outlines: SS papers.
The "W" in Franklin W. Dixon: *GHB*, 62.
The first "Fenton Hardy": Johnson, *Stratemeyer Pseudonyms and Series Books*, 98.
Location of "real" Bayport: *SSS*, 91–92.
Haileybury as Bayport: Interview by the author with Chris Oslund, Haileybury, Ontario, July 30, 2001. Oslund is curator of the Haileybury Heritage Museum, which details the history of the town and includes information about LM's career and life.
Calamities in HB books: *GHB*, 65
LM's mother's cooking: This is discussed in both of LM's memoirs.
Delicious meals in the books: *GHB*, 71.
Les as lover of good food: Interview by the author with NMP, Youngstown, NY, January 30, 2001.
ES's enthusiasm for *Tower Treasure:* ES to LM, January 4, 1927.
"Good yarn": ES to LM, January 7, 1927.
How to find Haileybury: ES to LM, May 3, 1927.
LM's invitation to ES: LM to ES, May 6, 1927.

CHAPTER 5: A WELL-OILED MACHINE

Description of *Tower Treasure* cover: *GHB*, 180.
LM impressed by *Tower Treasure: GHB*, 185.
Launching of the series: *GHB*, 182.
ES's advice about length of books and short manuscript: ES to LM, January 29, 1927.
"We're in a hurry": ES to LM, June 18, 1928.
LM requesting advance: LM to ES, July 6, 1927.
Announcement of *Maclean's* awards: "$1,000 Prize Story Awards," *Maclean's*, May 1, 1927 (page unknown).
Congratulations from ES: ES to LM, May 17, 1928.
Appeal of "Root-House": *GHB*, 179.
Excerpt from "Root-House": *Maclean's*, November 1, 1927, 3–5, 44–47.
Mystery Ranch summary: ES to LM, March 15, 1927.
Portrayal of clergy: ES to LM, March 23, 1927.
Payment for *Mystery Ranch:* ES to LM, March 25, 1929.
Portrayal of policemen: ES to LM, April 10, 1928.
"Bayport Bluecoats": *GHB*, 182.
LM on authority: *GHB*, 183.

REFERENCES

LM's view of women as writers and in workplace: Interview by author with NMP, Youngstown, NY, January 30, 2001.
Miss Flegg: *KHB*, 28–29.
Series "turning point": *GHB*, 185.
Aunt Gertrude as a favorite: *GBH*, 185–86.
Meeting Amy Arnold: Interviews by the author with Else Maddock, New Liskeard, Ontario, July 29, 2001, and NMP, Lewiston, NY, August 1, 2001.
Length of LM and Amy Arnold courtship: LM to Amy Arnold, March 21, 1926.
Kerchief: LM to Amy Arnold, August 1925 (undated).
Remembrances of autumn: LM to Amy Arnold, March 21, 1926.
Talking vs. letter writing: LM to Amy Arnold, March 21, 1926.
Kisses: LM to Amy Arnold, November 11, 1927.
Amy Arnold's letter writing: Interview by the author with NMP, January 30, 2001.
Amy Arnold's personality: Else Maddock interview; and interview by the author with Brian McFarlane, Toronto, Ontario, July 31, 2001.
Check from ES: This check was enclosed in a letter from ES to LM, April 25, 1928.

CHAPTER 6: THE GOLDEN HANDCUFFS

Publishing plans for HB: *GHB*, 187–88.
Hardy Boys as "sheet anchor": *GHB*, 189.
ES on story status: ES to LM, August 17, 1928.
Author of diaries: Interview by the author with NMP, August 1, 2001.
Amy's illness: Interview with NMP, August 1, 2001.
LM giving gifts on his birthday: Interview with NMP, August 1, 2001.
HB and Ted Scott sales: www.keeline.com.
Pay increase to $150: ES to LM, March 12, 1929.
Missing pages: ES to LM, May 27, 1929.
SS at peak production and SS as "gardener": *SSS*, 143.
Magazine legislation and new readers: Theodore Peterson discusses the history of American magazines at length in *Magazines in the Twentieth Century* (Urbana: University of Illinois Press, 1975), 2–4, 6–7.
Retailers and national marketing: Peterson, *Magazines*, 4.
Magazine publishers in lucrative position: Peterson, *Magazines*, 7.
Ads at lower rates: Peterson, *Magazines*, 7.
Saturday Evening Post history: Peterson, *Magazines*, 12.
Munsey quote: Peterson, *Magazines*, 21.
Professional attitude: *GHB*, 186–87.
LM's "entertainer's gift" *GHB*, 187.

CHAPTER 7: TOUGH TIMES

LM on poor magazine markets: LM to SS, October 15, 1930.

Mistakes in HB: *LH*, 63–68. Crawford notes that many of the errors in the series occurred in the late 1930s and early 1940s when LM temporarily stopped writing the books.

Announcement of ES's death: EDS to LM, May 12, 1930.

ES's will: *ES*, 11.

LM's condolence letter: LM to EDS, May 14, 1930.

HSA's life and comment in reunion book: *ES*, 12.

Status of SS in 1930: *ES*, 13.

Refusal by LM to write book: LM to HSA, January 1, 1931.

Praise of Perry Pierce book: HSA to LM, December 31, 1930.

Background of Perry Pierce: See Johnson, *Stratemeyer Pseudonyms and Series Books*, 80. James Keeline has indicated that it was Howard Garis who wrote the outline for the first in the Perry Pierce series. See www.keeline.com.

End of SS creative era: Johnson, *Stratemeyer Pseudonyms and Series Books*, xxix–xxx.

Baptism of Brian: LM noted the commotion caused by Pat in his diary. He also wrote in his diary about his and Amy's decision to name Brian "Bryan" two months after he was born. Brian discusses this in his autobiography, *Brian McFarlane's World of Hockey*, 8–9.

LM on capital punishment: Interview with NMP, August 1, 2001.

Article by LM on hanging: This appeared in the *Haileyburian* as "Haileybury Hanging a Creditable Affair," June 1933. Exact date and page number unknown.

"How Deep Is Down?": *Maclean's*, February 15, 1938, 9.

Maclean's prospector articles by LM: "A Canadian Eldorado," December 15, 1931, 12–13; and "It Wasn't All Luck," January 1, 1932, 22, 36–37.

LM's short-story characters: These appeared in *Maclean's* in the following stories: "Wakeville, Awake!" March 15, 1940, 5–6, 39–44; "The Voice of Oomph," June 15, 1940, 5–7, 34–38; "Grandpaw Foglesby's Leg," September 15, 1940, 12–13, 23–24; "Romance on Ice," February 11, 1937, 16–17, 27–40; "The Lunacy of Lucien," November 1, 1936, 12–13, 49, 52–53. "Grandpere" Poupet appears in LM's story "Grandpere Rides Again," *Country Gentleman*, January, 1939, 10–11, 56–58.

"Two-Fingered Finnegan": See "Romance on Ice."

"Wakeville, Awake!": This was a multipart series that appeared in *Maclean's* beginning on March 15, 1940, and continuing on April 1 and April 29 of that year.

Aunt Gertrude's comment and description of Wakeville: "Wakeville, Awake!" March 15, 1940, 6–7.

CHAPTER 8: THE CIRCLE GROWS

For more on the life and career of WAD, see John Lennox and Michelle Lacombe, eds., *Dear Bill: The Correspondence of William Arthur Deacon* (Toronto: University of Toronto Press, 1988) and Clara Thomas and John Lennox, *William Arthur Deacon: A Canadian Literary Life* (Toronto: University of Toronto Press, 1982).

WAD as writer's critic: See Lennox and Lacombe, *Dear Bill.*

WAD's autobiography: *My Vision of Canada* (Toronto: Ontario Publishing Co., 1933).

History of CAA: Lennox and Lacombe, *Dear Bill,* xix.

WAD's praise of LM: This appeared in a column by Deacon that was probably written in the late 1920s; Deacon praised LM personally in a letter to him, November 2, 1925.

Why LM doesn't write "literature": LM to WAD, April 28, 1930.

LM's affinity to Haileybury: LM to WAD, July 15, 1931.

Letter to the editor, *Mail and Empire:* This appeared on page 8 of the newspaper on August 28, 1931. It was dated and written by LM on July 28, 1931.

WAD on his own background: WAD to LM, July 17, 1931.

LM applying for other jobs: In a diary entry on April 22, 1932, LM indicated that he was considering answering a newspaper advertisement that sought reporters for a weekly newspaper. Whether he applied is unknown.

"Professional writer" definition: LM to WAD, July 22, 1931.

LM's mentors: LM to WAD, August 1931. LM mentions Cranston in his "Interview Notes," a series of facts and thoughts about his life that he put together for reporters in typewritten form in the early 1970s. They are among his personal papers.

LM seeking work with SS: LM to EDS, June 18, 1932.

HB sales figures: These were provided to the author by James Keeline.

Dana Girls series description: Included in a letter from SS to LM, January 5, 1933; the overall outline and proposal for the series is included among the SS papers.

LM request for pay advance: LM to EDS, June 1933.

Critique of Dana Girls book: EDS to LM, June 6, 1933.

SS asking for manuscript: EDS to LM, June 6, 1933, and July 20, 1933.

LM's apology to EDS: LM to EDS, July 1933.

History of Dana Girl series: See Johnson, *Stratemeyer Pseudonyms and Series Books.* James Keeline also addresses this in a memo to the author on April 30, 2003.

"Mighty rescue": LM to NMP, March 1965.

PMM's remembrances: PMM to LM, December 12, 1976.

McFarlane home life: Both BM and NMP recall that Pat as an adult had a tempestuous nature, and could be particularly argumentative with her father and others. Her father, however, usually tried to avoid arguments.

Canadian/American exchange rate: SS to LM, February 23, 1934.

CHAPTER 9: GOOD OR BAD BOOKS?

Seeking LM to write Dana Girls: SS to LM, August 7, 1934.

LM asking for pay increase: LM to SS, August 1934 (believed to be August 18).

REFERENCES

"Bondage": *GHB*, 197.

LM not comfortable as Carolyn Keene: *GHB*, 199.

Typical plot outlines: See Arthur Prager's *Rascals at Large* (Garden City, NY: Doubleday, 1971), 116–22, and *SSS*, 88.

Dana Girls meet HB: *GHB*, 199.

LM undecided by writing: LM to WAD, August 7, 1931.

WAD warning about complacency: WAD to LM, August 23, 1931.

WAD's vision of LM's novel: WAD to LM, August 4, 1934.

Murder Tree reviews: *Herald Tribune* book section, August 9, 1931, 10; *Saturday Review of Literature*, August 15, 1931, 60; *New York Times Review of Books*, August 16, 1931, 17.

LM on Cobalt: LM to WAD, August 7, 1931.

WAD on a powerful story, his "evangelism," and achieving success early: WAD to LM, August 7, 1931.

On poet MacDonald: NMP has memories of MacDonald performing magic in her home when she was a little girl, and his hobby was mentioned in *William Arthur Deacon: A Literary Life*, as was MacDonald's sour disposition, 77.

LM seeking books for library: LM to WAD, undated but believed to be January 1935.

LM on library "censorship": LM to WAD, undated, 1935.

Mathiews's article: See "Blowing Out the Boys' Brains," *Outlook*, November 18, 1914, 652–54.

The *Fortune* article about the syndicate was published in April 1934, 86–90. No author was listed, but syndicate researcher James Keeline believes it was written by staff writer Ayres Brinser, based on correspondence Keeline has read between Brinser and syndicate officials.

On the longevity of the *Fortune* article: See John T. Dizer, *Tom Swift and Company* (Jefferson, NC: McFarland, 1982), 17.

Banned books: On its website, the American Library Association posts the main reasons books were banned in the latter part of the twentieth century. The reasons include graphic sexuality, inappropriate language, and explicit violence. See www.ala.org/bbooks.

Conflict about "serious" fiction: Dizer, *Tom Swift and Company*, 15.

Children's reading tastes: E. B. White, "On Writing for Children," *Paris Review* 48 (Fall 1969).

"Under our intellectual radar": See Maria Tatar, "Reading Magic," *New York Times*, November 16, 2001, A23; Tim Morris, in "Returning to the Hardy Boys," *Raritan* 16 (Winter 1997): 123–42, offers his recollections of his early readings in Chicago.

Many adult writers have noted in journals and popular publications that it was series fiction that introduced them to the pleasures of reading overall. Many say it was the "forbidden nature" of the text that drew them to it. See, for example, Morris, "Returning to the Hardy Boys"; Thomas J. McCarthy, "De Gustibus Non Est Disputandum: I'm Still Irresistibly Drawn to the Hardy Boys," *America*, April 8, 2000, 6; Ken Donelson, "Nancy, Tom and Assorted Friends in the Stratemeyer Syndicate Then and Now," *Children's Literature* 7 (1978): 17–44; Anne Scott McLeod, "Secret in the Trash Bin: On the Perennial Popularity of Juvenile Series Books," *Children's Literature in Education* 15, no. 3 (1984): 127–40; Alison Lurie, *Don't Tell the Grown-ups: Subversive Children's Literature* (Toronto: Little, Brown and Company, 1990), x.

Mobile characters: Selma Lanes, *Down the Rabbit Hole: Adventures and Misadventures in the Realm of Children's Literature* (New York: Atheneum, 1971), 133.

HB archetype: Morris, "Returning to the Hardy Boys," 125.

Sales figures: These vary and are difficult to track down. See, for example, Donelson, "Nancy, Tom and Assorted Friends in the Stratemeyer Syndicate," 42; and Roger B. May, "Nancy Drew and Kin Still Surmount Scrapes—and Critics' Slurs," *Wall Street Journal*, January 15, 1975, 1–2. When Nancy Drew author Mildred Wirt Benson died in May 2002, it was estimated that the series had sold more than 200 million copies and was translated into seventeen languages since its inception in 1930.

"Fashions" in children's literature: See Lillian Smith, "An Approach to Criticism in Children's Literature," *School Activities and the Library* (1956): 1–3; and Carolyn Heilbrun, "For Children: Reform and the Reformers," *New York Times Book Review,* February 26, 1967, 26.

Offending librarians: Ervin J. Gaines, "Viewpoint," *Library Journal,* April 15, 1970, 145. See also Lanes, *Down the Rabbit Hole,* 153. LM made similar comments in a series of "Interview Notes" he wrote in the early 1970s.

Series fiction kept from the shelves: "County Libraries Banish Hardy Boys and Nancy Drew," *Windsor Star,* May 7, 1999. See www.Southam.com/windsorstar.

Series fiction in East Orange: Quoted by Peter Soderbaugh in "The Stratemeyer Strain: Educators and the Juvenile Series Books, 1900–1973," *Journal of Popular Culture* 7 (1974): 869.

"Heat" by Nancy Drew: This comment was made by Jan Freeman, young adult coordinator for the King County Library system in Oregon. She is quoted in May's *Wall Street Journal* article.

Comic books and romances: See Zena Sutherland and May Hill Arbuthnot, *Children and Books,* 7th ed. (Glenview, IL: Scott Foresmand, 1986), 59. Inglis is quoted on page 52.

Orwell's "Good Bad Books": This essay was originally published in the *Tribune* on November 2, 1945. It is reprinted in *The Collected Essays, Journalism and Letters of George Orwell (1945–1950),* ed. Sonia Orwell and Ian Angus (New York: Harcourt Brace and World, 1968), 19–22.

CHAPTER 10: THE BEST AND WORST OF TIMES

LM's drinking: Interview by the author with NMP, August 1, 2001.

LM's drinking later in life: Letters he wrote in middle age and beyond indicate that Les did not give up drinking completely, although his children said he never again drank in their home, nor was alcohol kept there. But there is evidence that he never had a drinking problem later in life and was a social drinker.

Life of pulp authors: Hugh Merrill, *The Red Hot Typewriter: The Life and Times of John D. MacDonald* (New York: Thomas Dunne Books/St. Martin's Minotaur, 2000), 45–47.

Moving to Whitby: Interview by the author with Brian McFarlane, July 31, 2001.

Celebration for the McFarlanes: The article appeared in the *New Liskeard Speaker*, October 1, 1936. It is referred to in Bruce Taylor's *Leslie McFarlane*, 40.

LM writing another HB book: LM to EDS, November 27, 1935.

LM mentioning hospitalization: LM to EDS, September 18, 1935.

"Fact checking" in series fiction and errors in some HB books: *LH*, 63; for more commentary on the errors in these five books, Crawford cites the following: John Seebeck, "The Great Hardys (What Made the Old Stories So Good?), Part 1: The Golden Era (1927–1932)," *Yellowback Library* 80 (February 1991): 5–9; John M. Enright, "Mr. McFarlane's Magic," in Fred Woodworth, ed., *Mystery & Adventure Series Review* (Special Edition) 4 (Spring 1981): 3–6; Donald J. Summar, "Leslie MacFarlane's [*sic*] Secret Warning; or the Hardy Boys at Sea," *Yellowback Library* 30 (November/December 1985): 3–6.

Mistakes in *Disappearing Floor: LH*, 64.

Mistakes in HB volumes 17–21: *LH*, 65.

Harriet Otis Smith: Memo, James Keeline to the author, May 10, 2003.

BM "stumbling" on his father's secret life as Franklin W. Dixon: See *Brian McFarlane's World of Hockey*, 18; LM also tells this story in his own autobiography.

The letter from F. Scott Fitzgerald to LM was written sometime in 1936. It is in the possession of NMP.

History of *Saturday Evening Post:* Weber, *Hired Pens*, 217–18.

Background of Fitzgerald: This was provided by Fitzgerald biographer Matthew Bruccoli and taken from the University of South Carolina website, www.usc.edu/fitzgerald.

Amy's unhappiness in Whitby: *LM*, 42. NMP also discussed this in an interview with the author, August 1, 2001.

LM's brothers: Interview by the author with Bertha McFarlane, widow of Dick McFarlane, July 30, 2001.

CHAPTER 11: NEW OPPORTUNITIES

The McFarlanes' home life: Both NMP and BM made these observations separately in interviews with the author.

CBC history: See the CBC website, www.CBC.ca.

LM's holiday poem: "A Canadian Christmas 1940," *Maclean's*, December 15, 1940, 9.

LM at draft board: *GHB*, 200.

REFERENCES

LM discussing politics: Interview by the author with NMP.

"How to Play a Harp": *Maclean's*, March 15, 1941, 24–25.

James Thurber wrote many humorous books, plays, and essays. Representative of his work in the 1930s and 1940s are *My Life and Hard Times* (New York: Harper & Brothers, 1933); *Men, Women and Dogs* (New York: Dodd, Mead, 1943); and *A Thurber Carnival* (New York: Modern Library, 1945).

"A Cat Called Claudius": *Maclean's*, July 1, 1942, 14–15, 26–31.

LM's children's daily lives: *Brian McFarlane's World of Hockey*, 18.

CHAPTER 12: AWAY FROM HOME

LM's knowledge of sports and writing: *Brian McFarlane's World of Hockey*, 25; NMP discussed her father's interest in writing during a CBC radio interview that aired July 19, 1998. BM also talks about it in his autobiography, 22.

LM's description of his family: LM to HSA, March 1944 (date unknown).

HSA's family: HSA to LM, March 31, 1944.

X Bar X Boys description: A description of the series can be found in Johnson, *Stratemeyer Pseudonyms and Series Books*, 123.

LM "as" James Cody Ferris: LM to HSA, December 13, 1942.

LM driving hard bargain: LM to HSA, July 9, 1942.

CBC history: Leonard Maltin, *Great American Broadcast* (New York: Dutton, 1997), 25, 30–31.

LM's move to Ottawa: Interview by the author with NMP, January 30, 2001.

BM as hockey player: *Brian McFarlane's World of Hockey*, 29–30.

Role of the National Film Board of Canada: *LM*, 55–56. Summaries of the film board films are available on the National Film Board's website, NFB.ca.

LM's role on the film board: LM mentions this in his "Interview Notes." See also *LM*, 55.

Why LM was hired at the NFB: *GHB*, 200.

LM's earnings in 1944: These are alluded to in LM's diary on April 20, 1945.

LM's children's activities: *Brian McFarlane's World of Hockey*, 34–35, 38.

CHAPTER 13: ON THE AIR

LM sending partial manuscript: LM to HSA, August 17, 1942.

LM writing *Flickering Torch:* LM to HSA, December 5, 1942.

LM's job on film board: LM to HSA, June 2, 1943.

LM working long days: LM to HSA, June 8, 1944.

LM turning down *Secret Panel:* LM to HSA, April 2, 1945.

Secret Panel authorship: James Keeline, Robert Crawford, and many others have debated the authorship of some Hardy Boys books, based on the text of the books.

REFERENCES

Amy McFarlane as author: LM to HSA, May 12, 1946.
Quality of *Phantom Freighter:* HSA to EDS, July 18, 1946.
Amy's writing abilities: Interview by the author with NMP, January 30, 2001.
LM bowing out as Franklin W. Dixon: *GHB*, 201–2.
LM enjoying travel: LM to PMM, undated, 1943.
LM on Banff: LM to PMM, undated, 1946.
BM as hockey player: *Brian McFarlane's World of Hockey*, 36.
PMM's romance: BM and NMP talked about this during interviews with the author. See also *Brian McFarlane's World of Hockey*, 36.
LM's advice to BM: LM to BM, August 8, 1951.
LM's advice to NMP about smoking and writing: LM to NMP, 1952 (undated) and 1949 (undated).
LM's vision of his family: LM to PMM, 1943 (undated).
LM's advice to PMM: LM to PMM, October 4, 1949.
LM's congratulations to PMM: LM to PMM, October 18, 1950.
LM on filmmaking: "Film Board Speaker Recalls Roaring '20s in Kirkland Lake," *Kirkland Lake Post*, July 1954.
Success of *Boy Who Stopped Niagara*: Geoff Jeffreys, "The Boy Who Stopped Niagara," in *National Home Monthly*, undated, but believed to have been written in 1947.

CHAPTER 14: A TRAGIC TIME

On teaching at Carleton: LM to NMP, undated, but believed to have been written in 1953.
LM congratulatory telegram: Telegram, LM to PMM, April 1, 1955.
Amy missing her children: Amy McFarlane to BM, 1951 (undated).
BM at college: *Brian McFarlane's World of Hockey*, 55–61, and LM to NPM, January 22, 1957, and 1952 (undated).
LM on a silent house: LM to NMP, September 1952 (undated).
LM on his closeness to NMP: LM to NMP, undated, but believed to be written in 1952, and January 22, 1957.
LM's advice on romance: LM to NMP, undated, but believed to be written in 1952.
LM on being "Charles": LM to NMP, March 1954 (undated).
LM's advice on Sunday school: LM to NMP, February 14, 1953.
LM's advice about writers facing rejection: LM to NMP, undated, but believed to have been written in 1954.
LM on his drinking as a young man: LM to NMP, undated, but believed to have been written in 1954.
LM's daughters' fears about his drinking: This is discussed in various letters from his daughters and NMP discussed it in interviews with the author.
LM on the dangers of drinking: Two letters, LM to NMP, undated, but believed to have been written in 1952 and 1954.

LM's nostalgia: LM to NMP, October 13, 1956.

Growth of television: See Peter Fornatale and Joshua E. Mills, *Radio in a Television Age* (Woodstock, NY: Overlook Press, 1980), 3–8; see also Margaret Blanchard, ed., *History of the Mass Media in the United States* (Chicago: Fitzroy Dearborn Publishers, 1998), 639–44.

LM's disappointment with Canadian television and his desire to own a set: LM to NMP, undated, but believed to have been written in 1953. Statistics on the history and growth of the CBC can be found on the CBC website, www.CBC.ca.

LM's views of "The Quest": LM to NMP, January 16, 1958.

LM's feelings about Amy's death: See letters from LM to NMP, October 8, 1955, and several written October 1955 (undated) and late in 1955 (undated).

LM on "insulin" script: LM to NMP, undated, but believed to have been written in late 1955.

LM's hospital doggerel: Included in a letter from LM to NMP in 1956 (undated).

LM's further depression over Amy's death: LM to NMP and Louis Perez, April 16, 1956.

LM's remembrance of Amy: LM to NMP and Louis Perez, April 19, 1956.

LM on Montreal and description of Bea Kenney: LM to BM, November 18, 1956.

LM's nostalgia about his family: LM to BM, November 18, 1956.

Bea's admirable qualities: LM to NMP, November 19, 1956.

CHAPTER 15: A GHOST EMERGES

LM's description of wedding: LM to NMP, undated, but believed to be mid-1956.

LM on telephone conversations: LM to NMP, June 14, 1957.

On "The Proud and the Beautiful": LM to NMP, undated, but believed to be mid-1956.

LM on Amy: LM to PMM, October 1956 (no date).

LM's encouragement for PMM: LM to PMM, February 4, 1967.

LM changing with the times: David Tom, "Whitby Man Writing TV Scripts," *Oshawa (Ontario) Times*, September 27, 1969, 1A.

Early history of television: Max Wilk, *The Golden Age of Television: Notes from the Survivors* (Chicago: Silver Spring Press, 1999), 11–24.

Some of the early years of the CBC are described in Stephen Cole's *Here's Looking at Us: Celebrating Fifty Years of CBC-TV* (Toronto: McClelland & Stewart, 2002).

LM providing draft of play: LM to NMP, June 13, 1956.

Canadians can't deliver: LM to NMP, August 1954 (no date).

CBC producer praises LM: LM to NMP, October 13, 1956.

LM traveling with Bea: LM to NMP, October 5, 1957.

The Twilight Zone is described on the CBC website.

REFERENCES

CBC official Hugh Gauntlett is quoted on the CBC website.

LM on aging: LM to NMP, August 26, 1959.

Number of professional writers in Canada: See Frank Rasky's column in *Liberty* magazine, January 1960.

LM on fiction writing: Quoted in George Brimmell, "Editor Writes Many TV Dramas Himself," *Toronto Telegram*, February 7, 1959.

LM on *Eye-Opener Man:* Brimmell, "Editor Writes Many TV Dramas Himself."

LM is described in detail in Rasky's *Liberty* column.

LM on "censorship": Quoted in the *Montreal Star,* "CBC Spurned by Sponsor," May 19, 1961. The show was reviewed several days later in the *Star.*

LM contented: LM to NMP, June 14, 1957.

LM as stepfather: Interview by the author with Kathy Palmer by telephone, August 25, 2002.

LM reviews Williams play: LM to NMP, January 16, 1958.

LM disdaining sex and violence in writing: He said this in a story by David Tom in the *Oshawa (Ontario) Times,* "Whitby Man Writing TV Scripts," September 27, 1969, 1A.

LM signing books as "Franklin W. Dixon": Quoted in a long profile of LM in the *Toronto Star Weekend* magazine by Bob Stall, "The Hardy Boys: The Ghost and the Old Books," December 15, 1973, 12–15.

LM on HB royalties: David Cobb, "He's Canada's Only Writer Who Works Full Time in TV," *Toronto Star,* date unknown, but believed to be 1962.

LM on future HB earnings: BM mentioned this briefly in an interview with the author; it is also mentioned in a 1997 article about LM, "Leslie McFarlane: The Canadian Writer Who Was Franklin W. Dixon," by Shane Peacock in the *Beaver,* June/July 1997, 27–31.

LM "as" Franklin W. Dixon: David Tom, "Whitby Man Writing TV Scripts," 1A.

CHAPTER 16: GHOSTS OF THEIR FORMER SELVES

HB and money: *GHB,* 205.

LM as father of famous sportscaster: LM to NMP, December 20, 1967.

LM on his son's success: LM to BM, April 18, 1971.

LM as "celebrity": LM to NMP, December 20, 1967.

LM's nature and life in Whitby: Interview by the author with Kathy Palmer.

LM on "rustic life" in Whitby: LM to NMP, May 5, 1962.

LM as wedding photographer: Interview by author with Anne Yarrow by telephone, September 8, 2002.

Conversations at dinner and LM's recipes: Interviews by author with Kathy Palmer and Anne Yarrow.

Whitby poems: Published in the *Whitby Weekly News,* "Inter-nationally [*sic*] Known Literary Figure Tells Rotary That Ideas Will Make the Town More Interesting." May 31, 1962, 1.

REFERENCES

"Wakeville, Awake!": This is the series by LM that appeared in *Maclean's*.

Making a living as a writer: Ralph Thomas, "24 Canadians Write for TV—Only Two Make a Living at It," *Toronto Star,* October 24, 1964, section 2, p. 23.

LM on rejections and problems at CBC: LM to NMP, undated, but believed to be 1962.

Story on non-union writers: Roy Shields, "Melodrama as Actors Strike at CBC," *Toronto Star,* September 30, 1965.

LM's casting Liberal vote: LM to NMP, May 5, 1962.

LM comments about Mencken: LM to NMP, October 7, 1974.

LM as "writer of entertainments": See his "Interview Notes." See also *The Last of the Great Picnics* (Toronto, Montreal: McClelland & Stewart, 1965).

Praise for *McGonigle Scores!:* Ted Reeves, "Ted Reeves Writes," *Toronto Telegram,* December 20, 1966, 14.

LM about writing from life experiences; loving drama; and describing "Padgett": LM to NMP, December 20, 1967.

Pooch the dog: Interview by the author with Kathy Palmer.

LM loving writing drama: LM noted in his "Interview Notes" that writing for radio was his favorite kind of writing. He occasionally wrote to his children in the 1960s that he was becoming disillusioned with writing for television.

SS and pseudonyms: LM to NMP, January 30, 1969.

On the Stratemeyers granting publicity: Memo, James Keeline to the author, May 11, 2003.

HSA interview: This article by Judy Klemesrud appeared in the *New York Times* on April 14, 1968.

Lack of diversity in series books: *LH,* 41.

Racism in HB books: Gerald O'Connor, "The Hardy Boys Revisited: A Study in Prejudices," in *Challenges in American Culture,* ed. Ray B. Browne, Larry N. Landrum, and William K. Bottorff (Bowling Green, OH: Bowling Green University Popular Press, 1970), 234–41.

LM and writing stereotypes: SS to LM, August 8, 1933, and February 1, 1935.

HB revisions: SS brief outlines for these revisions are available in the Stratemeyer collection at the New York Public Library.

Critics of the revisions: Cullen Murphy, "Starting Over," *Atlantic,* June 1991, 18, 20, 22. See also Morris Berman, *Twilight of American Culture* (New York: Norton, 2000), 46–47.

HB as "embalmed virtue": David Justin Ross, "The Mystery of the Missing Detectives," *Liberty,* November 1992, 69–73. In addition to Murphy, Berman, and Ross, others have written to criticize the revisions. See also Steve Burgess, "Perky Fellows in a Gay-Looking Speedwagon," Slate.com, October 7, 1999, and Philip Marchand's column in the *Toronto Star,* "Hardy Boys Mysteries for a TV Generation," August 5, 2000, M4.

Revised characters: See Burgess, "Perky Fellows."

LM on how to spot revised books: LM to NMP, December 8, 1963.

McFarlanes moving to Los Angeles: Interview by the author with Kathy Palmer. LM did not keep a regular diary during his time in Los Angeles, but he did keep a small journal to which he contributed brief passages. These passages served more as a travelogue than as a diary describing his feelings and thoughts.

LM on Los Angeles: LM to NMP, September 19, 1956.

LM on producers and "TV Land": LM to PMM, February 14, 1969.

LM as "barefoot boy" and quirks of Los Angeles residents: LM to BM, February 27, 1969.

LM on changed *Bonanza* script and disillusionment with California: LM to NMP, October 12, 1969.

Los Angeles as a jungle: LM to PMM, May 28, 1973.

CHAPTER 17: AT HOME AT THE TYPEWRITER

Epigraph: LM to grandson Jon Perez, March 3, 1973.

LM on getting gifts: Interview by the author with Kathy Palmer.

LM on Ranger Boys: LM to NMP, June 28, 1962.

CBC days over: LM to NMP, December 9, 1974.

LM research into Dickens: LM to NMP, November 2, 1972.

History repeating itself: LM to NMP, December 9, 1974.

LM remembering days as young writer: LM to NMP, January 30, 1975.

LM getting solace from work: LM to PMM, November 14, 1972, and LM to NMP, March 16, 1973.

LM on frustrations with HB memoir: LM to PMM, November 14, 1972, and LM to NMP, December 20, 1971.

LM on "where I came in": LM to NMP, April 26, 1974.

LM euphemisms for old age: LM to NMP, January 1, 1971.

LM on his birthday: LM to NMP, November 2, 1972.

LM on *I Am Curious (Yellow):* LM to NMP, November 14, 1973.

LM on modernizing Shakespeare and the permissive media: LM to NMP, June 12, 1971.

LM on habits of the elderly: LM to BM, 1973 (undated).

LM on contemporary authors: LM to PMM, September 14, 1975, and LM to NMP, August 6, 1975, and September 16, 1973.

LM on moving to Florida: LM to BM and family, February 18, 1973.

Affording move to Florida: Telephone interview by the author with Anne Yarrow, September 8, 2002.

LM on feeling worse as he entered his seventh decade: LM to PMM, September 14, 1975.

LM enjoying Florida: LM to BM and family, February 18, 1973, and LM to PMM and family, undated but believed to have been written in 1974.

"Letter from Paradise": This appeared in *Weekend* magazine on April 6, 1974.

LM and the mails: Interviews by the author with Kathy Palmer and Anne Yarrow.

Writers' club: Hugh Merrill talks about this club in his biography of Mac-

Donald, *The Red Hot Typewriter: The Life and Times of John D. MacDonald* (New York: Thomas Dunne Books, 2000), 77–78, 81.

LM's relationship with Svenson: LM to BM, January 23, 1975, and LM to PMM on February 9, 1975.

GHB publicity: Outlined in a news release for the book, which was published by Metheun. The release also promoted six Checkmate Series books LM wrote.

LM on his new novel: LM to NMP, August 6, 1975; to BM, September 13, 1975, and to PMM, September 14, 1975.

LM's optimism about his new manuscript: LM to Perez family, November 21, 1975.

LM describing *To Tell the Truth* and the tough book-publishing industry: LM to NMP, October 7, 1974.

LM on trouble getting work: LM to PMM, September 14, 1975.

LM upbeat about his health: LM to NMP, November 21, 1975.

LM on *GHB* reviews: LM to NMP, October 30, 1976.

GHB reviews: These appeared in the *Toronto Star,* 1976, date unknown.

LM on his seventy-fourth birthday and his cynicism about publishing industry: LM to NMP, October 30, 1976.

LM on his declining health: LM to BM, November 28, 1976.

LM on his mortality: LM to PMM, March 4, 1977.

LM on school named after him: LM to PMM, March 7, 1977.

Praising NMP's manuscript: LM to NMP, April 1, 1977.

Move to Minden: Interview by author with Anne Yarrow.

LM's further declining health: LM to NMP, July 18, 1977.

LM on writers writing forever: *GHB,* 204.

LM buying first round: Merrill, *Red Hot Typewriter,* 81.

CHAPTER 18: THE FINAL CHAPTER

HB "update": Ed Zuckerman, "The Great Hardy Boys Whodunit," *Rolling Stone,* September 9, 1976, 36–40; LM's resulting letter to the editor appeared in the magazine on October 21, 1976.

Stall's article appeared on December 15, 1973.

Grosset litigation: This lawsuit received much national publicity. For details, see two articles in *Publishers Weekly,* "Grosset Sues Simon & Schuster for $50-Million," May 7, 1979, 25; and "Judge Rules in Dispute over Nancy Drew, Tom Swift, et al.," June 27, 1980, 14.

Sales figures: "Nancy Drew and Kin Still Surmount Scrapes—and Critics' Slurs," *Wall Street Journal,* January 15, 1975, 1, 25.

Value of HB editions: The value and cost of the HB books are debated in many of the HB and series-fiction websites. For a summary, see "The Mystery of the Missing Detectives," *Liberty.*

HB parodies: Peter Kleinman and Larry Loman, "The Undiscovered

Notebooks of Franklin W. Dixon," *National Lampoon*, July 1985, 71–73; Will Jacobs and Charles Kaufman, "The Mystery of the Ghostwriter," *National Lampoon*, October 1984, available on the website, www.nationallampoon.com; "Junior Inquirer: Dumped by Bobbsey Twins, Hardy Boys Share New Love," *Mad*, November 1984, 39; see also a review of the play, *The Secret of the Old Queen*, "Gentle Parody of Hardy Boys Done," *Chicago Tribune*, June 7, 1999.

"Tribute" to Franklin W. Dixon: Hoff's *House on the Point* was published in 2002 by St. Martin's Minotaur.

HB current readership: David D. Kirkpatrick, "In Latest Hardy Boys Case, a Search for New Readers," *New York Times*, July 29, 2001, 1, 13.

HB in space: This was mentioned in Susan Clairmont's "Mystery at McFarlane Manor," *Hamilton (Ontario) Spectator*, August 1, 1998, C1.

Hiaasen's comments appeared in an interview in *Bon Appétit*, August 1997.

HB collector makes trek to Haileybury: His comments appeared in a Canadian Press wire story distributed on July 25, 1998.

PUBLISHED WORKS BY LESLIE MCFARLANE

UNDER HIS OWN NAME

Streets of Shadow (E. P. Dutton, 1930)*
The Murder Tree (E. P. Dutton, 1931)*
The Last of the Great Picnics (McClelland & Stewart, 1965)
McGonigle Scores! (McClelland & Stewart, 1966)
The Dynamite Flynns (Methuen, 1975)*
Agent of the Falcon (Methuen, 1975)*
The Mystery of Spider Lake (Methuen, 1975)*
Squeeze Play (Methuen, 1975)*
A Kid in Haileybury (Highway Book Shop, 1975)
The Snow Hawk (Methuen, 1976)*
Breakaway (Methuen, 1976)*
Ghost of the Hardy Boys (Two Continents/Methuen, 1976)

UNDER THE PSEUDONYM FRANKLIN W. DIXON

The Hardy Boys series, published by Grosset & Dunlap:

The Tower Treasure (1927)
The House on the Cliff (1927)
The Secret of the Old Mill (1927)
The Missing Chums (1928)
Hunting for Hidden Gold (1928)
The Shore Road Mystery (1928)
The Secret of the Caves (1929)
The Mystery of Cabin Island (1929)
The Great Airport Mystery (1930)
What Happened at Midnight (1931)
While the Clock Ticked (1932)
Footprints under the Window (1933)
The Mark on the Door (1934)
The Hidden Harbor Mystery (1935)
The Sinister Sign Post (1936)
A Figure in Hiding (1937)
The Secret Warning (1938)
The Flickering Torch Mystery (1943)
The Melted Coins (1944)

*Reprints of magazine stories.

The Short-Wave Mystery (1945)
The Phantom Freighter (1947)**

UNDER THE PSEUDONYM CAROLYN KEENE
The Dana Girls series, published by Grosset & Dunlap:

By the Light of the Study Lamp (1934)
The Secret at Lone Tree Cottage (1934)
In the Shadow of the Tower (1934)
A Three-Cornered Mystery (1935)

UNDER THE PSEUDONYM ROY ROCKWOOD
The Dave Fearless series, published by Garden City Publishers:

Dave Fearless under the Ocean (1926)
Dave Fearless in the Black Jungle (1926)
Dave Fearless near the South Pole (1926)
Dear Fearless among the Malay Pirates (1926)
Dave Fearless on the Ship of Mystery (1927)
Dave Fearless on the Lost Brig (1927)

UNDER THE PSEUDONYM CLINTON W. LOCKE
The Perry Pierce series, published by Henry Altemus Company:

Who Closed the Door, or Perry Pierce and the Old Storehouse Mystery (1931)

McFarlane also wrote or directed twenty-nine scripts for the National Film Board of Canada from 1944 to 1962; more than thirty television scripts for the Canadian Broadcasting Corporation from 1953 to 1971; and more than one hundred articles and short stories for numerous pulp and slick magazines from 1927 to 1938.

**Authorship of this is unclear. Leslie McFarlane told the Stratemeyer Syndicate that his wife, Amy, wrote it, but based on comments he and his relatives have made, it is believed he wrote it.

INDEX

Doyle, Arthur Conan, 248. *See also* Holmes, Sherlock
Drew, Nancy. *See* Nancy Drew (book series)

Editor & Publisher, 40

Farr, C. C., 1, 57, 256
Fearless, Dave. *See* Dave Fearless (book series); Rockwood, Roy
Fitzgerald, F. Scott, 32, 294; letter to Les, 153–54
Fortune (magazine), 5, 41, 50, 133–35

Galento, Tony (boxer), 160
Garis, Howard, 19–21, 35, 40, 95–96, 117, 138, 242
Garis, Roger, 48; as author of *My Father Was Uncle Wiggily*, 40
Ghost of the Hardy Boys. See McFarlane, Charles Leslie: on *Ghost of the Hardy Boys*
Goblin (magazine), 68, 80, 90
Granville, Bonita (actress), 176
Greene, Lorne, 184, 210, 250
Grosset & Dunlap, 19; lawsuit against Stratemeyer Syndicate, 276; as publisher of Hardy Boys series, 51–52; as publisher of series books, 97, 119, 176; relationship with Stratemeyer Syndicate, 22, 50, 242

The Haileyburian (newspaper), 23, 82–84, 100, 157
Haileybury, Ontario. *See* McFarlane, Charles Leslie: childhood in Haileybury
Haileybury fire of 1922, 10, 29–30, 256
Hardy, Bob (agent), 35, 66, 79, 99
Hardy Boys (book series): art for, 63–63; characters in, 53–55, 59, 65, 72; detective novels as models for, 50; early description/outlines of, 52–56; inception of, 47, 49;

media adaptations of, 277–78; parodies of, 278–79; revisions of and changes to (1959), 38, 243–49, 276–77; sales, longevity of, x, 64–65, 84, 115–16, 277, 279; *Tower Treasure* (first book), 49–50, 52, 55–57, 59, 61, 63, 243–44, 248, 277; violence/criminal activity in, 36; websites and newsletters related to, 280; "weird period" of, 149–50
Hemingway, Ernest, 24, 131, 154, 169; visit to Sudbury, 26
Hiassen, Carl, 280
"Hill of Gold" (short story), 45, 47
Holmes, Sherlock, 37, 140, 248

Jessup, Dick, 263
Joyce, James, 138, 260

Kantor, Mackinlay: as author, 187, 263; death of, 271; as friend of Les, 263, 271
Keene, Carolyn, 19, 21; Les as, 36, 116, 120, 125; Mildred Wirt as, 21, 116
Kenney, Beatrice Greenaway. *See* McFarlane, Beatrice Greenaway Kenney
Kid in Haileybury, A, 8, 12, 57, 72; idea for, 257
King, Stephen, 232, 259

LaBine, Gilbert, 103
Last of the Great Picnics, 240
Leacock, Stephen, 109
Lewis, Sinclair, 24, 70, 152
Liberty (magazine), 229–30
Lindbergh, Charles, 64
Louis, Joe, 160

MacDonald, Wilson, 130–31
Maclean's (magazine), 12, 30, 45, 67; fiction contest of, 67, 73, 84; Les's stories in, 78, 80, 90, 97, 102, 104, 106, 125, 141, 160, 162–64, 171,

237; Norah McFarlane's poetry in,
174

Mad magazine: gift subscriptions
from Les, 255; parody of Hardy
Boys, 278

Maddock, Else (sister-in-law), 73, 75,
154

Mail and Empire (newspaper), 108,
111

Mason, Bill, 25, 27, 31

Mathiews, Franklin K., 37–39, 133

McCauley, Bill (son-in-law), 194, 197

McCauley, Matthew (grandson),
202–3, 213–14, 281

McClelland & Stewart, 240–41, 257

McFarlane, Amy Arnold (first wife):
death of, 211–12; depression
problems, 80, 82, 99, 122–23,
141–45, 154–55, 159, 165, 171,
180, 205; early life of, 73; illnesses
of, 80–81; 91, 99, 107; life in Ottawa, 179–81, 215–16; life in
Whitby, 147–49, 154–55, 159–60,
179; marriage of, 73–74, 76–77,
148, 181; as wife and mother, 57,
78–80, 82–83, 90, 92, 120, 172,
175, 194–95, 203–5, 211

McFarlane, Beatrice Greenaway Kenney (second wife): birthday party
for Les, 258; daily life with Les,
230–31, 234–37, 241, 254; health
problems of, 266; introduction to
Les, 215, 218–19; life in Florida,
260–61; life in Los Angeles,
249–51; life in Whitby, 226, 262,
235–36

McFarlane, Bertha (sister-in-law), 17

McFarlane, Brian (son): as artist, 185;
as athlete, 173–75, 186, 193; as
baby, 97–98, 107, 120; birth of,
92, 97; broadcasting career of, 28,
181, 234–35, 281; childhood of,
121, 148, 151, 159, 165–67, 169,
174, 175–81; college years of,
203–4, 211; life in Ottawa, 181,
186, 192; life in Whitby, 147–49,

154–55, 159–60, 173; marriage
and family of, 203, 211, 215, 220;
as writer, 235, 281;

McFarlane, Charles Leslie "Les"
"Agent of the Hawk" (short story),
34

ancestry of, 13–14

as author of nonfiction, 99, 102–4

awards of: Academy Award nomination, 193; best Canadian playwright, 230; British Film
Academy Award, 184; IODE
award, 5; *Maclean's* fiction award,
67

Boy Who Stopped Niagara, The (film),
183, 191, 199–200, 296

on his Canadian identity, xi, 76,
130–31, 181, 227, 238, 240,
250, 260, 262

childhood in Haileybury, 4, 8–15, 17

on capital punishment, 100–101

as "Carolyn Keene," 36, 116, 120, 125

as college instructor, 202

death of, 271–72

diabetes/heart disease of, 261, 266,
269–71

diary, on importance of keeping,
77, 90, 141–42, 179, 193

drinking habits of, 82, 90–92, 108,
123, 141, 143, 148–49, 207–8

as "Franklin W. Dixon," xi, xii, 41,
50–52, 84, 150–51, 232–33,
255, 266, 273, 275

gallbladder operation, 214–15

on *Ghost of the Hardy Boys*, 242,
256–58, 264, 267–68

introduction to writing, 4–5, 17

as "James Cody Ferris," 177–78

Kid in Haileybury, A, 8, 12, 57, 72;
idea for, 257

on labor unions, 111–12, 239

Last of the Great Picnics, The, 240

life in Ottawa, 179–81, 186, 192,
215–16

life in Whitby: 147–49, 154–55,
159–60, 179, 226, 233–37, 262